ENDURING MOTIVES

ENDURING MOTIVES

The Archaeology of Tradition and Religion

in Native America

Edited by
Linea Sundstrom and Warren DeBoer

THE UNIVERSITY OF ALABAMA PRESS

Tuscaloosa

Copyright © 2012
The University of Alabama Press
Tuscaloosa, Alabama 35487-0380
All rights reserved
Manufactured in the United States of America

Conclusion copyright © Alice Beck Kehoe

Typeface: ACaslon

Cover design: Erin Bradley Dangar / Dangar Design

∞
The paper on which this book is printed meets the minimum requirements of
American National Standard for Information Sciences—Permanence of Paper for
Printed Library Materials, ANSI Z39.48-1984.

Library of Congress Cataloging-in-Publication Data

Enduring motives : the archaeology of tradition and religion in Native America /
edited by Linea Sundstrom and Warren DeBoer.
    p. cm.
  Includes bibliographical references and index.
  ISBN 978-0-8173-5715-3 (quality paper : alk. paper) — ISBN 978-0-8173-8621-4
(ebook)
1. Indians—Religion. 2. Indian cosmology. 3. Indians—Rites and ceremonies. 4.
Indians—Antiquities. 5. America—Antiquities. I. Sundstrom, Linea. II. DeBoer,
Warren R.
  E59.R38E54 2012
  299.7—dc23

                                                          2012010624

Dedicated to the memory of
Robert Leonard Hall, 1927–2012

His keen insight, meticulous research, generous spirit, and respect for all cultures have cleared a path for all those seeking to understand the complexity and beauty of ancient religious traditions in the Americas.

Contents

Figures

ENDURING MOTIVES

Introduction

Warren DeBoer and Linea Sundstrom

This volume was born in puzzlement. The concept of tradition, a term we use in the sense of long-term cultural continuity, plays a fundamental role in archaeology. This use of tradition does not imply stasis, nor does it hinge on whether the tempo of change is gradual or rapid, but it does require a mode of transmission that results in detectable continuity. In its instructional capacity at the individual level, tradition can be seen as an efficient mechanism for reducing the inconvenience of having to think too much in order to act and the palpable risks of thinking on one's own. Such an inertial role, of course, works best in a relatively unchanging or otherwise predictable environment of the kind that beaver dams (Morgan 1868) and human material culture are designed to secure (Odling-Smee et al. 2003). In the archaeological idiom of artifacts, tradition acts as a time-binding glue that holds together culture history, arguably archaeology's major contribution to world knowledge. Without tradition, prehistory crumbles into a jumble of curios (Willey and Phillips 1958).

The puzzle stems from the euphoria with which the collapse of culture history is seemingly welcomed in some academic quarters. The past, like all other cultural phenomena, of course, is a social product and thus embedded in "the social construction of reality," as a founding work would have it (Berger and Luckman 1966). Such construction, however, need not suggest that the past is mere fabrication, a retrodiction solely based upon present concerns, a resource to be plundered for contemporary purposes, or, to paraphrase that quintessential American, Henry Ford, "total bunk." Yet so much of today's anthropology, while paying homage to neglected histories, is flush with iconoclastic fervor and its supporting rhetoric that seem intent on historical erasure. The past and its cultural legacy thus assume interest to the extent that they are hotly contested, strategically contrived, selectively remembered or forgotten, creatively improvised, collectively hallucinated, totally reinvented by each child or each generation of children, dynamic and mercurial, or otherwise concocted in order to slight or problematize any symptom of inertia. Following Trouillot's (1995:xix) aphorism that "we are never as steeped in history as when we pretend not to be," this postmodern glorification of the unanchored can be seen as the flip side of the romantic quest for authenticity. The wished-for recurring motifs of tradition are replaced by the motives of tirelessly busy agents. All those folks who answered the ethnographer with "because that's the way we do it" were just being lazy, unreflective, or otherwise uncooperative.

The following chapters address this state of affairs, as it is somewhat unfairly sketched above, by examining archaeological traditions at work in the Americas. The contributors are archaeologists whose views are diverse and sometimes conflicting. As editors, we have not meddled to forge a consensus that does not exist. All the essays, however, implicate tradition and the modes and mechanisms by which it is transmitted. Emergent themes include the mnemonic roles and functions played by artifacts and the motor habits embodied in their production; the songs and chants that accompany and guide ritual performance; oral traditions, the variable fidelity with which they are passed on, and their use as historical documents; the clockwork stability of skyscapes that encode the stories of myth; toponym-dotted landscapes recalling events real and imagined; long-lived monuments that evoke memory, direct attention, and channel movement centuries after their construction; the caves, mountains, trees, and other "power places" where nature and supernature fleetingly touch; and the rock art and other fixtures that outlast individual lives. As this list suggests and as the subtitle of this volume indicates, religious belief and ritual comprise the chosen arena for these investigations.

Upon first consideration, this choice might appear to be apposite. There is a common supposition that religion is pervasively connected to other cultural domains and thereby is a locus for tenacious cultural persistence—that is, a good site for studying tradition. As an upper rung on Hawkes's inferential ladder, religion also presents an inviting challenge to archaeological inference, a challenge that is being taken up on numerous fronts (e.g., Fogelin 2008; Steadman 2009; VanPool et al. 2006; Whitley and Hays-Gilpin 2008). It is testimony to the overrated claims of human creativity that so many of us find ourselves independently participating in the same vogue.

The term *religion* raises polysemy to new heights, as indicated by Clifford Geertz's attempt at a covering definition: "something we circumambulate about" (Geertz 2005:2). Whether as activity or belief, religion always seems to evade capture in the flesh. Social sciences get around this impasse by reducing religion to something else. Thus we get an obfuscation or mystification (Marx), a psychological adaptation (Freud), a cross-modal central processor (Rappaport), a collective hallucination (Durkheim), a weird but catchy meme (Boyer), or any of numerous oils that keep the culture machine running. These reductions recount the history of anthropological fashions, but, as believers know, their gods are not vogue-chasers. None of this improves much on Tyler's simple "belief in supernatural beings," which covers such common topics as animism, witchcraft, and the intervention of ancestors on one's behalf. But enough of inadequate definitions; clarity is better sought in the actual interplay of tradition and religion as portrayed in the following chapters.

The first three chapters explore the creation and maintenance of cosmograms, or culture-specific symbolic representations of the universe. For openers, John E. Clark and Arlene Colman tie Postclassic Mesoamerican religious symbolism to ancient Olmec antecedents as found at San Lorenzo and La Venta. Here the links between ancestral and derived belief systems emerge from a wide array of observable elements: the structural arrangement of buildings, plazas, settlements, and settlement patterns; the layout of features to render microcosmic models; the use of colors to mark world quarters, zenith, nadir, and life and death; a basic tree/cross shape repeated in city plans and on sacred items; a composite crocodilian/tree symbol to represent the earth and sky; and the use of standard units of measure that seem to reflect mathematical calculations of solar and lunar cycles. The marshaled evidence indicates significant continuity over three millennia in many core concepts still current among indigenous peoples of the region. Some of these concepts have a more expansive pan-American or even global distribution. Such is the case of directional color symbolism, also widespread in North America and Asia (DeBoer 2005), the crocodilian Giver-of-Cultivated-Plants found in both Chavín and Olmec iconography and strongly echoed in Dakota mythology from the northern Great Plains (DeBoer 2006; Lathrap 1973; Oneroad and Skinner 2003:188–190; Roe 1982; Roe and Roe, this volume; Rowe 1962; Walker 1983:130–132), and a multitiered universe, disparate versions of which figure in such far-flung documents as the Ki'che' Mayan *Popol Vuh* and Dante's *Divine Comedy* (Nielsen and Reunert 2009).

Expanding on insights made by Robert Hall (1997), Linea Sundstrom coaxes the archaeological record of the northern Great Plains to yield a rich body of symbols and structures. Without city-states or monumental architecture of Mesoamerican scale, Sundstrom turns to more quotidian remains in order to reveal this symbolic order: the distribution of artifacts and features within earthlodges and tipis, the construction and form of ceremonial spaces such as sweatlodges, and the positioning of structures and sites in relation to landscape and sky. These data document a tiered universe, a tree or cross marking the world center, and the iconic association of life and death with sunrise and sunset. One might also add the power-laden loci of mountains and caves, with a cave atop a mountain constituting a double dose of power. These commonalities, many recalling the Mesoamerican cases described by Clark and Colman, intimate a deep-seated American tradition that is not necessarily linked to urbanism or stratified social organization, neither of which was present on the Great Plains in precontact times.

Perhaps inadvertently guided by an ancient Indo-European penchant for three, Peter G. Roe and Amy Roe's essay completes the artificial trisection of the Americas into North, Middle, and South. For those archaeologists who debunk the historicity of all oral traditions and regard ethnographic testimony as a problematic analogy rather than a living derivative, the Roes' essay is unsettling for it suggests that myths told by today's Shipibo—tropical forest people of the Peruvian Amazon—shed light on 3,000-year-old friezes and stelae adorning the site of Chavín de Huántar. These myths account for the origins of agriculture and are encoded in constellations (our Orion and Pleiades), whose appearance in the night sky marks the end of the dry season and the time for planting. The Roes argue that the initial layout of the Chavín ceremonial complex was aligned to the setting of the Pleiades, but later, from an earth-bound perspective, fell out of sync with the heavens and was appropriately abandoned.

The next four chapters focus on how people use objects to encode tradition and pass it on to future generations. One might at first relegate the Andean Staff God to the larger field of erect phalli, world trees, axes mundi, and related images that are so pandemic as to be candidates for cultural universality. Jeffrey Quilter, however, takes a more circumspect approach by questioning the extent to which form and meaning cohere in such long-lived motifs. His analysis identifies at least two major Staff God variants, each of which can be associated with a separate religious tradition developing from a common ancient root. This result reminds us that specific archaeological forms and their imputed meanings need not march around together, forever holding hands. Relative degrees of stasis and mutability should not be points of view but matters to be investigated.

To a background of coastal breezes buffeting cloud forest mists, Colin McEwan's portrayal of a Manteño ritual complex in Ecuador underscores the sensory aspects of place for enhancing ritual performance. Both stelae and the famed monolithic seats of Manabí province figure as props in this ritual theater and remind us that body postures, whether upright or enthroned, indeed comprise "body language" for mortals and gods alike. In a novel juxtaposition of phenomenological and structuralist approaches, McEwan goes on to show how this constructed landscape can be decoded to mark a string of complementary oppositions such as male/female, life/death, and rainy/dry season. Not stopping at the imposition of symbolic order upon an otherwise uncommunicative world, Manteño ritual precincts were also aligned to movements of the sun, the predictable habits of which could only help to stabilize an erratic and, in the case of Ecuador, earthquake-prone world.

At the San Juan conference that spawned this volume, the noted Caribbean archaeologist José Oliver explored the linked roles and practices of human and nonhuman agents as played out in pre-Columbian religion and ritual in Puerto Rico. It was unfortunate for us that this paper was destined for publication elsewhere (Oliver 2009), but themes addressed by Oliver carry over into this volume. Although human agency as variously rendered in Bourdieu (1977) and Giddens (1984) is now a standard part of archaeological discourse (e.g., Pauketat 2001), less attention has been paid to the nonhuman agents that populate the real world as it is imagined (Brown and Walker 2008). The very phrase *nonhuman agency* might seem oxymoronic, prompt Marxists to sense a mystifying fetishism at work, or strike the enlightened as a return to animism or other relic of primitive thought. As Oliver demonstrates, however, the carved objects the Taíno called *cemís* were not mere representations of spirits and ancestors. They were those beings. They kept genealogies, waged power struggles rivaling those of the Greek pantheon, favored or denied human needs, and manipulated human action in countless ways. To view these highly animated *cemís* as inert pieces of shaped wood, stone, or clay closes access to the Taíno world.

Attempting to work within a Hopi perspective and to define social groups and artifacts in a manner sensible to Hopi themselves, Wesley Bernardini shows that certain material objects can be much more than incidental mnemonic devices. In the capacity of portable palladia that evoke the histories of clans or subclans, these objects serve as central mechanisms in the maintenance and transmission of migration histories from generation to generation. The Hopi assiduously curate these long-lived religious objects and combine them with rock art sites, ruins of former settlements, and other durable fixtures to produce history-studded landscapes in which time is encoded in place (Bernardini 2005). This latter point is elaborated in Kelley Hays-Gilpin's essay. She notes how the imported categories often used by archaeologists, including the collective appellation "Hopi," may obscure or actively misrepresent Hopi understandings of their own historical traditions. In these traditions, place is privileged over time, or, perhaps better put, temporality is embedded in place, and each clan, subclan, or sodality may have its own distinct account of origins, subsequent movements, and the ownership of sacred objects and ceremonies acquired en route. Discussion of these matters requires discretion, because each clan is allowed to tell and to hear only its own stories. This secrecy, in turn, insulates the traditions from outside scrutiny or other meddling. In this case, notions of universal history or ecumenical religion do not even extend to the ethnolinguistic category "Hopi."

The three chapters that follow take on the question of how traditions can evolve over time without losing their core cultural significance. Never one to join a crowd, Stephen H. Lekson presents "A History of the Ancient Southwest" (Lekson 2009) that is disrupted repeatedly by catastrophic episodes of tradition-busting, systemic change. Such disruptions, typically of exogenous impetus, are not uncommon phenomena, but, as the late Claude Lévi-Strauss (1968:258) once remarked, stability is no less mysterious than dramatic upheavals. In any case, even the most tumultuous and tyrannical of new orders—Chaco, the Kachina Cult, or the Pecos Classification itself—did not achieve complete erasure. A fresh start in history is as rare as the fabled *tabula rasa* of ontogeny. Laziness, however, never makes memorable history, and Lekson prefers to view obstinate cultural persistence when it occurs as active resistance rather than passive inertia. Civilized Mesoamerica sent forth frothy chocolate drinks, copper bells, fancy feathers, and notions of High Culture to impress would-be Chichimec elites, but never completely assumed direct control over its northern frontiers. Mesoamerican-style political forms, even if presented in benevolent wrappings, rarely achieved long-term stability in the Southwest, and any prolonged reign of human tyranny or drought sent by angry gods brought forth Puebloan freedom-fighters of the kind sentimentally portrayed by Pierre Clastres (1987). The ancient Southwest probably witnessed several rehearsals for the Pueblo rebellion of 1680 in which latter-day Mesoamericans were routed and chased down the Camino Real.

After a peculiar episode in American archaeology during which explanation tended to be cast in myopically local, in situ terms, long-distance diffusion, both as event and process, is again an acceptable issue for debate. While Lekson sees few checkpoints along the Chichimec frontier, James Brown and John Kelly question any one-way nuclear–periphery model of cultural diffusion in which religious concepts and iconography spread from heavily populated, complexly organized centers such as the cities of ancient Mesoamerica to marginal areas such as the Southeast and Southwest. Brown and Kelly propose what they regard to be a more reasonable model of two-way exchange, sporadic vs. sustained interregional contact, and parallel development of traits from related root cultures. The latter point parallels the homology–analogy distinction made in evolutionary biology (Simpson 1944) and, from a different theoretical vantage, recalls the reasoning employed in the Kulturkreis school of the early twentieth century (Kluckhohn 1936).

Paintings and inscriptions on rocks, collectively known as rock art, have long challenged archaeologists with interpretive obstacles. Analytical methods developed for archaeological artifact assemblages and features having sedimentary contexts rarely transfer to rock art. At the same time, the human impulse to "see" shapes and designs as objects from one's affective world leads to many uninformed or bizarre speculations about these ancient images. Reacting to excesses in the alleged decipherment of ancient symbols, many archaeologists simply declared the topic off limits: a kind of Rorschach test or a futile attempt at paleopsychology. But rock art, like monumental architecture, has the quality of endurance. It can remain in place and be visible for centuries and millennia after its makers have died. This quality of endurance within a landscape is John Norder's starting point for exploring the meaning of rock paintings near Lake of the Woods in western Ontario. Bringing together quantitative observations of the placement of the paintings within the larger landscape and interviews with the First Nations community for whom the paintings remain an important aspect of landscape, Norder shows that rock art delineates a "landscape of presence and memory" that provides the group with its cultural identity and the individual with a map of the intersections of the visible and the invisible worlds within which she or he operates.

The final three chapters use innovative approaches to find evidence of ancient traditions in the archaeological record of later cultures. Cheryl Claassen takes a new look at artifact and faunal remains from Archaic sites in eastern North America in order to detect possible traces of ritual activities. She argues that seemingly mundane assemblages occurring in distinctive contexts represent ritual activities rather than mere food scraps generated by humans or other taphonomic agents. Although millennia separate Claassen's Archaic remains from ethnographic practice, it is noteworthy that her "distinctive contexts" are typically caves, those enduring "power points" juxtaposed between this world and its netherland. The study of swan remains by Lucretia and John Kelly (2007) can be profitably read alongside Claassen's contribution.

In his study of the Midéwiwin ceremonial society of the Great Lakes region, Warren DeBoer aligns with Lekson in questioning the role of archaeologists as sole arbiters of Native American history. Accepting the convention that real history includes only the period in which written documents were produced, archaeologists have consigned all preconquest Native American life to the vague realm of "prehistory" (Kehoe 1998). This remains a point of contention between modern First Nations and the archaeologists who study their ancestors. Descendant communities ask, why do Europeans have "history" while indigenous peoples have a negation? Even Eric Wolf's majestic *Europe and the People without History* (1982), written to redress this lack, can be misread to highlight indigenous peoples as heroic, but ultimately hapless, victims writhing in colonialist webs. DeBoer argues that archaeologists and ethnographers have wrongly concluded that the Midéwiwin was a postcontact religious movement that arose in response to the European fur trade. He combines early historic accounts, such as the Jesuit *Relations,* oral traditions, and toponomy, as well as archaeological evidence, to suggest that many elements of the organization, if not the Midéwiwin itself, can be tracked at least to Hopewell antecedents some 1,700 years ago. Claims for its historic genesis rest upon the tyranny of labels that carve up a continuum of tradition.

Robert L. Hall reminds us of the significant role that calendars play in religious socialization by enlisting time to commemorate and to ritually repeat significant holi[= holy]days or, in Zerubavel's (2003:46) expression, to establish "periodic fusion with the past." In his detailed investigation of Mesoamerican calendars, Hall reactivates the method of Tylerian "survivals" to show how relict beliefs and practices may be preserved in aspects of larger systems that have diverged considerably from earlier forms. In this case, he finds that contradictions in Classic Maya calendars can best be explained as holdovers from earlier systems that otherwise leave no trace. Evidence for these postulated precursors persists in the form of contradictory terms and metrics used for counting days, months, and years in derivative calendars, much as our own calendar carries day and month names taken from Roman and Nordic traditions. Hall's exegesis is ingenious, if hard going for the uninitiated, and should be compared to other reexaminations of calendar origins (e.g., Rice 2007).

If one theme unites all of these endeavors it is what indigenous people have known all along: that the Americas have a deep and complex history, rich in religious ideas and their tangible expressions. To find this history, archaeology needs to apply much more than shovels and screens. To know the past is exasperatingly difficult and all the help we can get should be enlisted: astronomy, iconography, myth studies, and detailed research into indigenous views of landscape and the cosmos. The tendency to reduce cultures to little more than food-getting, gene-spreading devices that eject pottery and stone tools to gratify future archaeologists guarantees an impoverished and unrealistic view of human life and is open to criticism as a handmaid of conquest, colonization, and religious conversion. A richer, more humanistic view of past cultures in the Americas reveals a set of "great ideas"—widespread cosmologies—adapted to a wide range of social and ecological circumstances.

References Cited

Berger, Peter L., and Thomas Luckman
    1966   *The Social Construction of Reality: A Treatise in the Sociology of Knowledge.* Doubleday, Garden City, New York.

Bernardini, Wesley
    2005   *Hopi Oral Tradition and the Archaeology of Identity.* University of Arizona Press, Tucson.

Bourdieu, Pierre
    1977   *Outline of a Theory of Practice.* Cambridge University Press, Cambridge.

Brown, Linda A., and William H. Walker
    2008   Prologue: Archaeology, Animism and Non-Human Agets. *Journal of Archaeological Method and Theory* 15:297–299.

Clastres, Pierre
    1987   *Society against the State.* Zone Books, New York.

DeBoer, Warren R.
    2005   Colors for a North American Past. *World Archaeology* 37:66–91.
    2006   Salient Representations of the American Past. In *A Pre-Columbian World*, edited by Jeffrey Quilter and Mary Miller, pp. 137–186. Dumbarton Oaks, Washington, D.C.

Fogelin, Lars (editor)
    2008   *Religion, Archaeology, and the Material World.* Occasional Paper 36. Center for Archaeological Investigations, Southern Illinois University, Carbondale.

Geertz, Clifford
    2005   Shifting Aims, Moving Targets: On the Anthropology of Religion. *Journal of the Royal Anthropological Institute* 11:1–15.

Giddens, Anthony
    1984   *The Constitution of Society: Outline of a Theory of Structuration.* University of California Press, Berkeley.

Hall, Robert L.
    1997   *An Archaeology of the Soul: North American Indian Belief and Ritual.* University of Illinois Press, Urbana.

Kehoe, Alice B.
    1998   *The Land of Prehistory: A Critical History of American Archaeology.* Routledge, New York.

Kelly, Lucretia S., and John E. Kelly
    2007   Swans in the American Bottom during the Emergent Mississippian and Mississippian. *Illinois Archaeology* 15-16:112–141.

Kluckhohn, Clyde
    1936   Some Reflections on the Method and Theory of the *Kulturkreislehre. American Anthropologist* 38:157–196.

Lathrap, Donald W.

1973   Gifts of the Cayman: Some Thoughts on the Subsistence Basis of Chavín. In *Variation in Anthropology: Essays in Honor of John C. McGregor*, edited by Donald W. Lathrap and Jody Douglas, pp. 91–105. Illinois Archaeological Survey, Urbana.

Lekson, Stephen H.

2009   *A History of the Ancient Southwest.* School for Advanced Research Press, Santa Fe, New Mexico.

Lévi-Strauss, Claude

1968   *Structural Anthropology.* Allen Lane, London.

Morgan, Lewis H.

1868   *The American Beaver and His Works.* Lippincott, Philadelphia.

Nielsen, Jesper, and Toke Sellner Reunert

2009   Dante's Heritage: Questioning the Multi-Layered Model of the Mesoamerican Universe. *Antiquity* 83:399–413.

Odling-Smee, F. John, Kevin Laland, and Marcus Feldman

2003   *Niche Construction: The Neglected Process in Evolution.* Princeton University Press, Princeton, New Jersey.

Oliver, José R.

2009   *Cacique and Cemí Idols: The Web Spun by Taíno Rulers between Hispaniola and Puerto Rico.* The University of Alabama Press, Tuscaloosa.

Oneroad, Amos E., and Alanson B. Skinner

2003   *Being Dakota: Tales and Traditions of the Sisseton and Wahpeton.* Edited by Laura L. Anderson. Minnesota Historical Society Press, St. Paul.

Pauketat, Timothy R. (editor)

2001   *The Archaeology of Tradition: Agency and History before and after Columbus.* University Presses of Florida, Gainesville.

Rice, Prudence M.

2007   *Maya Calendar Origins: Monuments, Mythistory, and the Materialization of Time.* University of Texas Press, Austin.

Roe, Peter G.

1982   *The Cosmic Zygote: Cosmology in the Amazon Basin.* Rutgers University Press, New Brunswick, New Jersey.

Rowe, John H.

1962   *Chavín Art: An Inquiry into Its Form and Meaning.* Museum of Primitive Art, New York.

Simpson, George G.

1944   *Tempo and Mode in Evolution.* Columbia University Press, New York.

Steadman, Sharon R.

2009   *Archaeology of Religion.* Left Coast Press, Walnut Creek, California.

Trouillot, Michel-Rolph

  1995   *Silencing the Past: Power and the Production of History.* Beacon Press, Boston.

VanPool, Christine S., Todd L. VanPool, and David A. Phillips Jr. (editors)

  2006   *Religion in the Prehistoric Southwest.* AltaMira, Lanham, Maryland.

Walker, James R.

  1983   *Lakota Myth.* Edited by Elaine A. Jahner. University of Nebraska Press, Lincoln.

Whitley, David S., and Kelley Hays-Gilpin (editors)

  2008   *Belief in the Past: Theoretical Approaches to the Archaeology of Religion.* Left Coast Press, Walnut Creek, California.

Willey, Gordon R., and Philip Phillips

  1958   *Method and Theory in American Archaeology.* University of Chicago Press, Chicago.

Wolf, Eric

  1982   *Europe and the People without History.* University of California Press, Berkeley.

Zerubavel, Eviatar

  2003   *Time Maps: Collective Memory and the Social Shape of the Past.* University of Chicago Press, Chicago.

Part I
Creating Continuity through Structure, Iconography, and Sacred Stories

1

Structure of the Mesoamerican Universe, from Aztec to Olmec

John E. Clark and Arlene Colman

Our original intent in this essay, which proved impractical, was to explicate Mesoamerican cosmological beliefs known for Postclassic Mesoamericans and then adduce archaeological evidence of these beliefs for the earliest city dwellers of Mesoamerica, the Olmecs. In the Spanish-language literature the beliefs of interest are known as a people's *cosmovisión,* a generous cognitive category that includes cosmogony, cosmography, and the nature of the gods, humans, and all other creatures, things, and animate forces of the universe (see Brundage 1979 for an excellent summary for the Aztecs). Several attempts to outline a minimum, shared cosmovision for the Aztecs and Maya at the time of the Spanish Conquest proved too vast for the historical exercise possible here, so we restrict attention to the slice of cosmological beliefs dealing with cosmography or "configurations of space" (Brotherston 1992:82)—notions about the structure of the heavens and the earth. We attempt to compare beliefs of the latest Mesoamericans at the time of the Conquest with those of their first civilized ancestors 3,000 years earlier. Looking at the shape and structure of the universe is an excellent place to begin evaluating similarities and differences between the cosmovisions of the first and last Mesoamericans because both built notions of space into their cities and offerings.

Details of Mesoamerican cosmography come from Native accounts recorded before the Conquest, or written soon thereafter, and from ethnographic descriptions of the descendants of Mesoamerican peoples (see López Austin 1994). Beliefs varied somewhat between groups, but there was broad agreement about the shape and organization of the universe, and these similarities appear to derive from a long tradition. The proposition of a shared tradition is built into the concept of Mesoamerica itself. Mesoamerica is a cultural-geographical term for a region of peoples who shared a common history of city living (Kirchhoff 1943, 1952, 1966). Continuities between early and late Mesoamericans have been known for centuries, and there is no doubt these peoples were part of a single tradition. This does not mean, however, that there were not significant changes through time in core beliefs. In fact, the definition of Mesoamerica as a historical-cultural phenomenon of high civilization dictates that fundamental changes necessarily occurred in the past to effect the transformation from egalitarian lifeways to urban living. Most of these changes probably happened during the emergence of civilization about 1500 B.C.E. What beliefs changed during this revolutionary transition, and how and why, are questions for another time. A first step for addressing the origins of core concepts is to document the earliest Mesoamerican cosmovision. We begin this task here by comparing archaeological indicators of Olmec concepts to those known for later periods. We avoid imposing Postclassic views on these earlier peoples, but we rely on concepts from the Postclassic period to inform the search for their possible beginnings. We first outline late Mesoamerican views on the configuration of the cosmos and then turn to possible archaeological manifestations of these beliefs as known for the Aztecs and Olmecs.

The Postclassic Universe

Mesoamerican myths record that the earth and its creatures have been divinely created and cataclysmically destroyed on multiple occasions. The Maya describe four creations and the Aztecs recount five. Aztecs believed they were living in the last age of the world, which they described as the Fifth Sun (for detailed summaries see Brundage 1979; de la Garza 1978; Gardner 1986; León-Portilla 1963; López Austin 1994; Monjarás-Ruiz 1987). The universe was a complex affair, and the earthly plane was its central pivot. Space extended in six directions from the center of the earth's surface: up, down, and to four directions. The earth was a disk of land floating on a sea. This sea extended out and up until it "merged with the sky, which then appeared to be the ceiling of a towering edifice. Sea and sky were thus one substance" (Brundage 1979:6).

Human beings, gods, creatures, and other beings each had their place in this universe, as specified during creation. For the Aztecs, the First Sun was ruled by their supreme deity, Tezcatlipoca, associated with the earth, moon, and jaguars: "The light of this original sun was only a half light. People existed in this age but were finally destroyed by a race of misshapen giants. Food consisted of acorns and pine nuts. The giants were finally consumed by jaguars and the feeble sun was stricken from the sky" (Brundage 1979:28). The Second Sun was ruled by Quetzalcoatl, a god associated with the planet

Venus, fertility, and wind. Food was "*acecentli*, a cornlike grain which grows in water" (León-Portilla 1963:42). This world was destroyed by winds, and the surviving people were turned into monkeys. Tlaloc, the rain god, ruled the third age. Food was *cincocopi*, a seed related to maize. The world was destroyed by fire, and survivors became turkeys (León-Portilla 1963:42). The fourth age was ruled by Chalchiuhtlicue, goddess of waters. Brundage (1979:28) describes that "the ending of this age was a peculiar horror for, as an accompaniment to the gushing up of the hitherto impounded waters of the earth, the sky collapsed and fell upon the earth. In the ensuing floods men turned into fish." In the fifth and current age, the god Nanahuatl "sacrificed himself to become the present sun. Maize was grown for the first time, fire was domesticated. . . . The full apparatus of culture appeared" (Brundage 1979:28). Humans were created from bones retrieved from the underworld by Quetzalcoatl. This world age will end with a large earthquake and hunger.

Aztecs believed that at the center of the earth was a cosmic tree, the axis mundi. Space extended vertically up the tree's trunk and branches to 9 or 13 levels of heaven (depending on the account and interpretation), and the tree's roots penetrated down 9 layers of dark and humid underworld. These two divisions of the vertical world were connected to the central, earthly plane by this center tree. Different layers were inhabited by different gods with diverse powers and propensities. Caves were openings to these other levels. "One of the fundamental concepts of the Aztec religion was the grouping of all beings according to the four cardinal points of the compass and the central direction, or up and down" (Caso 1958:10); these cardinal points also corresponded to different colors. Mercedes de la Garza (1978:55, translation by Clark) aptly summarizes the cyclical creation of Mesoamerican people in their evolving universe:

> The gods carried out the creation as a generative process realized by the Sun as the vital and divine cosmic principle, in which progressively appeared the four principal elements and diverse non-human entities, harmonized among themselves, while man, as the central part of the process, underwent successive transformations caused by the essential connection with the other entities of nature, to become a being that the gods needed to survive.

The Earthly Plane

For the Aztecs, the earth was the cleaved body of Cipactli, a fish/crocodile-like creature that floated on, and was surrounded by, the primeval sea. Half of Cipactli's body became the female earth and half the male sky (Bernal-García 2001; López Austin 1994:19, 25). Space extended horizontally in four directions from the earth and its central tree. An image from the Codex Fejéváry-Mayer shows the quincunx arrangement of the horizontal universe, with sky-supporting trees growing in each world quarter and in the central pivot, each tree with its bird, and each direction associated with a different color (see Miller and Taube 1993:187; Townsend 2000:133).

> The surface of the earth (*tlaltícpac*) is a great disk situated in the center of the universe and extending horizontally and vertically. Encircling the earth like a ring is an immense body of water (*téo-atl*), which makes the world *cem-á-nahuac*, "that-which-is-entirely-surrounded-by-water." Neither the land nor the great ring of water is considered to be amorphous or to possess undifferentiated qualities, for the universe is divided into four great quadrants of space whose common point of departure is the navel of the earth. From this point the four quadrants extend all the way out to the meeting place, on the horizon, of the heavens and the surrounding celestial water (*Ilhuíca-alt*). . . . Contemplating the passage of the sun, the Nahuas [Aztecs] described the cosmic quadrants from a position facing the West: "There where it sets, there is its home, in the land of the red color. To the left of the sun's path is the South, the direction of the blue color; opposite the region of the sun's house is the direction of light, fertility and life, symbolized by the color white; and finally, to the right of the sun's route, the black quadrant of the universe, the direction of the land of the dead, is to be seen" [León-Portilla 1963:57, 59].

Mary Miller and Karl Taube (1993:83–84) summarize things as follows: "The earth was also regarded as a flat four-sided field, with the four directions corresponding to each of the sides. For the Maya, this model is metaphorically compared to the quadrangular maize field."

Mountains, rivers, lakes, and caves were particularly important features of the earth's surface. Mountains and hills represented the scutes on the back of the leviathan that was the earth. The combination of mountain and water was also a key metaphor for civilized humanity.

> And they said that the mountains were only magic places, with earth, with rock on the surface; that they were only like ollas [ceramic jars] or like houses; that they were filled with the water which was there. If sometime it were necessary, the mountains would dissolve; the whole world would flood. And hence the people called their settlements *altépetl* ["water-mountain"]. They said, "This mountain, this river, springs from there, the womb of the mountain. For from there Chalchiuitlicue

sends it—offers it" [Fray Bernardino de Sahagún, Book 11, Chapter 12, in Dibble and Anderson 1963:247].

Upper Worlds

From a human perspective sky was unknown: "Unlike the realms of earth and underworld, which could be penetrated by humans, the sky was a source of mystery, a supernatural realm entirely distinct from that of human beings" (Miller and Taube 1993:153–154). As noted, there is some variation in the number of levels or divisions described for the celestial realm and its configuration. A postconquest, Aztec depiction from Vatican Codex A of the levels of the universe shows 13 levels stacked vertically (Caso 1958:61). Some scholars think that earlier views of the heavens conceived of 9 levels rather than 13; this would have made the levels of heaven symmetrical with the levels of the underworld.[1] Of earlier possibilities Walter Krickeberg (1968:39–40) argues,

> According to the most ancient version, the earth is a flat disk sandwiched between the bases of two immense step-pyramids; each step of the upper pyramid represents one hour of the day and one station of heaven, and each step of the nether pyramid represents one hour of the night and one station of hell. The stream which flows around the earth and round the bases of the two pyramids is called the Chicunaulapan, "nine stream," because there are nine heavens and nine underworlds.

Krickeberg also claims that the concept of the layers rather than a "stepped" concept is a later Aztec innovation: "The older idea is more logical; it fits in better with the idea that the sun climbs and descends a pyramid each day (and does the reverse every night), and it also coordinates spatial and temporal ideas better than does the idea of a layered universe" (Krickeberg 1968:40). Other views are that the Aztecs did have a pyramidal concept associated with 13 stations of heaven, with the seventh rather than the fifth level being the apex of the pyramid.

Most commentaries for the Aztec describe 13 separate and stacked layers of heaven, each the domain or abode of gods, and in some instances places for the afterlife existence of humans who died in certain ways. The two highest levels of heaven were "the place of duality" occupied by the original male–female duality, creator gods (León-Portilla 1963:59). The lowest level of heaven was the domain of the moon and clouds. Two groups of 400 stars each were in the second level, as were the numerous constellations. The sun ruled the third level of heaven, and he was aided in his travels across the arc of the sky by men who died in battle or sacrifice and by women who died in childbirth. The fourth level of the heavens was the domain of Venus. Comets and smoking stars were on the fifth level. Between these lower five levels and the two highest levels were the dwelling places of various gods and colors (León-Portilla 1963:59; Matos Moctezuma 2003:30).

The Aztecs had three other non-celestial places that received souls of the dead. Most persons went to the first of these, the underworld, as described below. Others went to two places that Spanish clerics equated with paradise. These two realms of the dead were Tlalocan and Chichihuacuauhco. Tlalocan was a hollow mountain so high that its peak was near the moon, meaning the first level of heaven (López Austin 1994:9, 52).

> Tlalocan, described by Sahagún as "the earthly paradise," was the second place of the dead. In this place "never is there a lack of green corn, squash, sprigs of amaranth, green chiles, tomatoes, string beans in pods, and flowers; there dwelled some gods called *Tlaloques.*" The pleasant destiny of going to *Tlalocan* befell those chosen by *Tláloc,* the god of rain. He called them by means of . . . death by drowning, lightning, dropsy, or gout. The individuals chosen by the god of rain were not cremated but were buried [León-Portilla 1963:125].

The third place for the dead was reserved for children: "It was called Chichihuacuauhco. The name . . . means 'in the wet-nurse tree.' To this place went the children who died before attaining the age of reason. There they were nourished by the milk which fell in drops from the tree" (León-Portilla 1963:127).

Lower Worlds

Most people who died went to the underworld. Details for this dark realm come from descriptions of the expected travels of the dead from the earth to the lowest level under the earth. Just as the highest heaven was ruled by a god and goddess pair, so was the lowest level under the earth. All the levels under the earth were known to the Aztecs as Mictlan. The god and goddess of death inhabited the ninth and lowest level. For the Maya, the underworld was known as Xibalba: "Xibalba, and the Maya Underworld in general, could be entered through a cave, or still, standing water . . . the Underworld geography includes at least two rivers and varies much like the geography of the surface world, and its realm is vast" (Miller and Taube 1993:177–178). In like manner, Mictlan had a complex geography that included mountains and streams. With the exceptions of the types of death mentioned above, "Persons who died a natural death went there, but on the road the dead had to overcome a number of obstacles. The company of a little dog was granted to the dead person; it was cremated along with the corpse. The Nahuas believed that the tests ended after four years, and that this also concluded the wandering existence of the dead" (León-Portilla 1963:124).

The entrance to Mictlan was a cave or caves (one for each of the world directions) that were hidden among the rocky crags of the mountains (Mendoza 1962:78). One descended toward Mictlan on very steep steps. Mictlan was conceived as a spacious and vast place without light or windows. It was a place of famine, desolation, and death. All that remained of the dead who went there was a skeleton of precious bones (Nicholson 1959:52). The soul/skeleton had to pass through four years of trials before it came to the lowest level of the underworld. To arrive there one had to first cross a river and travel through a narrow pass between two hills: "Then followed the place of the snake that guards the road, the place of the green lizard, the place of the eight wildernesses, crossing eight passes, the place of the razor-cold wind, crossing the Chicohahuapan River, and, finally, arrival at Mictlan" (Matos Moctezuma 2003:34; see also Sahagún in Anderson and Dibble 1978).

Tenochtitlan, the Aztec Center Place

Aztec beliefs about the cosmos were given spectacular material expression in their capital city of Tenochtitlan as well as in Native and Spanish maps of the city (see Matos Moctezuma 2003:19, 72). The Aztecs were the final, pre-Columbian immigrants to Mesoamerica. Their tribal lore recounts a pilgrimage lasting about two centuries from their northwest homeland in Aztlan, a community built on an island and a place of natural abundance. After generations of wandering, the Aztecs chose an island in the middle of the lake in the Valley of Mexico (currently Mexico City) for building their capital because it duplicated original conditions at Aztlan and fit expectations of tribal prophecies. Tenochtitlan was founded and built, after several life spans of searching, on promised ground, to a premeditated plan, in accordance with divine instruction, and as a miniature version of the cosmos (Townsend 2000). Tenochtitlan was a five-part city surrounded by water, with the sacred precinct at the center and extensions in four directions, as marked by causeways to the mainland (Matos Moctezuma 2003:30). Pyramids, plazas, and other special buildings were part of this plan.

Building the city to duplicate the cosmos was, of course, also a reenactment of creation, of bringing order out of chaos. The main ceremonial precinct was quadrangular and surrounded by an elevated, broad walkway. The scores of buildings and platforms enclosed by this wall were oriented to the cardinal directions (Clark 2010). The principal structures were a pair of tall pyramids placed side-by-side on the main east–west axis of the precinct and along the route of the sun's passage, facing west like the sun in transit. The summit temples of these twin pyramids were dedicated to the sun god and the rain god. Excavations in these buildings have revealed a complex history of dedicatory offerings and rebuilding episodes of the principal platforms, so cyclical re-creation was also part of their essence (see Broda et al. 1987; Matos Moctezuma 1988).

In Nahuatl, the Aztec language, the word for "city" is *altépetl* or "water-mountain," referring to the original mountain of abundance and the life-giving waters that flowed from the cave at its base (Bernal-García 1997, 2004, 2006; Bernal-García and García Zambrano 2006). Mountains were believed to be hollow and filled with water. Pyramids also represented sacred, hollow mountains overlying cave entrances to the underworld. Clouds and rains issued from mountains through caves; the original ancestors also came from caves. Myths associate the original mountain of creation with the central world tree at Tamoanchan, the place of abundance where gods and humans were created. Various places of this name are recorded in Aztec myths and legend-history, with the earliest one said by Fray Bernardino de Sahagún (Dibble and Anderson 1961:190–191; see also López Austin 1994:49, Figure 2.1, 231–239) to have been in the southern Gulf Coast region of modern Mexico, basically the Olmec heartland. We suspect that this placement of the original Tamoanchan is a legendary reference to Olmec cities built there over 2,000 years before the Aztecs intruded onto the Mesoamerican scene. One of the earliest Mesoamerican cities there was La Venta, and it was built around a large pyramid. Despite their different ages, locations, and cultures, La Venta is a close match for Tenochtitlan, perhaps because they both represented newly founded cities built from scratch and according to a similar cosmic scheme.

La Venta and Olmec Cosmography

La Venta was built by the Olmecs on a small, elongated island in the marshy coastal plain of western Tabasco, Mexico, about 900–850 B.C.E. and was abandoned about 400 B.C.E. This city was founded on virgin soil and built from scratch as an integrated whole and to a premeditated plan in this place that duplicated conditions later specified in Aztec myths (Clark 2012). Features that correspond to Postclassic cosmography are readily apparent in the site plan and in offerings found in the northern part of the site (Complex A), but they differ in some important respects. Concepts of a vertical and horizontal quadripartite cosmos were clearly in place at early La Venta and built into the public architecture. Offerings recovered in the limited excavations at the site reveal a concern with color symbolism associated with directions. Images on carved stone monuments and jade objects reveal knowledge of gods, kings, crocodile-like creatures, ancestral caves, and world centering. In the following sections, we list archaeological evidence that indicates the presence of these and other cosmological beliefs at early La Venta.

Quincunx and Quatrefoil

The horizontal plane of the earth was conceived as a center place extending in four cardinal directions and around a central tree or navel. This idea was represented as either a quatrefoil, in which the center place was implied, or as a quincunx, in which it was deliberately marked. Both configurations were clear in the layout of the city of La Venta and in some of its offerings. This message was fractally represented at the site, occurring at various scales in a variety of media. La Venta was originally constructed in a cruciform arrangement that extended in four directions from the principal plaza, as shown in Figure 1.1. As explained below, pyramids and platforms extended in six directions: up, down, and to four quarters (Clark 2008). The dominant construction was a 32-m-tall clay pyramid built at the northern edge of the plaza. This pyramid rests on a broad platform, and some evidence suggests that there were small mounds on each of the four corners of this platform, thus constituting a quincunx pattern within the site itself (see Clark 2001:186, Figure 2; Lowe 1998a:46, Figure 10). Other buildings spread out to the four earthly directions.

The most famous offerings at La Venta are a pair of large mosaic masks in the Ceremonial Court of Complex A, a square enclosure located just north of the main pyramid (Figure 1.1). These were part of multilayered offerings of serpentine blocks, with the final surfaces interpreted by some as stylized "jaguar mask" pavements. This interpretation was a clear case of a hypothesis in search of an object. Most scholars who saw jaguar faces in these masks were viewing the mosaics upside down, so they had little chance of making a correct identification. The images depicted by the mosaics are abstract rather than zoomorphic, and, in fact, the central elements of the masks constitute the standard Olmec quincunx, with a vertical bar flanked on both sides by two horizontal elements. Kent Reilly (1990:Figure 15) interprets this quincunx design as a symbol of the central world tree (vertical element) flanked by smaller trees or sprouting maize plants in the four quarters. On a more general level, this design is a cosmogram of the earth, its center, and its quarters. The same design is found inscribed on jade axes from the site (Drucker 1952:Figure 47; Drucker et al. 1959:Figure 35c, d).

Three known offerings at La Venta were laid out as cruciforms above square, serpentine pavements and are indicative of quatrefoils and perhaps world trees (Figure 1.2; Drucker 1952:Figure 10b; Drucker et al. 1959:Figure

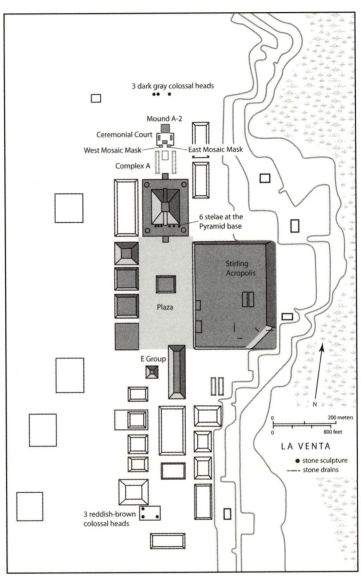

Figure 1.1. Map of La Venta. The probable early part of the site is shown in gray (redrawn from Clark 2012).

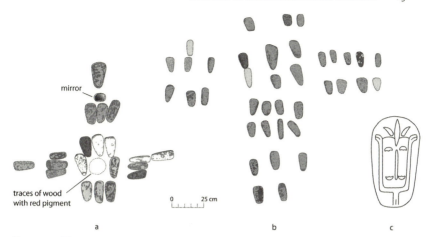

Figure 1.2. Three views of world trees at La Venta. Two are in the form of cruciform offerings—a, Offering 1943-E (redrawn from Wedel 1952:Plate 8b), and b, Offering 10 (redrawn from a photograph in the Heizer collection at the National Anthropological Archives, Smithsonian Institution, photo scan drucker_mesoamerica_laventa__x02)—and c shows the world tree on an incised axe (redrawn from Drucker 1952:Figure 47).

51 and Plate 47a; Wedel 1952:Figure 18 and Plate 8). Other quatrefoils appear to depict caves (Grove 2000). Centers coeval with La Venta have offerings laid out in quincunx patterns. At San Isidro, Chiapas, Offering 11 is a central ceramic bowl flanked on four sides by jade axes and ear spools (see Lowe 1981:245, Figure 13, 1998b:69, Figure 30; Taube 2000:301, Figure 3). Some of the earliest offerings in the Maya lowlands are cruciform arrangements involving jade axes and pots. Cache 7 at Seibal is a cruciform offering with jade axes (Sabloff 1975:230; Smith 1982:115–119, 243–245, Figure 188; Willey 1978:88–89, 97; Willey et al. 1975:44). Recently, a quincunx offering has been found at El Cival in northwestern Guatemala (Estrada-Belli 2004, 2006:Figure 3; Estrada-Belli et al. 2003). This offering, contemporaneous with those at La Venta, is elaborate and informative. Objects in the offering are horizontally and vertically placed and have clear color symbolism associated with different directions and levels. The lowest of three levels of the offering is a square hole excavated into bedrock, with a circular depression within and in the center of the hole, almost like a shallow posthole. Within this square were placed five upright axes in a quincunx arrangement, with the finest axe of the best jade in the center located above the circular hole; these standing axes were embedded in a layer of semipolished jade pebbles. The next level was a horizontal expansion of the central square hole in four directions to form a quincunx in the bedrock. A large water jar was

placed in each of these side chambers, and one was placed in the center, just above the arrangement of jades at the lower level. Four of the jars were black, and one was red. The red jar was placed in the south quarter of the quincunx. Francisco Estrada-Belli (2004, 2006) postulates that this offering was buried and that a central pole, representing a world tree, was erected directly above the center of the offering, thereby constituting a third level. The offering was placed in the plaza and on the east–west axis between two of the principal buildings of the plaza.

An even earlier quatrefoil is known from La Blanca, an early city on the westernmost part of the Guatemala coast. La Blanca began earlier than La Venta and had a large pyramid about the same size and configuration as La Venta's that may have been the precursor of and inspiration for the pyramid at La Venta. Unfortunately, most of the pyramid at La Blanca was destroyed in the late 1960s and carted away to make an elevated road to the beach (Love 1991, 2002). Just to the east of this pyramid, investigators found a painted, rammed-clay sculpture nearly 2 m wide of an elaborate quatrefoil in the shape of a four-petaled flower (Love and Guernsey 2007). This horizontal sculpture dates to about 900 B.C.E. and demonstrates the antiquity of this notion. The clay sculpture is similar to Monument 9 from the highland Mexico site of Chalcatzingo (Benson and de la Fuente 1996:164, No. 37; Grove 1984:48, Figure 8; Grove and Angulo 1987:125, Figure 9.17).

The arrangement of four buildings around a central patio or plaza also conforms to the quincunx pattern. These arrangements are older than La Venta and precede the beginning of Mesoamerica as cultural practices of city living. For example, the early ceremonial center of Paso de la Amada on the coast of Chiapas, Mexico, about 60 km northwest of La Blanca, had major buildings arranged on four sides of a rectangular plaza by 1650 B.C.E. (Clark 2004a:65, Figure 2.6). A quincunx arrangement of four platforms around a sunken patio is also known for San Lorenzo, the predecessor of La Venta in the Gulf Coast lowlands (Cyphers et al. 2006:23, Figure 1.3). One of the most spectacular examples of quincunx architecture of this early period comes from the highland site of Teopantecuanitlan in Guerrero, located southwest of Chalcatzingo. A sunken, square patio dating to about 900 B.C.E. there was surrounded by an elevated walkway. Four massive limestone sculptures were placed on the walkway walls facing the patio, and on the floor of the patio was a miniature ball court, an elongated structure (Martínez Donjuán 1994, 2010). Overall, the arrangement of walls, sculptures, and ball court is remarkably similar to the quincunx image on the large mosaic masks at La Venta. Quatrefoil and quincunx arrangements of buildings and offerings were widely known and clearly go back to the beginning of Mesoamerica by 1500 B.C.E. and probably well before. They appear to have been old concepts from a tribal past that were preserved throughout Mesoamerican history, even up until the present day.

Cipactli as Primeval Monster

Mesoamerican myth views the earth as half the body of a monstrous saurian creature, Cipactli. The earth is her elongated body floating in a vast sea. The geographic circumstances of La Venta fit this notion perfectly. La Venta is situated on an elongated salt dome on the Gulf Coast of Tabasco, Mexico, about 15 km south of the current shore of the Atlantic Ocean. This north–south trending eminence is 10 to 12 m high (Drucker 1952:6) and is surrounded on all sides by a vast swamp. The heavy rains and floods of 2007 raised the water many meters and nearly submerged this island and its lowest mounds in a literal sea. We suspect this place was selected as the site to build a special city because of these very features of natural hydrology and symbolic geography. C. A. Burland (1968:20) suggested that the "whole architectural complex . . . could be taken to represent the head of an enormous alligator. . . . The pyramid would be the main part of the head, with basalt pillars [in Complex A] as the rows of teeth lining the jaws and the two 'jaguar' mounds forming the nostrils. One is led to wonder whether this might not be Mother Earth, or Cipactli, as she was called in later times by the Aztecs." This analogy is intriguing but need not have been this precise; the shape of the island is sufficient. If the Olmecs at La Venta selected this ground for their new city with primal myths in mind, the platforms erected at La Venta would have represented mountains on the earth monster, or back-plates on the crocodile.

    Images of crocodiles or caimans are known in Olmec art, and a case has been made that this was one of the primary images of the Olmecs and a representation of their gods (Stocker et al. 1980). A sandstone sarcophagus found at La Venta in the northern part of the site depicts a crocodile-like creature with vegetation growing out of its back (Covarrubias 1957:70, Figure 30; Drucker 1952:Plate 2; Grove 1992:160, Figure 10; Reilly 1990:Figure 8, 1994:128, Figure 4, 1999:33, Figure 1.11). Clearly, crocodilian and saurian creatures were represented at La Venta and its predecessor San Lorenzo. On the basis of current evidence, however, it is not clear whether these images represented the concepts of Cipactli as mother earth. Slightly later images of crocodilians show them as world trees, with the snout of the creature in the earth, the vertical body of the creature as a tree trunk, and branches growing out of the tail (see Clark and Moreno 2007:Figures 13.7 and 13.24; Miller and Taube 1993:49; Norman 1973:Plates 41 and 42, 1976:133, Figure 3.26; Reilly 1990:Figure 14). In short, there appear to have been at least two ideas associated with crocodiles, both related to the earth and vegetation.

Directions and Colors

The La Venta Olmec are famous for the patterned use of brightly colored clays in their offerings (see illustration in Coe 1968:65), a practice that may have derived from, and be indicative of, a directional color system. Colored clays and stones appear in matched sets indicative of binary pairs (see De-Boer 2005), and these may have been integral to a quadripartite scheme of world directions. The evidence is ambiguous but promising. Potential color symbolism tied to directions is evident in monument placements and the composition of offerings at La Venta. As illustrated in Figure 1.1, mounds at the site were regularly spaced and oriented to the cardinal directions. The main axis of the site is 8 degrees west of north (Drucker et al. 1959:14, Figure 5). Most excavation at the site occurred in the sector north of the main pyramid and is known as Complex A; about 50 percent of it has been excavated (Heizer 1968:12). Offerings were found there along the principal north–south axis or arranged symmetrically on both sides of this axis. The regularity of the placement of offerings in three-dimensional space is an archaeologist's dream because they are so predictable.[2] Because only a small part of the whole site has been excavated, however, assessments of any directional and color symbolism at the site are necessarily limited to Complex A in the northern part of the site.

Unlike the main pyramids at Aztec Tenochtitlan, which faced west, the principal pyramid at La Venta faced south onto the main plaza. At the opposite end of this plaza was a pair of platforms known as an E-Group. This arrangement of mounds, well known in the Maya area, consists of a low pyramid located about 50 m west of a long mound of about the same height (Clark 2012; Clark and Hansen 2001). E-Groups are thought to have been built for observing the passage of the sun throughout the year and for calculating solstices and equinoxes for various calendar cycles kept by Mesoamericans (Lowe 1989:62, Figure 4.10). The east–west axis at La Venta was clearly important, as were observations of the sun, but these observations appear to have been associated with the E-Group rather than the main pyramid. At the southern base of the main pyramid, six tall, carved stone monuments or stelae flanked a central stairway. Those on the eastern side were of various kinds of greenish stones: gneiss, schist, and serpentine. The three monuments west of the stairs were carved of grayish andesite and basalt, so colors of the monuments were clearly being associated with different directions (González Lauck 2010), with a contrast between green and black (dark gray). Stone slabs on the southern base of the pyramid, but north of the standing stelae, were of white limestone (González Lauck 1997). The grouping of stone monuments also shows a north–south contrast. Three colossal

stone heads of volcanic stone were placed in an east–west line at the northern edge of the city, and three even larger stone monuments of pebble con-
glomerate were placed at its southern edge. The northern monuments are
dark gray (black), and the southern monuments are reddish-brown. This suggests a red vs. black/gray contrast between south and north. There was a clear
distinction in the raw materials used for these monuments, with one of the
characteristics involved being color. Parallel contrasts were noted for facing
stones lining the base of the southwest platform of Complex A. Along the
north, east, and west sides of the lower slope of this platform very carefully
squared basalt blocks were placed end to end in a long row in a yellowish-
red clay fill. On the south side, the row of basalt blocks continued. However, behind the row, carved rectangular blocks of green polished serpentine were placed on end, tilted back at a slight angle. Roughly shaped basalt
blocks were then also placed on end on top of the outer layer of well-shaped
and finished basalt blocks. The rough basalt blocks covered the top of the inner serpentine blocks and the finished basalt blocks covered the lower half
of these same green blocks (Drucker et al. 1959:88–89, Figure 26, Plates 12,
13). This arrangement of blocks provides a color scheme of green on the interior, touching the yellowish-red clay fill, and gray on the outside of the green
blocks, for an inside–outside sequence of red/yellow, green, and black. The
distribution of stone monuments at the edges and middle of La Venta can be
read (counterclockwise) as the same color scheme of south (red), east (green),
black (north), and black (west).

The pair of mosaic masks in the Ceremonial Court provides another instance of color distinctions by direction. The centers of these masks were 20.6
m apart. As described more fully below, these masks were complementary
images. They were made up of upper layers of worked green serpentine blocks
set in yellowish clay. Excavation under the southwest mask showed that it
rested on 28 layers of serpentine rubble, with the underlying layers of stone
separated by thin layers of binding clay. Exploration under the southeast
mask also revealed the presence of underlying serpentine rubble.[3] The clays
used to decorate the upper two images were contrasting colors. As illustrated
in Figure 1.3, the rectangular masks have a lower fringe of four diamond-
shaped elements with possible "tassels" associated with them, probably a representation of vegetation (see Reilly 1994:134, Figure 10), and an upper element, just below the cleft, that looks like a recumbent letter E. The mosaic
mask discovered in 1943 on the eastern side of the site axis is known as Pavement 1 and Massive Offering 4. Waldo Wedel (1952:59) summarizes its striking colors: "The blocks of green serpentine set in asphalt on a yellow clay bed,
with a purplish-red veined background for the appendages along the south,
presented a most striking picture, particularly so when the entire surface was

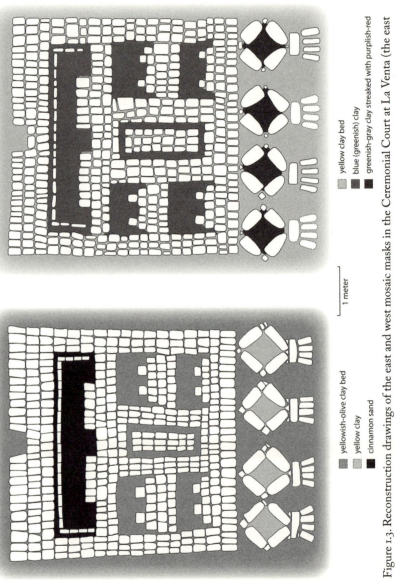

West Mask

East Mask

1 meter

yellowish-olive clay bed
yellow clay
cinnamon sand

yellow clay bed
blue (greenish) clay
greenish-gray clay streaked with purplish-red

Figure 1.3. Reconstruction drawings of the east and west mosaic masks in the Ceremonial Court at La Venta (the east mask is redrawn from Wedel 1952:Figure 20; the west mask is redrawn from Drucker et al. 1959:Figure 29).

cleaned with water and the colors came out in all their richness."[4] This description glosses over his earlier detail that the area within each diamond-shaped element was filled with "greenish-gray clay mottled and streaked with purplish red" (Wedel 1952:59). Stirling (1943:322) presents a slightly different picture of tamped blue clay in the upper, open elements; the southern elements were filled with green and red, which contrasted with the yellow background and blue/green interior of the northern elements.[5] The mosaic mask on the western side of the site axis was excavated a decade later. The serpentine blocks for this mask were set in a matrix of "yellowish-olive clay" (Drucker et al. 1959:93). Drucker and colleagues (1959:94–95) state that the "centers of the diamond-shaped appendages at the [bottom] were filled with clay, slightly more yellowish in color than that of the matrix in which the mosaic was set."[6] In contrast, the upper element, or reclining E (also known as a double-merlon) was filled with cinnamon-colored sand (Drucker et al. 1959:94). Each mask had a north–south color contrast, and they were contrasting pairs. The western mask was red to yellow, north to south, and the eastern mask was yellow to green/red, north to south. It appears possible that the central portions of both the eastern and western masks were set in the same yellowish-olive clay. The diamond appendages at the bottom edge of these masks, however, were clearly distinct, with yellow being associated with the west and green/red with the east. The reddish fringe at the southern end of the southeast mask correlates with other evidence at La Venta that red relates to the south. It probably had many more meanings, as well.[7]

One feature recorded for the western mask, but not the eastern one, was a narrow clay wall around the stylized mask about 1.5 m tall (Figure 1.4). This was of brightly colored clay that contrasted with the clay fill around it. The northern, western, and southern sections of this wall were of red clay mottled with splotches of green, and the eastern part of the wall was of greenish clay with splotches of red clay (Drucker et al. 1959:99).[8] Again we see the association of green with the east. The sequence of colors (inside to outside) associated with the mask was green, yellow (the clay the serpentine blocks rested on), and red (the raised wall).

It is worth pointing out that another mosaic mask (Pavement 2) was found at La Venta on the centerline of the site but about 50 m south of the pair just described (as measured from the clefts from mask to mask). Unlike the other mosaics, the southern mask consists of a single layer of serpentine blocks, and it lacks the four fringed diamonds along its southern edge. Some of the stones of this mosaic were missing, so the absence of a decorative fringe is not definitive. This mask may have been a solitary offering in which contrasts were incorporated into the same representation. Unlike the northern pavements, Pavement 2 had a different matrix: "In the north part of the pavement,

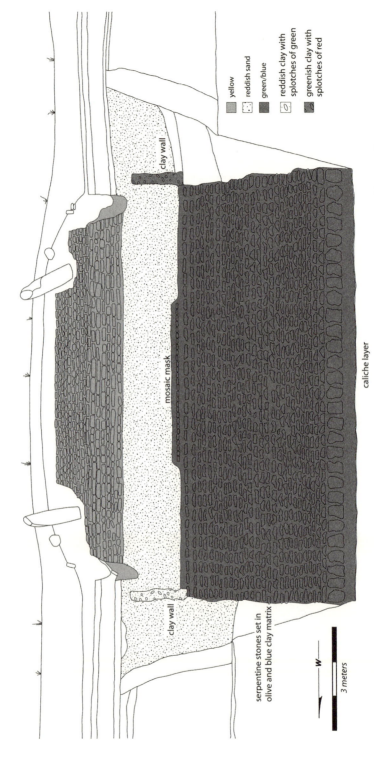

Figure 1.4. Schematic east–west cross section of Massive Offering 1 at La Venta (redrawn from Drucker et al. 1959:Figure 27).

yellow

reddish sand

green/blue

reddish clay with splotches of green

greenish clay with splotches of red

clay wall

mosaic mask

caliche layer

clay wall

serpentine stones set in olive and blue clay matrix

W

3 meters

the stones had been laid in or on a bed of clay; to the south, many lay directly on sand. The blocks on the north, furthermore, had generally a smooth, worn appearance that was missing, or at least was much less noticeable, on those in the south portions" (Wedel 1952:75). Whether the yellow matrix of this offering was a deliberate color contrast with the northern masks is unclear. The mosaic masks may have represented a triad. If there were four masks, the northern mask was removed anciently. There is no evidence of a northern mask in the expected position. We suppose that the three masks represent separate offerings, with the two flanking the center line in Complex A being created at the same time as a contrasting pair.

The Vertical Universe

The presence of a 32-m-high pyramid at La Venta is sufficient proof that the Olmecs there were concerned with vertical dimensions. As noted, this pyramid was likely a copy of an earlier one erected at the coastal Guatemalan site of La Blanca (Clark 2012; Love 1991, 2002). Much has been made of La Venta's pyramid, and various configurations have been postulated for it. When the layout of the site was first sketched, it was assumed that the pyramid was four-sided, like most pyramids known for Mesoamerica (Blom and La Farge 1926:84, Figure 68; Drucker 1952:Figures 1 and 4; Gillespie 2011; González Lauck 1997). A later map by the Berkeley project showed the mound as a fluted cone, and Robert Heizer (1968) postulated that it was purposely made in this manner to mimic a volcano, the mountain that it may have represented. John Graham and Mark Johnson (1979) suggested straight sides with stairways on each of the four sides of the pyramid. Their reconstructed plan was prepared soon after the mapping season of 1968. It was shown to Heizer, but he preferred his original interpretation of the structure as a truncated cone. Excavations by Rebecca González Lauck (1989, 1996, 1997) along the southern base of this great mound verified Graham and Johnson's (1979:Figure 1) portrayal; the pyramid was straight-sided rather than fluted. The fluted appearance is a consequence of centuries of erosion of a clay structure. Graham and Johnson (1979) also considered that the mound may have had inset corners, thus lending itself to the current pattern of erosion, an interpretation with which González Lauck concurs. It is not known whether this earth and clay mound was a stepped pyramid because the interior of this pyramid has not been explored. It has not been determined whether its final form and size represent the accretion of various building episodes or were established in a single building event. We suspect various building episodes were involved. The outermost layer on this pyramid dates to about 500 B.C.E., a century before La Venta was abandoned (González Lauck 1996:75, 1997:93).

As evident with the twin Aztec pyramids at Tenochtitlan, different levels of vertical heavens could be symbolized by stepped pyramids. The earliest pyramids known for Mesoamerica were made of earth and clay, and most are melted cones today. Excavations at some pyramids contemporaneous with La Venta show they had multiple, vertically stacked bodies (Clark 2012); some low clay mounds in the northern part of La Venta were stepped platforms (Drucker 1952:29, Figure 11; Drucker et al. 1959:Figures 10 and 11; Wedel 1952: 40–42, Figure 15), and we suspect the great pyramid was too.

The most spectacular evidence of concepts of verticality at La Venta are the mosaic masks and their associated features (Figure 1.3). So much has been made of the so-called jaguar masks and the enormous quantity of serpentine that each appears to rest on that it generally escapes notice that these masks were the middle elements of massive offerings that extended both above and below them (Coe 1968:65; Drucker et al. 1959:Figures 26–29; Reilly 1999:24, Figure 1.7; Wedel 1952:Figures 18–20). As mentioned, the central design of the masks themselves represents a quincunx and symbol of the earth and its central tree rather than a stylized jaguar. We propose that these masks depict the face of the earth, with complementary representations on the east and west sides of the central site axis. Heizer and his Berkeley team succeeded in getting to the bottom of Massive Offering 1 in one corner. Excavators of the eastern mask gave up trying to hack their way through the stone rubble substructure after going down 60 cm (Wedel 1952:56).

Before describing these twin offerings, it is worth pointing out that neither offering has been tested adequately. It is not known how deep the rock rubble extends below the eastern mask. If it is like its western counterpart, it should be about 4.6 m thick. What, if anything, lies beneath the center of either of these buried stone mounds?[9] These offerings show similarities in overall structure, with color variations between them indicative of paired contrasts. Another factor to keep in mind is that these paired masks were excavated by different archaeologists in different decades, so we cannot vouch for the accuracy of some described differences. They could represent variant perceptions rather than physical differences. Sufficient contrasts are clear between the masks that one should be cautious in extrapolating features from one to the other to compensate for missing information.

Figure 1.4 presents a hypothetical reconstruction of the western mask. This mosaic was precisely placed as the middle horizontal element of a complex vertical feature; it had layers of serpentine below it and layers of adobe brick above it. The layers of green rock below the mask contrasted with the yellow adobes embedded in red clay mortar above it. The upper adobe structure was at least 16 courses high and may have been higher. The bricks were laid horizontally in geometric patterns, but the excavators did not record many details (Drucker et al. 1959:90). The sides of this upper structure were tapered. When originally constructed, this brick platform was 2.25 m thick, with 2 m rising above the surface of the plaza (Drucker 1952:31). Between the lower level of the adobe mound and the upper surface of the mask was a thick layer of mottled pinkish clay mixed with sand (see Coe 1968:65). For the eastern mask, this intermediate fill layer is described as sandy with some clay but also of a mottled pinkish color. The adobe structure above the western mask was mainly yellow bricks set in red clay mortar (Drucker et al. 1959:90). The clay taken out of the hole in which the offering was placed was yellow (Drucker et al. 1959:82), so these adobes could have been made with clay taken from the very pit they subsequently capped. The adobes in the eastern platform were "olive-gray to greenish and yellowish in color, and they had been set in reddish clay" (Wedel 1952:55). The adobes in this mound appear to have tended toward green, with the one on west favoring yellow.[10] This directional color symbolism conforms to evidence mentioned above for the association of green with the east and perhaps yellow with the west.[11] The 16-plus layers of adobe bricks of the eastern platform together were at least 2.25 m thick, and the pinkish fill below them to the upper surface of the mosaic mask was another 2 m (Wedel 1952:55). About 15–20 cm below the adobe platform was a cruciform offering of greenstone axes and a hematite mirror that probably represented a world tree (see below).

In 1942, Philip Drucker (1952:31) placed a 1-by-2-m pit in the center of the western platform. He uncovered six serpentine celts in two different lots; two celts were on the north side of his trench and the other four on the east side, both found "under the bricks." Drucker continued his excavation another 1.4 m below these and did not encounter the mosaic mask, so the axes beneath the bricks under the western platform were probably about in the same position as the greenstone axes were under the eastern platform. The six celts beneath the western platform were embedded in two different masses of very hard, dark, olive-brown clay that retained grass impressions (Drucker 1952:31). Although no special arrangement amid the two sets of celts was recognized, it is certain they were not in the same arrangement as those found below the eastern platform (Drucker and Heizer 1965:55). Also, the axes in the east were not embedded or placed on clay. Another difference between the two masks is represented by a small stone statuette found at the southwest corner of the western mask and in the same clay envelope as the mosaic. The figure had been decapitated (Drucker et al. 1959:212, Figure 63). Excavations of the eastern mask did not extend much beyond the mask itself, so we cannot verify or deny the presence of corner offerings. For the moment, the two different kinds of offerings conform to the complementary patterns already noted for the pair of masks, so we would not be surprised if these were the only special offerings associated with the masks. We remain curious about the possibility of center offerings under the thick stone platforms below the masks.

One striking difference between the masks is that the mosaic for the western mask was enveloped in a layer of olive-colored clay about 30 cm thick. No such clay covering is mentioned for the eastern mask. Rather, the reddish sandy fill above the eastern mask appears to have rested right on top of the mask itself. Based on excavation descriptions, one of the principal differences between the paired masks is that the western one had a thick layer of clay above it and also underneath the adobe platform; the eastern mask did not. Underlying the clay envelope for the western mask was a "slightly darker colored olive clay" in which the serpentine blocks were embedded (Drucker et al. 1959:95). The serpentine rubble under the eastern mask appears also to have been held together with the same tough clay (Wedel 1952:56). No further information is available for the eastern mask, so all insights and speculations come from the excavations of the western mask. Twenty-eight layers of serpentine rubble mixed with some other stones underlay the mask. If one just counts layers of stone, including the mask, there are 29 or 28.5 layers of stone. This count appears to be an obvious reference to lunar cycles. This would associate the moon with at least the western portion of the underworld.

In its horizontal arrangement the western mask tapers from top to bottom (north to south), much like jade axes, while the face of the eastern mask is more square and slightly shorter (Figure 1.3). The number of blocks in each mask appears to be significant, but this complicated topic is not addressed here. Because of the difficulty of the excavation, only one corner of the stone platform beneath the western mask was exposed. The walls of the buried stone platform were vertical. From the stonework and orientation of stones, and their fit in the original offering pit, it is obvious that the stone masons started each layer of stone at the southern edge and worked north. The ancient artisans who put this together were able to keep each of the successive layers level. Drucker and his coauthors (1959:96, Figures 26 and 27) remark that the size of the stones increased as a function of depth. The stones in the lowermost level were the largest, and they were set on end. There are some indications of distinctions made for different layers, as indicated by different colors of clay and/or treatment and orientation of the stones. The eighth layer of stones under the mask, for example, was of cut blocks placed horizontally, like those used in the upper mask (Drucker et al. 1959:96–97). We would not be surprised if these were arranged in a special pattern, but not enough of this level was exposed to make this determination. Layers 15 and 16 below the mask were embedded in blue rather than olive-green clay. Below this level, the excavators noticed more blue clay mixed with the green, but they did not specify whether these were separate layers (Drucker et al. 1959:97). The lowermost level of stones was placed on top of a 30-cm-thick layer of "gun-metal blue" clay that included bits of vegetation that likely was a swamp subsoil or gley material (Drucker et al. 1959:95).[12] Under this was a thin gray layer of caliche-like material; it is not clear in the descriptions whether this was a natural layer or manmade. Colors may have been significant in the vertical divisions, but it may have been the sources of the clays that were more significant, with some coming from the nearby swamp and the olive-green and red clays of unspecified, nonlocal origin and geologic context. In any event, the layers below the mosaic masks were demarcated by clear vertical distinctions, with the lowest layers perhaps indicating a watery origin of the clay. The two clearest distinctions, from top to bottom, occurred at eight-layer intervals, or about one-fourth increments from the mask to the bottom of the offering pit. From bottom to top, the main color sequence was white, blue-green, red, and yellow. This sequence inverts that noted above for the basal facing stones of the southern edge of the adobe mound capping this offering.

The La Venta Olmec left some indications of aspects of their cosmovision with the twin mask offerings. The most complete data are for the western mask. Swamp clay was the first layer of material placed in the bottom of a nearly 7-m-deep offering pit and above a layer of caliche. Over this were placed 28 layers of green stones cemented together with green and blue clays, with some sequential differences in them. For some layers stones were set vertically; for others they were laid horizontally. On top of this stone platform was laid out an image of the earth, likely the stylized image of a crocodilian rather than a jaguar (Clark 2004b). The mask represented the vertical transition from stone to clay. The uppermost layers of this offering were 16 or more courses of yellow bricks, perhaps made from clay from the same hole that the serpentine was placed in, so some of the vertical symbolism may have involved the symbolic inversion of building the stacked layers of the overworld with clay from the underworld, and constructing the underworld with stone from the overworld.

To summarize, the mosaic masks at La Venta are a matched, complementary pair. Both have stone structures built below them and clay structures built to a height of 4.6 m above them. The massive rectangular blocks of light-green rock on which the masks rested were underground platforms. The stone platform beneath the western mask was 4.6 m deep; the 4.6-m depth of the layered rock is also the maximum width of the two mosaic masks. In its entirety, the western platform was about 12 by 9 m in length and width; it consisted of 1,000 tons of imported serpentine cobbles and blocks imbedded in different colors of clay, the color depending on vertical position. The unexcavated buried platform beneath the eastern mask is assumed to be of comparable size. We consider this a good guess because the observed difference between the two masks concerns subtle features rather than basic structure. It does not require much imagination to view these subterranean platforms as green-stone pyramids constructed in the underworld. Small, multilevel platforms of adobe bricks were built directly above these interred, stone mounds. These are the only cases of which we are aware of paired mounds being built one above the other as part of a single vertical series—one in the underworld and one in the overworld. There were two masks but four platforms. For each set of platforms and their mediating mask there were three major levels of different kinds of fill, with vertical levels most clearly marked in the uppermost and lowermost layers. If one considers the masks as earth images and representations of the surface of the earth, then the vertical universe was depicted as equally partitioned between underworld and overworld, but made of different stuff. Each of these major divisions was further divided into vertical layers. The eastern set was associated with an axe offering that represented a world tree with a polished iron-ore mirror hung above its cross piece. The western mask was associated with a decapitated stone figurine, a possible representation of death. This kneeling figure of an adult male was not an accidental inclusion in the fill. On the basis of the current evidence, our best guess for a directional color scheme at La Venta is center—green, north—white/black, east—green/red, south—red/yellow, and west—yellow/black.[13]

Warren DeBoer (2005) described the color symbolism of world directions for pre-Columbian peoples in the Americas and determined broad patterns that correspond to latitudinal zones. Our proposal for the La Venta Olmec does not conform to DeBoer's reconstruction of the likely directional symbolism for Mesoamericans. He postulated that the variety of systems recorded for the Aztecs, Zapotecs, and Maya derived from a color circuit of white/north, red/east, yellow/south, and blue-green/west. The ambiguous data from La Venta could be read as conforming to this scheme, but we think the evidence is better for an association of green with center and east and red with south. Evidence for directional colors for the west and north is less clear. There are multiple evidentiary and logical difficulties with our reconstruction of the color of the Olmec universe, which become clear when considered in conjunction with DeBoer's detailed arguments. We inferred directional colors from the relative placement of features at La Venta and from elements within individual features, so there are questions of the reference points and the scale at which the color code should be interpreted. An even more serious challenge is the presumed connection between beliefs and practices. DeBoer describes Navajo sandpaintings in which the meaning of images comes from manipulation of the standard, understood symbolism to signal contrasts and deviations from the natural state of affairs.[14] In a situation in which directional symbolism is reconstructed inductively from archaeological data (i.e., from what peoples actually did rather than from what they believed or understood), more information is needed to confirm the cognitive model of directional symbolism (see DeBoer 2005:83). For the moment, insufficient information is available for La Venta to verify the directional color scheme hypothesized here. The contrasts of paired objects and features at La Venta suggest that the colors of things and their locations in vertical and horizontal space mattered.

For vertical data we get a sequential color scheme. For horizontal colors, it is not clear how the colors were understood—whether in a clockwise or counterclockwise color circuit (see DeBoer 2005). Vertical color symbolism is evident on the interior north wall of the offering pit excavated for Massive Offering 2.[15] The sides of this pit were given a smooth, flat finish using a yellowish sandy-clay plaster. Presumably, the sides were then painted in horizontal bands (there are only data for a short stretch of the northern face). The excavators discovered the thin layer of paints by chance when they returned to La Venta in 1967 to collect new carbon samples so they could better date the offerings and architecture (Heizer et al. 1968). The initial excavation of this offering in 1955 missed this detail (Drucker et al. 1959). In 1967, only the top 5.5 feet (1.67 m) of this 4.95-m-deep offering pit was excavated, so information is only available for the upper third of the northern wall. The upper band was 16 inches high (40.6 cm) and painted purplish-red. The next band below it was 15 inches high (38.1 cm, listed as 40.6 cm by the excavators) and lacked color. Perhaps this stripe was painted with some organic pigment that has disappeared. Below this noncolored strip was an 18-inch (45.7 cm) band of black (or deep brownish-black), and below this was an 18-inch (45.7 cm) band of purplish-red, the same color as the uppermost one. How extensive this painting is we cannot say, but there are signs that the west wall of the pit was also painted (Heizer et al. 1968:11).[16] If we just deal with what the excavators saw rather than imagined, the color sequence from top to bottom is red, yellow (color of the clay walls), black, and red. Related to our reconstructed horizontal scheme, these colors would represent south, west, and north, with the green east missing from the sequence. Green was well represented in the offering placed in the pit itself. It would be interesting to see whether each wall had the same bands of colors, and in the same sequence.

The regularity of these bands is also of interest and merits investigation. It is remarkable that the four upper strips are 1.67 m in height all together, because this was the standard unit of measure for later Mesoamericans (Clark 2010), and it is one of two basic measurement units reported for La Venta based on other data (Clark 2001, 2008). The offering pit was three of these macro-units deep, with at least the upper level being segregated into four horizontal, stacked bands. If the same regularity persists to the bottom of the pit, there would be 12 horizontal bands in this representation of an underworld. If every fourth band were red (the known pattern), then the bands would constitute four groups of three bands each. This would make the natural triad unit 1.24 m tall. We cannot pursue this topic in detail here, but it seems clear that the Olmecs placed offerings and buildings at La Venta to correspond to notions of vertical and horizontal divisions, each associated with colors or color contrasts, and that each of these may also have had precise dimensions related to it rather than just relational ones.

Axis Mundi and World Trees

We mentioned tree images in discussing site layout and offerings. La Venta has the shape of a northward-oriented cross with a short east–west crossbar. This assessment is based on remnants of public platforms of the main ceremonial center rather than the distribution of domestic middens and houses at the site. As mentioned, the offering (1943-E) of greenstone axes associated with the eastern mosaic mask has a cross shape.[17] Other offerings of jade and serpentine axes at the site associated with other massive offerings have a cross or tree shape (Figure 1.2). It is worth mentioning that these would have been green trees. As described for the later Maya, the green tree was the central tree of the universe. These same cruciform symbols have been interpreted on incised Olmec axes as corn plants that are shown as emerging from the cleft in the top of the head (Reilly 1990; Taube 2000). The vertical arrangement of the cruciform axe offering above the eastern mosaic mask may have expressed this same vertical relationship of cruciform tree/maize plant emerging from the cleft head of the earth image. By extension, it would associate the growing maize plant with the east in possible contrast with a representation of death in the west, as indicated by the decapitated stone figurine.

Mountains, Caves, and Water

The correspondence of the main pyramid at La Venta to a mountain is obvious, as is the surrounding swamp to a primordial sea. As for caves, these are well represented at La Venta in monumental sculptures. The oldest Olmec thrones were large boxlike forms having thick tablelike tops. In the early literature they were called "altars." An Olmec image painted in Oxtotlilan Cave in Guerrero shows a king or god-impersonator seated on top of one of these devices, thereby indicating they were thrones rather than altars (Grove 1970; Reilly 1990:Figure 11, 2002:53, Figure 4.10). Early Olmec thrones are particularly interesting because below the thick slab of stone at the top, for many, there was a recessed niche wherein sits an adult male, sometimes shown holding a lax infant, perhaps a dead and/or sacrificed baby. These seated males are thought to represent royal ancestors to the kings who once sat on the thrones (Clark 1997; Gillespie 1993, 1999, 2000; Grove 1973, 2000). The ancestor emerges from a niche thought to be a cave. Other Olmec art, especially Monument 1 from Chalcatzingo (Grove 1984:Plate IV, 2000; Grove and Angulo 1987:119, Figure 9.7), clearly shows that these niches represented caves and that caves were also the sources of winds and life-giving rains.

Like its predecessor city at San Lorenzo (see Coe and Diehl 1980:119–125, Figures 82–93), La Venta had a special drainage system internal to the central part of the city (within the Stirling Acropolis) to deal with rain. Special drains were made of elongated, U-shaped pieces of basalt covered with basalt lids to keep the system enclosed. A large stone basin was found at La Venta for catching and perhaps preserving water running through this drain system. Stone drains and large stone tubs are known for other cities contemporary to late La Venta. Much remains to be discovered, but at this point it is clear that water management within the city center of La Venta was important. Also, the earliest Ceremonial Court floors were purposely graded to manage water. Shallow open gutters, crowns, and drains were added in subsequent floorings (Drucker et al. 1959:22–24).

Cycles of Creation and Renewal

Given the limited excavation information for most of La Venta, not much can be demonstrated for construction cycles of mounds. Heizer (1960:220, 1962:311) argued that the northern part of La Venta was periodically renewed every 52 or 104 years. Four major building episodes were identified, and the few radiocarbon dates obtained suggested approximate century-long intervals for these activities (Heizer 1960:220, 1961:45, 1962:311). At present, such chronological precision and building periodicity cannot be confirmed. Excavations at La Venta showed numerous episodes of reflooring and rebuilding that Heizer attempted to explain by recourse to later Mesoamerican calendrical and ritual practices. The periodicity of these events was retrodicted from Aztec practices of creating the world anew at the end of every 52-year Calendar Round.[18] As of this writing, it is still not known whether the great pyramid at La Venta was built in stages over time. Based on analogous pyramids from coeval centers in Mesoamerica from adjacent regions, we suspect it was (Clark 2012).

Altépetl

One idea that must have been new with the founding of Mesoamerican civilization was that of "city." We have considered evidence from the structured space of cities as indicative of cosmographic concepts. It is appropriate, therefore, to consider the concept of city itself. For the Aztecs, this concept was represented by an ironic couplet signaling a metaphor that referenced creation and the emergence of humans from caves: cities were "water-mountains." We have argued that La Venta was founded in the middle of a sea and that it had an internal water system. La Venta was a mountain surrounded by water—as well as a mountain full of water. The same can be claimed with greater confidence for its predecessor at San Lorenzo (see below). We propose that the pyramid at La Venta symbolized a water-mountain and that the site was Tamoanchan—the place of creation and abundance mentioned by Sahagún.

But the mythical place of Tamoanchan is likely even earlier. The first city in Mesoamerica evolved by 1500 B.C.E. at San Lorenzo, Veracruz, and was located 100 km southwest of La Venta (Clark 2007). At first glance, San Lorenzo appears to have been radically different from La Venta. The early architecture at San Lorenzo lies buried under later occupation, so few features have thus far been identified. However, the fact that 2 m of late midden could obscure San Lorenzo's original site plan of public buildings indicates the absence of tall mounds for this early city.

The signal differences between La Venta and San Lorenzo may be the physical form given to cities built on virtual islands. We propose that shared features of their physical geography could have carried metaphorical meaning similar to, or ancestral to, the Postclassic concept of water-mountain. For example, the city center of San Lorenzo was built on top of a 50-m-high plateau. In essence, the whole center was a carved mountain about 60 ha in extent. By 1100 B.C.E., San Lorenzo was surrounded by another 640 ha of residential terraces and habitation zones (Cyphers 2009, 2010:37; Symonds et al. 2002). María Elena Bernal-García (1989, 2006) argues that the whole plateau was a sacred mountain (see also Cyphers 2010:38). Specifically, it was a water-mountain—a mountain full of water as well as a mountain surrounded by water. The top of the plateau had a subterranean system of stone drains, some connected to springs (Coe and Diehl 1980; Cyphers 1999, 2010; Cyphers and Zurita-Noguera 2006). During early Olmec times, two arms of the Coatzacoalcos River ran on both sides of the plateau, making San Lorenzo an island (Cyphers 1996:62). The city was abandoned about 1000 B.C.E. Ann Cyphers (1996:71) argues that the river may have shifted course at this time, leading to the collapse of the city and the state society centered there. La Venta was founded about a century after the demise of San Lorenzo, perhaps by disenfranchised Olmecs looking for a promising, or promised, new homeland that duplicated conditions of their, by then, legendary first city.

San Lorenzo may have been Mesoamerica's original Tamoanchan and *altépetl.* The Mesoamerican tradition of kingship and social stratification started there by 1350 B.C.E. (Clark 1997, 2004b, 2007; Coe and Diehl 1980; Cyphers 1996, 2010). Unlike their descendants at La Venta centuries later, the first villagers at San Lorenzo created a city by transforming and building over earlier forms of community, beginning with a small hamlet at 1750 B.C.E., a later village and town, and eventually a city. City life was born and evolved at San Lorenzo. In contrast, it was a prerequisite for founding La Venta. The de novo conditions of La Venta's founding, we think, is the principal reason that Mesoamerican cosmography is much more apparent there than at San Lorenzo (cf. Gillespie 2011). When the city was built at San Lorenzo, the plateau was shaped, cut, and extended to form a rough cross pattern oriented to the cardinal directions (Clark 2008). The most extensive modification appears to have been to the eastern bluff, with a principal axis running perpendicular east–west along the short dimension of the city. At later La Venta, north was privileged over east. More investigation is needed at both cities to recover crucial details. It is sufficiently clear that some principles of site organization at La Venta were present earlier at San Lorenzo and some of its predecessors. For the moment, however, the clearest early manifestation in Mesoamerica of an ordered horizontal and vertical universe partitioned into quarters is found at La Venta.

The Rest of the Olmec Cosmos

The configuration of space is just one of the many topics related to Olmec cosmology, and it is probably the most accessible archaeologically. Much excavation needs to be carried out at La Venta and San Lorenzo to clarify the early physical manifestations of these concepts in Mesoamerica. Pending issues of cosmovision concern time and the nature of various kinds of beings in the Olmec universe. In other essays, Clark has suggested that some Mesoamerican cities were precisely built and that their horizontal and vertical dimensions related to important counts in their ritual and solar calendars (Clark 2001, 2008, 2010, 2012). That is to say, cities such as Tenochtitlan, Teotihuacan, Monte Albán, and La Venta were configured according to the seven sectors of the horizontal and vertical universe as well as to the precise dimensions of time within that universe (Clark 2001, 2004a). For the moment, claims for La Venta remain unsubstantiated and incompletely justified because details of building histories are lacking.

Some of the most precise measurement data come from the offering pits and offerings in the northern sector of the site in Complex A. The well-known mosaic masks are rectangles with singular properties. The proportions of their sides are 3:4, which gives them a diagonal of 5. The natural unit of this simple form is about 1.55 m. In short, the masks represent the union of two standard 3:4:5 triangles. We based our proposed La Venta measuring unit of 154 cm on data from the massive offerings in Complex A (Clark 2001:201). In this linear system, the size of the stone platform under the western mask would have been eight units long, six units wide, and three units high. The top of the adobe platform above the mask would have been another three units. Translating site and feature dimensions into the La Venta Olmec system of linear measurement will be an enormous task fraught with logical challenges. The point we stress here is that concerns of time and number were likely as important as direction and color and that one would do well to heed these details in investigations of Mesoamerican sites.

More difficult topics worth pursuing involve the nature of the various kinds of beings or creatures that once populated the Olmec cosmos. A case has been made for kings and gods (Clark 2004b) and shamans, animal alter egos, and souls (Furst 1968, 1995; Gutiérrez and Pye 2010; Reilly 1989, 1995). All these hypotheses are based on iconographic comparisons of Olmec representations with those of Mesoamerican peoples who lived 2,000 years later, and so are highly speculative. One debate we find especially interesting and important concerns the presence or absence of gods. Creation of a formal pantheon was certainly one of the major innovations of Mesoamerican peoples. How and when did this happen? The supposition that Olmecs had gods goes back to the very beginning of their identification as a culture (Beyer 1927; Covarrubias 1942, 1946, 1957; Saville 1900, 1929), but the idea did not become a topic of debate until the antiquity of the Olmecs had been established with radiocarbon dates. Michael Coe (1968, 1972, 1973) and his students (Joralemon 1971, 1976, 1988, 1996; Taube 1992, 1995, 1996, 2004) describe a small pantheon of gods going back to the early Olmec city at San Lorenzo (also Clark 2004b, 2007, 2012; Reilly 2002). Joyce Marcus (1989) and others argue, largely on theoretical grounds, that these early societies lacked gods and that the images archaeologists interpret as Olmec gods represented animate forces of nature (Flannery and Marcus 2000; Kubler 1972, 1973; Pohorilenko 1975, 1977, 1990; Proskouriakoff 1978). The nature of the supernatural world, the entities that inhabited it, and their relations to humans are surely some of the more important issues awaiting resolution to round out the picture of Olmec cosmology. These relate to fundamental issues of being, agency, and what it meant to be an Olmec or a Mesoamerican 3,000 years ago, issues that, in turn, relate to the structural and cognitive possibilities for historic change. It is not clear at present how such issues can be approached or resolved archaeologically, but they merit the best future efforts of those investigating early Mesoamerican cultures.

Acknowledgments

We received generous and helpful comments from Warren DeBoer and two anonymous reviewers, for which we are grateful. We also thank Kisslan Chan for his artwork.

Notes

1. Jesper Nielsen and Toke Sellner Reunert (2009) make a strong case that the vertical cosmos attributed to the Aztecs and other Mesoamerican peoples is a European imposition of Dante's *Divine Comedy* on Native beliefs. They argue that Aztec beliefs indicate an overworld and underworld organized horizontally, with different stations and features. We became aware of their argument as we were making the final edits to this chapter and so did not have the opportunity to take their argument into account. We promote the widely published view here of a multilayered Mesoamerican heaven and hell. Nielsen and Reunert's proposal rests on sufficient ethnohistorical documentation to be taken seriously but not enough to make a compelling case. One clear statement in Sahagún suggests the concept of stacked layers of heaven is pre-Columbian:

> And so wise were [the Toltecs that] they understood the stars which were in the heavens; they gave them names and understood their influence. And they understood well the movements of the heavens; their orbits they learned from the stars. And they understood that there were many divisions of the heavens; they said there were twelve divisions. There existed, there dwelt, the true god and his consort. The name of the god of the heavens was Ome tecutli, and the name of his consort, the woman of the heavens, was Ome cihuatl; that is to say, they were lords, they were rulers, over the twelve heavens [Dibble and Anderson 1961:168–169].

In other texts, Sahagún mentions that the creator gods were "[above] the nine heavens" (Dibble and Anderson 1969:174, 202; see Séjourné 2004:155). The verticality of the pre-Columbian Mesoamerican cosmos merits serious investigation and debate. We suspect that it will prove irresolvable based on historic documentation alone and that final resolution will depend on facts recovered archaeologically, such as those reported here for La Venta, Tabasco.

2. This symmetry is emphasized in how the 1955 excavators found Offering 11. Offering 9 was found first in Mound A-2 while cutting a shoveling platform back from the main trench on the site axis. "Since by itself it was so obviously off center," the excavators explained, "we put our centerline hypothesis to the test by measuring off a corresponding point on the opposite side of the trench and excavating down to

the level of Offering 9. Offering 11 was found exactly where measurements predicted it should be. This, we decided, is the way archeology ought to turn out all the time" (Drucker et al. 1959:177).

3. Wedel (1952:56) mentions serpentine rubble below the southeast mask: "Underlying the asphalt was an exceedingly tough brownish-yellow clay, 5 to 7 cm thick, below which, in turn, was a compact stone rubble consisting of irregular fragments of serpentine and other rock held together with more clay. This rubble underlay the entire pavement, extending beyond it in all directions to and beyond the edge of our excavations. The stone fragments were so thoroughly compacted and interlocked as to be almost impossible to remove; and we finally gave up our attempts to get through the mass when 60 cm below its surface, we found ourselves still in the rubble. Even here it was so compact that a pick could be driven only a few centimeters into it. There is, thus, no way of telling at this time how much deeper the rubble continued; but what we saw represented an extraordinarily solid foundation for the pavement and all that lay above."

4. Philip Drucker et al. (1959:93) claim that the black color Wedel calls "asphalt" is a chemical precipitate of manganese rather than asphalt.

5. Past perceptions and descriptions of colors are problematic. In some descriptions Stirling identified blue whereas Drucker saw olive or even olive-brown for the same material. It also seems odd that Wedel would leave out the blue hue in his description. He does say the appendages were filled with greenish-gray clay and perhaps the same color was used in the open elements. The color "gun-metal blue" was used by the 1955 excavators (Drucker et al. 1959:95) to describe the clay at the bottom of the rubble.

6. These diamond elements are to the south of the nearly square, abstract design and actually are the bottom of the design. Drucker et al. (1959) viewed and published the southwest mask upside down but amended their mistake in a subsequent publication (Heizer 1964:48). As typical of Olmec figures, the cleft is at the top of the head. Carved axes found at La Venta positioned vertically have the cleft at the top of the head in upright position. When placed horizontally, the head was north and the bottom of the image south, as with the mosaic mask images.

7. Red and yellow were both associated with human burials and death. In all of the La Venta offerings considered human burials (Colman 2010) red cinnabar is present. Structures that contained burials—the basalt tomb, the sarcophagus, and the cist tomb—were all packed with red clay. Other burials not enclosed by stone were often covered with a yellow clay cap (Offering Nos. 3, 5, and 6). The yellow clay cap may have been associated more with the act of burying offerings since four other offerings, not considered human burials, were also capped with yellow clay (Offering Nos. 9, 11, 10, and 12). A vertical distinction may have existed for the two colors: yellow/up, red/down.

8. The color symbolism of this wall reminds us of the water jars buried in the El

Cival cache in which three of the directions, and the center, had similar black jars, with only one direction offset as a different color, in this case, a red jar in the south. The association of red with the south could have been the same for the two sites.

9. Heizer et al. (1968:8) returned to the site in July 1967 and found beads under the serpentine pavement of Massive Offering 2 under Mound A-2. We would not be surprised if similar offerings of scattered jades underlay the serpentine layers beneath the large mosaic masks.

10. The final assessment of the brick color for the western mound was based on a horizontal exposure of the bricks. It is not clear whether this is the color once the surface was dried by the sun or whether it is the color wet. In his earlier test pit through this structure, Drucker (1952:31) described the bricks as "olive-brown clay," a description that parallels that for the eastern platform. Hence, it is possible that there was no significant difference in the color of the paired adobe mounds and that differences can be attributed to the perceptions of different investigators.

11. Heizer argues for the same directional color symbolism on the basis of other evidence that merits comment. He stresses the absence of jade offerings in the western platform and interprets the overall pattern in a way that complements the analysis advanced here:

> Within the palisaded court area were three low platform mounds, one centrally located at the south, and two oppositely paired on the east and west sides. Only in the east mound were ritual jade offerings found, and the large number of these contrasts strongly with their complete absence in the west mound. Here again is evidence of an activity and belief pattern, perhaps having something to do with a color directional concept in terms of jade-green-east, but once more we can only speculate on the significance of the observed differences [Heizer 1962:312].

> Only in the east mound and the eastern half of the south mound were jade offerings found, and the large number of these contrasts strongly with their total absence in the western half of the south mound and in the western mound [Heizer 1961:49].

There are two problematic aspects to these descriptions. Heizer appears to have forgotten about the six serpentine celts found under the western platform (see text). We presume these were green. If he was making a distinction between jade and serpentine, this is not apparent or supportable in terms of his claims for colors. Most of the jade and serpentine offerings at La Venta were found in caches along the central axis rather than to the east of it. We agree with Heizer's overall approach to consider the types of offerings found in each sector of the site, and there are significant differences. The northeast platform in Complex A had three burials, each with a jade maskette, ear spools, beads, and ceramic vessels. In the paired northwest mound, only pottery was found (Colman 2010; Drucker 1952; Drucker et al. 1959).

12. At least one other offering is associated with blue clay. Within the basalt tomb (Monument 7) a platform built of clay and covered with large flat limestone flags was coated with a thin layer of blue clay (Stirling and Stirling 1942). Above the blue clay rested cinnabar and the burial bundles with all their goods (Offering 1942-A). Drucker's (1952:23) description of the clay differs from Matthew Stirling's. Drucker describes the clay as heavy olive-brown or swamp muck. Ironically, these two men excavated this feature together, so their disparate descriptions demonstrate how details may be reflections of perception. Other offerings encased in Drucker's "olive-brown" clay include the cruciform celts (Offering 1942-C) in the same mound (A-2) as the basalt tomb and the six celts (Offering 1942-E) positioned in the fill above the western mask of Massive Offering 1. The clay associated with the six celts retained impressions of straw or grass, possibly pointing to its origin as swamp muck. In all cases, this material was used as a lowermost, foundation layer for an offering.

13. The equation of red with a southern direction is evident in three of the offerings incorporating pigment (Offering Nos. 9, 10, and 11); a deep purplish-red cinnabar was placed at the south end of these offerings. In four offerings (Offering Nos. 1943-E, 1943-N, 9, and 11) that include a hematite mirror as part of the arrangement, the mirror was positioned to the north, supporting an equation of gray or shiny (white) with the northern direction.

14. Offering 12 is an example of possible inversion of color symbolism. This offering on the centerline in the fill above Massive Offering 3 consisted of two round, lens-shaped masses of bright-colored material (20-cm diameter by 1 cm thick) at the bottom of a small pit. The pigment on the west was bright green malachite and the material on the east was very bright purplish-red cinnabar. No artifacts were found with the offering. The pit was plastered over with yellow clay. This offering documents the pairing of red and green colors on the east–west axis, but inverts the relationship described for other monuments.

15. Massive Offering 2 is a single layer of serpentine blocks placed on a bright-red sandy-clay bed at the bottom of an approximately 15-m (north–south) by 6-m (east–west) by 5-m deep pit below Mound A-2, a stepped platform on the north end of Complex A. These blocks were prepared rectangles with rounded corners and a smoothed and polished upper surface (Drucker et al. 1959:128–129). The cruciform offering of celts discovered in 1942 (Offering 1942-D) and Offerings 9 and 11 were placed in the fill above the serpentine pavement.

16. Much of the painted walls in this pit may still exist, so it will be interesting in the future to determine the vertical alternation of colors with the use of modern techniques for detecting chemicals that may have been part of organic paints.

17. The three cruciform celt arrangements discovered at La Venta are all placed on different-colored beds (Colman 2010). The cruciform (Offering 1943-E) associ-

ated with the eastern mask (Pavement No. 1) did not have a specially prepared bed for the celts (Wedel 1952:55). Instead, the axes were laid directly on the light mottled pinkish sand mixed with whitish clay. The cruciform arrangement (Offering 10) associated with Massive Offering 3 to the north was laid out on a special bed of reddish-clay and was plastered over with a layer of yellow sandy clay (Drucker et al. 1959:185). Also, a small area at the extreme south end of this arrangement was covered with deep-purple material (possibly a pigment or a form of cinnabar; Drucker et al. 1959:185). The third cruciform cache (Offering 1942-C) was placed above Massive Offering 2 in Mound A-2. These axes were embedded in a layer of compact olive-brown clay (see Note 12) (Drucker 1952:27).

18. We have avoided addressing topics of time here because of lack of space. The Calendar Round was a period of 18,980 days and represented the concatenation of a solar calendar of 365 days and a ritual calendar of 260 days. Any given combination of a ritual day with a solar day would only occur once every 52 years (for good discussions of Mesoamerican calendars, see Coe 2005; Sharer and Traxler 2006).

References Cited

Anderson, Arthur J. O., and Charles E. Dibble (translators)

1978   *Florentine Codex: General History of the Things of New Spain by Fray Bernardino de Sahagún: Book 3—The Origins of the Gods.* 2nd ed. Monographs of the School of American Research and The Museum of New Mexico 14, Part 4. School of American Research, Santa Fe, New Mexico.

Benson, Elizabeth P., and Beatriz de la Fuente (editors)

1996   *Olmec Art of Ancient Mexico.* National Gallery of Art, Washington, D.C.

Bernal-García, María Elena

1989   Tzatza: Olmec Mountains and the Ruler's Ritual Speech. In *Seventh Palenque Round Table, 1989 Vol IX,* edited by Merle Greene Robertson and Virginia M. Fields, pp. 113–123. Pre-Columbian Art Research Institute, San Francisco.

1997   From Mountain to Toponym in the *Historia Tolteca-Chichimeca.* In *Latin American Indian Literatures, Messages and Meanings: Papers from the Twelfth Annual Symposium, LAILA,* edited by Mary H. Preuss, pp. 85–102. Labyrinthos, Lancaster, California.

2001   The Life and Bounty of the Mesoamerican Sacred Mountain. In *Indigenous Traditions and Ecology: The Interbeing of Cosmology and Community,* edited by J. A. Grim, pp. 235–349. Center for the Study of World Religions, Harvard Divinity School, Cambridge, Massachusetts.

2004   Chollollan: de Montaña a Topónimo de Paraje y Ciudad. In *La Ciudad: Problema Integral de Preservación Patrimonial,* edited by L. Noelle, pp. 103–121. UNAM, Mexico.

2006   Tu Agua, Tu Cerro, Tu Flor: Orígenes y Metamorfosis Conceptuales del

Altepetl de Cholula, Siglos XII y XVI. In *Territorialidad y Paisaje en el Alte-petl del Siglo XVI,* edited by F. Fernández Christlieb and A. J. García Zam-brano, pp. 231–349. Fondo de Cultura Económica, Mexico.

Bernal-García, María Elena, and Ángel Julián García Zambrano

2006   El Altepetl Colonial y sus Antecedentes Prehispánicos: Contexto Teórico-Historiográfico. In *Territorialidad y Paisaje en el Altepetl del Siglo XVI,* ed-ited by F. Fernández Christlieb and A. J. García Zambrano, pp. 31–113. Fondo de Cultura Económica, Mexico.

Beyer, Hermann

1927   Review of Blom and La Farge, *Tribes and Temples. El México Antiguo* 2: 305–313.

Blom, Frans, and Oliver La Farge

1926   *Tribes and Temples: A Record of the Expedition to Middle America Conducted by the Tulane University of Louisiana in 1925.* Tulane University, New Or-leans.

Broda, Johanna, Davíd Carrasco, and Eduardo Matos Moctezuma

1987   *The Great Temple of Tenochtitlan: Center and Periphery in the Aztec World.* University of California Press, Berkeley.

Brotherston, Gordon

1992   *Book of the Fourth World: Reading the Native Americas through Their Litera-ture.* Cambridge University Press, Cambridge.

Brundage, Burr Cartwright

1979   *The Fifth Sun: Aztec Gods, Aztec World.* University of Texas Press, Austin.

Burland, C. A.

1968   *The Gods of Mexico.* Capricorn Books, New York.

Caso, Alfonso

1958   *The Aztecs: People of the Sun.* University of Oklahoma Press, Norman.

Clark, John E.

1997   The Arts of Government in Early Mesoamerica. *Annual Review of Anthro-pology* 26:211–234.

2001   Ciudades Tempranas Olmecas. In *Reconstruyendo la Ciudad Maya: El Ur-banismo en las Sociedades Antiguas,* edited by A. Ciudad Ruiz, M. J. I. Ponce de León, and M. d. C. Martínez Martínez, pp. 183–210. Sociedad Española de Estudios Mayas, Madrid.

2004a   Mesoamerica Goes Public: Early Ceremonial Centers, Leaders, and Com-munities. In *Mesoamerican Archaeology,* edited by Julia Hendon and Rose-mary Joyce, pp. 43–72. Blackwell, Oxford.

2004b   The Birth of Mesoamerican Metaphysics: Sedentism, Engagement, and Moral Superiority. In *Rethinking Materiality: The Engagement of Mind with the Material World,* edited by E. DeMarrais, C. Gosden, and C. Renfrew, pp. 205–224. Cambridge University Press, Cambridge.

2007   Mesoamerica's First State. In *The Political Economy of Ancient Mesoamerica: Transformations during the Formative and Classic Periods,* edited by V. L. Scarborough and J. E. Clark, pp. 11–46. University of New Mexico Press, Albuquerque.

2008   Cities and Towns of the Olmec. In *Encyclopaedia of the History of Science, Technology, and Medicine in Non-Western Cultures,* 2nd ed., edited by Helaine Selin, Vol. 1, pp. 554–558. Springer, Dordrecht, Netherlands.

2010   Aztec Dimensions of Holiness. In *The Archaeology of Measurement: Comprehending Heaven, Earth, and Time in Ancient Societies,* edited by Iain Morley and Colin Renfrew, pp. 150–169. Cambridge University Press, Cambridge.

2012   Western Kingdoms of the Middle Preclassic. In *Early Maya States,* edited by R. Sharer and L. Traxler. University Museum, Philadelphia.

Clark, John E., and Richard D. Hansen

2001   The Architecture of Early Kingship: Comparative Perspectives on the Origins of the Maya Royal Court. In *The Maya Royal Court,* edited by T. Inomata and S. D. Houston, pp. 1–45. Westview Press, Boulder, Colorado.

Clark, John E., and Ayax Moreno

2007   Redrawing the Izapa Monuments. In *Archaeology, Art, and Ethnogenesis in Mesoamerican Prehistory: Papers in Honor of Gareth W. Lowe,* edited by L. S. Lowe and M. E. Pye, pp. 277–319. Papers of the New World Archaeological Foundation 68. Brigham Young University, Provo, Utah.

Coe, Michael D.

1968   *America's First Civilization.* American Heritage, New York.

1972   Olmec Jaguars and Olmec Kings. In *The Cult of the Feline,* edited by Elizabeth P. Benson, pp. 1–12. Dumbarton Oaks, Washington, D.C.

1973   The Iconology of Olmec Art. In *The Iconography of Middle American Sculpture,* edited by Dudley T. Easby Jr., pp. 1–12. Metropolitan Museum of Art, New York.

2005   *The Maya.* 7th ed. Thames and Hudson, London.

Coe, Michael D., and Richard A. Diehl

1980   *In the Land of the Olmec.* University of Texas Press, Austin.

Colman, Arlene

2010   The Construction of Complex A at La Venta, Tabasco: A History of Buildings, Burials, Offerings, and Stone Monuments. Unpublished M.A. thesis, Department of Anthropology, Brigham Young University, Provo, Utah.

Covarrubias, Miguel

1942   Origen y Desarrollo del Estilo Artístico "Olmeca." In *Mayas y Olmecas: Segunda Reunión de Mesa Redonda sobre Problemas Antropológicos de México y Centro América,* pp. 46–49. Talleres de la Editorial Stylo, Mexico.

1946   El Arte Olmeca o de La Venta. *Cuadernos Americanos* 4:154–179.

1957   *Indian Art of Mexico and Central America.* Alfred A. Knopf, New York.

Cyphers, Ann

  1996   Reconstructing Olmec Life at San Lorenzo. In *Olmec Art of Ancient Mexico,* edited by Elizabeth P. Benson and Beatriz de la Fuente, pp. 61–71. National Gallery of Art, Washington, D.C.

  1999   From Stone to Symbols: Olmec Art in Social Context at San Lorenzo Tenochtitlán. In *Social Patterns in Pre-classic Mesoamerica,* edited by D. C. Grove and R. A. Joyce, pp. 155–181. Dumbarton Oaks, Washington, D.C.

  2009   Bad-Year Economics and the San Lorenzo Olmec. Public lecture, Dumbarton Oaks, Washington, D.C., November 5.

  2010   San Lorenzo. In *Olmec: Colossal Masterworks of Ancient Mexico,* edited by K. Berrin and V. M. Fields, pp. 34–43. Fine Arts Museums of San Francisco and Los Angeles County Museum of Art, California.

Cyphers, Ann, Alejandro Hernández-Portilla, Marisol Varela-Gómez, and Lilia Grégor-López

  2006   Cosmological and Sociopolitical Synergy in Preclassic Architecture. In *Precolumbian Water Management: Ideology, Ritual, and Power,* edited by L. J. Lucero and B. W. Fash, pp. 17–32. University of Arizona Press, Tucson.

Cyphers, Ann, and Judith Zurita-Noguera

  2006   A Land That Tastes of Water. In *Precolumbian Water Management: Ideology, Ritual, and Power,* edited by L. J. Lucero and B. W. Fash, pp. 33–66. University of Arizona Press, Tucson.

DeBoer, Warren R.

  2005   Colors for a North American Past. *World Archaeology* 37:66–91.

de la Garza, Mercedes

  1978   *El Hombre en el Pensamiento Religioso Náhuatl y Maya.* UNAM, Mexico.

Dibble, Charles E., and Arthur J. O. Anderson (translators)

  1961   *Florentine Codex: General History of the Things of New Spain by Fray Bernardino de Sahagún: Book 10—The People.* Monographs of the School of American Research and The Museum of New Mexico 14, Part 11. School of American Research, Santa Fe, New Mexico.

  1963   *Florentine Codex: General History of the Things of New Spain by Fray Bernardino de Sahagún: Book 11—Earthly Things.* Monographs of the School of American Research and The Museum of New Mexico 14, Part 12, The School of American Research, Santa Fe, New Mexico.

  1969   *Florentine Codex: General History of the Things of New Spain by Fray Bernardino de Sahagún: Book 6—Rhetoric and Moral Philosophy.* Monographs of the School of American Research and The Museum of New Mexico 14, Part 7, The School of American Research, Santa Fe, New Mexico.

Drucker, Philip

  1952   *La Venta, Tabasco: A Study of Olmec Ceramics and Art.* Bulletin 153, Bureau of American Ethnology. U.S. Government Printing Office, Washington, D.C.

Drucker, Philip, and Robert F. Heizer

1965   Commentary on W. R. Coe and Robert Stuckenrath's View of *Excavations at La Venta, Tabasco, 1955. The Kroeber Anthropological Society Papers* 33:37–69.

Drucker, Philip, Robert F. Heizer, and Robert J. Squier

1959   *Excavations at La Venta Tabasco, 1955.* Bulletin 170, Bureau of American Ethnology. U.S. Government Printing Office, Washington, D.C.

Estrada-Belli, Francisco

2004   Cival, La Sufricaya and Homul: The Long History of Maya Political Power and Settlement in the Holmul Region. Paper presented at the II Belize Archaeology Symposium, Belize City.

2006   Lightning Sky, Rain, and the Maize God: The Ideology of Preclassic Maya Rulers at Cival, Peten, Guatemala. *Ancient Mesoamerica* 17:57–78.

Estrada-Belli, Francisco, Jeremy Bauer, Molly Morgan, and Angel Chavez

2003   Symbols of Early Maya Kingship at Cival, Petén, Guatemala. *Antiquity* online 77(298).

Flannery, Kent V., and Joyce Marcus

2000   Formative Mexican Chiefdoms and the Myth of the "Mother Culture." *Journal of Anthropological Archaeology* 19:1–37.

Furst, Peter T.

1968   The Olmec Were-Jaguar Motif in the Light of Ethnographic Reality. In *Dumbarton Oaks Conference on the Olmec,* edited by Elizabeth P. Benson, pp. 143–174. Dumbarton Oaks, Washington, D.C.

1995   Shamanism, Transformation, and Olmec Art. In *The Olmec World: Ritual and Rulership,* edited by Elizabeth P. Benson, pp. 69–81. Art Museum, Princeton University, Princeton, New Jersey.

Gardner, Brant

1986   Reconstructing the Ethnohistory of Myth: A Structural Study of the Aztec "Legend of the Suns." In *Symbol and Meaning beyond the Closed Community: Essays in Mesoamerican Ideas,* edited by G. H. Gossen, pp. 19–34. Institute for Mesoamerican Studies, State University of New York, Albany.

Gillespie, Susan D.

1993   Power, Pathways, and Appropriations in Mesoamerican Art. In *Imagery and Creativity: Ethnoaesthetics and Art Worlds in the Americas,* edited by D. S. Whitten and N. E. Whitten, pp. 67–107. University of Arizona Press, Tucson.

1999   Olmec Thrones as Ancestral Altars: The Two Sides of Power. In *Material Symbols: Culture and Economy in Prehistory,* edited by John E. Robb, pp. 244–253. Occasional Paper 26. Center for Archaeological Investigations, Southern Illinois University, Carbondale.

2000   The Monuments of Laguna de los Cerros and Its Hinterland. In *Olmec Art and Archaeology in Mesoamerica,* edited by John E. Clark and Mary E. Pye, pp. 95–115. National Gallery of Art, Washington, D.C.

2011   Archaeological Drawings as Re-presentations: The Maps of Complex A, La Venta, Mexico. *Latin American Antiquity* 22:3–36.

González Lauck, Rebecca

1989   Recientes Investigaciones en La Venta, Tabasco. In *El Preclássico o Formativo Avances y Perspectivas,* edited by Martha Carmona Macías, pp. 81–90. Instituto Nacional de Antropología e Historia, Mexico.

1996   La Venta: An Olmec Capital. In *Olmec Art of Ancient Mexico,* edited by Elizabeth P. Benson and Beatriz de la Fuente, pp. 73–81. National Gallery of Art, Washington, D.C.

1997   Acerca de Pirámides de Tierra y Seres Sobrenaturales: Observaciones Preliminares en Torno al Edificio C-1, La Venta, Tabasco. *Arqueología, Segunda Época* 17:79–97.

2010   The Architectural Setting of Olmec Sculpture Clusters at La Venta, Tabasco. In *The Place of Stone Monuments: Context, Use, and Meaning in Mesoamerica's Preclassic Transition,* edited by J. Guernsey, J. E. Clark, and B. Arroyo, pp. 129–148. Dumbarton Oaks, Washington, D.C.

Graham, John A., and Mark Johnson

1979   The Great Mound of La Venta. In *Studies in Ancient Mesoamerica, IV.* Contributions of the University of California Archaeological Research Facility, No. 41, pp. 1–6. Department of Anthropology, University of California, Berkeley.

Grove, David C.

1970   *The Olmec Paintings of Oxtotitlan Cave, Guerrero, Mexico.* Studies in Pre-Columbian Art and Archaeology 6. Dumbarton Oaks, Washington, D.C.

1973   Olmec Altars and Myths. *Archaeology* 26(2):128–135.

1984   *Chalcatzingo: Excavations on the Olmec Frontier.* Thames and Hudson, London.

1992   The Olmec Legacy. *National Geographic Research and Exploration* 8(2): 148–165.

2000   Faces of the Earth at Chalcatzingo, Mexico: Serpents, Caves, and Mountains in Middle Formative Period Iconography. In *Olmec Art and Archaeology in Mesoamerica,* edited by John E. Clark and Mary E. Pye, pp. 277–295. National Gallery of Art, Washington, D.C.

Grove, David C., and Jorge Angulo

1987   A Catalog and Description of Chalcatzingo's Monuments. In *Ancient Chalcatzingo,* edited by David C. Grove, pp. 114–131. University of Texas Press, Austin.

Gutiérrez, Gerardo, and Mary E. Pye

2010   The Iconography of the Nahual: Human-Animal Transformations in Preclassic Guerrero and Morelos. In *The Place of Stone Monuments: Context, Use, and Meaning in Mesoamerica's Preclassic Transition,* edited by J. Guernsey, J. E. Clark, and B. Arroyo, pp. 27–54. Dumbarton Oaks, Washington, D.C.

Heizer, Robert F.

1960   Agriculture and the Theocratic State in Lowland Southeastern Mexico. *American Antiquity* 26:215–222.

1961   Inferences on the Nature of Olmec Society Based upon Data from the La Venta Site. *Kroeber Anthropological Society Papers* 25:43–57. University of California, Berkeley.

1962   The Possible Sociopolitical Structure of the La Venta Olmec. *Aketn des 34 Internationales Amerikanisten Kongresses,* pp. 310–317. Verlag Ferdinand Berger, Horn, Austria.

1964   Some Interim Remarks on the Coe-Stuckenrath Review. *Kroeber Anthropological Society Papers* 31:45–50. University of California, Berkeley.

1968   New Observations on La Venta. In *Dumbarton Oaks Conference on the Olmec,* edited by Elizabeth P. Benson, pp. 9–36. Dumbarton Oaks, Washington, D.C.

Heizer, Robert F., Philip Drucker, and John A. Graham

1968   Investigations at La Venta, 1967. In *Papers in Mesoamerican Archaeology.* Contributions of the University of California Archaeological Research Facility, No. 5, pp. 1–34. Department of Anthropology, University of California, Berkeley.

Joralemon, Peter David

1971   *A Study of Olmec Iconography.* Studies in Pre-Columbian Art and Archaeology 7. Dumbarton Oaks, Washington, D.C.

1976   The Olmec Dragon: A Study in Pre-Columbian Iconography. In *Origins of Religious Art and Iconography in Preclassic Mesoamerica,* edited by Henry B. Nicholson, pp. 17–71. UCLA Latin American Center Publications, Los Angeles.

1988   The Olmec. In *The Face of Ancient America: The Wally and Brenda Zollman Collection of Precolumbian Art,* edited by Lee A. Parsons, John B. Carlson, and Peter David Joralemon, pp. 9–50. Indiana University Press, Bloomington.

1996   In Search of the Olmec Cosmos: Reconstructing the World View of Mexico's First Civilization. In *Olmec Art of Ancient Mexico,* edited by Elizabeth P. Benson and Beatriz de la Fuente, pp. 51–59. National Gallery of Art, Washington, D.C.

Kirchhoff, Paul

1943   Mesoamérica: sus límites geográficos, composición étnica y caracteres culturales. *Acta Americana* 1:92–107.

1952   Mesoamerica: Its Geographic Limits, Ethnic Composition and Cultural Characteristics. In *Heritage of Conquest: The Ethnology of Middle America,* edited by S. Tax, pp. 17–30. Free Press Publishers, Glencoe, Illinois.

1966   Mesoamerica: Its Geographic Limits, Ethnic Composition and Cultural Characteristics [translation of 1943 original]. In *Ancient Mesoamerica: Selected Reading,* edited by John A. Graham, pp. 1–14. Peek Publications, Palo Alto, California.

Krickeberg, Walter

1968   Mesoamerica. In *Pre-Columbian American Religions,* translated by Stanley Davis and edited by W. Krickeberg, H. Trimborn, W. Müller, and O. Zerries, pp. 7–82. Holt, Rinehart, and Winston, New York.

Kubler, George

1972   Jaguars in the Valley of Mexico. In *The Cult of the Feline,* edited by Elizabeth P. Benson, pp. 19–44. Dumbarton Oaks, Washington, D.C.

1973   Science and Humanism among Americanists. In *The Iconography of Middle American Sculpture,* edited by Dudley T. Easby Jr., pp. 163–167. Metropolitan Museum of Art, New York.

León-Portilla, Miguel

1963   *Aztec Thought and Culture.* University of Oklahoma Press, Norman.

López Austin, Alfredo

1994   *Tamoanchan y Tlalocan.* Fondo de Cultura Económico, Mexico.

Love, Michael W.

1991   Style and Social Complexity in Formative Mesoamerica. In *The Formation of Complex Society in Southeastern Mesoamerica,* edited by W. R. Fowler Jr., pp. 47–76. CRC Press, Boca Raton, Florida.

2002   *Early Complex Society in Pacific Guatemala: Settlements and Chronology of the Río Naranjo, Guatemala.* Papers of the New World Archaeological Foundation 66. Brigham Young University Press, Provo, Utah.

Love, Michael W., and Julia Guernsey

2007   Monument 3 from La Blanca, Guatemala: A Middle Preclassic Earthen Structure and Its Ritual Associations. *Antiquity* 81:920–932.

Lowe, Gareth W.

1981   Olmec Horizons Defined in Mound 20, San Isidro, Chiapas. In *The Olmec and Their Neighbors,* edited by Elizabeth P. Benson, pp. 231–255. Dumbarton Oaks, Washington, D.C.

1989   The Heartland Olmec: Evolution of Material Culture. In *Regional Perspectives on the Olmec,* edited by R. J. Sharer and D. C. Grove, pp. 33–67. Cambridge University Press, Cambridge.

1998a   *Los Olmecas de San Isidro en Malpaso, Chiapas.* Instituto Nacional de Antropología e Historia, Mexico.

1998b   *Mesoamérica Olmeca: Diez Preguntas.* INAH Colección Científica, 370. Mexico City.

Marcus, Joyce

1989   Zapotec Chiefdoms and the Nature of Formative Religion. In *Regional*

Perspectives on the Olmec, edited by R. J. Sharer and D. C. Grove, pp. 148–197. Cambridge University Press, Cambridge.

Martínez Donjuán, Guadalupe

1994   Los Olmecas en el Estado de Guerrero. In *Los Olmecas en Mesoamérica,* edited by J. E. Clark, pp. 143–163. Citibank, Mexico City.

2010   The Sculpture from Teopantecuanitlan, Guerrero, Mexico. In *The Place of Stone Monuments: Context, Use, and Meaning in Mesoamerica's Preclassic Transition,* edited by J. Guernsey, J. E. Clark, and B. Arroyo, pp. 55–76. Dumbarton Oaks, Washington, D.C.

Matos Moctezuma, Eduardo

1988   *The Great Temple of the Aztecs: Treasures of Tenochtitlan.* Thames and Hudson, London.

2003   Aztec History and Cosmovision. In *Moctezuma's Mexico: Visions of the Aztec World,* edited by D. Carrasco and E. Matos Moctezuma, pp. 3–97. University of Colorado Press, Boulder.

Mendoza, Vicente T.

1962   El Plano o Mundo Inferior, Mictlan, Xibalba, Nith y Hel. *Estudios de Cultura Nahuatl* 3:75–99.

Miller, Mary, and Karl Taube

1993   *An Illustrated Dictionary of the Gods and Symbols of Ancient Mexico and the Maya.* Thames and Hudson, London.

Monjarás-Ruiz, Jesús (editor)

1987   *Mitos Cosmogónicos del México Antiguo.* INAH, Mexico.

Nicholson, Irene

1959   *Firefly in the Night: A Study of Ancient Mexican Poetry and Symbolism.* Faber and Faber, London.

Nielsen, Jesper, and Toke Sellner Reunert

2009   Dante's Heritage: Questioning the Multi-Layered Model of the Mesoamerican Universe. *Antiquity* 83:399–413.

Norman, V. Garth

1973   *Izapa Sculpture: Part 1—Album.* Papers of the New World Archaeological Foundation 30. Provo, Utah.

1976   *Izapa Sculpture: Part 2—Text.* Papers of the New World Archaeological Foundation 30. Provo, Utah.

Pohorilenko, Anatole

1975   The "Mechanics" of the Olmec Representational System: The Interaction of Material and Conceptual Complexes. *Human Mosaic* 8(1):81–105.

1977   On the Question of Olmec Deities. *Journal of New World Archaeology* 2(1):1–16.

1990   *The Structure and Periodization of the Olmec Representational System.* Unpublished Ph.D. dissertation, Department of Anthropology, Tulane University, New Orleans.

Proskouriakoff, Tatiana

1978   Olmec Gods and Maya God-Glyphs, Codex Wauchope. *Human Mosaic* 12:113–117.

Reilly, F. Kent, III

1989   The Shaman in Transformation Pose: A Study of the Theme of Rulership in Olmec Art. *Record of The Art Museum, Princeton University* 48(2):4–21.

1990   Cosmos and Rulership: The Function of Olmec-Style Symbols in Formative Period Mesoamerica. *Visible Language* 24(1):12–37.

1994   Enclosed Ritual Spaces and the Watery Underworld in Formative Period Architecture: New Observations on the Function of La Venta Complex A. In *Seventh Palenque Round Table, 1986,* edited by V. M. Fields, pp. 125–135. Pre-Columbian Art Research Institute, San Francisco.

1995   Art, Ritual, and Rulership in the Olmec World. In *The Olmec World: Ritual and Rulership,* edited by Elizabeth P. Benson, pp. 27–45. Art Museum, Princeton University, Princeton, New Jersey.

1999   Mountains of Creation and Underworld Portals: The Ritual Function of Olmec Architecture at La Venta, Tabasco. In *Mesoamerican Architecture as a Cultural Symbol,* edited by J. K. Kowalski, pp. 14–39. Oxford University Press, Oxford.

2002   The Landscape of Creation: Architecture, Tomb, and Monument Placement in the Olmec Site of La Venta. In *Heart of Creation: The Mesoamerican World and the Legacy of Linda Schele,* edited by Andrea Stone, pp. 34–65. The University of Alabama Press, Tuscaloosa.

Sabloff, Jeremy A.

1975   *Excavations at Seibal: Ceramics.* Memoirs of the Peabody Museum of Archaeology and Ethnology, Vol. 13, No. 2. Harvard University, Cambridge, Massachusetts.

Saville, Marshall H.

1900   A Votive Adze of Jadeite from Mexico. *Monumental Records,* pp. 138–140. Monumental Records Association, London.

1929   Votive Axes from Ancient Mexico. *Indian Notes* 6:266–299, 335–342. Museum of the American Indian, Heye Foundation, New York.

Séjourné, Laurette

2004   *Cosmogonía de Mesoamérica.* Siglo Veintiuno Editores, Mexico.

Sharer, Robert J., and Loa Traxler

2006   *The Ancient Maya.* 6th ed. Stanford University Press, Palo Alto, California.

Smith, A. Ledyard

1982   *Excavations at Seibal, Department of Peten, Guatemala: Major Architecture and Caches.* Memoirs of the Peabody Museum of Archaeology and Ethnology, Vol. 15, No. 1. Harvard University, Cambridge, Massachusetts.

Stirling, Matthew W.

 1943   La Venta's Green Stone Tigers. *The National Geographic Magazine* 84(3): 321–328.

Stirling, Matthew W., and Marion Stirling

 1942   Finding Jewels of Jade in a Mexican Swamp. *The National Geographic Magazine* 82(5):635–661.

Stocker, Terry, Sarah Meltzoff, and Steve Armsy

 1980   Crocodilians and Olmecs: Further Interpretations in Formative Period Iconography. *American Antiquity* 454:740–758.

Symonds, Stacey, Ann Cyphers, and Roberto Lunagómez

 2002   *Asentamiento Prehispánico en San Lorenzo Tenochtitlán.* UNAM, Mexico City.

Taube, Karl A.

 1992   *The Major Gods of Ancient Yucatan.* Studies in Pre-Columbian Art and Archaeology 32. Dumbarton Oaks, Washington, D.C.

 1995   The Rainmakers: The Olmec and Their Contribution to Mesoamerican Belief and Ritual. In *The Olmec World: Ritual and Rulership,* edited by Elizabeth P. Benson, pp. 83–103. Art Museum, Princeton University, Princeton, New Jersey.

 1996   The Olmec Maize God: The Face of Corn in Formative Mesoamerica. *RES: Anthropology and Aesthetics* 29/30:39–81.

 2000   Lightning Celts and Corn Fetishes: The Formative Olmec and the Development of Maize Symbolism in Mesoamerica and the American Southwest. In *Olmec Art and Archaeology in Mesoamerica,* edited by John E. Clark and Mary E. Pye, pp. 297–337. National Gallery of Art, Washington, D.C.

 2004   *Olmec Art at Dumbarton Oaks.* Pre-Columbian Art at Dumbarton Oaks 2. Dumbarton Oaks, Washington, D.C.

Townsend, Richard F.

 2000   *The Aztecs.* Rev. ed. Thames and Hudson, London.

Wedel, Waldo R.

 1952   Structural Investigations in 1943. In *La Venta, Tabasco: A Study of Olmec Ceramics and Art,* by Philip Drucker, pp. 34–79. Bulletin 153, Bureau of American Ethnology. U.S. Government Printing Office, Washington, D.C.

Willey, Gordon R.

 1978   *Excavations at Seibal: Artifacts.* Memoirs of the Peabody Museum of Archaeology and Ethnology, Vol. 14, No. 1. Harvard University, Cambridge, Massachusetts.

Willey, Gordon R., A. Ledyard Smith, Gair Tourtellot III, and Ian Graham

 1975   *Excavations at Seibal: Introduction, the Site and Its Setting.* Memoirs of the Peabody Museum of Archaeology and Ethnology, Vol. 13, No. 1. Harvard University, Cambridge, Massachusetts.

2
Will the Circle Be Unbroken?
The Roots of Plains Indian Views of the Cosmos

Linea Sundstrom

The indigenous religion of the northern Great Plains that non-Native observers encountered in the nineteenth century was a complex mix of elements, most of which had parallels in northern (Algonquian) and southeastern (Siouan and Caddoan) Native cultures. While it may be impossible to reconstruct the points of origin and paths of diffusion of these elements, I suggest here that those occurring over wide areas likely represent traditions of great historical depth. Further, some widespread traits that occur within both the northern and the southeastern traditions may represent the remnants of even older religious traditions. Such sets of traits appear to have been retained as peoples left their homelands for new areas over the centuries or millennia. While these groups and factions thereof subsequently adopted Christianity to various degrees during the contact period, my focus here is on those beliefs and practices retained to this day that have clear precontact antecedents.[1]

I examine the question of retention and mixing of ancient religious traditions on the northern Great Plains by looking at cosmograms, or symbol sets that encode beliefs about how the universe is structured. As one example, I examine how northern (Algonquian) and southeastern (Siouan) derived groups view the Black Hills, an isolated mountain range on the border of South Dakota and Wyoming, and suggest that these perceptions reflect the distinct ancestral belief systems of these groups, as well as beliefs common to both.

Northern and Southeastern Roots of Great Plains Groups

Algonquian-speaking groups of the northern Great Plains include the Blackfoot alliance, comprising the Siksikawa, Pikuni, and Kainai nations; the Chey-

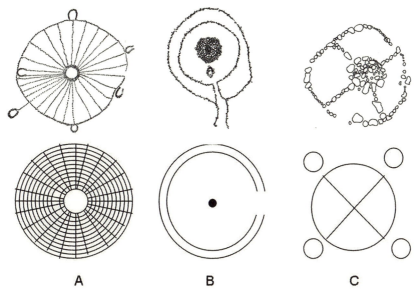

A   **B**   **C**

Figure 2.1. Symbolic structures of ceremonial grounds, houses, and objects serving as cosmograms on the northern Great Plains; the top row shows boulder alignments, the bottom row shows schematics of the basic forms: (a) netted circle (Big Horn Medicine Wheel, Wyoming, from a 1903 drawing by Stephen Chapman Simms [Simms 1903]); (b) circle open to the east or south (Sundial Medicine Wheel, Alberta, from website www.royalalbertamuseum.ca, courtesy of the Royal Alberta Museum); (c) quincunx (unnamed medicine wheel, South Dakota, from field notes on file, South Dakota State Historical Society, Archaeological Research Center, Rapid City).

enne nation with its Tsistsistas and Sutai divisions; and the Arapaho and Gros Ventre nations. The ancestors of Algonquian speakers appear to have first arrived in the northern Great Plains by way of northern Canada at an unknown date at least 2,000 years ago. The Tsistsistas appear to have arrived most recently, during the mid-eighteenth century. These Algonquian groups brought with them several important religious ideas, including ritual animal trapping, embodiment of animal spirits, reverence for albino or white animals, and shamanism as it was originally defined for subarctic and arctic Europe and North America, including shaking-tent rituals and using drums to induce a trance state (Schlesier 1987). Most of these Algonquian groups have an Earth-diver origin story. The primary symbolic structure of their ceremonial grounds and ceremonial objects is a netted or spoked circle or a walled circular enclosure with a small opening to the east or with no opening at all (Figure 2.1a; Hall 1997; Schlesier 1987, 2002). Their most important constellations are associated with stories of hunting and escape from monsters (bears, bulls, or a giant head), the story of the dog husband, the story of the poor children, and the story of Star Boy/Scarface (Barbeau 1965:195–199; Dorsey and Kroeber 1903: 152–160; Josselin de Jong 1915:32–38; Kehoe 1996; Kroeber 1900:182–183; McClintock 1910:281; Mooney 1896:1015; Schlesier 1987; Schwartz 1988:88–89; Stone 1982:7). They recognize the Corona Borealis constellation as the Camp Circle or Spider's (Trickster's) Lodge (Dorsey 1905: 62; McClintock 1910:281, 500).[2]

From the woodlands of what is now the southeastern United States came speakers of Siouan and Caddoan languages. The Siouans primarily followed the Mississippi and Missouri rivers to the northern Great Plains, while the Caddoans tracked farther west on their migrations. These Siouan- and Caddoan-speaking peoples appear in the northern Plains in historic times as the Mandan, Hidatsa, Arikara, Dakota, Nakota, Lakota, Assiniboine, Absoroka (Crow), and Skiri Pawnee. They brought with them concepts of a world organized into halves or moieties. Their ceremonies include earth-stamping dances and ritual adoption. Their primary symbolic structure is a circle or two concentric rings open to the east or south (Figure 2.1b; Dorsey 1894; Walker 1980). Most Siouan origin stories speak of emergence from an underground world; however, the Pawnee tie their origins to the stars (Dorsey 1906:13–14). The principal Siouan and Caddoan constellations are called the Litter or Bier, the Hand (which they share with the Algonquian-speakers), the Bear Lodge, and one whose name is variously translated as the Deer's Head, the Third-Born Relative, or Three Deer (Buechel 1983:132, 334, 486, 578; Buechel and Manhart 1998:233; Clark 1885:386; Deloria 1992:122; Dorsey 1888:389, 394, 1894:379, 1895:130; Fletcher and La Flesche 1911:110, 177–178; Goodman 1992; Mekeel 1931; Oneroad and Skinner 2003:161; Smith 1949:145; Waggoner ca. 1930:18–20; Zitkala Sa 1901:95). The latter constellation is one of a series thought to represent the parts of a quadruped, including the head, tail, and backbone. The Lakota/Dakota term for the Backbone constellation (Orion's Belt) seems to refer not to the spine, but to a hearth board (the platform used with a fire drill to ignite tinder using friction; see Buechel 1983; Ullrich 2008); this is the same constellation called the Hearthboard in Mesoamerica (Hall 1997:163; Milbrath 1999). The Caddoan Skiri Pawnee trace their ancestry to the south and maintain a complex star-based cosmology and religious practices that formerly included occasional human sacrifice. Another Caddoan group, the Arikara, moved to the middle Missouri River but maintained close ties with the Skiri Pawnee.

Long before they completed their gradual migration westward to the Plains, Siouan and Algonquian groups had met in the woodlands covering the vast region from the Atlantic to the Great Plains. Their history and traditions reflect this long association. More recently, Siouan, Caddoan, and Algonquian peoples lived together and formed alliances along the central portion of the

Missouri River during the contact era. The long history of these groups interacting in the Woodlands and Plains has tangled the threads of their respective ancient belief systems (Wissler 1908). Some Siouans tell Earth-diver creation stories, and some Algonquians tell earth-emergence origin stories. While maintaining their specific core set of northern and southern constellations, these groups also recognize constellations from each other's traditions. The northern-derived shaking-tent ritual called *Yuwipi* is an important element in Lakota religion today, while the Algonquian-speaking groups apparently adopted elements of the Scalp or Victory Dance from their Siouan and Caddoan neighbors.

Among elements that Algonquian and Siouan-Caddoan have in common are the sweatlodge ceremony; an earth-renewal ceremony involving a circular dance structure with a center tree or pole; a division of the universe into upper, lower, and surface layers, as well as four horizontal quadrants (Figure 2.1c); recognition of four and seven as the principal sacred numbers; belief in transmigration of souls; belief in animal spirit homes below the earth's surface; sacred pipes; and mounded earth altars with designs created in colored mineral powders.

Cosmograms as Indicators of Religious Tradition

The most direct link between tradition, defined as beliefs that remain intact and relevant over long periods, and archaeology is the cosmogram. A cosmogram is anything that expresses a belief system in terms of natural or built things. A cosmogram boils the universe down to its essence, as it were, and expresses it in terms of a set of basic symbols that are easily recognized through the sense of sight, sound, smell, or touch. Although things like songs, poetry, myths, and rituals can be cosmograms, most American archaeologists outside of Mesoamerica have confined themselves to more tangible, visible cosmograms, such as tools, items of dress, ritual paraphernalia, dwellings, and ceremonial grounds.

Cosmograms vary in size, complexity, and accessibility. Some may be instantly recognizable to anyone with a basic knowledge of his or her culture. Others require specialized learning for their correct or complete interpretation. Some cosmograms are mapped onto the natural world, for example, by recognizing prominent stars or constellations as illustrating religious stories or precepts. Beliefs can also be mapped onto the landscape, based on physical characteristics of natural features or on a perceived historical link to formative cultural events. On a smaller scale, the shape, colors, and markings of plants and animals can be symbols of beliefs. For example, in the Americas, the turtle is often believed to embody the shape of the earth's surface, with its four legs representing the four directions. In Mississippian iconography, a water spider also embodies the four directions, while the cross on its abdomen is the sacred central fire from which new life arises (Howard 1968:57).

Cosmograms both reflect and reinforce fundamental beliefs. The constant interaction between people and the cosmograms that pervade their environment is a primary means of maintaining religious traditions, passing them along from generation to generation as young and old encounter and remember or learn the symbols that surround them. The conscious learning that takes place in childhood becomes internalized over time, such that perceptions of cosmic structure may be interwoven into human creations on a subconscious level. The individual may identify a weaving, pottery design, or building as "right" or "wrong" without being able to articulate why one is good and the other bad (Bunzel 1929). In other words, one's aesthetics of form, pattern, and color is informed on a subconscious level by perceptions of the universe that find pervasive expression in one's surroundings. To find tradition, then, archaeologists need to look for cosmograms in the culture under study however they may define that culture.

As an example from the Western European tradition, consider how ceremonial, public space is constructed. In the Western religious tradition that reached its most exact material expression during the Middle Ages, society and religion were viewed as hierarchical and dichotomous. Hierarchy was a matter of one's wealth, education, and political power and incorporated a series of gradations, such as king, lord, knight, vassal, and serf, or God, pope, cardinal, bishop, monsignor, priest, and congregant. Dichotomy, by contrast, drew a line between the sacred and the profane, the person invested with power and the ordinary citizen, the teacher and the pupil. These organizing structures are expressed in architecture in premodern churches, courtrooms, and schoolrooms, and in modern lecture halls. These cultural spaces take the form of a single large enclosed rectangular room, with a small antechamber at one end through which the public enters the larger space. At the opposite end is a raised platform or stage that only persons of authority are allowed to enter. This restricted area may be further designated by a barrier such as the communion rail in a church or the bar in a courtroom. Seating (or in the Medieval church, standing) is in parallel rows extending back from the raised area. The more prestigious seats are nearer the raised area. This design thus incorporates hierarchy in the ranks of pews and dichotomy in the separation of the public and restricted spaces. This structure can be traced back to ancient Classical and Semitic cultures. With the rise of bureaucratized Christianity, this structure is superimposed on the Latin cross in construction of cathedrals, such that the raised space occupies the center of the cross and the public space occupies the long axis of the cross.

The Cross, Sun Dance Pole, and Milky Way as Spirit Road

In seeking fundamental religious traditions in the Americas, it is reasonable to hypothesize that universal or widely distributed cosmograms represent the oldest beliefs and that these cosmograms have been locally adapted to new beliefs. In the northern Great Plains, the Sun Dance pole with its forked top and crosspiece of bunched willows is explicitly linked to the Milky Way as the path traveled by dead souls (Catches and Catches 1997:116–117). The same idea is expressed in the forked sticks carried by mourners in the Osage Mourning Dance, in the forked poles used to support burial platforms, in the forked sticks used to stir the soup served at the Lakota Soul Release ceremony, and in the placement of dead bodies, the placenta, and a girl's first menstrual bundle in the forks of trees (Catches and Catches 1997:116–117; Clark 1885:91–92, 135, 194–196; Fletcher 1884:298, 304; Grinnell 1896; Hassrick 1964:302, 312; Hilger 1952:18, 20, 1970:282; Lowie 1935:66; Petter 1915:16a, 23; Shimkin 1953; Standing Bear 1933:211; Walker 1980:79, 246).

Circle Opening to the East

A northern Plains cosmogram consisting of a circle with an opening on the east similarly expresses both ubiquitous, old beliefs and more restricted and perhaps newer beliefs (Hall 1985, 1997). The general belief is that the earth is a disk that can be split into halves along a north–south or an east–west axis or split into quarters corresponding to the cardinal or semicardinal directions. In this system, birth is associated with the east and death with the west. For example, Sun Dancers enter the ceremonial ground from the east, but lie down on the west side for their symbolic death through piercing and thirsting. Following the ceremony, the Sun Dancers and spectators exit through the east, as if reborn.

The same pattern shows up in more prosaic contexts. For example, formal encampments consist of a circle of tipis with a gap on the east side and surrounding an open plaza that sometimes has a larger, communal lodge in the center. If more than one group is camping together, they form their camps into a great circle. People in a state of transition, such as newlywed couples, may place their tipis just outside or inside the main circle. Households and bands follow a set order of placing their tipis and camps within the circles. Some tribal and band names refer to their position in the large camp circle. It is not difficult to imagine how this might play out archaeologically in sites where circles of rocks mark the former location of tipis (see Kehoe 1960; Oetelaar 2003).

Like all cosmograms, however, the circle embeds several layers of meaning

(Hall 1997). North and south are not just halves of the sky; each has particular religious associations. One of two oppositional pairs is associated with one or the other direction: north, south; east, west; zenith, nadir; sun, moon; cold, heat; male, female; winter, summer; death, life; upward movement, downward movement; inward movement, outward movement; bison, corn or deer (Anderson 2001:100; Fletcher and La Flesche 1911:134; Kehoe 1996; Moore 1984; Petter 1915:211, 422–423; Walker 1917:108).[3] One of the clearest expressions of this is in the circular houses used on the northern Great Plains, whether earthlodges or tipis (Oetelaar 2000, 2003; Weltfish 1977:63–64). A Pawnee story explains the form of the earthlodge in the words of the creator-being, Tirawa:

> Cut four sticks and set them in a circle. Cut some poles to lay across the sticks. Four of the upright forks must form a parallelogram, with the longest sides extending east and west. The posts that are set in the ground to uphold the lodge represent the four gods who hold up the heavens in the northeast, northwest, southwest, and southeast. There are minor gods between these, with powers that connect the power of one god to another. There is also an outer circle of many gods, and you shall cut poles to represent them; their power also extends from one god to another. The south side of the lodge will be for the men, for the men will be strong and so they must be on the right. The north side shall be for the women, for they are not as strong as the men and so must be on the left. The entrance of the lodge shall always face the east, for the lodge that you are to build shall breathe as if human. Five posts are on the south side representing the five branches of the man: two legs, two arms, and head. The five forks at the north also stand for the five branches of the woman. You shall net willows together. These shall be thrown upon the east side of the four posts that stand for the gods in heaven. These netted willows represent the ribs of the gods that the posts represent. When the lodge is complete, dig in the center for the fireplace and I will give you fire-sticks so that you can make your fire. These fire-sticks belong to the sun. When you make the fireplace, dig up the dirt in the center of the lodge and take it out and place it in front of the lodge in the form of a mound, so that when the sun shall rise in the east he will see that mound. Fire will do many things for you. After you have completed the fireplace, make the ground even inside of the lodge, leaving only one small mound in the west for an altar. Kill a buffalo and place the skull on the altar. Though the skull has no life in it, I, Tirawa, or the spirit of the buffalo will be present there when the rays of the sun shine upon it. For this reason always keep the skull on the

altar, facing east, so that the first rays of the sun, as it enters the lodge, will shine upon it [Dorsey 1906:14–15].

The orientation of the tipi and earthlodge results in persons moving from east to west when retiring for the night, at the "death" of day and the symbolic death of sleep (Weltfish 1977:63–64). In the morning, one emerges in an easterly direction to greet the new sun. The tipi represents a woman, one's "second mother" (Old Horn and McCleary 1995:55). The tunnel-like entrance of the earthlodge and the ovoid, restricted doorway of the tipi symbolically replicate the birth canal and vagina, so that each person is reborn in the morning to a new day. A similar pattern holds for the sweatlodge, which also requires one to emerge toward the east by crawling through a narrow opening. It can be easily seen that the lodge, earthlodge, and sweatlodge, each with its podlike shape and central hearth, are symbolic wombs (Weltfish 1977:63–64). Certain mound-shaped mountains, such as Bear Butte, are also seen as dens, pods, or wombs from which new life emerges (Bowers 1963:435; Parks and Wedel 1985; Wallaertt 2006). On a smaller scale, the cache pits and pottery vessels used in the earthlodges were also womb-shaped vessels that contained and protected ritual paraphernalia, foodstuffs, and seeds for the following year's planting, just as the earthlodge itself sheltered the life of the people (Sundstrom 2009).

The Quartered Circle

The quartered circle so common in Great Plains religious iconography is found throughout Central and North America. In Mesoamerica it most often takes the form of the quincunx: that is, a figure with four equally spaced points with a fifth point in the center of the square they form (e.g., the first pages of the Fejéváry-Mayer and Medoza codices). Although the basic form is square, it is easily accommodated into circular form by combining the circle with two or more crossed lines passing through the center point. While the divided circle takes many forms on the northern Plains, these always start with two equally spaced lines. This gives four points at which the straight lines intersect the circle. Another circular format for this apparently very ancient cosmogram places four points just outside the circle at the cardinal or semicardinal directions.

The Black Hills as Cosmogram

Taking the Black Hills as an example of a northern Plains ritual landscape, we find three historic patterns of distribution of sacred sites. The first and the earliest of these in the ethnographic literature contains only two features: Bear Butte, lying just outside the northeastern Black Hills, and Devils

Tower or Bear Lodge Butte, lying just outside the northwestern Black Hills. These are Kiowa sacred sites (Harrington 1939; Sundstrom 1997). They are igneous features within a landscape otherwise lacking anything resembling volcanism. They form a simple line or arc at the northern end of the Black Hills, and thus do not fit the cosmograms described above. The second pattern consists of caves as sacred sites. Another likely Kiowa shrine, based on archaeological evidence, is located in the northwestern foothills at a fissure cave (Sundstrom 2004:142–148).

With the later Cheyenne and Lakota occupation of the Black Hills, the third pattern of sacred landscape emerges. The igneous intrusives that were sacred to the Kiowa continue to be held sacred, but they are part of a circular quincunx cosmogram. Rather than being perceived as a line or arc across the northern end of the Black Hills range, these two features make up the northern two points of the quincunx (Figure 2.2). The ethnographic literature is silent on the location of the southern points, except to the extent of noting that there were four sacred peaks arranged around the periphery of the mountain range. The most likely candidate for the southwestern point is Inyan Kara Mountain. The southeastern point could be Battle Mountain, which was said to be an important landmark for the Cheyenne and Lakota, or any of several other peaks. The oval-shaped domal mountain range itself is the circle. There are several possibilities for the central point. The most geographically logical is Harney Peak, the highest of the Black Hills peaks and the highest point between the Rockies and the east coast. Although Harney Peak is named as the center of the world in *Black Elk Speaks,* the famous account of an Oglala holy man's vision and life (Neihardt 1932), it receives only one possible mention in the mythology of groups occupying the region. That refers to the presence of an owl-like monster there, not to the mountain as a world center. Another possible center would be the high, treeless meadows, known as prairies or "balds," that occupy the geographic center of the main uplift. We know from ethnographic accounts that these places were (and are) sacred to Lakota people and by conjecture that they were associated with the elk and, by extension, with the Four Winds.

Another possibility is Wind Cave. Although caves occur on all sides of the Black Hills, Wind Cave is among the largest and has the most easily discerned "breath." With 120 miles of passageways (as mapped to date) and an opening barely large enough to squeeze through, the cave creates strong air currents going in and out depending on the differences in barometric pressure inside and outside the cave. Lakota today assert that Wind Cave is the earth opening from which they emerged to become a people (Albers 2002). While a cave may seem counterintuitive for a center point, this pattern does show up elsewhere. For example, many of the great temple complexes in

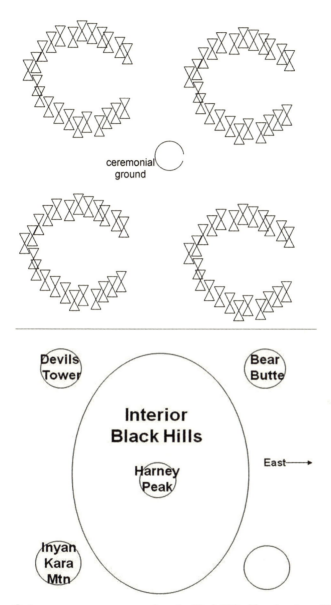

Figure 2.2. Quincunx cosmogram mapped on the Black Hills. Top, drawing of four-village encampment adapted from Standing Bear 1933:121; bottom, idealized drawing of Black Hills showing arrangement of four "sky pillars" and center point.

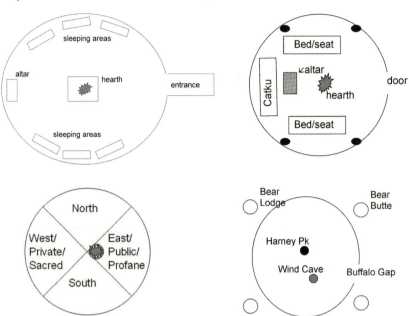

Figure 2.3. Quartered circle cosmogram as expressed in structure of earthlodge and tipi and as mapped on the Black Hills. Top left, arrangement of typical Hidatsa earthlodge; top right, arrangement of tipi with *catku* or seat of honor at back; bottom left, schematized diagram of arrangement of space in Plains dwellings; bottom right, idealized drawing of Black Hills showing relationship to quartered circle or quincunx cosmogram.

Mesoamerica were constructed over caves or sinkholes (Miller and Taube 1993:57; Taube 2001). In the Cheyenne Massaum ceremony, the center point is a hole dug in the center of the lodge (Schlesier 1987:7, 93). Further, the cave as center links to another very widespread belief—namely, that the spirits of animals live in a world under the ground from which they emerge periodically to renew the herds so that people will have food (Beckwith 1938:22–23, 157–158; Bowers 1950:171–172, 1963:127, 437; Dorsey and Kroeber 1903:145, 176; Hoebel 1978:89; LaPointe 1976:80; Lowie 1918:216; Schultz 1962:59–60). As with the tipi, earthlodge, and sweatlodge, the east-facing entrance of Wind Cave is a narrow oval opening from which life emerged to face the rising sun. In this case, the huge geologic dome forming the Black Hills is the womb-shaped container that incubates this life (Figure 2.3).

Very little is known of the archaeology of Wind Cave. An early National Park Service administrator noted that numerous artifacts were found around the natural entrance to the cave, but he neither counted nor described them.

He did, however, record that the Indians told him the cave was the "home of the Four Winds" and the home of the buffalo spirits, as well as of the Lakota culture hero White Buffalo Calf Woman (Freeland 1938; Koller 1970). The convergence point of the four winds is, of course, the center of the world. Such "breathing" caves are also considered the home of the winds in Maya tradition (Miller and Taube 1993:85). A face paint for the Cheyenne world-renewal ceremony provides another version of this cosmogram. Here four triangles pointing inward from the edge of the face represent the four sky pillars and a cross upon the nose represents the center at which the four winds converge. The person's breath thus represents the winds.

The Black Hills as Animal Trap or Racetrack

The Black Hills are a cosmogram of another belief complex involving animal drives and mythological races between animals and humans. This is expressed in the open circle cosmogram described above (Figure 2.4). The Cheyenne and Lakota stories of the Great Race between the Two-Leggeds and the Four-Leggeds probably originated in proto-Algonquian cultures of the far north, but the story as told today is firmly emplaced in the Black Hills. The racetrack is preserved as an area of low red beds surrounding the high interior granites and limestones of the central Black Hills and walled in by high sandstone cliffs that form the outer rim of the mountains. The presumably earlier, Cheyenne, version of the story, says that the Buffalo Gap was the starting and ending point of the race, while the Lakota version places this at Devils Tower, one of the four sky pillars of the Black Hills quincunx. This example shows how easily more than one belief can be mapped onto a landscape and meshed with an earlier cosmogram. Other examples of this pattern of a circle open on one side with or without a pathway leading to it are widely scattered throughout the northern Great Plains. For example, the Sundial and Roy Rivers medicine wheels in Alberta have two central cairns and a runway opening to the south.

Arapaho camped in sheltered mountain parks in winter; these closed parks were called "game bags," in reference to the game trapping enclosures they resembled (Anderson 2001:8). The same idea is expressed in the Great Race story, in which all the animals and humans race around inside the circle formed by the high sandstone cliffs rimming the Black Hills (Stands in Timber and Liberty 1967:22). Bison and people did, in fact, migrate to the sheltered interior valley of the Black Hills through the great Buffalo Gap on the east side of the mountains as winter approached (Turner 1974:20). Small medicine wheels have been found in former Cheyenne territory in South Dakota, including one just outside the eastern Black Hills.

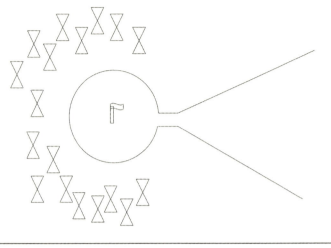

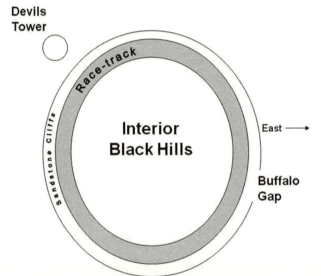

Figure 2.4. Animal trap or open circle cosmogram as mapped on the Black Hills. Top, an Assiniboine bison trap by Edwin Denig (adapted from an 1854 drawing); bottom, idealized drawing of Black Hills showing opening on the east side at Buffalo Gap.

Northern and Southern Traditions in Constellations

The Lakota carried the cosmogram to the sky in naming certain constellations for natural features in the Black Hills, including the Race Track and the Bear Lodge (known today as Devils Tower). Other Lakota constellations correspond to a general southern, Siouan–Caddoan astronomy. The Cheyenne, by contrast, seem to have retained a general northern, Algonquian astronomy. Their constellations neither refer to the Black Hills nor correspond with those of groups that entered the area from the south. Significantly, Ursa Major (the Big Dipper) is uniformly known to the Siouans and Caddoans as the Person-Carrier, referring to a litter or a funeral bier. Since so many Siouan and Caddoan beliefs and practices have parallels in Mesoamerica, I expected to find something similar in the Mesoamerican zodiac. I did not find the specific name in the Mesoamerican material; however, I did discover that the earliest name recorded for this constellation in the Middle East was the Bier (Allen 1899:433). It is not clear whether this indicates a northern hemisphere–wide, and likely very old, belief or is simply coincidental.[4]

Ursa Major is known as Seven Macaw by some groups in Mesoamerica. This name refers to a king, and the story associated with it, like that related by Lakota, involves kings, battles between brother-princes, biers, decapitation, and ritual mourning (Clark 1885:386; Waggoner ca. 1930).[5] This is not too surprising for Mesoamerica, but it is hard to reconcile with the nonstate, egalitarian Lakota society of the northern Great Plains without drawing a historical connection between the two regions. The Lakota had neither burial biers nor kings, but at the time of contact with non-Natives, they practiced ritual mourning rites with parallels to those known from Mesoamerica, including ritual death of captives or mourners, the capture of heads or scalps to acquire psychopomps for their recently deceased loved ones, and ritual piercing by male mourners. Most strikingly, the southern (Siouan and Caddoan) traditions consistently link Ursa Major to warfare (Buechel and Manhart 1998), while the northern (Algonquian) tradition associates this constellation with stories of hunting or people escaping from monsters.

Northern and Southern Traditions in Petroforms

Turning to petroforms, a northern and a southern tradition can again be recognized. The features known as medicine wheels are largely restricted in their distribution to areas of the northern Plains dominated by Algonquian-speaking groups. Research at two such sites, the Big Horn Medicine Wheel and the Moose Mountain Medicine Wheel, has demonstrated that they can be used to mark the heliacal rising of the bright stars Alderbaran, Rigel, Sirius, and Fomalhaut, as well as sunrise at summer solstice (Eddy 1981; Kehoe and Kehoe 1979; Robinson 1981; Schlesier 1987:83–87). These stars—much like the points of sunrise and sunset at the solstices and equinoxes—mark four points on the horizon corresponding to the semicardinal directions. These appear to reflect a tradition that goes back some 2,000 years. While the religious symbolism of all northern Great Plains people is permeated by the quartered circle, there is a distinct preference among the northern-derived Cheyenne to base this on the semicardinal directions (Powell 1969; Schlesier 1987), while the southern-derived Lakota tend to base theirs on the cardinal directions.

The classic medicine wheel is a closed circle with interior lines. It is the "dream-catcher" writ large. In other words, it represents a net or snare, in this case for capturing spirits. The Big Horn Medicine Wheel contains 28 interior lines or spokes (Grey 1963; Simms 1903); others contain four or eight interior lines (Brumley 1985:210, 1988; Sundstrom 2005). The Massaum lodge of the Cheyenne takes the same shape: it is a large, doorless tipi with 28 poles built around a base of four poles placed at the semicardinal directions (Schlesier 2002:390). People impersonating animal spirits are drawn from the animal spirit dens under Bear Butte into this enclosure, much as the Cheyenne animal priests lured actual antelope and bison into similar structures (Schlesier 1987:52–58, 81, 100). The Spirit Lance used by some Cheyenne holy men is a miniature version of the netted circle snare (Grinnell 1923:314, 1962:6, 28, 85; Schlesier 2002:390–391), and the small netted hoop used in the Pikuni hoop and pole game sometimes contains 28 spokes (Culin 1907:Figure 582). The hoop and pole game refers explicitly to killing bison; the netted hoop used there and in other contexts can symbolize abundance of food (Hoebel 1978:46).

Hall (1997) treats the circle with interior lines—that is, the netted hoop—and the circle open on one side as variants of a single cosmogram related to earth renewal and spirit capture. The overlapping forms and meanings of these two symbols may indicate that they are indeed just regional variations on a single theme, but they may also indicate the melding of two belief systems at their points of closest similarity. I lean toward the latter explanation, given the apparent correlation between the netted hoop and Algonquian-speaking groups, who consistently interpret these symbols as traps. As Hall (1997) notes, other indigenous American groups also had the concept of trapping of supernatural power, but they often created different visual symbols for it, including the rainbow.

Implications for Archaeology

What does this mean in terms of archaeology? It suggests that settlement patterns, dwelling types, and ceremonial structures can be expected to have served as cosmograms in the past as they did in historic times and still do today. For example, bisected stone circles in Canada have been recognized as possible remains of structures used in the shaking-tent ceremonies recorded for northern Plains Algonquians and some of their neighbors (Vickers 1988:93, cited in Brink et al. 2003:235–236). In seeking cosmograms, it is important to be cognizant of different scales of magnitude (Sundstrom 2000:124–125). It is also important to recognize that cosmograms frequently collapse three dimensions into two and that a cosmogram may "work" in more than one dimension (Nagy 1994; Petter 1915:422–423; Schlesier 1987). The quartered circle that divides the earth's surface into four quadrants and a center can be tilted on its east–west axis such that north becomes up and south becomes down. The same quartered circle can be pushed upward in the center to give the sky's dome, the earthlodge, and the sweatlodge. In a tipi camp or earthlodge settlement, the most sacred lodge is likely to have been placed at the west side, opposite the opening, or in the center of the camp circle or settlement, the position within a tipi or earthlodge occupied by the seat of honor, altar, or hearth (Anderson 2001:94).

Within archaeological sites, we may be able to recognize regular patterns in the arrangement of camps and villages that reflect beliefs about the organization of the world. Features and activity areas may be distributed within house remains according to the age and sex of those using the structure. On the scale of landscape, sacred sites might eventually be identified by the discovery of clusters of vision quest stations, petroforms, or places with artifacts left as offerings associated with natural features that formed parts of cosmograms, such as mountain peaks or caves.

For example, examination of records on file at the South Dakota State Historical Society, Archaeological Research Center (Rapid City) and Wyoming State Archaeologist's Office (Laramie) shows that in the Black Hills, almost all rock art sites are in the foothills and outer ring of peaks, the area encompassing Bear Butte, Devils Tower, Inyan Kara Mountain, and Buffalo Gap, and bordering the Race Track. Of these, sites that appear to have been made in a religious context date to the Archaic period, in excess of 2,000 years ago. A buffalo jump site lies just inside Buffalo Gap, reflecting both the real function of this feature as a gateway into the sheltered interior valleys and beliefs that the gap was formed by bison emerging from Wind Cave and running out to the prairies east of the Black Hills. Material from this site was radiocarbon dated at 920 years before present; however, older strata may be present, as well. At the time Wind Cave was developed for tourism, numerous artifacts were noted near its natural entrance; unfortunately, we do not know the age of these items. Many archaeological sites have been recorded at Bear Butte, Devils Tower, and Inyan Kara. Other sites of probable ceremonial use (medicine wheel and vision quest features) are also concentrated in the outer portions of the mountain range, just where indigenous stories recorded in the postcontact era would predict. By contrast, very little archaeological material has been found on or near Harney Peak, suggesting that indigenous religious traditions surrounding it are fairly recent. While present data are inadequate to assess whether these site distributions are related to recent and present indigenous views of the Black Hills, the pattern raises the possibility that old and fundamental religious beliefs are expressed in the landscape use patterns observable in the archaeological record.

Conclusion

In conclusion, the archaeological footprints of settlements, houses, and sacred sites, along with ritual objects and sacred stories, reflect complex, and probably ancient, ideas about how the universe is structured. The way in which interior spaces are allocated within a tipi or earthlodge, the arrangement of houses and ceremonial structures within a village, and concepts of how various landscape features relate to one another are visualized in terms of a group's most basic beliefs about the world in which they live and die. In the northern Great Plains, differences in how northern vs. southeastern-derived groups visualize the structure of the sky—that is, how they group stars into constellations that illustrate sacred stories—suggest that groups maintained religious traditions for centuries, if not millennia.

The ideas presented here are more suggestive than conclusive. The lines between northern and southern traditions have been blurred by the passage of time and displacement of Native peoples. Nevertheless, these patterns may play out as archaeologists take a closer look at the intersection of mythology, material culture, and features of the natural world. Once we become more adept at finding cosmograms at all scales of magnitude and in both the built and the natural environment, we can begin to trace out a picture of ancient cultures that finally gets beyond subsistence and resource extraction to the real heart of what makes people human.

Notes

1. My use of present tense in describing these beliefs and practices acknowledges their currency within the groups under discussion but is not meant to imply that everyone within these groups follows these older traditions or to negate the adoption of Christian systems of belief and practice among some members of the groups under discussion.

2. The Siouan-speaking Crow recognize the northern set of constellations, including the Camp Circle, and associate Ursa Major with a monster story, perhaps reflecting their long association with the more northern and western groups, in particular those of the Blackfoot alliance. The Siouan-speaking Ponca recognized the Camp Circle but not the other northern constellations (Howard 1965:75, 103).

3. The cardinal directions and zenith and nadir also have color associations; however, these are not consistent from group to group (see DeBoer 2005).

4. One can speculate a connection between this and a very old European name for Ursa Major, Charles Wain, or the churl's wagon, given its possible identification with the hearse wagon or the even older Bronze Age practice of burying a wagon with the deceased person; however, the origins of this term for the constellation are lost to history.

5. The Litter or Bier constellation seems to be linked to the origins of the Kit Fox society and the Hunka ceremony, as Hall (1997:166) has proposed, based on a link between the crooked staff and the form of Ursa Major. Sometimes the captive/adoptee was carried in on a litter for the Hunka ceremony. The stories cited here say it was a "fox" king on the litter or bier. Just as Mesoamerican Jaguar warriors wore jaguar skins, Kit Fox society members wore kit fox skins in the form of a poncho. Hall (1997) cites the Lakota historian No Flesh in saying that the Hunka ceremony originated with a chief who was mourning the deaths of his four sons, all Kit Fox society members (Walker 1980:193–195).

References Cited

Albers, Patricia

2002   *The Home of the Buffalo: An Ethnographic and Ethnohistoric Study of Cultural Affiliations to Wind Cave National Park.* Report prepared for U.S. Department of the Interior, National Park Service, Wind Cave National Park, Hot Springs, South Dakota.

Allen, Richard Hinckley

1899   *Star-Names and Their Meanings.* G. E. Stechert, New York.

Anderson, Jeffry D.

2001   *The Four Hills of Life: Northern Arapaho Knowledge and Life Movement.* University of Nebraska Press, Lincoln.

Barbeau, Marius

1965   *Indian Days on the Western Prairies.* Bulletin 163, Anthropological Series 46. National Museum of Canada, Ottawa. Reprint of 1960 edition.

Beckwith, Martha Warren

1938   *Mandan-Hidatsa Myths and Ceremonies.* Memoirs of the American Folklore Society, Vol. 32. Reprinted 1969 by Kraus Reprint, New York.

Bowers, Alfred W.

1950   *Mandan Social and Ceremonial Organization.* University of Chicago Press, Chicago. Reprinted 1991 by University of Idaho Press, Moscow.

1963   *Hidatsa Social and Ceremonial Organization.* Bulletin 194, Bureau of American Ethnology, Smithsonian Institution. U.S. Government Printing Office, Washington, D.C.

Brink, Jack W., Kristine Wright-Fedyniak, and Dean Wetzel

2003   A Review of Certain Stone Alignments and Rock Cairns in Alberta Archaeology. In *Archaeology in Alberta: A View from the New Millennium,* edited by Jack W. Brink and John F. Dormaar, pp. 208–241. Archaeological Society of Alberta, Medicine Hat, Canada.

Brumley, John H.

1985   The Ellis Site (EcOp-4): A Late Prehistoric Burial Lodge/Medicine Wheel Site in Southeastern Alberta. In *Contributions to Plains Prehistory: The 1984*

Victoria Symposium, edited by David Burley, pp. 180–232. Occasional Paper 26. Archaeological Survey of Alberta, Edmonton.

1988   *Medicine Wheels on the Northern Plains: A Summary and Appraisal.* Manuscript Series 12. Archaeological Survey of Alberta, Edmonton.

Buechel, Eugene

1983   *A Dictionary–Oie Wowapi Wan of Teton Sioux.* Edited by Paul Manhart. Red Cloud Indian School, Holy Rosary Mission, Pine Ridge, South Dakota.

Buechel, Eugene, and Paul I. Manhart

1998   *Lakota Tales and Texts in Translation.* Tipi Press, Chamberlain, South Dakota.

Bunzel, Ruth

1929   *The Pueblo Potter: A Study of Creative Imagination in Primitive Art.* Contributions to Anthropology 8. Columbia University, New York.

Catches, Pete, Sr., and Peter Catches

1997   *Oceti Wakan, Sacred Fireplace.* Oceti Wakan, Pine Ridge, South Dakota.

Clark, William Philo

1885   *The Indian Sign Language.* Hammersly, Philadelphia. Reprinted 1982 by University of Nebraska Press, Lincoln.

Culin, Stuart

1907   *Games of the North American Indians.* Bureau of American Ethnology Annual Report 24. U.S. Government Printing Office, Washington, D.C.

DeBoer, Warren R.

2005   Colors for a North American Past. *World Archaeology* 37:66–91.

Deloria, Ella C.

1992   *Dakota Texts.* University of South Dakota Press, Vermillion. Originally published 1932, Publications of the American Ethnological Society 14, New York.

Dorsey, George A.

1905   *The Cheyenne.* Publication 99, Anthropological Series Vol. 9(1). Field Columbian Museum, Chicago.

1906   *The Pawnee Mythology, Part I.* Publication 59. Carnegie Institution of Washington, D.C.

Dorsey, George A., and Alfred L. Kroeber

1903   *Traditions of the Arapahos.* Publication 81, Anthropological Series Vol. 5. Field Columbian Museum, Chicago.

Dorsey, James Owen

1888   *Osage Traditions.* Bureau of American Ethnology Annual Report 6, pp. 373–397. U.S. Government Printing Office, Washington, D.C.

1894   *A Study of Siouan Cults.* Bureau of American Ethnology Annual Report 11, pp. 351–544. U.S. Government Printing Office, Washington, D.C.

1895   Kwapa Folk-Lore. *Journal of American Folk-Lore* 8(29):130–131.

Eddy, John A.

1981   Medicine Wheels and Plains Indian Astronomy. In *Astronomy of the Ancients,* edited by K. Brecher and M. Feirtag, pp. 1–24. MIT Press, Cambridge, Massachusetts.

Fletcher, Alice C.

1884   *The Shadow or Ghost Lodge: A Ceremony of the Ogalalla Sioux.* Annual Report 16-17, Vol. 3(3-4), pp. 296–307. Peabody Museum of American Archaeology and Ethnology, Cambridge, Massachusetts.

Fletcher, Alice C., and Francis La Flesche

1911   *The Omaha Tribe.* Smithsonian Institution Bureau of American Ethnology Annual Report 27. U.S. Government Printing Office, Washington, D.C.

Freeland, Edward D.

1938   Some Caves of the Black Hills. *The Black Hills Engineer,* December 1938, 272–277. South Dakota School of Mines and Technology, Rapid City.

Goodman, Ronald

1992   *Lakota Star Knowledge: Studies in Lakota Stellar Theology.* Sinte Gleska University, Rosebud, South Dakota.

Grey, Don

1963   The Big Horn Medicine Wheel Site, 48BH302. *Plains Anthropologist* 8:27–40.

Grinnell, George Bird

1896   Childbirth among the Black Feet. *American Anthropologist* 9:286–287.

1923   *The Cheyenne Indians: Their History and Ways of Life.* 2 vols. Yale University Press, New Haven, Connecticut. Reprinted 1972 by University of Nebraska Press, Lincoln.

1962   *By Cheyenne Campfires.* Yale University Press, New Haven, Connecticut. Originally published 1926.

Hall, Robert L.

1985   Medicine Wheels, Sun Circles, and the Magic of World Center Shrines. *Plains Anthropologist* 30:181–193.

1997   *An Archaeology of the Soul: North American Indian Belief and Ritual.* University of Illinois Press, Urbana.

Harrington, John P.

1939   Kiowa Memories of the Northland. In *So Live the Works of Man,* edited by Donald D. Brand and Fred E. Harvey, pp. 169, 174–176. University of New Mexico Press, Albuquerque.

Hassrick, Royal B.

1964   *The Sioux: Life and Customs of a Warrior Society.* University of Oklahoma Press, Norman.

Hilger, M. Inez

1952   *Arapaho Child Life and Its Cultural Background.* Bulletin 148, Bureau of American Ethnology. U.S. Government Printing Office, Washington, D.C.

1970   Notes on Crow Culture. *Baessler-Archiv,* Neue Folge 18:253–294.

Hoebel, E. Adamson

1978   *The Cheyennes: Indians of the Great Plains.* 2nd ed. Holt Rinehart and Winston, New York.

Howard, James H.

1965   *The Ponca Tribe.* Bulletin 195, Bureau of American Ethnology. U.S. Government Printing Office, Washington, D.C.

1968   *The Southeastern Ceremonial Complex and Its Interpretation.* Memoir 6. Missouri Archaeological Society, Columbia.

Josselin de Jong, J. P. B., de

1915   *Blackfoot Texts.* J. Muller, Amsterdam.

Kehoe, Alice B.

1996   Ethnoastronomy of the North American Plains. In *Songs from the Sky: Indigenous Astronomical and Cosmological Traditions of the World,* edited by Von Del Chamberlain, John B. Carlson, and M. Jane Young, pp. 127–139. Ocarina Press, Bognor Regis, England.

Kehoe, Thomas F.

1960   *Stone Tipi Rings in North-Central Montana and the Adjacent Portions of Alberta, Canada: The Historical, Ethnological, and Archaeological Aspects.* Bulletin 173, Bureau of American Ethnology. U.S. Government Printing Office, Washington, D.C.

Kehoe, Thomas F., and Alice B. Kehoe

1979   *Solstice-Aligned Boulder Configurations in Saskatchewan.* Mercury Series, Canadian Ethnology Service, Paper 48. National Museum of Man, Ottawa, Canada.

Koller, Joe

1970   Wind Cave. *Wi-Iyohi, Bulletin of the South Dakota Historical Society* 23(10).

Kroeber, Alfred L.

1900   Cheyenne Tales. *Journal of American Folk-Lore* 13:161–190.

LaPointe, James

1976   *Legends of the Lakota.* Indian Historian Press, San Francisco.

Lowie, Robert H.

1918   Myths and Traditions of the Crow Indians. *Anthropological Papers of the American Museum of Natural History* 11(8).

1935   *The Crow Indians.* Farrar and Rinehart, New York.

McClintock, Walter

1910   *The Old North Trail.* London.

Mekeel, H. Scudder

1931   Unpublished field notes, White Clay District, Pine Ridge Indian Reservation, South Dakota. On file at American Museum of Natural History, New York.

Milbrath, Susan

    1999   *Star Gods of the Maya: Astronomy in Art, Folklore, and Calendars.* University of Texas Press, Austin.

Miller, Mary, and Karl Taube

    1993   *An Illustrated Dictionary of the Gods and Symbols of Ancient Mexico and the Maya.* Thames and Hudson, London.

Mooney, James

    1896   *The Ghost-Dance Religion and the Sioux Outbreak of 1890.* Bureau of American Ethnology Annual Report 14. U.S. Government Printing Office, Washington, D.C. Reprinted 1991 by University of Nebraska Press, Lincoln.

Moore, John H.

    1984   Cheyenne Names and Cosmology. *American Ethnologist* 11(2):291–312.

Nagy, Imre

    1994   Cheyenne Shields and the Cosmological Background. *American Indian Art Magazine* 19(3):38–47, 104.

Neihardt, John G.

    1932   *Black Elk Speaks.* William Morrow, New York. Reprinted 1961 and 1979 by University of Nebraska Press, Lincoln.

Oetelaar, Gerald A.

    2000   Beyond Activity Areas: Structure and Symbolism in the Organization and Use of Space inside Tipis. *Plains Anthropologist* 45:35–61.

    2003   Tipi Rings and Alberta Archaeology: A Brief Overview. In *Archaeology in Alberta: A View from the New Millennium,* edited by Jack W. Brink and John F. Dormaar, pp. 104–130, Archaeological Society of Alberta, Medicine Hat, Canada.

Old Horn, Dale D., and Timothy P. McCleary

    1995   *Apsáalooke Social and Family Structure.* Little Big Horn College, Crow Agency, Montana.

Oneroad, Amos E., and Alanson B. Skinner

    2003   *Being Dakota: Tales and Traditions of the Sisseton and Wahpeton.* Edited by Laura L. Anderson. Minnesota Historical Society Press, St. Paul.

Parks, Douglas R., and Waldo R. Wedel

    1985   Pawnee Geography: Historical and Sacred. *Great Plains Quarterly* 5:170.

Petter, Rodolphe

    1915   *English-Cheyenne Dictionary.* Kettle Falls, Montana.

Powell, Peter J.

    1969   *Sweet Medicine.* 2 vols. University of Oklahoma Press, Norman.

Robinson, Jack H.

    1981   Astronomical Alignments at the Fort Smith Medicine Wheel. *Archaeoastronomy* 4(3):15–23.

Schlesier, Karl H.

1987   *The Wolves of Heaven: Cheyenne Shamanism, Ceremonies, and Prehistoric Origins.* University of Oklahoma Press, Norman.

2002   On the Big Horn Medicine Wheel: A Comment on Matthew Liebman, *Plains Anthropologist* 47:61–71. *Plains Anthropologist* 47:387–392.

Schultz, James Willard

1962   *Blackfeet and Buffalo.* University of Oklahoma Press, Norman.

Schwartz, Warren E.

1988   *The Last Contrary: The Story of Wesley Whiteman (Black Bear).* Center for Western Studies, Augustana College, Sioux Falls, South Dakota.

Shimkin, D. B.

1953   *The Wind River Shoshone Sun Dance.* Anthropological Paper 41, Bureau of American Ethnology. U.S. Government Printing Office, Washington, D.C.

Simms, Stephen Chapman

1903   A Wheel-Shaped Stone Monument in Wyoming. *American Anthropologist* 5:107–110.

Smith, Decost

1949   *Red Indian Experiences.* George Allen and Unwin, London.

Standing Bear, Luther

1933   *Land of the Spotted Eagle.* Houghton-Mifflin, Boston.

Stands in Timber, John, and Margot Liberty

1967   *Cheyenne Memories.* University of Nebraska Press, Lincoln.

Stone, Richard

1982   *First Encounters: Indian Legends of Devils Tower.* Sand Creek Printing, Belle Fourche, South Dakota.

Sundstrom, Linea

1997   The Sacred Black Hills: An Ethnohistorical Review. *Great Plains Quarterly* 17:185–212.

2000   Cheyenne Pronghorn Procurement and Ceremony. *Plains Anthropologist* 45:119–132.

2004   *Storied Stone: Indian Rock Art of the Black Hills Country.* University of Oklahoma Press, Norman.

2005   *Boulder Effigy Sites in South Dakota: History, Description, and Evaluation.* South Dakota Historical Preservation Office, Pierre.

2009   Coils of Meaning: Women, Corn, Shell, Pottery, and the Below World in the Northern Plains. In *Que(e)rying Archaeology,* edited by Susan Terendy, Natasha Lyons, and Michelle Janse-Smekal, pp. 256–263. Proceedings of the 37th Annual Chacmool Conference, Department of Anthropology, University of Calgary, Calgary, Alberta, Canada.

Taube, Karl A.

2001   The Breath of Life: The Symbolism of Wind in Mesoamerica and the

American Southwest. In *The Road to Aztlan: Art from a Mythic Homeland,* edited by Virginia M. Fields and Victor Zamudio-Taylor, pp. 102–123. Los Angeles County Museum of Art, Los Angeles, California.

Turner, Ronald W.

1974   *Mammals of the Black Hills of South Dakota and Wyoming.* Miscellaneous Publication 60. University of Kansas Museum of Natural History, Lawrence.

Ullrich, Jan (editor)

2008   *New Lakota Dictionary.* Lakota Language Consortium, Bloomington, Indiana.

Vickers, J. Roderick

1988   1986 Majorville Inventory Project. Unpublished permit 86-29 report. On file with the Heritage Resource Management Branch, Alberta Community Development, Edmonton, Alberta, Canada.

Waggoner, Josephine

ca. 1930   *My Land, My People, My Story.* Privately published.

Walker, James R.

1917   The Sun Dance of the Oglala. *Anthropological Papers of the American Museum of Natural History* 16(2):53–221.

1980   *Lakota Belief and Ritual.* Edited by Raymond J. DeMallie and Elaine A. Jahner. University of Nebraska Press, Lincoln.

Wallaertt, Hélène

2006   Beads and a Vision: Waking Dreams and Induced Dreams as a Source of Knowledge for Beadwork Making: An Ethnographic Account from Sioux Country. *Plains Anthropologist* 51:3–15.

Weltfish, Gene

1977   *The Lost Universe: Pawnee Life and Culture.* University of Nebraska Press, Lincoln. Originally published 1965, Basic Books, New York.

Wissler, Clark

1908   Ethnographical Problems of the Missouri Saskatchewan Area. *American Anthropologist* n.s. 10:197–207.

Zitkala Sa

1901   *Old Indian Legends.* Ginn, Boston.

3
Of Iron Steamship Anacondas and Black Cayman Canoes
Lowland Mythology as a Rosetta Stone for Formative Iconography

Peter G. Roe and Amy Roe

Enduring (Myth)themes and Systemic Change: An Overview

The overarching topics of this volume are the enduring themes that have guided Amerindian cultures over vast stretches of time, space, and societies, and the alterations those themes have undergone as the natural byproduct of continuous, and often catastrophic, cultural and environmental change.

Because the western hemisphere is essentially a set of vertically and tenuously connected island continents, there is an underlying unity to the linguistics, physical anthropology, and social development of these relatively isolated worlds before they were violently reintegrated into, and often obliterated by, the larger human story. This unity can be superficially belied by the welter of languages, cultures, adaptations, and specific histories that the autochthonous inhabitants of the Americas exhibit. Yet despite the range of environments and levels of social and political integration among these myriad populations, some themes persist even into the modern day, and do so from the remotest antiquity. One theme, in particular, stands out.

A reverence for nature, evident in a persistently animistic worldview, is common to Amerindian societies, regardless of the level of social, political, or technical integration they have achieved. In their ethos, all the things of culture were modeled upon, and derived from, the world of nature. These worlds did not exist in static opposition to each other but in an endlessly dynamic dualism that focused on the liminal overlapping categories between otherwise opposed entities, a phenomenon called dual-triadic dualism (Roe 1995a). Such a view effectively connected the worlds of humans with the worlds of geological, hydrological, and climatological forms, as well as the animals, birds, and plants that inhabited them, via bridges or ladders of intergrading concepts. In turn, this animistic ontology of nature worship was generated by a cultural epistemology of altered states of consciousness from dreams to trance and visions that revealed hidden realities that were, and are, regarded as more real, more perfect (a form of "primitive Platonism") than the empirical patterns perceived by the waking senses (Roe 1989).

In this metaphorically amphibian chapter, we attempt to reflect some of the complexity of that world by combining archaeological interpretation, archaeoastronomy and ethnoastronomy, and traditional ethnographic fieldwork. We examine one such importation of culture, the horticultural way of life, from the world of nature via one such overlap category, withholding protocultural custodians, mostly dawn were-creatures who withheld the secret of cultigens, which they acquired *naturally,* from questing humans and their culture hero deities. We do this with reference to the first true multimedia, multiregional, and multiethnic civilization (Lavallée 2000) of ancient Peru, Chavín. The aesthetic signature of this seminal civilization was an art style (Roe 1974; Rowe 1967) that flourished from 1200 to 200 B.C.E., as part of a regional cult (Burger 1992) that spread throughout the northern and central Andes and coast, and the civilization's related sacred polities. We will do that by offering a new meta-narrative (Roe and Roe 2010), the story behind the story, for the physical location, construction, orientation, and history of the monumental stone architecture, and its associated stone sculpture, of the primate type site of Chavín de Huántar in the Callejón de Conchucos of the northeastern Andes.

We attempt to do so by affirming a 3,200-year pattern of cultural continuity, with appropriate change but without significant symbolic or iconic disjunctions, or radical changes of meaning, in the astral mythologies of at least two jungle tribes removed both in time and environmental zones from that ancient highland civilization. These reference groups are the current ethnographic Amahuaca and Shipibo Indians of the eastern slopes of the Andes. They are both egalitarian Panoan tribes within the watershed of the Upper Amazon, the same watershed Chavín de Huántar was located within. These enduring themes and persistent narratives will allow us to partially explicate the content of the heretofore little understood Chavín religion (Burger 2008:692) and its attendant myths carved in stone on the famously enigmatic monumental sculpture that the site is noted for, esoteric artwork, an aesthetic system that has successfully resisted generations of Andeanists' attempts to decipher it (Roe 2008).

Specifically, we examine two well-known and complex pieces of monolithic stone carving, the in situ principal cult image of the Lanzón and the later and spatially altered, but thematically related, Tello Obelisk, and decode them, image by image, using modern texts recorded from our living consultants in the jungle in their own language (Panoan). Next, we take one central mytheme from the ancient iconography and the modern oral tradition, the "cayman canoe," the giant New World mythic crocodilian naturefact-artifact, and chart its further mythological transformations. We then present heretofore-unpublished verbal texts from our corpus that show how ancient themes transmute into stories of giant *paiche* fish to nineteenth-century *garreta* (iron-hulled steamboats) and modern *mestizo* jail cells and courts! In all this feverish change, the ancient mythemes and their primal paradigmatic (deep structural) meanings remain largely intact, with elements and actions that call up images and sequences from the first transition to settled horticulture in the New World Neolithic or Formative period.

The Narrative Approach to Cultural Archaeology: Voices of Ancient Consultants

The narrative approach we use is cultural archaeology (Roe 1993a); recently Bill Keegan (2007) has independently coined the same term for a similar exercise in melding direct historical ethnographic analogy with archaeology. Central to cultural archaeology are three key perspectives: first, a systems view of culture in which ideas matter as much as techno-economic imperatives and the structure of society and, second, that these ideas are articulated in powerful narratives, meaningful stories full of explanatory power. They are central myths, sacred stories believed to be true (Roe 1988), about the origin, functioning, and fate of the universe and all the beings, spiritual and natural, that inhabit it. Third, the continuity of such myths can carry their concepts across deep time and over vast stretches of space, accommodating change as they go, but resisting fundamental alterations in meaning.

By listening to the narrators of modern myths from the *montaña*, we can interpret the mythological "texts" (the inscribed monuments themselves) that the ancient Chavín artists left behind. The *montaña* comprises the moderately high jungle that runs along the eastern slopes of the Andes from Ecuador in the north to Bolivia in the south; it lies above the *hylea*, or low jungle of the Amazon, and below the even higher *ceja* fog forest that stretches just beneath the Andean cordillera. This medial zone shares many items of material culture and ideology with the highlands immediately to the west, resulting from millennia of interaction.

A key astral myth from that liminal jungle realm spans a remarkable 3,200 years of cultural continuity. It is incised into granite on several key monoliths from the ancient highland cult center of Chavín de Huántar. Indeed, its various characters, and the scenes in which they figure, are arranged sequentially, from top to bottom, one frame at a time, on these monuments just like storyboards (Roe and Roe 2010:54), the cartoonlike drawn cells used to plan the development of modern films. Bourget (2006:7–8) has independently used this concept for the pictorial narratives of Moche fine-line paintings. The Mochica are a succeeding culture on the north coast that displays a high degree of iconographic continuity with Chavín (see Quilter, this volume), largely because it evolved out of Cupisnique, north coastal Chavín, with admixtures from the post-Chavín Salinar and Virú cultures (Castillo Butters and Uceda Castillo 2008:710).

The Chavín de Huántar site, although located in the northeastern Andes, actually falls within the watershed of the Upper Amazon and was situated there to bridge the three biomes of Peru: the humid jungle to the east, the semiarid highlands in the center, and the desert coast to the west. It functioned as the primary pilgrimage center of a regional cult (Burger 1992) that endured from 1200 to 200 B.C.E.

We compare the ancient site's iconography and architectural orientations with the astral mythology we recorded, transcribed, and translated from the modern Shipibo, Panoan-speaking "Canoe Indians" of the main river floodplain of the central Ucayali River, a major southern tributary of the Upper Amazon. The Shipibo dwell in the *montaña* of eastern Peru, approximately 200 km, as the harpy eagle flies, from Chavín (a mere four days' walk, albeit over rough terrain) and at almost the same latitude. In their jungle fastness, the Shipibo have been relatively protected, until recently, from the traumas of the Conquest and subsequent colonization and Christianization. Hence, they have preserved tales that have long since disappeared or, rather, were extirpated from the more accessible Andes and coast. Those surviving lowland myths not only form the meta-narrative for the ancient Andean site, but they also act as oral Rosetta stones to decode, motif-by-motif, many elements carved into the monumental sculptures associated with the Old and New Temples at the site, as well as their archaeoastronomical orientation.

Continuity vs. Discontinuity: Andean vs. Amazonian Culture Geographic Areas

While some may question this interpretivist approach because it transcends the hermetic boundaries of modern academic area studies and their quoting-circles (Andeanist/Amazonianist), we argue that such distinctions are anachronistic when applied to the remote Formative Period of the central and northern Andes (the Formative includes the Preceramic and Initial periods of horticultural and ceramic-using prehistory in this region, as well as the Early Horizon—roughly 3500–200 B.C.E.). This was a time when these culture-geographic areas remained in much closer contact than they were in during the late Incaic-Colonial and modern Quechua periods, the eras that formed the current areal disciplines (see Burger 1992:104 and Raymond 1988:279 for similar observations on the pitfalls of applying modern academic impermeable cultural divisions back to the ancient Formative).

Indeed, recent and important discoveries in the *ceja* zone of Ecuador just to the north, at the sites of Pechinche (2800 B.C.E.) and Santa Ana-la Florida, dating to the Early Formative (2300 B.C.E.), down to Valdivia, Machalilla, and Cotocollao (and the neighboring Peruvian *oriente* site of Bagua), demonstrate the extent to which the "Andean" tradition owes its inception to the Amazon. This northern region (including the tributaries of the lower Marañon, itself another affluent of the Upper Amazon that the Mosna River, which Chavín de Huántar is located along, drains into as it flows to the north and east) is where the Andean chain lowers and narrows, allowing Amazonian influences to reach the Ecuadorian coast, and from thence to the Peruvian north coast and highlands. Such influences continue via the Huayurco site in the Peruvian *oriente* at 1500 B.C.E. (Zeidler 2008:481). Taken together, these northern sites made the Chavín cultural style possible, including the use of *yopó* hallucinogenic snuff as documented in early miniature avimorphic and theriomorphic (often feline) ground-and-polished incised stone mortars, shamanic transformation, and the *recto-verso* imagery (Valdez 2008:881–882) that goes with that visionary experience; the importance of *Strombus* gastropods (conches) and *Spondylus* pelecypods (bivalves) as ritual offerings (Valdez 2008:879); the very stirrup-spout bottles, usually destined for ritual inhumation, that became the hallmark of Chavín (Valdez 2008:884); as well as the specific iconography of avian, serpent, and feline figures, which "suggests the early existence of an ideological scheme that would further evolve into the Formative Andean traditions" (Valdez 2008:884).

As Guffroy (2008:893) states, "these elements also attest the early appearance, in the eastern slopes, of religious representations and ritual activities that formed part, several centuries later, of the basic components of the Cupisnique and Chavín religion in northern Peru." This assessment is particularly significant because, in a new perspective, Bischof (2008) has argued that the sites that betray this tropical forest imagery in northern Peru, like Huaca Prieta, Pampa de las Llamas, La Galgada, Kuntur Wasi, and Pacopampa, form the iconographic substrate of Cupisnique (north coastal Chavín) and thus can be considered proto-Chavín. He identifies these images as Phase A, a refinement of the Rowe (1967) Chavín seriation. We differ slightly from him by believing that these forms are directly developmental to Phase A, as defined by the Lanzón, the principal cult object at Chavín de Huántar (Burger 2008:692).

Moreover, from its very definition by Julio C. Tello (1923) almost a century ago, the Chavín phenomenon has been recognized as drawing significantly upon the flora and fauna of the Amazon (Tello 1960), as well as its human denizens' shamanic practices and cosmology (Roe 1982a). Today, Andeanists like Richard Burger (1992:150, 2008:694), Daniel Morales Chocano (2008:158), and Gary Urton (2008:218) recognize that all of the major, and most of the minor, supernaturals that populated the Chavín pantheon were the large carnivores and raptors of the wet tropical forest. Why would these carnivorous creatures and lowland cultigens appear in the monuments of a highland society that subsisted on llamas and potatoes? Burger writes, "The supernaturals represented draw upon the features of powerful and dangerous carnivores such as the jaguar, anaconda, harpy eagle and cayman, frequently combining the features to produce hybrids [like the caymanic dragon] unknown in the natural world. Moreover, the natural habitats of these creatures were the forested eastern slopes and tropical lowlands far to the east, a world radically different from the intermontane valley environment in which Chavín de Huántar is situated" (Burger 2008:690, 692). The attraction of the exotic and mysterious in the religious experience, the figuring of these predators as the major icons in the hallucinogenic visions derived from the ritual ingestion of lowland psychotropic drugs, as well as the fearsome beauty and the compelling affective response such powerful and beautiful, yet deadly, creatures elicit in humans all contribute to this apparent anomaly of jungle natural icons in the Andes.

In addition, these icons were arranged in precisely the same order as they are in the current lowlands, as the "Masters" and "Mistresses" (the giant natural paragons, which the modern Shipibo would call *Ibo*, "owning," as in dominating—literally "eating"—but also generating, as in procreating, the creatures of each plane) of the three superimposed cosmic worlds (Lathrap 1985:246; Roe 1982a:Figure 3). As Burger (2008:692) summarizes, in addition to the Lanzón as the "principal god" and cult image, "there were also the supernaturals associated with the celestial sphere [Sky World], often with the features of harpy eagles or hawks, sometimes shown as the guardians or assistants of the principal deity [as in the Black and White Portal]. Worship also involved the supernatural forces present in the world inhabited by humans and animals [Earth World]; these were often depicted as jaguars [or werejaguars]. The forces associated with the [Sub-Aquatic] Underworld, and the water that circulated through it, were represented on the sculptures by fanged anaconda-like serpents or cat-snakes [*à la* Roe 1974]."

For Chavín actors, as for modern lowlanders (Roe 1990), the human body was a microcosm of the universe at large (the macrocosm). The Tello Obelisk Dragons were also seen as cosmological bodies and had a similar somatic geography of adornment and corporeal elements that corresponded with the views of the structure of the universe held by the artists who carved them. These artists' conceptions were "strikingly similar to the divisions and organization of body segments by means of body decoration found among the Yekuana of the Upper Orinoco River basin . . . [and on] body ornaments among the Suya [of Central Brazil]" (Urton 2008:232).

Just as the human body and the bodies of the artistic creations of the Chavín style reflect the cosmos, so too did their body politic. The general social principles of opposition and alliance that are deducible from the monuments at Chavín de Huántar find parallels among the distant Bororo and other lowland groups of Central Brazil, according to Morales Chocano (2008: 154–158). If Andeanists can find ethnographic analogs to Chavín as far afield in the Amazon as the Guianas and Central Brazil, then surely the use of lowland parallels with groups like the Amahuaca and Shipibo from the *montaña*, with its long history of interaction with, and propinquity to, the neighboring sierra (Raymond 1988; Raymond et al. 1975), is even less problematic.

Animal and plant icons, and their significance, were not the only things that diffused from the jungle to Chavín de Huántar. Iconographic evidence indicates that unique *montaña* feathered back-racks (Roe 1990), and highly prized *chonta* serrated war spears, were traded from the jungle to the sierra since they were part of the accoutrements being paraded by Chavín warriors on a recently discovered cornice fragment (Rick 2008:Figure 1.15) from the site. Everything from probable jaguar bones, used for bone-working (Burger 1984:213), to a piranha mandible (Burger 1988:132), employed as a cutting implement, has been recovered from the faunal remains. Were the preservation conditions better, there would have doubtless been excavated the remains of jaguar and ocelot pelts as well as the spectacular plumes of the scarlet macaw and other gaudy tropical forest birds, items we already know were being traded to other highland and coastal sites since the Preceramic.

In addition, there is the problem of using a specific lowland myth to illuminate the art and architecture of Chavín de Huántar. If the mythic icons that decorate the site are Amazonian, if their cosmological ordering and conceptual patterning are Amazonian, and if, as Chavín specialists from Lumbreras (2005:243) to Burger (2008:692) recognize, the intricate carving on the monoliths renders them myths carved in stone, then it is not a conceptual leap to suggest that certain of the myths illustrated on the monuments may also have been of Amazonian origin. Andeanists have already made that leap before us: "perhaps the Chavín de Huántar cult also adopted some of its myths and beliefs from these Amazonian sources" (Burger and Salazar-Burger 1980:27).

There is also the potential problem of disjunction (Kubler 1962), the possible disassociation of form and meaning over time (Grieder 1975), specifically during the interval from the end of the Chavín horizon at 200 B.C.E.

to the arrival of the Shipibo's ancestors in the form of the Cumancaya tradition on the Upper Ucayali at 800 c.e., with its evidence of trade with the Andes in the form of a cache of pure native copper axes and spokeshaves (Raymond et al. 1975)—the sort of items that would have been traded to the lowlands in exchange for the animal pelts, bird feathers, and tropical wood items that went from the jungle to the sierra cited above, and from thence to the modern Shipibo narrator who told one of us the myth in 1978. Can the ethnographic tale narrated in the modern oral tradition and the ancient myth carved in stone at the archaeological site be cognate versions of the same story? As we will see, the high degree of fit between the two media, despite their differing spatio-temporal placement, is the best case for such continuity so far discovered.

It is very fortunate that a myth from an adjacent South American region meets all the criteria needed to interpret the Lanzón and the Tello Obelisk, as well as a number of related monoliths at Chavín de Huántar. In this myth a cayman canoe carried two culture hero passengers, one of whom loses a leg (or legs) to his hungry barque, while the other escapes by means of a magical connection between the earth and sky planes, both also being transformed into birds (and, again, one loses a leg to the cayman's maw). This myth also includes the origin of the Pleiades, Hyades, and Orion and the importance of these asterisms (closely spaced, easily recognizable groupings of stars using naked-eye astronomy) at Chavín for horticulture (Lathrap 1973). The *montaña* offered such a myth, collected from two, not just one, jungle tribes, one in the interior (the Amahuaca), the other on the main river (the Shipibo), by two independent investigators (Roe 1993b, 2005; Woodside 1979) decades apart.

Our argument for continuity, rather than disjunction, in ideology does not rest on the isomorphism of a narrative in two related media (verbal and plastic arts) alone, or on iconography by itself, unsupported by other vectors of evidence. Through an examination of ancient astronomical data, we have discovered that the entire ceremonial complex at Chavín de Huántar corresponds precisely with the heliacal setting of the Pleiades. Such archaeoastronomical evidence further reinforces our arguments for continuity since the modern myth concerns precisely the same constellation and its associated asterisms. Our findings also reinforce other evidence concerning the importance of the Pleiades at the site (Burger 2008:688). Thus, a whole suite of congruent vectors of evidence, from geographic and latitudinal propinquity, similarities in oral tradition, archaeoastronomy and ethnoastronomy, architectural orientation, configuration, and the iconography that adorned it, all cohere to argue for the endurance of powerful themes in South Amerindian thought, lowland, highland, and coastal, ancient and modern alike.

As to the methodology of this study, art historical–inspired close visual analysis, when it is coupled with structural and componential analysis from anthropology, helps to eliminate equivalences that are not really comparable, thus highlighting the false disjunctions introduced by Western students into a continuous South Amerindian tradition. For example, Roe (2008:Figure 7.11) has already demonstrated that the generic "staffs" held by the Black and White Portal winged Raptor Guardians on either side of the entrance to the New Temple were actually weaponry (as are many of the objects held by Chavín supernaturals). Specifically, they were an atlatl (spear-thrower) and its dart. Thus we agree with Quilter (this volume) that the use of "staff" is an inappropriate ethnographic analog based on historic Quechua custom, itself a product of acculturation with Spanish practice—just like the English who gave staffs of office to Indian "captains" in their efforts to increase their indirect rule in the Guianas (Menezes 1977)—and thus a true case of iconic disjunction. This is yet another example of what we call below the "Quechua Tyranny," applying analogy from the last surviving cultural tradition to one of the earliest, despite the numerous disjunctions that have occurred between them.

Instead, we maintain that iconic continuity from the weaponry of the ancient Chavín supernaturals like the Snarling Were-Jaguar Warrior God/Goddess (aka Smiling Staff God and Goddess) persists from Chavín only down to Tiahuanaco/Huari [Wari] Middle Horizon times circa 1000 C.E., in the southern highlands, and to just the Moche and their similarly snarling Were-Jaguar Gods (Wrinkle Face and his cohort) on the north coast to 600–800 C.E. Then a real iconic and symbolic disjunction occurs (from Huari-Tiahuanaco to Inca and post-Inca, the Quechua heritage) and between Moche and Chimu (Castillo Butters and Uceda Castillo 2008:724–725), as the iconography shifted from the representational and anthropomorphic to the geometric and decorative, and from the sacred to the profane. If this is so, the irony is obvious; the Inca and Quechua analogs that most Andeanists use to decode Chavín are the most disjunctive, and therefore the least appropriate analogs, compared with those from the jungle offered here.

Applying modern Quechua ethnographic analogy to ancient Chavín reflects two common, but largely unacknowledged, problems in archaeology and cultural anthropology: flattened, two-dimensional time in the former, and secondary ethnocentrism in the latter. In archaeology, there is always the tendency to decode the societies of remote antiquity using the latest surviving culture from those regions at European contact. Thus all the earliest Pre-Maipuran Arawak societies of the Caribbean are traditionally reconstructed using their most recent descendants, the Taíno Indians of Columbus's arrival: the "Taíno Tyranny" (Roe 1991b). The same could be said of

Peruvian prehistory, the realm of the "Inca Tyranny." While such a view flattens time, compressing everything into the span of the latest occupants of a long and highly disjunctive chronological column (Roe 1994), it is understandable given the much greater data and better preservation conditions obtainable from these latest actors on the stage of prehistory. But as excavation progresses this two-dimensional time-scape dissipates and a whole host of distinctive cultures appear in long chronological columns. Nevertheless, the protohistoric ruler is often still applied to prehistory.

The second difficulty involves cultural anthropology. This is the tendency of fieldworkers to unconsciously assimilate the ethnic perspectives (the ethnoanthropology) of the groups they study. In essence, some Andeanists have internalized the ethnocentrism and narrowed geographical frameworks of the highlanders they have worked among, lowlanders being merely colorful and marginal *chunchos*, "feathered Indian savages," exotic but utterly alien remnants of a "precivilized world," compared to the "civilized" Inca and their Andean descendants (Heckman 2003:113).

We hasten to point out that neither of these difficulties circumscribes the perspectives of the Andeanists cited in this study. Instead, their phytomorphic simile is a useful compromise, being first employed by Tello (1923) and then by Burger (1984:2). While they regard the organic growth of Chavín as authentically Andean in its trunk, they nevertheless also acknowledge that some of its main roots lie in the jungle to the north (Ecuador) and to the east (the Peruvian *montaña*). Therefore, let us now examine one of those still-vibrant roots.

Sacred Architecture as the Stony Stage for Ceremonial Reenactments

The Chavín de Huántar site has a ceremonial core composed of a gigantic stone-faced truncated pyramid that, through a complex sequence of at least five major rebuildings and additions, is composed (firstly) of an Old Temple with three layers that step back toward a flat summit with twin small shrines. Projecting forward on either side of the facade of this artificial mountain are two wings that, in plan view, turn the temple into a U-shaped pyramid modeled on earlier complexes from the coast (Burger and Salazar-Burger 2008). In the middle of the wings is a sunken circular court with a stairway leading to a hidden cruciform gallery in the interior of the main body of the structure. In the very center of that gallery stands a large L-shaped monolith called the Lanzón (Figure 3.1a), a therianthropic fanged being with a Medusa's head of writhing snakes (Figure 3.1b). Other galleries, including narrow acoustic galleries that turn tumbling water into a roar like the low-pitched infrasonic vocalizations of the cayman and the anaconda, which current *montaña* dwellers like the Canelos Quichua liken to thunder and emulate with giant hollow signal drums (Whitten 1976:219), honeycomb the building and extend down into the circular court area. The sides of that court are faced with two levels of stone plaques. On the upper row are bas-relief sculptures of were-jaguar anthropomorphs, including the San Pedro Bearer (Figure 3.1d), who holds his namesake columnar cactus, a mescaline-rich hallucinogenic plant, in his right hand while marching with his companions (others blowing the *Strombus fututo* trumpet) toward the monumental stairway of the Old Temple and the entombed Lanzón. Below the fanged humanoids, a set of profile jaguars pad in the same direction, the probable theriomorphic shamanic transformations or familiars of the therianthropomorphs above them (Burger 2008:687–688).

According to the prominent Peruvian Chavín archaeologist Luís Lumbreras (1989:30), the sunken plaza's first excavator, in the center of that court may have stood the second, smaller, but even more elaborately carved, L-shaped monolith, the Tello Obelisk (Figure 3.1e). Incised and excised into its sides, in bas-relief, are dual consort caymanic dragons (Figure 3.1f, for the male). The male covering the female (as in coitus), both are carved emerging vertically, on either side of their monolith, out of the center of the artificial "lake" of the paved sunken plaza. A host of lesser figures jostle with, and reside inside of, the X-ray depicted bodies of these monsters. This motley crew includes only one humanoid twin set. The simpler of the twins has his legs disappearing into the profile neck-mouth of the dragons while he gesticulates wildly, as if he is being devoured. The more elaborate twin is contorted into a U shape, leaping from near the dragons' fishlike tails to grab a rope motif. This is the same motif held by the Lanzón (Figure 3.1b; the holding is implied given the primitive pictorial conventions of this earliest phase of the art style). This later divine humanoid also sports teeth similar to those of the Lanzón, but displays, instead of snaky locks, an elaborate headdress (Figure 3.1g).

That crown represents the "demonic" nocturnal flower of the San Pedro cactus (*Trichocereus pachanoi*). This identification is based on a number of botanical observations such as the fringe of short, bevel-edged petals ringing the flower's castellum. These fringing petals, in turn, are surrounded by fewer, but much longer thin and pointed petals, arranged radially around the outside of the flower (Figure 3.1i). Such a dual structure exactly conforms to the design of the elaborate leaping figure's carved headdress (Figure 3.1h), with its inner ring of numerous short petals = feathers surrounding the castellum-equivalent cap that forms the base of the headdress. A simple frontal face appears inside that castellum, perhaps indicating the San Pedro's in-dwelling and animating spirit. In the original, these short feathers, if the lowland "language of the plumes" (Roe 1990) was applied, would have been the white

Figure 1

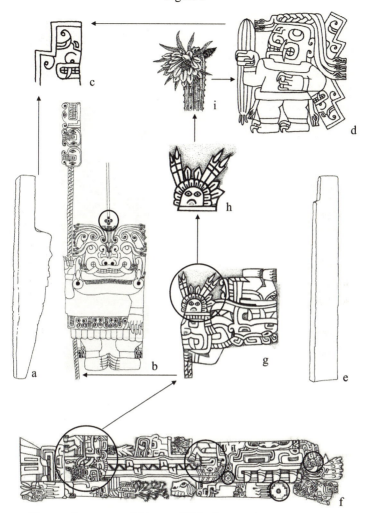

Figure 3.1. The transformations of Alcyone, "Elder Brother, Pleiades," in Chavín monumental sculpture: (a) outline of the Lanzón (Old Temple cruciform gallery) showing its L shape (abstracted from Tello 1960:Figure 30); (b) rollout drawing of the were-anthropomorphic Alcyone carved into the Lanzón (modified from Burger 1992:Figure 140); (c) the lower back-rack profile face of the San Pedro Bearer; (d) the San Pedro Bearer as the Phase C–D Transition version of Alcyone, from a square plaque in the circular sunken plaza within the U-shaped arms of the Old Temple (modified from Roe 1978 and Rick 2008:Figure 1.16); (e) outline of the Tello Obelisk, another L-shaped monolith, which represents the caymanic Dragon Canoe (abstracted from Tello 1960: Figure 31, middle); (f) reconstruction of the male from the Tello Obelisk; (g) enlarged and rotated drawing of Alcyone (from the female Dragon) showing his longer Sky Rope segment and elaborate San Pedro flower-feather headdress with the face of its indwelling spirit in the castellum cap of the crown; (h) Alcyone's feather headdress in the form of the San Pedro crown; (i) San Pedro cactus in nocturnal flower with short, white fringing petals around the castellum and the longer projecting thin red petals.

feathers of the harpy eagle, just like the white inner petals of the flower. The few long and thin "feathers" that project outward from the headdress could have been scarlet macaw tail plumes, burning red like the long petals of the San Pedro flower. These elongated feather-petals have been "kenned" (a stock visual metaphor commonly used in Chavín art—see Rowe 1967) as plan-view bat finger-wing digits with long, pointed fingernail = claw elements (compare them with the profile-view finger-wing and nail elements of the little bats seated on the dragons' backs on the Tello—Figure 3.2a, b). A natural linkage unites these two motifs, crouching bats and flower-headdresses, because the large and showy night-blooming San Pedro flower is bat-pollinated (Roe and Roe 2010:Figure 5a, b).

San Pedro is the same columnar cactus carried by the other fanged anthropomorph already referred to (Figure 3.1d). He bears ophidian hair like the Lanzón, but it is now carefully arranged in a braided coiffure. This later San Pedro Bearer also displays a back-rack of the sort used exclusively by *montaña* warriors. His is composed of two L-shaped profile fanged heads of the Lanzón (Figure 3.1c), signaling a relationship between the two theomorphs.

The two little bats sit within U-shaped plazas on the backs of the two dragons. These motifs resemble miniature profile views of the circular sunken plaza, in the center of which the Tello and its dragons were likely erected. Based on this web of mutual associations, the San Pedro Bearer appears to be linked with both the Lanzón and the Tello's elaborately decorated Sky Rope Leaper. All of these characters appear to be interconnected, diachronic manifestations of the same figure as he appears in succeeding phases of the art style's evolution.

To employ our modified version of the Rowe (1967) sculptural seriation (Roe 1974, 1978, 1982b, 2008; Roe and Roe 2010), this supreme being took the following style-phase manifestations—what the Ye'cuana (Yekuana) would call his *Damodedes*, or periodic embodiments (Guss 1989), where he acts out various episodes of his religious odyssey or holds key elements of his defining accoutrements: Phase A = Lanzón, Phase B (no representations recovered as yet), Phase C = Tello's Sky Rope Leaper, Phase C–D Transition, the San Pedro Bearer, Phase D = the Shell Bearer (aka the Smiling God), and Phase E = the Were-Jaguar Warrior. The latter is also known as the Staff God, seen on the Raimondi stela (Quilter, this volume). The "staffs" he holds are actually bundled darts kenned as dual subjugated dragons, the very dragon consorts of the Tello Obelisk, his ancient cannibal parents—but that is another paper.

This figure, in his original form of the in situ Lanzón, has already been called the principal deity of the site and his image the site's principal cult image (Burger 2008:689). The placement of his various manifestations in the

Figure 2

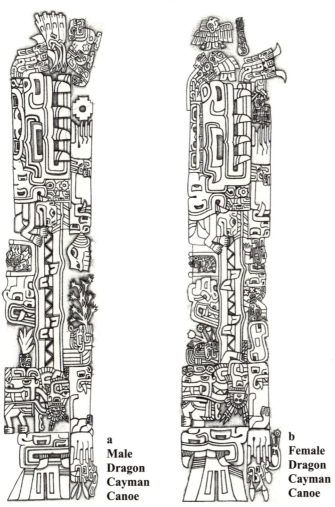

a
**Male
Dragon
Cayman
Canoe**

b
**Female
Dragon
Cayman
Canoe**

Figure 3.2. The twin caymanic dragon canoes of the Tello Obelisk, separated and reconstructed based on site visits and digital photography (compare with their original relationship and condition in the Rowe rubbing-derived rollout in Burger 1992:Figure 141): (a) the male dragon cayman canoe, the manifestation of the "Sub-Aquatic Seducer and Bringer of Cultigens and Hallucinogens"; (b) his consort, the female dragon cayman canoe, the "Rainbow Dragon."

temple complex recapitulated an important myth of this deity's origin, functioning, and fate, a myth certainly reenacted annually by priests in elaborate calendrical rituals that used the Old Temple as a dynamic lithic stage.

To appreciate this myth, consider the series of plants that grow from the dragons' bodies or sprout from the trophy heads they drag along behind them. Donald Lathrap, a lowland specialist who developed the Ucayali sequences (Lathrap 1970), the succession of prehistoric cultures in the *montaña* from the Tutishcainyo ceramics of the Initial Period to the ancestors of the modern Shipibo in late prehistoric times, the Cumancaya tradition, first called attention to a seemingly anomalous aspect of Chavín de Huántar's iconography as a highland site. Despite the Chavín population's subsistence on llamas and potatoes (Miller and Burger 1995), the Tello Obelisk, one of the site's key monuments, nevertheless portrays plants that are jungle cultigens, like manioc, chili peppers, and peanuts. Moreover, he noted that the creature they decorated was the largest jungle reptile, the giant black cayman (Lathrap 1973). This is a position most Andeanists, like Richard Burger (1992:150) and Gary Urton (2008:218), now accept.

Moreover, the dragons reveal multiple cut slices of the multilobed San Pedro cactus (Roe and Roe 2010:Figure 18) in precisely the same form that modern coastal shamans prepare it for boiling to extract a mescaline-rich psychotropic tea. These San Pedro slices (shown as multipointed figures, a circular hole in the center representing the cactus's pithy core; Figure 3.1f, right) appear in a number of contexts on the monolith. One of them dangles from the dragons' dual-view forehead frontal faces' trifid serpentine tongue (Figure 3.1f, far right). In this complex, esoteric art, an opaque dualism rules, so in addition to the main figure's profile face, which is easily visible as the dragon paddles by, above it, on the level of its forehead, appears a frontal face of the same caymanic dragon arriving, only his eyes, nose, and agnathic jaw visible; the tongue of this jaw lolls sideways over the dragon's nose. Another San Pedro slice hangs from the tip of his earring (Figure 3.1f, middle right, behind the profile head's jaw), and one may even be present as one of the polysemic readings of the similar *chakana* (Andean cross) cosmogram in front of his hand (Figure 3.1f, lower right, his holding it is implied). These identifications are not new but date back to Cané's (1983:6, 8) insights; what is new is our identification of the San Pedro flower on the monument as well as its slices.

Thus, we can now add a coastal and highland hallucinogenic "food" (of the gods and shamans), San Pedro cactus, to the staple foods of the peasants that the dual dragons bore. The coastal cactus is itself probably a regional mythic substitute for the jungle hallucinogenic vine, *ayahuasca*, which is viewed as an ophidian Sky Rope in the lowlands. That is the same rope grasped by the Lanzón and the U-shaped leaping San Pedro flower-bearer on the Tello.

Indeed, all these major theomorphs of the Chavín pantheon derived from the large animals of the tropical rain forest; they are not Andean or coastal life forms. Moreover, they were all the apical predators in their respective niches, for this was a sanguinary religion based on human sacrifice and blood offerings (Burger 2008:689, associated with the Lanzón), ritual cannibalism (Burger 1992:108, from Pacopampa Chavín levels; Burger 2008:688, from the Ofrendas Gallery at Chavín de Huántar), and the Trophy Head Cult (Cordy-Collins 2001; Roe 1974:Figure 4b). These are appropriate ritual practices to venerate such carnivorous gods. The blood they spilled was likened to the flowing water needed to nourish the thirsty crops in the arid highlands and coast.

Their carnivorous nature also explains why Chavín gods and goddesses appear to snarl. Contrary to the peaceful label adopted by the prominent Andeanist John H. Rowe, the originator of a qualitative seriation of the style (Rowe 1967; see also Roe 1974), these bloody gods and goddesses do not smile; they grimace. Indicative of the difference between a smile and a snarl are the multiple lines on the margins of the nose and the bunched flesh above the noses of Chavín deities (Roe 1974:Figures 13–15). This wrinkling effect can only be produced, in felines (Roe 1974:Figure 24b) as in humans, by a snarl that exposes the canines. One can evoke Darwin's (1998 [1872]:185–186) classic characterization of this expression as involving "a virulent set frown," where "the wings of the nostrils are somewhat raised to allow of a free indraught of air, and this is a highly characteristic sign of indignation, and there is almost always a frown on the brow," or, again, the "lowered and strongly wrinkled brows" (Darwin 1998 [1872]:188) of equally angry subjects. For precisely such a lowered and wrinkled brow and flaring nostrils, accompanied by the exposed canines of a snarl, see Rowe 1967, Figure 21, the Shell Bearer, the last preserved manifestation of the principal deity at the site. Fear, mystery, and exoticism are essential to religion's affective power, and what better place from which to borrow one's gods than the occult jungle; this mining of the jungle for its fearsome animistic supernaturals, and seeking the wisdom of the shamans in the deep forest, is an ongoing process in the *montaña* even today (Whitten 1976:149).

After the Old Temple was built, a massive New Temple was annexed to it on the south at double the scale, together with its own large square sunken plaza. The court was centered on the Black and White Portal with its Raptor Columns (Roe 2008) and its dual hidden stairways entering the middle of the New Temple's facade. That addition (or series of additions, see Kembel

2008; Kembel and Rick 2004) maintained the same orientation as the Old Temple to which it was joined.

In 1982, Peter Roe published a cosmological meta-model for the Formative worldview of lowland central and northern South America, a vision of the universe that dated back to at least the second millennium B.C.E., the time of Chavín (Roe 1982a:Figure 3). It postulated a triple-tiered cosmology composed of a series of floating, superimposed, disk-shaped cosmic levels: a bright blue aerial Sky World; a green and verdant Earth World in the middle inhabited by humans; and a cold, black, and wet Sub-Aquatic Underworld. This cosmos accounts for the Shipibo diurnal journey of the Sun with his fiery macaw-feather headdress, in a charred black, vulture-paddled canoe, from eastern rising to zenith strength and western setting. At night, this cosmos literally turns itself inside out, like flipping a black, polished jet Chavín mirror, to reveal the sub-aquatic world of twinkling stars-as-fish and other aquatic life forms (water birds) and artifacts (canoes) as asterisms, all floating in a foaming Milky Way (Roe 2005). That nocturnal stream is the same "river" that flows from west to east underneath one's feet during the day. At night it brings the Sun from the west, from whence he set as a dying old man, to the east, where he will rise again every day, once more strong, youthful and life-giving.

Each level of this jungle religious tradition's worldview mimics the appropriate stratum of the triple-tiered rain forest canopy upon which it was modeled, from the dark understory of palms to midlevel deciduous trees and the upper story of forest giants. Each cosmic platter is ruled by its dual (Master and Mistress) consort pairs of natural icons. Together, they compose the "Terrible Trinity" of the largest apical raptors and carnivores of the main Amazonian floodplain. These are the huge harpy eagle (*Harpia harpyja*) and lesser hawk (his younger brother) in the Sky World, the fear-inspiring jaguar (*Panthera onca*, in both yellow and black pelage variants) of the Earth World, and the dreaded composite dual dragons of the dark, wet, and cold Underworld. To compose the latter mythical beast, the bifid tongue of the immense anaconda (*Eunectes murinus gigas*) is appended to the body of the gigantic black cayman (*Melanosuchus niger*). This composite monster is furnished with the tail of the flesh-stripping piranha (*Pygocentrus natterei*, Serrasalmidae). Like other lowland dragons (Varese 1968), this chimerical creature is so labeled by acculturated Indians when they translate their conceptions into English or Spanish (Roe 1989).

All natural icons are paired, like humans. Using the lowland myths in which these mega–life forms appear as a gloss, the Chavín consort pair materializes as a male Sub-Aquatic Seducer Dragon (Figure 3.2a) and a female Rainbow Dragon (Figure 3.2b) arching from an aqueous Underworld into the sky during the rainy season. Each of these fearsome pairs rule their respective sanguinary domain. Men, repelled yet fascinated and admiring, model themselves, as fierce warriors or capable hunters, deadly sorcerers or curing shamans, upon these fearsome feathered, furry, or scaly paragons (Roe 1998).

Since this model was published, it has independently been confirmed at the Pacopampa site (Morales Chocano 1995, 2008), another major Chavín ceremonial center, which is coeval with Chavín de Huántar (Burger 2008: 698). There the Peruvian excavator discovered the telltale triple-tiered set of platter worlds with apical predator or raptor masters of each level carved into artificial terraces cut into a modified natural mountain (Morales Chocano 2008:Figure 5.8). As expected, the three cosmic levels of the Old Temple at the type site of Chavín de Huántar can now also be shown to repeat the same pattern (Burger 1992:107; Roe and Roe 2010:51–52). Thus, from the point of view of architecture and its associated monoliths alone, it is appropriate to use *montaña* myth to decode the monuments at Chavín, so many carved "myths in stone" (Burger 2008:692). Such direct historical analogy is reinforced by the near thematic identity between those tales and the monuments' ancient iconography.

These toothy creatures, jaguars and dragons, were not just monsters. Using a kind of dualism that the site itself reconfirms (opposed dual plazas, dual pyramids, dual pyramid-surmounting shrines, portals with dual colors and decorating figures, but with interdigitated shared traits, a form of systematic overlapping categories that makes this dualism dynamic), these creatures were also protocultural custodians, one of the overlap categories between culture and nature as seen from the viewpoint of culture (Roe 1995a). Such dawn-creatures had defining human cultural possessions, like artistic designs, cultigens, and fire, but employed them naturally. That is, they were the mere keepers of cultural traits, and could not generate them via the transmission of learned skills that defines true culture. For example, the dragon had fire, but instead of using the cultural technology of fire sticks and the principle of friction, he held fire in his belly naturally, merely vomiting it up when he wanted to cook and swallowing it back down again when he was finished. Moreover, he and the others behaved in a distinctly noncultural manner; they were stingy. The prime virtue all over the lowlands, ruled as it is by reciprocity, is to be generous. In contrast, they were the opposite of generous. They did not want to share their possessions with the protohumans of this first unfolding of the universe, nor with the latter's culture heroes, the Magical Twins. Therefore, the myths specify that, using helpful avian intermediaries, these treasures had to be stolen, as war booty, ripped from the very bodies of these withholding creatures and transferred to people. Thus the world of culture came from the spoils of the domain of nature. This act of cultural appropria-

tion was achieved by killing, and dismembering, the reluctant donors themselves and carrying away their severed body parts as trophies or body art, just
as warriors did to their anticultural (subhuman) enemies (Roe 1974:Figure
28e) before pacification.

Every authority who has studied Chavín recognizes that monoliths like
the Tello Obelisk are "myths in carved stone," so many lithic "texts" (Burger
2008:692; Lumbreras 2005:243), but which myth and how is the text to be
read? Urton (2008:221) underscores this central problem of dealing with iconography alone: "Only if we were to have access to Chavín narratives, which
would allow us to move beyond, or behind, iconographic comparisons and
substitutions could we follow the cumulative chains of ever more complex
and indirect comparisons that are the hallmark of 'kennings' in literature."

Reconstructing the Myth: Iconography and Narrative Analysis

Using archaeological evidence from the Chavín site, iconographic elements
of the Lanzón and Tello Obelisk, and ethnographic *montaña* narratives, we
are able to reconstruct the myth of the Tello as it might have been told by
Chavín narrators in the first millennium B.C.E. Such ethnoarchaeological
methodology builds upon Quilter's (2005:36–39) reconstruction of a pilgrim's
visit to the Lanzón in the Old Temple in his book *Treasures of the Andes* and
his narrative approach to cultural archaeology.

Figure 3.1 provides a partial storyboard comparison of the separate elements on the Tello Obelisk and modern Shipibo myths originally published
in *The Cosmic Zygote* (Roe 1982a) and further supplemented by ethnoastronomical fieldwork (Roe 1993b, 2005). These myths recount the primal thiev-
ery of cultigens from the bodies of withholding dragons, initiating the horticultural way of life.

A synthesis of these two stories recounts the following tale of boyhood
adventure and danger, and explains the origins of some of the most prominent astronomical features of the night sky for South Amerindians. These
asterisms govern the changing of the seasons and the organization of the
yearly subsistence cycle.

The story starts at the beginning of time, before there were humans or animals as we know them today. The only creatures were dawn-creatures that
fused the ancestral traits of humans and animals together into monstrous
composite beings, the first of which was the male were-caymanic dragon.
This ancestor of human and animal life had a body composed of a giant black
cayman, out of whose fearsome mouth darted an anaconda's bifid tongue.
His tail was that of a piranha and he was adorned with human-style anklets
and bracelets composed of curling snakes.

The male dragon lived a lonely life in a giant oxbow lake off the main channel of the Amazon. As the Master of Fish, he vomited them from his stomach in a thunderous roar and then pursued them as food. Replete after feeding, he crawled up upon the sandy beach of the lake and discovered a beautiful huge and round peanut growing on the ground near the shore. Overcome with lust, he repeatedly copulated with it, impregnating it with his offspring, the Magical Twins and their six peanut siblings.

Rudely interrupting the conception of these culture heroes, another were-caymanic dragon came around the bend—an equally lustful female. A witness to the passion between the male and the peanut womb, she became flooded with jealousy, desiring to be the eager recipient of his attentions. Rushing forward, she grabbed her rival in her powerful jaws, cracking and swallowing it so forcefully that it displaced her collared cat-snake clitoris to her backbone, ejaculating her own bottle gourd progeny. The peanut womb lodged in the female dragon's abdomen, appearing on the Tello Obelisk complete with the two eye souls (caya) of the fetal Magical Twins, who anxiously peer out at either end of their translucent prison.

The female dragon actually killed the peanut womb, breaking it during ingestion, forcing the premature birth of the Magical Twins via postmortem cesarean section. The female dragon also imprisoned the peanut sibling companions of the Magical Twins, the remaining six stars of the Pleiades, hanging them from the roof of her nest. They appear on the uppermost part of the Tello Obelisk, suspended in an X-ray depicted bottle gourd, while she is frozen in an upward leap still striving to devour them too.

The Magical Twins grew up precociously to become were-deities, culture heroes. Elder Brother, born first, became Alcyone, the brightest star of the Pleiades. Wise Elder Brother bore somatic signs of his father's parentage, giant cayman dagger teeth and hair of writhing serpents. Filled with shamanic wisdom, Elder Brother fed on the blood offered him by his vampire bat minions and wore a showy diadem crown of San Pedro flower-feathers, the longer elements of which appeared like the elongated finger-wings of its bat pollinators. Younger Brother, Orion, was foolish and heedless of his older brother's constraining advice, wishing just to fulfill his unbridled, infantile desires.

Unaware that the female dragon had killed their mother, the Magical Twins escape and go on an odyssey in search of their mother's murderer, to exact revenge ("return the harm"). Liberating their peanut siblings from their bottle-gourd prison, they set out on their journey, accompanied by their guide, yellow jaguar—ancient enemy of the caymanic dragon and friend to early earthly creatures. The yellow jaguar guide appears at the top of the Tello Obelisk, pursued by the male dragon. A second luckless jaguar lies dismembered, being digested in the belly of the female dragon, surrounded by the flowers of *ayahuasca*, on the Tello Obelisk, while the severed trophy head of yet a third is carried on her back. Voracious, she is also shown devouring a lesser spectacled cayman in her gut and carrying a severed cayman trophy head on her serrated back. The equally hungry male bears another jaguar's severed trophy head on his ridged dorsal region.

While on their journey, the party becomes increasingly hungry. Arriving at the oxbow lake, they see the succulent first cultigens of manioc, *achira*, bottle gourds, chili peppers, and peanuts growing on the other side of the lake. The dragons, who sprouted these cultigens from their very bodies, had planted them in their garden. These same cultigens can be seen sprouting on the Tello Obelisk, *achira* above the backbone of the male, manioc ejaculating from his collared cat-snake penis, and peanuts germinating from the trophy head of one of his victims, which he drags along clutched in his clawed foot. On the female the same naturefact garden flourishes: the bottle gourd and its flowers are being ejaculated from her displaced collared cat-snake clitoris (in the jungle a woman's clitoris is regarded as her penis or "tooth"), now displaced above her backbone, while chili peppers germinate from the crown and mouth of the trophy head of one of her victims, which she drags along, held firm in her clawed foot.

Ravenous with hunger, the Magical Twins and their companions want to get to the other side of the lake to eat the cultigens, but they cannot swim. They see the giant black cayman canoe swimming in the middle of the lake. The cayman canoe is the Tello Obelisk itself, comprising both the male and female caymanic dragons. Thus the story of the meeting with the Magical Twins is also repeated, using the redundancy of myth, depicted on both sides of the Tello Obelisk.

Seeing the cayman canoe, the Magical Twins and their companions yell to hail what they hope will be their conveyance. The reptilian barque turns and approaches the shore, its glaring eyes, nostrils, upper lip, and lolling tongue visible in a bow wave, also seen approaching in the forehead frontal faces on both the male and female dragons of the Tello Obelisk; their main figure profile faces depict the dragons swimming by.

Arriving at the shore, the cayman canoe offers to take the party across as his/her passengers. The Magical Twins agree to go, leaving their companions stranded behind on the shore. Elder Brother enters first, cautiously stepping to the stern of the canoe and sitting down gingerly. He cautions his younger brother not to insult his host and to tread lightly as he enters. Disregarding this advice, Younger Brother jumps into the canoe, stomping painfully on the snout-prow of the cayman canoe, angering him/her. Nevertheless, they set off on their voyage. The respective locations of the Elder and Younger Brothers on the Tello Obelisk recapitulates the way the story develops, with early episodes near the snout and later episodes in proximity to the tail, thus enabling a reading of the monument from top to bottom.

Elder Brother whispers to Younger Brother that he should avoid making any reference to the horrible flatulence of his host-boat. Sure enough, halfway across the lake, Younger Brother loudly protests the foul stench bubbling up from beneath the cayman's undulating tail. Enraged, the cayman canoe launches itself vertically out of the water, in a mighty breach, raising its head upward to devour its passengers. The vertical leap of the cayman canoe is depicted architecturally by the Tello's vertical placement with the tail below, on ground-level, and the head upward toward the sky. It is believed to have been originally located in the center of the circular sunken plaza, which may have been seasonally flooded using the acoustic water canal entering it from the Old Temple's facade to form the dual dragons' ritual lake on the advent of the rainy season.

Terrified, Elder Brother prudently transforms himself into a powerful giant harpy eagle and flies vertically away, unscathed. Appropriately, this same harpy eagle is depicted at the very top of the Tello Obelisk, flying intact with wings spread and looking upward. It is pursued by the hungry female's snapping jaws, and in front of them, the equally voracious jaws of her piranha minion, a fierce "jaguar of the waters" (a role indicated by its feline head).

Meanwhile, the equally alarmed Younger Brother makes the foolish mistake of transforming into the smaller and weaker hawk. Before he can fly away, the pursuing female cayman leaps up and snaps her jaws shut on one of his legs, biting it off. This bloody action is illustrated on the top of the female dragon, just below the eagle, by the badly damaged hawk missing its legs. This wretched bird is carved right in front of her grasping clawed front foot, as if it were about to be captured; one of its severed legs with talons attached is still visible lying in front of it.

The trauma of this attack causes Younger Brother to retransform back into his human form; the cayman attacks again, but this time with his/her neck-mouth, which swallows the remaining half of Younger Brother's body. Younger Brother, grimacing at this assault, flails his arms about wildly. This gory scene is depicted on both the male and female dragons of the Tello Obelisk as the inverted body of Younger Brother disappears into the profile agnathic neck-mouth of the dual dragons.

Using the redundancy of myth, the Magical Twins get a second opportunity to escape the cayman canoe. Elder Brother flies back and retrieves the wounded body of Younger Brother. The junior sibling's lower extremities are still lodged in the stomachs of the dragons. Elder Brother, in his winged form, returns Younger Brother's body to the shore and brings him back to life, amidst their grieving peanut sibling companions, who have been helplessly watching the mayhem from the beach. Elder Brother asks one of his siblings, white sloth (who does *not* appear on the monolith, appearing instead in the modern narratives), to use his sharp-tined *chonta* palm spear (of the sort depicted in the recently recovered warrior lintel at Chavín) to pierce the bottom of the cayman's lake. Indeed, the Tello itself can be metaphorically regarded as that lance itself (the real Lanzón), penetrating the middle of the circular "lake" of the semisubterranean plaza. Meanwhile, the cayman has submerged to lodge his/her food at the bottom of the lake to tenderize it and feed upon it later, as is crocodilians' wont. After the lake bed is pierced, all the water drains out from the lake via the spear hole, leaving the cayman helpless and stranded on the muddy bottom. Elder Brother, retransformed into a humanoid, marches down and kills the giant reptile, extracting his brother's leg and cutting out the cayman's mandible as a trophy, which he carries with him back up to the shore.

Weary from these travails, Elder Brother decides to escape this earthly plane and find safety in the heavens. Returning to the now-inert cayman canoe and using its body as a springboard, he contorts himself into a U and launches himself upward from the stern of the reptilian barque, grabbing ahold of a twin-strand Sky Rope. This is really a living, ophidian rope composed of the intertwined bodies of two giant serpents that are hanging from the sky, supported by their fangs, which are piercing the cloud layer. Elder Brother, sporting a San Pedro flower headdress, appears on both the male and female dragons of the Tello Obelisk at the base of their continuous mouth-band spine, and just above their pelvis and tail, his right hand grasping the Sky Rope. In the act of ascending this flexible "ladder," he transforms into Alcyone, the brightest star of the Pleiades, along with his peanut sibling companions, who together form the remaining six stars of the Pleiades. Seven now in number, they age rapidly in the coldness of space, their hair turning white in the process, thus yielding the present white fuzzy appearance of the asterism.

Following Elder Brother up the Sky Rope is the cayman canoe with its still-snapping jaws, now reanimated after death and transformed into the V-shaped Hyades. Finally, limping up the swaying armature, ascends the mutilated Younger Brother, who transforms into Orion, the One-Legged Hunter, a pan-Amazonian constellation.

The Shipibo and the Amahuaca myths cohere remarkably well with the ancient Chavín lithic "text." One of the few differences is that while in modern myths the sexed caymans alternate (the Canelos Quichua, for example, use an old "grandmother" cayman, *Apamama* [Whitten 1976:53], whereas the Shipibo to the south employ a male cayman), the Tello forms their prototype by having both sexes appear simultaneously. Other details of the myth not pictured on the Tello would doubtlessly have been supplied by the rituals and ceremonies, some accompanied by music and dancing, which flowed around and by this standing axis mundi.

While the original carvers would have heard this myth in a dialect of Arawak, one of the most ancient and widespread of Amazonian language families (the Arawakan Campa and Machiguenga are still in contact with Andean peoples via an ongoing trade network in the uppermost tributaries of the Pachitea), we at least know the later Panoan names for the mythic actors on the Tello. The Gourd Siblings are the *shopan baquëbo*. The wise Elder Brother is *Huishmabo* (the "white-haired" principal deity, Alcyone of the Pleiades). Since there is a polysemic linkage between hair-petals-feathers in the lowlands, this "white hair" could refer to his white harpy eagle feather headdress. The foolish Younger Brother is *Quishioma* ("without lower leg," the belt of Orion and descending stars, the One-Legged Hunter). The murderous caymanic dragon canoe is *huiso capë nonti* ("black cayman canoe," Lévi-Strauss's [1981] Irascible Ferryman).

Now, just as in the myth and in precisely that order, the three asterisms rise in the night sky, first the Pleiades, then the ever-pursuing open, snapping jaws of the Hyades, followed by the still-wounded Orion, limping behind. As Shipibo narrators say, "You doubt the story? Just look up." Then, roughly six months later, they set, urged on by shamans who fast for "one Pleiades period," *huestiora huishmabo*, half the year, to ensure their timely arrival and departure. The heliacal (dawn) setting of the Pleiades in the west gives shamans three weeks' notice, time enough to advise people to prepare the fields (by cutting and burning the slash-and-burn gardens in the jungle to plant the dragon's crop, manioc, and by turning the earth with foot plow in the highlands, for the equivalent carbohydrate source, potatoes) before the rains of the wet season arrive (*Jënëtian*, "Wet Time," when the dragon surfaces). The rising water of the resultant floods makes hunting easier since the game retreats to high ground, thus concentrating and making themselves easy prey. The Pleiades rise just before the onset of the dry season (*Baritian*, "Sun Times," when the dragons dive), when the oxbow lakes empty and the water levels drop in the river channels, thus concentrating the fish, making their capture easier. Therefore, in their linked journey across the night sky, these asterisms not only determine the whole horticultural year, equally helpful for growing manioc in the originating lowlands as for raising potatoes in the neighboring Andes, but also the entire protein (game/fish) capture cycle.

Myth and the Astronomical Orientation of Chavín de Huántar

Pursuing this myth into the Andean highlands during 2006–2007, we examined the Tello Obelisk in the National Museum in Lima (the monument has now been returned to the type site to adorn a new museum) and conducted archaeoastronomical fieldwork at its putative location at Chavín de Huántar. Our examination of this monolith and the Lanzón included detailed digital photography, accompanied by documentary sketches of the uncovered monuments. This allowed us to correct the original Tello Atlas, which had been produced by Rowe via a rubbing (Rowe 1967:Figures 6, 7). The partial results of our work are the two reconstructions of the complete dragons that adorn each side of the obelisk (Figure 3.2a, b). The Tello appears to correspond exceptionally closely to the *montaña* myth of the origin of food crops, which was also the origin myth for the Pleiades, Hyades, and Orion.

We were not, in fact, the first to make the observation that the oral myth and the stone myth corresponded so well. The ethnoastronomer Joseph Woodside (1979) also recognized this linkage after examining the cognate, but more fragmentary, myths of the Panoan Amahuaca, "backwoods" (interfluvial) cousins of the Shipibo. Through a more comprehensive study of Shipibo ethnoastronomy (Roe 2005), recording some 81 of their mythic variants, while at the same time redrawing and correcting the earlier rollouts of the original monolith, we offer more specific linkages between the two. This ethnoastronomical work in the jungle provided the problem orientation to revisit the Chavín de Huántar site and test Lumbreras's (1989:30) placement of the Tello in the middle of the circular plaza.

Older maps often have the whole architectural complex of Chavín de Huántar aligned to the cardinal directions (although see the curious difference between the orientations of the two north arrows in Burger 1992:Figure 120). But Rick's (2005) and Kembel's (Kembel 2008; Kembel and Rick 2004) recent GPS mapping of the site revealed that the alignment deviates from north by 15 degrees west. The Andeanist ethnoastronomer Gary Urton had earlier noted that such an alignment appeared to orient the Old Temple and circular court central axis to the setting of the Pleiades (Burger 1992:132). But lacking the meta-narrative of the lowland myths, and not having conducted a sextant survey, which would have revealed key breaks in the encircling mountain wall sufficient to make accurate low-angle setting predictions possible, he assumed that a Pleiades setting alignment was not viable.

To test Urton's original judgement that the mountains would have blocked observations of the Pleiades, we utilized a sextant equipped with an artificial bubble horizon, along with a transit, in the middle of the sunken circular court. A 360-degree survey revealed a break in the mountain wall surrounding the site, a perfect window, just to the west-northwest of the sunken circular court and in alignment with the facade of the Old Temple. Our subsequent computer-based simulation using Starry Night software reconfirmed that this valley to the west, together with a notch cut in its southern margin, an ancient path descending into the valley, corresponded to an ideal, low viewing angle of the heliacal setting of the Pleiades between 1100 B.C.E. and 900 B.C.E.

A sight line established from the center of the sunken circular court (where the Tello Obelisk may have originally stood as an L-shaped gun-sight gnomon) precisely bisects the middle of the seven-riser (like the seven stars of the asterism) Pleiades stairway that ascends from it and approaches the facade of the Old Temple. The sight line extends onto, and exactly in line with, the long axis of the cruciform gallery buried in the bowels of the Old Temple, where the Lanzón lies hidden. It then continues beyond the artificial mountain that was the Old Temple's truncated step-pyramid (three levels for the three world planes) to the real mountain behind it. At that point the sight line cuts right through the notch in the side of the mountain where an ancient path winds down into the valley. Therefore, while other alignments, such as that to the summer solstice, are also possible from the sunken court (Lumbreras 1989:137; Rick 2008:Figure 1.8), the entire site and the complete architectural assemblage (both Old and New Temple, for we also took sextant readings from the center of the large square sunken plaza) was oriented, not to the cardinal points, but to the heliacal setting of the Pleiades behind the Old Temple at 1000 B.C.E. The moment of that descent marked the advent of the rains in both the verdant jungle to the east and the seasonally arid Andes at this latitude. Indeed, it first tracked that event as far back as the end of the second millennium B.C.E., when the Old Temple was erected around the L-shaped Lanzón gnomon itself circa 1200 B.C.E.

The Lanzón is possibly the first in a long series of such L-shaped gnomons, ideal as cross-hairs for celestial sightings, from the Lanzón at 1200 B.C.E. to the Tello at approximately 900–800 B.C.E., and thence to the 400–300 B.C.E. L-shaped female Were-Feline Goddess gnomon at Pacopampa (Lyon 1979:Plate XXVII). From there this type of instrument descends to the iconographically distinct, but culturally distantly affiliated, L-shaped monoliths of the Yaya-Mama tradition in the southern highlands near Lake Titicaca at 400 B.C.E. (Quilter 2005:99), and thence to Pucará at 250 B.C.E., and eventually down to the fourteenth-century C.E. *Intihuatana* stone of the Incas at Machu Picchu. Since there are many ways to carve stelae, and these L-shaped stelae are unique (in all the world) to the northern and southern Andes, in cultures that also share other iconographic traits, and ones that form an internally consistent chronological pattern, this thematic connection between them seems plausible. Quilter also apparently thinks so since he suggests that "the notched post [of the *Intihuatana*] recalls the Lanzón and Tello Obelisk of Chavín de Huántar and may have been an astronomical sighting device as well as a ritual object" (Quilter 2005:179).

Astronomy was therefore central to the ceremonial functioning of the U-shaped temple itself. Priests, able to make the calculations that announced the arrival of the rains using these alignments, would have allayed the anxiety of peasants coming as pilgrims to the site. In that manner the astronomical specialists would thus have ritually regulated the peasants' entire subsistence round. This conferred upon them the authority (but not yet the power) to direct the construction and manage the ceremonies of the center for their own material well-being and prestige, as well as for the satisfaction of their lay public.

At last, when the tilt of the earth on its axis made accurate sightings no longer possible, the Tello was moved to a new location, probably in the center of the large square sunken plaza of the New Temple (it was found in that plaza's southeastern corner), there to continue the observations, though with decreasing accuracy. Finally, centuries later, when the vast stone astronomical instrument no longer worked to the precision required, the site was abandoned. Squatters from later cultures, Huaylas and Requay, built hovels in the ruins. Yet memories of the glories of the site, and the cult practices performed at it, continued through the colonial and into the modern period (Burger 2008:681–682).

Mythic Substitutions within Enduring Themes: The Narrative Evolves

Mythic substitutions (Roe 2005) are systemic alterations in the variants (from one ethnic group to another) or versions (one personal rendition vs. a differing one from another narrator within the same ethnic group) of sacred tales that replace certain actors with others. This may be done for a host of reasons, beginning with the search for novelty to keep an audience's interest (most students of myth ignore the obvious fact that these sacred tales are also a form of verbal art and therefore must obey the aesthetic imperative of creativity, usually within traditional theme and variation constraints). Another reason for a novel substitution may be when the mythic action moves into a new realm or episode (as when the tapir replaces the dragon when the locus of activity shifts from the water to the land). Most relevant to the present argument are the mythic substitutions that occur when local ecology, and the species found therein, differs from that where the myth originated.

This is easiest to recognize when the myths, as here, are projected onto the largest canvas of all, the night sky (as the origin of asterisms and constellations). Some of the well-known Andean asterisms can best be viewed as local highland mythic substitutes for much more widespread Amazonian asterisms simply because the lowland natural icons that they represent do not extend their habitats into the highlands. For example, the Andean Dark Cloud (negative) asterisms of the Llama, whose eyes are Alpha and Beta Centauri, are chased through the path of the Milky Way by a black puma, which is the Coal Sack (Urton 1981), whereas in the jungle they are deer chased and killed by a black jaguar instead of a puma; one of the fallen eyes of the deer is also known as Alpha Centauri (Roe 2005).

The same mythic substitutions occur elsewhere. For example, in the xerophytic Gran Chaco to the south the mighty anaconda of the "bathing in the blood of the Dragon" mytheme is replaced by the humble lungfish (locally called an eel) in the Ishir (Chamacoco) myths of Orion as the One-Legged Hunter (Escobar 2007:73). In the more distant Caribbean where big cats are absent in the impoverished fauna of the Greater Antilles, the lowly dog becomes a species of domesticated jaguar in myth and material culture (Roe 1995b).

These syntagmatic changes (character and episode arrangement) are not disjunctions if the paradigmatic relations (deep structural oppositions, congruences, or transformations) of the tale remain unaltered. The same acts of mythic substitution can occur with the technology or social relations that appear in sacred narratives. One major alteration between the ancient Chavín "stone myth" of the Tello Obelisk and the modern Amahuaca or Shipibo narratives, for example, is the change from the Sky Rope as a means of celestial ascent on the monolith to the Chain or Ladder of Arrows in the Panoan myths. However, both motifs, Chain of Arrows and Sky Rope, are recombinatorial variants today for that celestial escape (Roe 1991a). Furthermore, arrows could not have existed as a mytheme in Chavín art, verbal or visual, because they did not yet exist in the highlands. Bows and arrows do not appear until Huari times, in Conchapata iconography at 1000 C.E., probably via contact with jungle Indians. Instead, Chavín artists and warriors utilized the available atlatl and darts technology. Both mythemes are interchangeable means of ascent from Earth World to Sky World in a triple-tiered cosmology.

Moche fine-line painting iconography, from a Chavín successor culture, shows a congruent three-leveled world with the Sun God (Golte 2009:Figure 2.3) and his companions such as the Hawk Deity ascending from Earth World to Sky World (represented by the quintessentially Chavín double-headed collared cat-snake) via a Sky Ladder made by spiders (Golte 2009: Figure 13.44). There he was carried through the sky on his coastal conveyance, a sedan chair, flown by hummingbirds and hawks (Disselhoff and Linné 1961:Figure 27; see Golte 2009:Figure 2.2 for the whole scene), just like the lowland Shipibo Sun God (*Barin Rios*), who reaches the sky via a Ladder of Arrows, climbing into his canoe to be paddled across the sky by his scorched black turkey vulture paddlers, while shamans visit his burning realm on the backs of their celestial mounts, scarlet hummingbirds (Roe 1982a, 1993b, 2005). Because Moche was at least partially a Cupisnique-Chavín descendant civilization with many iconographic traits and figures in common (Benson 1975: 105 n. 1; Castillo Butters and Uceda Castillo 2008:710; Quilter, this volume; Rowe 1971), the existence of such a Tello Obelisk–congruent cosmology in its art reinforces the multitiered reconstruction we have proposed for the Chavín worldview.

Another example of syntagmatic change is the alteration of the peanut womb of the Tello's tale into the gourd womb of the Shipibo account. Both are round and hollow fruitlike naturefacts whose shapes within the lowland form code lend themselves to be treated as First Women icons by ethnic groups from the Yanomamö of Venezuela (Chagnon 1997:104–105) to the Urubu of eastern Brazil (Huxley 1956), and nearly everyone (including the Shipibo) in between. Roe (1991b) has already linked such shape categories to the androcentric theory of conception ubiquitous in the Amazon whereby men appropriate the gestational role of women by regarding them as just the passive recipients (the container) into which men repeatedly ejaculate to literally construct the fetus. Such an ethnophysiological theory illuminates hitherto arcane cultural practices ranging from the *couvade* to male postpartum food taboos, and even plural genitors among the Shipibo and other Amazonian groups.

A last difference between the Shipibo *Huishmabo* myth and the Tello Obelisk story is the mythic substitution of the Elder Brother's huge harpy eagle avian transform (Tello) with the tiny hummingbird (Shipibo). Although the diets of these two species are completely different, as are their sizes, appearances, comportments, and colors, just like the Younger Brother's avian transforms—the ferocious hawk (Tello) becoming the timid tinamou (Shipibo)—these are another example of syntagmatic change rather than disjunction.

The hummingbird, for example, is one of the fiercest, most belligerent of birds, belying its diminutive size. It is fiercely territorial in the male, doing combat with rivals using its long, phallic, spearlike beak. Thus for its size it is as good a masculine icon as the mighty harpy. Indeed, it is the frequent companion of victorious warriors in Chavín-descendant Moche iconography, where it appears alongside the equally ferocious hawk (Alva and Donnan 1993:Figure 137; Donnan and McClelland 1999:Figure 1.20). Moreover, it is a diurnal bird, like the eagle, the daytime being the realm of men, and is the bearer of the Sun God's litter in his celestial travels through the Moche Sky World (Golte 2009:29). This is a task that it shares with the Hawk Warrior (Donnan and McClelland 1999:Figure 4.107). It is also naturally decorated with light/bright celestial colors like the eagle (scarlet vs. white) that men favor in their war headdresses (Roe 1990, 1995c). Lastly, both martial birds are strong and swift fliers, the eagle noted for its vertical flight powering through the jungle canopy (just like its placement and attitude on the Tello) and the hummingbird for its dazzling speed and miraculous hovering capability. The latter characteristics stand both avian transforms in good stead on the Tello, as well as in the Shipibo myth, allowing Elder Brother to safely escape the threatening jaws of the pursuing cayman canoe.

The mythic substitution of the tinamou for the ancient hawk is more complex but also raises issues of continuity rather than disjunction in the evolution of oral narratives. A diachronic study of folklore (Hammel 1972) suggests that, over time, generations of narrators unconsciously seek to perfect the syntagmatics of a tale through the ever-greater achievement of balance and symmetry, while leaving the paradigmatic structure unaltered. This Chavín–Panoan example offers precisely the same pattern, but over an even deeper range of time. The first Chavín example from the Tello embodies an opposition that comes from a jungle-based repertoire of tales. Roe (1982a) has already shown how the hawk is regarded as the younger brother of the eagle, subsidiary to it (the first hawk being created from a single falling feather of a giant harpy eagle ogre, *Ani Tëtë* ["Big Eagle"], upon the latter's death at the hands of besieged humans). Thus the oppositionary formula Elder Brother : Eagle :: Younger Brother : Hawk establishes the primordial relations on the Tello.

In the Chavín variant of the myth, both bird avatars are carnivores (raptors), since the Magical Twins, being born of the dragon, share not only his serpent coiffure but also his dietary preferences (hence Elder Brother's big canines). The hawk, a fierce and fleet raptor and the alter ego of warriors, becomes a victim mauled by his arch subaquatic enemy. How can a ferocious raptor become victimized in the Chavín myth? While clearly not as victorious as the harpy eagle in the story, the avian transform of Younger Brother also changes over time into the ill-flying, ground-dwelling, drab-colored feminine bird, the tinamou, a shy vegetarian. Through this mythic substitution, it becomes much easier to believe that the Younger Brother transform can actually be caught by the pursuing cayman canoe (the nadir in the struggling, oscillating flight path of the tinamou brings him dangerously close to the surface of the water), but it also coheres better with the paradigmatic imperatives that carnivores eat herbivores, just as aerial and terrestrial birds oppose subaquatic life forms. As the story has evolved over time, the contrasts have become even starker, making the story more believable.

The main characters in the myths also continue to evolve and take on new roles in other stories. For example, the cayman canoe has continued to transform in Shipibo mythology. The three myths transcribed below illustrate the continued mythic substitution of the cayman canoe into, first, the nineteenth-century steamship and then into the modern court system and water jail of the *mestizos*. In the second myth, the function of the cayman canoe is assumed by the giant Amazonian otter who transforms in the story into the thunder jaguar. The final myth, recasting the first, shows yet another example of the mythic substitution of the cayman canoe, the huge *paiche* Fish Canoe. These myths elaborate the subaquatic seducer aspect of Dragon A of the Tello by focusing on the lethal consequences of marital infidelity, a trait still tied to his function as the bringer of manioc, and other cultigens like *piqui* fruit, by groups all over the Amazon, from the Trío of the Guianas (Rivière 1969:260–261) to the Mehinaku of central Brazil (Gregor and Ash 1986). In essence, this is another expression of his stinginess, the dragon's reluctance to share his women lovers with men, and hence the necessity of his death at their hands. This ancient Formative figure of the reptilian barque is thus kept alive and adapted to new metaphors, through many transformations, and serves as an illustration of the enduring themes of Amazonian and Andean thought.

Modern Transformations of the Ancient Dragon Canoe: The Shipibo Texts

CONSULTANT: Ricardo Vargas; AGE: circa 28; SEX: Male; VILLAGE: San Francisco de Yarinacocha; DATE: August 10, 1986; TITLE: "The *Acoro* That Carried Off a Man," NARRATIVE 51, Field Notebook 4.

They say that there was a man who was an *Onan* (a shaman, literally a "Knower" or *Onaya*, "One with Knowledge") who wanted to steal the woman of another man who was also an *Onan*. The (would-be seducer) tried to kill the other shaman but his songs did not work. Then he said, "now I'm going to make a *Yoshi* (a malignant spirit) carry away that person." But that man also had a wife and he passed his time singing songs (to get the other one also). One day the intended victim said to his wife, "I am going to kill *huamë*" (a giant fish, see below) and he started for the water. "When are you coming back?" asked his wife; "I will come back in the afternoon, wait for me (here)." Then he left, but he did not return at the specified time. It was getting on toward night but still he didn't return. (Using a *huamë* as bait) the *Jënën Yoshinbo* ("Water Spirits, group of") had carried him into the water. Instantly they took him beneath the surface. (They did so just as easily) as we enter our *bachi* (the cotton mosquito bar, a rectangular tentlike structure, literally, an "egg" that one must crawl into at night for protection on the Mosquito River). Arriving there, (the kidnapped shaman) looked around. The *Yoshinbo* (the spirits sent by the would-be adulterer) spoke to him, "now we will go to where the chiefs are." Then the *Yoshinbo* took him there (just as they do before the judges of this world). They arrived there and the man was seated. He also had his *Yoshi* (spirit) who asked (on his behalf), "Why have they carried you here?" They were inside a huge boat, the (*Acoro*) launch (the "non-ordinary steamboat," which carries its victims prisoner, swallowed whole inside its iron belly with its hard, black ribs. It is a mythic transform of the traditional *jënën roni*, "water boas," but much bigger, like the anaconda itself). Then inside of it the chiefs questioned him. (After that) they determined that he had no guilt. He was just there because of a matter concerning (a rivalry over) his wife. "We will take you to *ani paro* (the "big water," the Amazon to the north) downriver, just to visit the *Yoshinbo* who live there," they told him. They (then) carried him downriver in the (*Acoro*) launch. Although the river meanders (constantly) the (powerful) launch went straight through, cutting all of the meanders off at their necks. The man stayed there with them for three moons, but then the *Yoshi* of the *Acoro* launch said, "Your mother and your wife are thinking of you and crying. Your children are suffering, let's go." (The man went with them), and they arrived back to where the chiefs were. The chiefs cancelled the charges (note the acculturative analogy here; the accusations were like the charges leveled in a *mestizo* court). (They said), "We will go to your house to see your mother and wife and to leave you there. The man who wanted to get rid of you (by sending us against you) is now with your wife."

Then they (the spirits) and the man journeyed (to his place). Arriving there his sons yelled (to his mother), "Grandmother, look, Papa is coming there," for they had seen him first. (Disbelieving them) the grandmother responded, "Your papa is not coming. How could he arrive when the *Yoshinbo* have carried him away?" "But look, Grandmother, Papa is arriving," the children insisted. Then she turned her head and saw that her son was (indeed) coming. He was not pallid or transparent (as are the spirits of the returning dead, the *mahua yoshinbo*). He was normal. Looking at him, his mother wept (with joy), as did his sons. Then the man asked about his wife. His mother answered, "She has already remarried (to your rival)." Later, when night was beginning to fall, the man's *Yoshinbo* (spirit helpers) came.

Arriving there, they told him, "Let's go once more, come on." After they said that, he returned with the (*Jënën*) *Yoshinbo* (Water Spirits). Arriving at their place (under the water), his *Yoshinbo* (friends) said, "Let's return the harm. You were held tightly as a prisoner even though you had not committed any crime." Thus they spoke to the man. "Now we will begin action against your accuser," they resolved. The other shaman was (also) a fisherman of *huamë*. Therefore, he (usually) left early in the morning to kill *huamë*.

The man whom he had falsely accused could see him as clearly as one can see (somebody) in our own world (even though he was looking up from beneath the surface of the water). He watched as his enemy left his port. His foe was paddling along. Then the (*Jënë*) *Yoshi* said to the man, "Roll two cigars of tobacco." (He did so) and (the *Yoshi*) blew on them (to make them potent; Shipibo tobacco shamans use the strong native tobacco as a real hallucinogen). (At that moment) the man noticed a *huamë* coming along, which the other (his rival) was to harpoon (because of its flat, armored head the only way to kill a *paiche* was with a heavy harpoon). He placed one cigar behind the fin on one side of the *huamë*'s head (like large, rod-style ear plugs) and the other cigar in the same place under the fin of the other side. The *huamë* (now strengthened) was ready to carry away (his enemy) in the same way that it had carried the man himself beneath the waters. When the cigars had been placed on it, the *huamë* (allowed itself to be) harpooned by the guilty man. But then the *huamë* pulled him beneath the surface. They (the Water Spirits) made him a prisoner there, shutting him up in the (*Acoro*) launch. The chiefs incarcerated him, and advised him, "For what you have done, we will carry you off to *ani paro* downriver, so that the *Yoshinbo* who live there can eat you." (The journey to the "Great Water" is conceived to be a journey to the Land of the Dead where the man's *caya,* permanent eye soul, will be judged, and in this case, consumed.) Then they addressed the innocent man, "Now you have returned the harm (and avenged yourself), now leave," and the man left.

CONSULTANT: Juana; AGE: circa 35; SEX: Female; VILLAGE: Nuevo Destino; DATE: June 21, 1986; TITLE: "The Man the *Jënën Ino* Tried to Kill," NARRATIVE 56, Field Notebook 4.

They say that in ancient times a man had a *chaiconi* (a spirit familiar, sometimes used to refer to either friendly backwoods Panoans like the Amahuaca, or even a *mestizo*) friend or brother-in-law. (They lived) in a tiny village. (But) the (*chaiconi*) was cuckolding him with his wife. Because of that the *chaiconi* thought, "Now I will make the *ino* ("jaguar," although in this case it is the huge Amazonian otter, *jënën ino,* at 2 m long, a mustelid classified as a feline by the Shipibo because of its general shape, long tail, and ferocious interlocking canines, see Roe 1998) grab this man." Thinking this, he addressed (them) directly (in a spell). "I want you *ino* to grab hold of that man (for me)." After he had uttered those words the (*chaiconi*) left to go fishing and he brought (back) good fish to eat. When he was carrying them (his intended victim) asked him, "Where did you catch (those)?" The other answered his question (to lure him), "I caught them in *Jënën Ino Iyan* ("Water Jaguar," i.e., the giant otter, "Lake"). (It was) from there that I got them. Why don't you go there to fish?"

After (the evil spirit) said that, the (hapless) man left at dawn of the (next) day. He arrived at the lake when night was approaching. Then the *jënën ino* saw him and (launched) its attack, sending *coni* (electric eels) (in great quantities) and making the water (level) rise alarmingly. After the spate of the *coni* had arrived, *huamë* (*paiche*) and *ronin ëhua* ("boa, giant," the anaconda) also (came). With (such a mass) of those fish (all wriggling together) the man could no longer paddle. It was (very) dangerous. At that moment the man was frightened and thought, "Now the *jënën ino* will eat me." Thinking this, he grabbed his *chicaro* (his heavy *paiche* harpoon) and climbed up into a (low hanging) *hona* (a mangrove tree branch). Thus armed, he sat and waited. (Then) he saw just arriving beneath him (the *ino*), swimming in the water to attack him. As it was swimming by the man looked and saw its tail raised, ready to strike (the water's surface). He fixed the tail in his sights, aimed, and hit it (with his *chicaro*). As soon as he struck it the danger abated and the water (level) subsided. (When the water had all disappeared) and it was very dry, the (*ino*) was left stranded, pinned there by the *chicaro*. Then the man spit his saliva into the air for (the *ino*) to smell. Upon smelling his odor, it turned into a man. Having once threatened to kill him, the *ino* man (who was now submissive) said, "You have made me into your *ochiti* ("dog"). I did not seek to kill you for the sport of it. Rather, your enemy sent you here so that I could attack and kill you. Now you have (defeated me) and made me your *ochiti*. You must come with me." Saying this, he carried the man to (his village) and gave him his *poi* ("sister") in marriage.

After the man and (giant otter) woman were united, the man stayed with the (giant otter people) for I don't know how many days, but it was a long time. He became like them. Then his otter *chai* ("brother-in-law") said to him, "I will take you to see your (former) wife." The other man had sent the *ino* to attack him. (The victim) saw that that man was now living with his woman. He returned another day to spy on them (and formulated a plan). Then he said to his *chai*, "Tomorrow when the sun begins to descend, wait for them when they come." Thus he spoke to his *chai*. When the sun began to descend, (the man's *chai*) carried the husband there so that he could return the harm he had suffered (and get his revenge). (The guilty couple's) path left their port and ran for some distance (to their hut). It was the path (they always) used. Halfway down the path there was a tree. Beneath it the *chai* placed an *acónpano* (a poisonous viper, smaller than the fer-de-lance). Putting it there he told the husband, "That is for your woman." Then the two of them left and hid underneath a *nonti* ("wooden dugout canoe") tipped upside down (at the port). Then the *chai* turned himself into a *huiso capë* (a black cayman) while his *chai* (the husband) looked on from a distance. After these preparations the (man) remained there, watching. Then his enemy and his former wife came playfully (down) to bathe. When they were bathing (the woman climbed onto the canoe). The *huiso capë* latched onto the original enemy, the (new) husband of his (former) wife (and dragged him beneath the surface of the water). He had hold of the man's calf (and drowned him). The waves from their struggles pitched the woman into the water. Completely terrified, the woman (scrambled out of the water and) fled back up the path toward her hut. As she was running on the path, halfway there, the *acónpano* bit (her). In arranging that, the (slighted) man had killed both his (ex-) wife and her (new) husband in the same day.

CONSULTANT: Bahuanmëtsa (Manuel Rengifo); AGE: circa 45, SEX: Male; VILLAGE: San Francisco de Yarinacocha; DATE: August 17, 1982; TITLE: *Huamëntita* ("Paiche Mother" or "Mistress of *Paiche*"); NARRATIVE 78, Field Notebook 5.

At one time there were many *huamë* (*paiche*) in Yarinacocha (*Jëpëshiyan*, from *Jëpë*, the Yarina palm, *Phytelephas microcarpa*, and *iyan*, "lake"). But then a *medico* (shaman, an *onaya*) who was a Cocama (the historical Tupian-speaking enemies of the Shipibo, the descendants of the Caimito Polychrome Horizon style who entered the Ucayali from the Upper Amazon to the north in late Prehistoric times; most modern *mestizos* are their acculturated nominally Catholic, Spanish-speaking, rural Peruvian descendants. They have continued their animosity toward the Shipibo, who are still visibly and culturally Indians), he sent the *tita* (literally, "mother," but in this case the giant supernatural "Mistress" of all the natural related life forms, who are her *baquëbo*, "children") of the *huamë* away to another lake, or river, because he was mad that the people were killing too many. Then he sent much *huama* ("water hyacinth"; note the intentional homonyms: *huamë*, the fish, which can act like an obstruction, and *huama*, the water hyacinths, that also do) to form impenetrable floating beds as an affliction on canoeists. He sent them from their home on Cashibocaño (the small rivulet near Yarinacocha, the entrance to the backwoods home of the cannibal Cashibo, traditional Panoan enemies of the Shipibo, and therefore the origin of all such afflictions).

Discussion

These myths establish a number of iconic vectors that show that the dragon canoe is alive and well through a welter of recombinatorial variants, aquatic devouring life forms that range from titanic mythic anacondas (*Acoro*) to giant fish (*huamë*) to large Amazonian otters (*jënën ino*) and huge black caymans (*huiso capë*), all of which can assume human shape at will and also act as shamanic power animals, spirit helpers, or familiars as well as natural antagonists and anticultural ogres.

The *Acoro* is the mythical giant anaconda (*Eunectes murinus gigas*), the *Ibo* ("Master") of all the lesser water boas (*jënën roninbo*) and the electric eels (*coni*). A powerful aquatic constrictor, but now supersized to extraordinary dimensions, it is one component, in this case a recombinatorial variant, of the Formative dragon.

The *huamë* is the huge amphibian-like Paleozoic fish (it has functional lungs as well as gills), the archaic *Arapaima gigas*, or the *paiche*, as it is locally known. It is the largest of the freshwater fishes in the Amazonian river system and its thick fillets provided the basis for the salted-fish trade throughout the Amazon. Its considerable stores of rendered oil were also used in cooking and its raspy tongue employed as a file. Sadly, it is now overfished and nearly extinct. In Shipibo ethnotaxonomy, it is classed with the huge armor-headed catfish and the manatee as the quintessential food fish. As a carnivore that stalks its prey by ambush, it also appears in myths as supernatural bait, drawing victims and malefactors alike to their deaths, much like the black cayman. Moreover, it is a mouthbreeder and therefore a suitable natural metaphor for the devouring mother, caymanic Dragon B of the Tello.

The *jënën ino* has a wide, flat, spatulate tail with which it strikes the water, causing tidal waves that swamp canoes so that it can devour the hapless canoeists. It is the giant, six-foot-long freshwater Amazonian otter, but clearly appears here in an even larger, supernatural form, like the *Acoro*. This water jaguar, although a mustelid, is a part of the Shipibo ethnotaxonomic unit of *inobo*, "jaguars, group of." It may also be related to the water = thunder jaguar mytheme of the *nai ino*, the giant black sky jaguar that lives in the dark, threatening cumulus clouds, the bringer of tempests and high wind. Its flashing eyes are lightning bolts and its earthquaking roars are thunder. This thunder jaguar is a much-feared cannibal spirit in Shipibo cosmology, and many a fisherman has told us about his narrow escape from this terrifying celestial beast. The same mytheme of the thunder jaguar is present throughout the lowlands of South America and extends from the intermediate area all the way to the Atlantic watershed of Costa Rica.

Many of the paradigmatic elements of the ancient Chavín tale remain in these modern transformations of the dragon: most centrally, they are dragon canoes that swallow persons whole, holding them in the water jails of their ribs and stomach just like the ancient Tello Obelisk dragons imprisoned their swallowed victims. These sacred animals act like *Ibos*, masters of the species they hunt, and are capable of punishing excessive utilization of them, like the masters of the Chavín cosmos. In one important sense, the modern forms are the inverse of the ancient ones. Instead of being stingy, they stand for the golden mean of careful utilization, just like the Master of Animals of the northwest Amazon (Reichel-Dolmatoff 1971).

Another enduring element is the water as a one-way mirror that can be flipped to yield hidden knowledge, just as ancient Chavín supernaturals flip upside down in anatropic imagery (Torres 2008:Figure 9.20). Actual polished jet mirrors were important elements in Chavín material culture. In addition to the Water-Mirror, the sharing of hallucinogens, and large aquatic creatures that drown their victims and then devour them whole, other enduring natural icons are also part of this primordial assemblage.

Principal among them are snakes as the minions and accoutrements of the cayman (as its ophidian ropes, ligatures like anklets or bracelets, or writhing hair). The powerful coils of the constrictors and the poison of the pit vipers can be added as dangers to the tearing teeth of the larger devouring cayman, in both ancient Chavín iconography and in modern Shipibo myth. Lastly, tidal waves, thunder, destructive winds, and deadly lightning can reinforce the dragon's life-taking capabilities through a mythic substitute, the giant water jaguar. All these figures unite the "water gyre" (Roe 1982a) that connects the cold subaquatic waters with the falling rain and fire from the Cloud World above, just as the Rainbow Dragon did on the Tello.

Conclusions: The Dragon Canoe Glides Off into the Sunset

In all these countless permutations culture endures; cosmic structures and key myths remain, not static, but ever adapting to changing technology (from atlatls to bow and arrows, from canoes to steamships), evolving-devolving society (from egalitarian tribes to stratified states and back down again to modern pacified tribes), and even surviving the precession of the equinoxes and the cataclysm of conquest, while always retelling the same never-ending story on a paradigmatic level.

As the myths recorded above from our Shipibo corpus indicate, by the nineteenth century, when Rubber Boom contact penetrated the Ucayali in earnest, the black scaly hull of the cayman canoe spawns a new manifestation, the *Acoro*, the giant black anaconda iron-hulled *garreta*. These were the steamboats that plied the Ucayali, their lighted portals the glaring eyes of the dragon, their puffing steam its thunderous roar, and in their bellies the malignant ophidian water spirits, *jënën yoshinbo*. These dragonic "passengers" dragged hapless canoeists to their death by swallowing them whole in the whirlpools caused by the animated steamboats' churning wakes, the roiling waters behind the steamers interpreted as the frantic circling of the iron dragon's water boa and cayman familiars.

Finally, in the twentieth and twenty-first centuries, a time of increased Peruvian national hegemonic intrusion into the *selva* ("jungle"), as well as massive highlander in-migration, the iron ribs of the *Acoro* transformed into the iron bars of the *jënën carcel* (the latter word from the Spanish), meaning the "water jail." This is the filthy pen in which Indians are imprisoned by the *mestizo* authorities.

Ancient paradigmatic structures are not immutable, but continually transform via an endless set of mythic substitutions (ceiba trees to San Pedro cactus, eagles to hummingbirds, hawks to tinamous, black dragon canoes to steamboats with black iron hulls and prisons with black iron bars), all employing the same culture logic of dynamic dualism and systemically overlapping liminal categories (Roe 1995a). This perspective, as we hope this brief excursion through 3,200 years of collective memory has demonstrated, gives life and meaning to inert ancient monuments. In a field where archaeologists look down to study the ground, there are advantages to looking around, investigating natural history, ethnohistory, and ethnography, as well as looking upwards toward the sky for information and inspiration.

It has been a long and tortuous journey, indeed, from ancient Chavín engraved stone idols like the Lanzón and the Tello Obelisk beginning in the second millennium B.C.E. to the water jail of the third millennium C.E., but the myth endures, morphing, seeking ever greater clarity, symmetry, and power. Ideas not only matter, they refuse to die. Via San Pedro, *yopó,* and the other hallucinogenic foods these dragons brought, myths are "good to think." They are also, through the ritual regulation of protein and carbohydrate they oversaw, good to eat.

The diving of the caymanic dragons, which comprised the Tello Obelisk, still instantiates their role as Master/Mistress of Fish during the dry season in the *montaña,* by making fishing productive via the concentration of aquatic fauna in the shrinking rivers and lakes. In a similar manner their rising (surfacing) announces the coming of the rainy season and the rainbows that arch through the sky, and the floods they accompany, that make hunting terrestrial game productive by restricting their mobility and concentrating their numbers.

Similarly, the celestial diving of the caymanic dragons beneath the horizon heralds the rains that will make the planting of both manioc (in the lowlands) and potatoes (in the neighboring highlands) productive, and their harvesting in the dry season successful. Together, this protein supply (fish/game) and carbohydrate source (starchy manioc/potatoes) comprise the South Amerindian "sandwich" or "stew" of a complete diet. The ability to ritually regulate this subsistence round conferred influence upon jungle shamans and real authority upon ancient Andean Chavín priests making, in turn, the ceremonial centers they manned the focus of pan-regional pilgrimage and powerful public ceremonies replaying the discordant harmony of the heavens. When the stars shifted with the passing of centuries, the stone astronomical instrument lost its function and had to be abandoned, but the narratives that determined its construction, orientation, and functioning live on in the shelter of the myth's original home, the lush and verdant jungle, both of the biome and the mind.

References Cited

Alva, Walter, and Christopher Donnan

1993   *Royal Tombs of Sipan.* Fowler Museum of Cultural History, University of California, Los Angeles.

Benson, Elizabeth P.

1975   Death-Associated Figures on Mochica Pottery. In *Death and the Afterlife in Pre-Columbian America,* edited by Elizabeth P. Benson, pp. 105–144. Dumbarton Oaks Research Library and Collection, Washington, D.C.

Bischof, Henning

2008   Context and Contents of Early Chavín Art. In *Chavín: Art, Architecture and Culture,* edited by William J. Conklin and Jeffrey Quilter, pp. 107–141. Cotsen Institute of Archaeology, University of California, Los Angeles.

Bourget, Steve

2006   *Sex, Death, and Sacrifice in Moche Religion and Visual Culture.* University of Texas Press, Austin.

Burger, Richard L.

1984   *The Prehistoric Occupation of Chavín de Huántar, Peru.* University of California Publications in Anthropology Vol. 14. University of California Press, Berkeley.

1988   Unity and Heterogeneity within the Chavín Horizon. In *Peruvian Prehistory: An Overview of Pre-Inca and Inca Society,* edited by Richard W. Keatinge, pp. 99–144. Cambridge University Press, Cambridge.

1992   *Chavin and the Origins of Andean Civilization.* Thames and Hudson, London.

2008   Chavín de Huántar and Its Sphere of Influence. In *Handbook of South American Archaeology,* edited by Helaine Silverman and William H. Isbell, pp. 681–703. Springer, New York.

Burger, Richard L., and Lucy Salazar-Burger

1980   Ritual and Religion at Huaricoto. *Archaeology* 33(6):26–32.

2008   The Manchay Culture and the Coastal Inspiration for Highland Chavín Civilization. In *Chavín: Art, Architecture and Culture,* edited by William J. Conklin and Jeffrey Quilter, pp. 85–105. Cotsen Institute of Archaeology, University of California, Los Angeles.

Cané, Ralph

1983   El Obelisco Tello de Chavín. *Boletín de Lima* 26:1–28.

Castillo Butters, Luis Jaime, and Santiago Uceda Castillo

2008   The Mochicas. In *Handbook of South American Archaeology,* edited by Helaine Silverman and William H. Isbell, pp. 707–729. Springer, New York.

Chagnon, Napoleon A.

1997   *Yanomamö.* 5th ed. Harcourt Brace College Publishers, Fort Worth, Texas.

Cordy-Collins, Alana

2001   Decapitation in Cupisnique and Early Moche Societies. In *Ritual Sacrifice in Ancient Peru,* edited by Elizabeth P. Benson and Anita G. Cook, pp. 21–33. University of Texas Press, Austin.

Darwin, Charles

1998   *The Expression of the Emotions in Man and Animals and the Autobiography.*
[1872]   Introduction by Steven Pinker. The Folio Society, London.

Disselhoff, Hans D., and Sigvald Linné

1961   *Art of the World, Ancient America.* Methuen, London.

Donnan, Christopher B., and Donna McClelland

1999   *Moche Fineline Painting: Its Evolution and Its Artists.* UCLA Fowler Museum of Cultural History, Los Angeles.

Escobar, Ticio

2007   *The Curse of Nemur: In Search of the Art, Myth and Ritual of the Ishir.* University of Pittsburgh Press, Pittsburgh.

Golte, Jürgen

2009   *Moche: Cosmología y Sociedad, Una Interpretación Iconográfica.* IEP, Instituto de Estudios Peruanos, Centro de Estudios Regionales Andinos Bartolomé de las Casas, Lima, Peru.

Gregor, Thomas A., and David Ash

1986   *Mehinacu.* VHS educational film. Color, 52 min. Disappearing World Series, Granada Television International. Gastown Productions, Thomas Howe Associates, Vancouver, British Columbia, Canada.

Grieder, Terence

1975   The Interpretation of Ancient Symbols. *American Anthropologist* 77:849–855.

Guffroy, Jean

2008   Cultural Boundaries and Crossings: Ecuador and Peru. In *Handbook of South American Archaeology,* edited by Helaine Silverman and William H. Isbell, pp. 889–902. Springer, New York.

Guss, David M.

1989   *To Weave and to Sing: Art, Symbol, and Narrative in the South American Rain Forest.* University of California Press, Berkeley.

Hammel, Eugene A.

1972   *The Myth of Structural Analysis: Lévi-Strauss and the Three Bears.* Addison-Wesley Module in Anthropology. Addison-Wesley, Reading, Massachusetts.

Heckman, Andrea M.

2003   *Woven Stories: Andean Textiles and Rituals.* University of New Mexico Press, Albuquerque.

Huxley, Francis

1956   *Affable Savages: An Anthropologist among the Urubu Indians of Brazil.* Capricorn Books, New York.

Keegan, William F.

2007   *Taíno Indian Myth and Practice: The Arrival of the Stranger King.* University Press of Florida, Gainesville.

Kembel, Silvia Rodríguez

2008   The Architecture at the Monumental Center of Chavín de Huántar: Sequence, Transformations, and Chronology. In *Chavín: Art, Architecture and Culture,* edited by William J. Conklin and Jeffrey Quilter, pp. 35–81. Cotsen Institute of Archaeology, University of California, Los Angeles.

Kembel, Silvia Rodríguez, and John W. Rick

2004   Building Authority at Chavín de Huántar: Models of Social Organization and Development in the Initial Period and Early Horizon. In *Andean Archaeology,* edited by Helaine Silverman, pp. 51–76. Blackwell, Malden, Massachusetts.

Kubler, George

1962   *The Art and Architecture of Ancient America: The Mexican, Maya, and Andean Peoples.* Penguin, Baltimore, Maryland.

Lathrap, Donald W.

1970   *The Upper Amazon.* Praeger, New York.

1973   Gifts of the Cayman: Some Thoughts on the Subsistence Basis of Chavín. In *Variation in Anthropology: Essays in Honor of John C. McGregor,* edited by Donald W. Lathrap and Jody Douglas, pp. 91–105. Illinois Archaeological Survey, Urbana.

1985   Jaws: The Control of Power in the Early Nuclear American Ceremonial Center. In *Early Ceremonial Architecture in the Andes,* edited by Christopher B. Donnan, pp. 241–267. Dumbarton Oaks Research Library and Collection, Washington, D.C.

Lavallée, Danièle

2000   *The First South Americans: The Peopling of a Continent from the Earliest Evidence to High Culture.* Translated by Paul G. Bahn. University of Utah Press, Salt Lake City.

Lévi-Strauss, Claude

1981   *The Naked Man: Introduction to a Science of Mythology 4.* Translated by John and Doreen Weightman. Harper and Row, New York.

Lumbreras, Luís G.

1989   *Chavín de Huántar en el Nacimiento de la Civilización Andina.* Ediciones INDEA, Instituto Andina de Estudios Arqueológicos, Lima, Peru.

2005   *Arqueología y Sociedad.* Edited by Enrique González Carré and Carlos Del Águila. IEP, Instituto de Estudios Peruanos, Lima, Peru.

Lyon, Patricia J.
  1979   Female Supernaturals in Ancient Peru. *Ñawpa Pacha* 16:95–140, Plates XXVII–XXXIV.

Menezes, Sister Mary Noel
  1977   *British Policy towards the Amerindians in British Guiana 1803–1873.* Oxford at the Clarendon Press, Oxford.

Miller, George, and Richard L. Burger
  1995   Our Father the Cayman, Our Dinner the Llama: Animal Utilization at Chavin de Huantar, Peru. *American Antiquity* 60:421–458.

Morales Chocano, Daniel R.
  1995   Estructura Dual y Tripartita en la Arquitectura de Pacopampa y en la Iconografía de Chavín y Nazca. *Investigaciones Sociales* 1(1):83–102. Revista del Instituto de Investigaciones Historico Sociales, Universidad Nacional Mayor de San Marcos, Lima, Peru.
  2008   The Importance of Pacopampa Architecture and Iconography in the Central Andean Formative. In *Chavín: Art, Architecture and Culture,* edited by William J. Conklin and Jeffrey Quilter, pp. 143–160. Cotsen Institute of Archaeology, University of California, Los Angeles.

Quilter, Jeffrey
  2005   *Treasures of the Andes: The Glories of Inca and Pre-Columbian South America.* Duncan Baird, London.

Raymond, J. Scott
  1988   A View from the Tropical Forest. In *Peruvian Prehistory: An Overview of Pre-Inca and Inca Society,* edited by Richard W. Keatinge, pp. 279–300. Cambridge University Press, Cambridge.

Raymond, J. Scott, Warren R. DeBoer, and Peter G. Roe
  1975   *Cumancaya: A Peruvian Ceramic Tradition.* Occasional Papers 2. Department of Archaeology, University of Calgary, Calgary, Alberta, Canada.

Reichel-Dolmatoff, Gerardo
  1971   *Amazonian Cosmos: The Sexual and Religious Symbolism of the Tukano Indians.* University of Chicago Press, Chicago.

Rick, John W.
  2005   The Evolution of Authority and Power at Chavín de Huántar, Peru. In *Foundations of Power in the Prehispanic Andes,* edited by Kevin J. Vaughn, Dennis Ogburn, and Christina A. Conlee, pp. 71–89. Archeological Papers of the American Anthropological Association 14. American Anthropological Association, Arlington, Virginia.
  2008   Context, Construction, and Ritual in the Development of Authority at Chavín de Huántar. In *Chavín: Art, Architecture and Culture,* edited by William J. Conklin and Jeffrey Quilter, pp. 3–34. Cotsen Institute of Archaeology, University of California, Los Angeles.

Rivière, Peter G.

1969   *Marriage among the Trio: A Principle of Social Organization.* Oxford University Press, London.

Roe, Peter G.

1974   *A Further Exploration of the Rowe Chavín Seriation and Its Implications for North Central Coast Chronology.* Studies in Pre-Columbian Art and Archaeology 13. Dumbarton Oaks Research Library and Collection, Trustees for Harvard University, Washington, D.C.

1978   Recent Discoveries in Chavín Art. *El Dorado* 3(1):1–41.

1982a   *The Cosmic Zygote: Cosmology in the Amazon Basin.* Rutgers University Press, New Brunswick, New Jersey.

1982b   Cupisnique Pottery: A Cache from Tembladera. In *Pre-Columbian Art History: Selected Readings,* 2nd ed., edited by Alana Cordy-Collins, pp. 231–253. Peek Publications, Palo Alto, California.

1988   The *Jo_ho Nahuanbo* Are All Wet and Undercooked: Shipibo Views of the Whiteman and the Incas in Myth, Legend and History. In *Rethinking History and Myth: Indigenous South American Perspectives on the Past,* edited by Jonathan Hill, pp. 106–135. University of Illinois Press, Urbana.

1989   Of Rainbow Dragons and the Origins of Designs: The Waiwai *Urufiri* and the Shipibo *Ronin ëhua. Latin American Indian Literatures Journal* 5(1):1–67.

1990   The Language of the Plumes: "Implicit Mythology" in Shipibo, Cashinahua and Waiwai Feather Adornments. In *L.A.I.L. Speaks! Selected Papers from the Seventh International Symposium, Albuquerque, 1989,* edited by Mary H. Preuss, pp. 105–136, Plates A–F. Labyrinthos, Culver City, California.

1991a   *Panó Huëtsa Nëtë:* The Armadillo as Scaly Discoverer of the Lower World in Shipibo and Comparative Lowland South Amerindian Perspective. *Latin American Indian Literatures Journal* 7(1):20–72.

1991b   The Best Enemy Is a Killed, Drilled, and Decorative Enemy: Human Corporeal Art (Frontal Bone Pectorals, Belt Ornaments, Carved Humeri and Pierced Teeth). In *Pre-Columbian Puerto Rico: Proceedings of the 13th International Congress for Caribbean Archaeology, Curaçao, Netherlands Antilles, 1989,* Part 2, pp. 854–873. Reports of the Archaeological-Anthropological Institute of the Netherlands Antilles 9, Curaçao.

1993a   Apuntes para una Arqueología Cultural: Preguntando a los Informantes Muertos sobre la Estructura y Significación del Arte Precolombino de las Antillas Mayores. Paper presented at the Tercer Congreso Nacional de Arqueología, "Dr. Narciso Alberti Bosch." Museo del Hombre Dominicano, Santo Domingo, Dominican Republic.

1993b   The Pleiades in Comparative Perspective: The Waiwai *Shirkoimo* and the Shipibo *Huishmabo.* In *Astronomies and Cultures: Selected Papers from Oxford*

3, International Conference on Archaeoastronomy, edited by Clive Ruggles and Nick Saunders, pp. 296–328. University Press of Colorado, Boulder.

1994   Ethnology and Archaeology: Symbolic and Systemic Disjunction or Continuity? In *A History of Latin American Archaeology,* edited by Augusto Oyuela-Caycedo, pp. 183–208. World Archaeology Series. Avebury, Aldershot, England.

1995a   Style, Society, Myth and Structure. In *Style, Society, and Person,* edited by Christopher Carr and Jill E. Neitzel, pp. 27–76. Plenum, New York.

1995b   Eternal Companions: Amerindian Dogs from Tierra Firma to the Antilles. In *Actas del XV Congreso Internacional de Arqueología del Caribe,* edited by Ricardo E. Alegría and Miguel Rodríguez, pp. 155–172. Centro de Estudios Avanzados de Puerto Rico y el Caribe, La Fundación Puertorriqueña de las Humanidades, and La Universidad del Turabo, San Juan.

1995c   *Arts of the Amazon.* Edited by Barbara Braun. Thames and Hudson, London.

1998   Paragon or Peril? The Jaguar in Amazonian Indian Society. In *Icons of Power: Feline Symbolism in the Americas,* edited by Nicholas J. Saunders, pp. 171–202. Routledge, London.

2005   Mythic Substitution and the Stars: Aspects of Shipibo and Quechua Ethnoastronomy Compared. In *Songs from the Sky: Indigenous Astronomical and Cosmological Traditions of the World,* edited by Von Del Chamberlain, John B. Carlson, and M. Jane Young, pp. 193–227. Also published in *Archaeoastronomy: The Journal of the Center for Archaeoastronomy* 12–13, 1996. Ocarina Books, Bognor Regis, U.K., and Center for Archaeoastronomy, College Park, Maryland.

2008   How to Build a Raptor: Why the Dumbarton Oaks "Scaled Cayman" Callango Textile Is Really a Jaguaroid Harpy Eagle. In *Chavín: Art, Architecture and Culture,* edited by William J. Conklin and Jeffrey Quilter, pp. 179–214. Cotsen Institute of Archaeology, University of California, Los Angeles.

Roe, Peter G., and Amy W. Roe

2010   Riding the Cayman Canoe: The Iconography of Bats in Chavín Art. In *Adventures in Pre-Columbian Studies: Essays in Honor of Elizabeth P. Benson,* edited by Julie Jones, pp. 50–74. The Anthropological Society of Washington, Washington, D.C.

Rowe, John H.

1967   Form and Meaning in Chavín Art. In *Peruvian Archaeology: Selected Readings,* edited by John H. Rowe and Dorothy Menzel, pp. 72–103. Peek Publications, Palo Alto, California.

1971   The Influence of Chavín Art on Later Styles. In *Dumbarton Oaks Conference on Chavín,* edited by Elizabeth P. Benson, pp. 101–124. Dumbarton Oaks Research Library and Collection, Washington, D.C.

Tello, Julio C.

  1923   Wira Kocha. *Inca* 1(1):93–320; 1(3):583–606.

  1960   *Chavín: Cultura matriz de la Civilización Adina,* edited by Toribio Mejia Xesspe. Universidad de San Marcos, Lima, Peru.

Torres, Constantino Manuel

  2008   Chavín's Shamanic Pharmacopoeia: The Iconographic Evidence. In *Chavín: Art, Architecture and Culture,* edited by William J. Conklin and Jeffrey Quilter, pp. 239–259. Cotsen Institute of Archaeology, University of California, Los Angeles.

Urton, Gary

  1981   *At the Crossroads of the Earth and the Sky: An Andean Cosmology.* University of Texas Press, Austin.

  2008   The Body of Meaning in Chavín Art. In *Chavín: Art, Architecture and Culture,* edited by William J. Conklin and Jeffrey Quilter, pp. 217–236. Cotsen Institute of Archaeology, University of California, Los Angeles.

Valdez, Francisco

  2008   Interzonal Relationships in Ecuador. In *Handbook of South American Archaeology,* edited by Helaine Silverman and William H. Isbell, pp. 865–888. Springer, New York.

Varese, Stefano

  1968   *La Sal de los Ceros: Notas Etnográficas e Históricas sobre los Campa de la Selva del Perú.* Universidad Peruana de Ciencias y Tecnología, Lima, Peru.

Whitten, Norman E., Jr.

  1976   *Sacha Runa: Ethnicity and Adaptation of Ecuadorian Jungle Quichua.* University of Illinois Press, Urbana.

Woodside, Joseph H.

  1979   Amahuaca Star Lore and the Obelisk Tello. Unpublished manuscript, Department of Anthropology, University of Minnesota, Minneapolis.

Zeidler, James A.

  2008   The Ecuadorian Formative. In *Handbook of South American Archaeology,* edited by Helaine Silverman and William H. Isbell, pp. 459–488. Springer, New York.

Part II
Encoding Tradition in Place and Object

4
The Staff God
Icon and Image in Andean Art

Jeffrey Quilter

Many Andean scholars have seen the image of the Staff God as having great antiquity and representing a basic religious concept that has undergone various transformations while remaining essentially the same, an intriguing, compelling, and yet dubious proposition. It has been claimed, for example, that an image on a gourd from the Late Preceramic Period (ca. 2000 B.C.E.) is the Staff God (Haas et al. 2003) and many scholars see the Staff God as the forerunner of the principal Inca gods, as William Isbell and Patricia Knobloch (2006:307) note in a recent review of Staff God imagery from the Middle Horizon (ca. 650–1000 C.E.). The notion that there are long-lasting ideas and practices in Andean culture is sometimes referred to as "Lo Andino" ("The Andean," as in the Andean Way). Archaeological evidence does suggest great longevity for many practices while the identification of origins remains difficult and the parallel issue of the origin and continuity of ideas more difficult to confirm when posited, as in the case of Staff Gods.

The touchstone for reference to Staff Gods is the Raimondi Stone from Chavín de Huántar, in the central highlands of Peru (Burger 1992:174–175) (Figure 4.1). Although the Staff God of the Gate of the Sun at the Middle Horizon site of Tiwanaku, on the Bolivian side of Lake Titicaca, may be a fair rival in its popularity of portrayal and its iconic role as an emblem for the site and culture, the Raimondi figure, being older, may claim precedence and iconic stature in the history of the study of Andean art and archaeology, as well. Finely carved on a highly polished granite ashlar (1.98 m × .74 cm × 17 cm), this late-phase Chavín figure is posed frontally with splayed legs and feet, holding a staff in each hand. The arms are bent, perhaps a concession to the width of the stone, but the out-turned grasping hands seem deliberately executed. The eccentric eyes suggest a trance state, despite the figure's facing forward. An elaborate headdress towers above the anthropomorphic form of the god. As is well known, viewing the image upside down reveals the headdress to be composed of a series of interlinked monster heads.

The staffs themselves consist (from bottom to top) of two serpent heads from one of which rises a column of volutes, while from the other rises a braid motif. This patterning is interrupted by a reversed agnathic monster head. The volute and braid designs beginning behind the basal heads do not continue up the shafts of the staffs. Instead, the central segments are plain and unadorned.

Proceeding upward from between the two basal heads in the center of each staff are two rows of rectangles. These represent a stylized, closed maw, judging from similar motifs elsewhere in the carving. This design also is not continued upwards, past the hands, but the focus on the center of the shafts is maintained by the depiction of a series of interlocked, upwardly rising volutes. Another reversed agnathic head tops the staffs, from the mouth of which comes a spray of volutes. In the center of the sprays are two small serpents. Whereas the bottom serpents are arranged head-to-head, these more simply rendered snakes are chin-to-chin and from their mouths more volutes are emitted.

Staff God or Staffs God?

Having examined the objects held by the Chavín Staff God in detail, it may be asked whether he holds two, four, or six staffs. Is the viewer seeing in each hand one staff, splayed to show all of the details around a curved form? Or do the jawless heads depict the bindings of two staffs, each represented by the basal serpent heads? Or are there three staffs in each hand, each bundle comprising the two serpent-ended staffs plus the mouth element between them, as a third?

It may be a dubious exercise to attempt to discern artistic intent, in this case. If artistic conventions were well known among those privileged to view this carving, then the number of held objects would have been clear. Given that Chavín art was designed to dazzle and confuse the viewer, however, we may cautiously infer that the apparent ambiguity created by the carving was intentional and that many contemporary viewers were as uncertain as we are as to the resolution of this issue.

Whether two staffs or more are represented in the carving, we may propose that a viewer not attuned to the conventions of Chavín art would have a twofold impression in looking at the staffs on the Raimondi Stone. The first impression is that the figure holds two staffs, one in each hand. Further contemplation would make the viewer reconsider whether more staffs are represented if the viewer were able or cared to contemplate such matters. The conditions under which this or most other ancient Andean art was

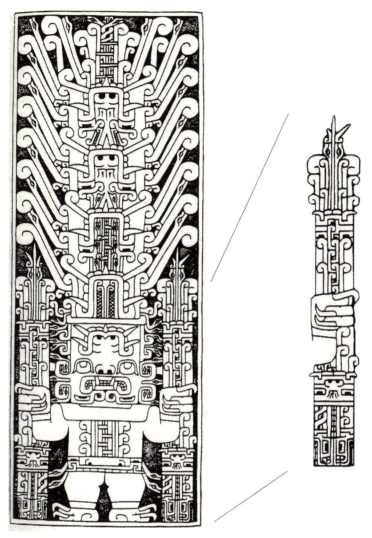

Figure 4.1. The Raimondi Stone (Burger 1992:175, Figure 176) and detail of the staff held in the left hand of the deity.

observed—drunken, hallucinating, terrified, exalted—are matters of some import and matters of which we know very little but which would have much bearing on understanding what the art, itself, as well as its production and reception were all about.

What Are the "Staffs"?

Whether the objects held in the deity's hands are single or multiple ones, they appear to emit light and, perhaps, smoke. The twin serpents rising upwards from the tops of the objects are the same creatures shown extending outwards at angles from the Staff God's headdress. These thin snakes are similar to motifs shown at similar angles sprouting from a figure seen in late Moche fine-line painting that used to be known as the Rayed Deity but now is known as the Warrior Lord. In a previous essay, I suggested that the serpents represented light rays based on the metallic plaque shirts associated with the Moche figures (Quilter 1990).

While it is supposition, I believe it is not unreasonable to propose continuity between the iconography of this late Chavín carving and the Moche imagery, although I have made the interpretive argument backwards, "upstreaming." Although snakes-as-rays become prominent in late Moche, the art style itself began shortly after the demise of Chavín so that continuity in symbolism is feasible. Indeed, Santiago Uceda Castillo (2010:140) has suggested that Moche gods were strongly related to Cupisnique divinities that, in turn, were related to the gods of Chavín. The fact that similar snakes are commonly shown being emitted from or wrapped around eyes in phases AB, C–D, and D in Roe's Chavín art seriation (Roe 1974:72, Chart III) may lend support to the proposal that these serpents represent light: light rays are emitted out of the headdress of the Staff God and out of the objects he holds, as well.

As a further interpretation, if the thin serpents are light rays, then the volutes may be interpreted as stylized puffs of smoke. One interpretation of the light and, possibly, smoke at the top of the staffs might be that the deity is holding torches. It is quite possible, however, that the reference to fire is metaphorical rather than literal and that the message was that the Principal Deity was powerful, emitting light and smoke as a sign of his omnipotence. Perhaps the single most important point of this study of the image on the Raimondi Stone is that we cannot say, for certain, that the deity holds staffs. If he does hold torches and is engaged in the emission of light, fire, smoke, or some combination of these, we may ask whether this is merely to emphasize the power of the deity or whether the reference is more specific, such as to a particular aspect of the god, as in the case of the Inca deity, Illapa, associated with thunder and lightning, or to a particular part of a larger narrative in which the deity took part (e.g., Roe and Roe, this volume).

Variations on the Staff Figure

Richard Burger (1992) proposes that the Staff God is a spectacular example of one of several representations of the Principal Deity of Chavín de Huántar. Much has been made of the fact that the image of the Lanzón, a large in situ statue at the heart of the temple, which was its principal cult object, represents a figure similar to the Staff God. While the Lanzón may have

Figure 4.2. The Principal Deity and friends. Gate of the Sun, Tiwanaku (Chávez 2004:93, Figure 3.27a–c).

been the most sacred cult object, the engraving of the god was made to conform to the surface of the three-dimensional stone, whereas in other depictions, especially those on flat surfaces, the artist had more freedom in representing the image.

Whenever images were made on relatively flat surfaces, the preferred style of rendering the figure was in the front-facing, splayed-legs position, as can be seen, for example, in the "Medusa" figure, another version of the Principal Deity. Parenthetically, we may wonder: if the snake rays are light, then what are the tangled snakes-as-hair? Given that the Medusa holds seashells and that the hair is tangled as if wet, the image may represent an underwater, subterranean, and maritime aspect of the Great God of Chavín, and the snakes may represent either a diminished amount of light or the twisting reflections of light under water.

Another, later, pivotal version of the Staff God is that of the Gate of the Sun at Tiwanaku (Figure 4.2, center). A close examination of this figure reveals that it also does not hold staffs. The right hand appears to hold a spear-thrower and the left a bifurcated object. Some of the "attendants" that flank the principal figure may hold staffs (Figure 4.2, left), while others hold the bifurcated objects, perhaps spear-thrower darts in a quiver.

Sergio Chávez (2004) suggests that the iconography of Tiwanaku derives from the Yaya-Mama religious tradition, a regional cult developed and continued at the site of Pucará. Interestingly, a Pucará-style stone carving of a human–avian figure was made in the full frontal position. The figure holds what appear to be true staffs—that is, single poles. Although the finial of one of these objects has been lost due to damage, the other shows a plain shaft topped by a bird head (Chávez 2004:80, Figure 39a, b). Nevertheless, if the two most-cited examples of the Staff God do not carry staffs, can we sustain the concept?

I am a proponent of searching for widespread, long-lasting patterns in

Native American culture (Quilter and Miller 2006), looking for continuities rather than disjunctions. Nevertheless, such searches may result in identifying discontinuities. I believe that this is the case for Staff Gods. The term has become a generic one used indiscriminately for a host of different figures that share some common features but not staffs. I have even heard Moche front-facing images that hold trophy heads and crescentic knives referred to as Staff Gods, without a staff in sight!

We do know that office holders in Andean communities today and in recent times bear staffs of office (Salomon 2001). But simply because this has been the case recently does not necessarily mean that staffs, per se, were the chief paraphernalia of high offices in the past. We might consider the role of long sticks in general from a comparative perspective.

Sticks and stones were among the first weapons used by primates, as studies of chimpanzees show (Van Lawick-Goodall 1968). As one of the most elemental of weapons, the staff held a special place in the martial arts of Medieval Europe. It was seen as a highly effective weapon but also one belonging to commoners—swords were for the gentry—although by its ancient pedigree and association with yeoman stock, it held a place of special esteem as the "noblest of weapons" (Brown 1997). Friar Tuck wielded a quarterstaff, as did monks in Asia. The simplicity of the weapon was its great advantage, but it conferred no status on those who wielded it. Sticks as weapons then, are as old as humanity and, while venerable, were commonly conceived of as old-fashioned and autochthonous but not as cutting-edge martial technology.

Given the status of stick weapons, it would seem highly unusual for a deity to wield a staff unless he or she were construed as a god of the poor and downtrodden: Jesus is sometimes depicted as a shepherd with a crook specifically to cast him as a god of the lowliest of the low, as shepherds indeed were viewed. As an aid to walking, a staff may also confer the status of a venerable elder, implying the wisdom or, at least, authority that often comes with age. We might expect old gods to use a staff or staffs, perhaps, but the actual depiction of staffs seems scant in the art of ancient America. Powerful gods would have powerful weapons, if they needed weapons at all.

Rather than see the Staff God as a recurring figure throughout the art and religion of ancient America, I suggest that we are viewing a conventionalized form that serves as a template on which to place more specific symbolism. In other words, we are confronting a situation of disjunction, as delineated by George Kubler (1962): the *putti* of Classical art were identical in form to Christian angels but were fundamentally different in their symbolism. In the case of Staff Gods, there is even less similarity between different gods because the main feature that they share in common is a posture. The long tradition in the Andes and in South America, perhaps, is not in Staff Gods but in a more elemental form of representation, the full frontal figure, commonly with splayed legs, out-turned feet, and bent arms.

Full Frontal Figures

What the various figures labeled as Staff Gods share is a common stance. The figure faces forward, the legs are bent, the feet are often splayed, and the arms also are bent out to the sides. Personages in similar positions are known as hocker (derived from "squat") figures, although the legs are often more bent and the hands are commonly held higher (see Graham 2003). I do not believe that the Staff Gods we commonly see are hocker figures, but I think that something similar is occurring in both images. Graham suggests that hocker figures are tied to concepts of female fertility and birth. It is also true, however, that the squat, condensed position allows for the presentation of the full human form in a much smaller, more compact area than the linear, roughly rectangular shape of a standing figure. Nevertheless, there seems to be a gradation of stance between some figures that appear to be generally related to Staff Gods, such as the various Decapitator Gods of the Moche and the more erect figures such as at Chavín and Tiwanaku.

The stance of the staff gods, like that of the hocker figures, is one of potential. Bent knees indicate a state of being both grounded and ready to spring. For the case of the Staff Gods, we may wonder whether the turned-out legs and splayed feet have less to do with showing a specific, awkward posture than with showing bent knees in general. Without recourse to perspective, a profile view would be the only way to show bent legs. In Asian martial arts, including tai chi, the "at rest" posture requires slightly bent legs in order to allow for a literal springing into action. Locked knees cannot be moved except by the action of the hips, as in the "goose step," and more fluid and powerful motion is only derived by body movement if the knees revert to a bent position. The bent-knee position shown in many figures in Andean art may thus be referencing the potential for movement of the figure and, perhaps, its actual movement beyond the moment captured in the image. This, indeed, raises issues of the consideration of the representation of time and narrative in even apparently static imagery in Andean art, but these cannot be followed in the present essay beyond this point.

In combination with the latent energy of bent legs, the front-facing position with bent arms, to the sides, is full of potential movement but nevertheless also is static. This is especially emphasized in the case of the Tiwanaku figure flanked by running attendants in profile. The position of facing forward with arms to the side is thus both vulnerable and confrontational as a kind of hieratic dare, and the latent energy in both legs and arms might be read as a warning to those considering taking the dare; thus, this posture offers a note of menace in the image.

The argument has just been presented that the front-facing figure is full of latent power. But slight variations in the representation can offer very different meanings. Consider the almost universally recognized position of surrender: front-facing with bent arms and open hands, usually with palms facing forward. Legs may or may not be bent but they are often slightly spread apart. This is not only an image of surrender but also a sign of peaceful intent because it demonstrates to the viewer that the person assuming the posture is not bearing weapons. We may circle back to the consideration of Staff Gods, then, in noting that holding anything in the hand(s), especially sticks, spear throwers, and the like, is the critical difference in representing an anthropomorphic figure as powerful, whether in terms of physical aggression or in regard to spiritual power.

Most important of all, perhaps, is that front-facing figures are those who are prepared to interact with the viewer. The position insists on an encounter. Any other position places the viewer as an observer to the figure being represented. In this, of course, the key issue is the orientation of the face of the representation. If the body is moving at an angle away from the viewer but the head is turned toward him or her, the position suggests a recognition of presence with the option, perhaps, of the figure reorienting to face the viewer directly. The full frontal figure, however, suggests full engagement with the person viewing it and that engagement may be friendly, hostile, or neutral.

The front-facing god figures, with their outspread arms and legs, are ideally positioned to maximize the display of clothing, jewelry, and other adornments. Although the Maya are famous for their representational art style with its emphasis on line (Herring 2005), many stelae are carved less in the round than "on the square." That is to say, the cross sections of stelae often are rectangular. The fronts of these blocks of stone commonly bear the image of a personage. Even in cases where the figure is more fully carved, both they and the men carved on blocky stelae are often obscured by the dense amounts of clothing, jewelry, and other paraphernalia covering the human form. More often than not, it appears that the regalia are more significant than the personage.

Long thin objects play important roles in Native American religions, and they are commonly symbols of authority. These include the calumet, bilobed arrows, ceremonial axes, spear-throwers, bows, arrows, and staffs of different kinds (Figure 4.3). But these vary significantly across time and space. There may be some way to see connections in the symbolism of these objects, although we must remember that stafflike batons are not only ancient but

Figure 4.3. A Staff God? Engraving on a conch shell (*Busycon sinistrum*) from Spiro Mound, Oklahoma, Caddoan Mississippian culture, circa 1350–1400 C.E. (Craig C style). (Philip Phillips and James A. Brown, *Pre-Columbian Shell Engravings from the Craig Mound at Spiro, Oklahoma*, Vol. 6. Peabody Museum Press. Copyright 1982 by the President and Fellows of Harvard College.)

functionally draw attention to themselves simply due to their size, as well as their common potential as striking weapons.

Conclusions

My conclusion for this brief consideration of Staff Gods is that it might be best to retire the term altogether. Archaeology, like most disciplines, is divided into splitters and lumpers, and each approach has its own advantages and disadvantages. In the case of Staff Gods, however, I believe that continued use of the term prevents us from seeing and understanding the development of different religious traditions in Peru in which the form of representational styles may have continued but the content likely was considerably different, albeit with potential continuities that need to be demonstrated rather than assumed.

The fact that a front-facing figure has been found depicted on a gourd from the Late Preceramic Period (Haas et al. 2003) does not mean that there is an unbroken line of continuity in the iconic content or meaning of the image portrayed, although it is striking that the formal features of this kind of representation have such great antiquity. Isbell and Knobloch (2006), for example, argue that the "classic" Middle Horizon "staff gods" are more likely derived from the Rayed Head motif of Provincial Pucará art and religion, a distinctively southern Andean tradition that was contemporaneous with Chavín, but likely not strongly influenced by it.

In other words, this is a case in which we must heed the words of George Kubler regarding disjunctions in meaning, even while the forms remain the same. But I think that while we may have to abandon the notion of Staff Gods, we may wish to consider the significance of a widespread, long-lasting convention of front-facing figures with bent legs, splayed feet, and bent arms. Indeed, one of the striking recurrences in the hocker-staff figure complex is the apparent concern with showing the entire body. This too may be an important convention widespread in the ancient Americas. Given that the taking of body parts, especially the head, was a common practice among so many people, there may have been an impetus in art to be sure to include all of the body of a god or ruler, even if various parts had to be reduced in order to portray them all, as an indication of the wholeness or completeness of the figure represented. Indeed, the interrelation between the Provincial Pucará Rayed Head motif and the full-figure Middle Horizon Staff Gods may be important in the very fact that the former is only a head while the latter is a body, even though they share many similar features. Other exceptions to the rule of full-body, frontal portrayal may be noteworthy in what they attempt to achieve by ignoring it.

References Cited

Brown, Terry
   1997   *English Martial Arts.* Anglo-Saxon Books, Hockwold-cum-Wilton, England.
Burger, Richard L.
   1992   *Chavin and the Origins of Andean Civilization.* Thames and Hudson, London.
Chávez, Sergio J.
   2004   The Yaya-Mama Religious Tradition as an Antecedent of Tiwanaku. In *Tiwanaku: Ancestors of the Inca,* edited by Margaret Young-Sánchez, pp. 70–93. Denver Art Museum and University of Nebraska Press, Lincoln.
Graham, Mark Miller
   2003   Creation Imagery in the Goldwork of Costa Rica, Panama, and Colombia. In *Gold and Power in Ancient Costa Rica, Panama, and Colombia,* edited by

Jeffrey Quilter and John Hoopes, pp. 279–299. Dumbarton Oaks Research Library and Collection, Washington, D.C.

Haas, Jonathan, Winifred Creamer, and Alvaro Ruiz

2003   Gourd Lord. *Archaeology* May/June 56:9.

Herring, Adam

2005   *Art and Writing in the Maya Cities, A.D. 600–800.* Cambridge University Press, Cambridge.

Isbell, William H., and Patricia J. Knobloch

2006   Missing Links, Imaginary Links: Staff God Imagery in the South Andean Past. In *Andean Archaeology III, North and South,* edited by William H. Isbell and Helaine Silverman, pp. 307–351. Springer, New York.

Kubler, George

1962   *The Shape of Time: Remarks on the History of Things.* Yale University Press, New Haven, Connecticut.

Phillips, Philip, and James A. Brown

1982   *Pre-Columbian Shell Engravings from the Craig Mound at Spiro, Oklahoma,* Vol. 6. Peabody Museum Press, Harvard University, Cambridge, Massachusetts.

Quilter, Jeffrey

1990   The Moche Revolt of the Objects. *Latin American Antiquity* 1:42–65.

Quilter, Jeffrey, and Mary Miller (editors)

2006   *A Pre-Columbian World: Searching for a Unitary Vision of Ancient America.* Dumbarton Oaks Research Library and Collection, Washington, D.C.

Roe, Peter G.

1974   *A Further Exploration of the Rowe Chavín Seriation and Its Implications for North Central Coast Chronology.* Studies in Pre-Columbian Art and Archaeology 13. Dumbarton Oaks Research Library and Collection, Washington, D.C.

Salomon, Frank

2001   How an Andean "Writing without Words" Works. *Current Anthropology* 42:1–27.

Uceda Castillo, Santiago

2010   Theocracy and Secularism: Relationships between the Temple and Urban Nucleus and Political Change at the Huacas de Moche. In *New Perspectives on Moche Political Organization,* edited by Jeffrey Quilter and Luis Jaime Castillo B., pp. 132–158. Dumbarton Oaks Research Library and Collection, Washington, D.C.

Van Lawick-Goodall, Jane

1968   The Behaviour of Free-Living Chimpanzees in the Gombe Stream Reserve. *Animal Behaviour Monographs* 1:161–311.

5
On Being and Becoming

Ruminations on the Genesis, Evolution,
and Maintenance of the Cerro Jaboncillo
Ceremonial Center, Ecuador

Colin McEwan

Throughout the Americas diverse ancient religious traditions have engendered collective acts of devotion and worship celebrated in carefully chosen landscape settings. Recognized routes and inherent temporal rhythms helped guide participants' journeys from their communities of origin to periodic gatherings at prescribed locations that were frequently timed to coincide with key times in the seasonal cycle. At many sites the repetition of esoteric ritual and public pageantry gradually found formal expression in the built environment, ranging from temples, pyramids, and plazas to palaces and administrative complexes. Where the material signature of shared protocols and ritual performance becomes visibly inscribed in the art and architecture of sacred places, these are conventionally described as ceremonial or cult centers. The early Formative U-shaped complexes and sunken circular plazas that emerged in the coastal valleys of northern Peru, for example, find parallels in the rectangular sunken plazas of the Yaya-Mama tradition in the southern Andean highlands (e.g., Chávez 2004; Williams 1985). In due course local shrines were superceded by large, planned, and architecturally elaborate sites such as Chavín de Huántar and Tiwanaku where the art styles that encode religious beliefs became firmly established as powerful instruments of instruction and persuasion (e.g., Burger 2008).

Why are certain locations selected in the first place, and why might their inherent qualities be conducive to continued religious interest and use over the longer term? Why do certain motifs such as the so-called Staff God and the Displayed Female become centrally embedded in the iconography of some of the best-known styles? What role do ceremonial centers play in shaping the continued development of the art and architecture of a given tradition? How do architectural, stylistic, and aesthetic conventions become established, and how do architects and artisans alike reconcile the tension between prescriptive stylistic templates and the tendency for these to meta-morphose and evolve? While the imperative to forge and maintain a rec-ognizable visual corpus surely serves as a powerful incentive to ensure that long-established precedents are followed, how can this be squared with the kind of dynamic, innovative creativity that is the hallmark of evolving icono-graphic traditions?

This chapter explores some of these questions from one of South America's less well-known religious traditions by focusing on Cerro Jaboncillo, a hilltop ceremonial complex in southern Manabí, on Ecuador's Pacific coast. This was the preeminent regional locus of a corpus of stone sculpture com-prising seats, stelae, and anthropomorphic and zoomorphic sculpture, as well as ceramic figurines principally attributed to the Manteño culture (800–1500 C.E.) (McEwan 2004; McEwan and Delgado-Espinoza 2008; see also Estrada 1957, 1962; Holm 1992). By the time of first European contact, the Manteño had successfully forged a powerful confederation of polities known as Señorios that controlled long-distance maritime trade by balsa raft. Soon after European contact in the early sixteenth century, the Señorios suffered precipitate social collapse leading to the wholesale abandonment of towns and ceremonial centers alike. Centuries later a substantial number of the larger stone sculptures were recorded and then removed from Cerro Jabon-cillo and adjacent hilltops by the American researcher Marshall H. Saville (Saville 1907, 1910). He also excavated ceramic figurines in different styles on Cerro Jaboncillo. Several of these portray high-status males seated on stools chewing coca, and the range of styles represented suggests that the ritual consumption of coca had been practiced for 1,500 years or more in this set-ting by earlier coastal Ecuadorian cultures.

Using information extracted from Saville's *Antiquities of Manabí* (1907, 1910), together with his unpublished field notes, I have been able to map the ritual topography of the site and, insofar as the available information per-mits, to reconstruct the architectural contexts for the specialized corpus of stone sculpture. This is complemented by an analysis of the stela iconography outlined below that helps to explain why this hilltop site was revered and to account for its enduring viability and elaboration as a ceremonial center. I suggest that this kind of integrated approach contributes to a broader un-derstanding of the genesis and evolution of ceremonial centers in their land-scape settings and the role they play in maintaining autochthonous religious traditions.

Hilltop Sites and the Dry-Season/Wet-Season Cycle

The choice of the plateau summit of Cerro Jaboncillo as the locus for Man-teño ceremonial activity underlines the special character of this and similar nearby hilltops lying between 600 and 800 m above sea level. At these loca-

Figure 5.1. Seat found in situ at Cerro Jaboncillo; photo by Marshall Saville in 1906. (M. H. Saville, *The Antiquities of Manabí, Ecuador: Final Report*, 1910, Heye Foundation, New York, pl. XVII.)

tions, a permanent verdure of cloud forest is sustained by year-round coastal fog (*garua*), presenting a marked contrast with the xerophytic vegetation of the dry tropical forest on the surrounding coastal plain below. In southern Manabí the riverbeds are mostly dry for 10 months of the year and depend upon the seasonal rains to be replenished. Today, as in the past, the dry-to-wet-season transition that occurs annually in late December is of critical importance for the planting and maturation of the crops. The temporal turning point represented by the reversal of the sun's movement across the horizon around the December solstice would have been matched by a ritual concern with the approaching transition from the dry season to the essential winter rains upon which the earth's fertility and the life of human communities ultimately depended. With the arrival of the rains, the moist green mantle on the plateau summits seems to spill downslope and turn the parched brown vegetation on the coastal plain into a verdant sea of green.

Manteño Stone Seats at Cerro Jaboncillo

The exceptional assemblage of stone sculpture comprising seats, stelae, and anthropomorphic and zoomorphic sculpture suggests that Cerro Jaboncillo and adjacent hilltops were once important settings for significant seasonal ritual events (Figure 5.1). Saville noted what he described as two great classes

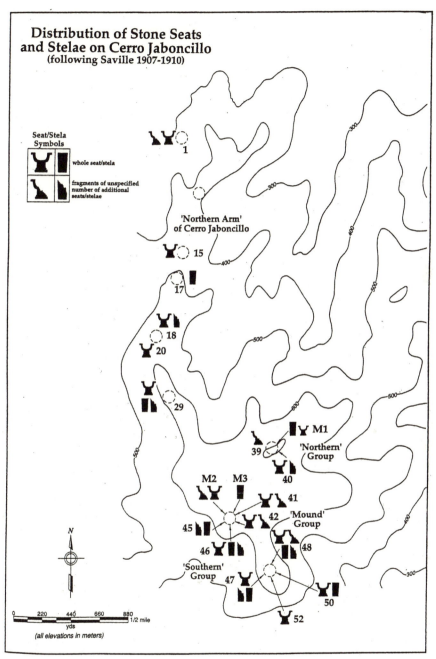

**Distribution of Stone Seats
and Stelae on Cerro Jaboncillo**
(following Saville 1907-1910)

Seat/Stela
Symbols

whole seat/stela

fragments of unspecified
number of additional
seats/stelae

1

'Northern Arm'
of Cerro Jaboncillo

15

17

18

20

29

39   M1

'Northern'
Group

40

M2   M3   41

45   42   'Mound'
Group

46   48

'Southern'
Group   47

50

52

N

0   220   440   660   880
yds   1/2 mile
(all elevations in meters)

Figure 5.2. Location of seats and stelae at Cerro Jaboncillo. (Reconstructed from Saville's
field notes.)

of U-shaped stone seats: those with male figures on hands and knees and those with crouching felines. Both anthropomorphic and feline seats are found at Cerro Jaboncillo and were clearly used in conjunction with each other. In at least one case, anthropomorphic and zoomorphic seats have been found within the confines of the same structure, perhaps expressing a distinction between opposing moieties (Figure 5.2). The range of sizes suggests a hierarchy of seats perhaps indicative of social ranking and status. There may also have been seats in wood, metal, or even ceramic for which little or no evidence now exists. There is a prima facie case for a formal seating arrangement but no direct evidence for what such an arrangement may have been like.

The seats are evidently much more numerous than the stelae, and demonstrable iconographic relationships link them. The fact that they are found together, along with other sculpture and pottery figurines in architectural contexts on Cerro Jaboncillo, confirms that they are integral elements of a cohering ritual complex.

Seats in Architectural Context at Agua Blanca

Although we can tell little of the precise layout of the seats within the structures at Cerro Jaboncillo, more secure evidence has been obtained from another Manteño site, Agua Blanca, some 70 km south and once the principal town of the Señorío of Salangome. Here areal excavation of selected structures has demonstrated the existence of ordered arrangements of seats within architectural contexts. At one structure (MIV-C4-2.2) a row of seats has been discovered in situ along the length of one wall. The greatest number of seats is concentrated at MIV-C4-5.1, the largest public structure at this site. In this building it is estimated that some 20 seats in all were probably arranged along the side walls facing each other across the interior space. The long axis and principal entrance of the building are oriented on the December solstice sunrise. Horizon-based solar observations may therefore have governed the timing of the principal festivals and seating rituals revolving around the temporal axis of the solstices. This was also the turning point of the year in the seasonal cycle: the critical transition from dry season to wet season. As the sun "sat in his seat," it is suggested that so too did human beings engage in formal seating rituals to establish social order and affirm anew the social hierarchy.

Standing and Seated Nude Males

Many Manteño pottery figurines are known to have come from Cerro Jaboncillo and adjacent hilltop sites, among the most striking being large *incensarios* featuring a modeled figure sitting on a stool resting on an annular base (Figure 5.3).[1] The figure is invariably a naked male, sitting in a formal pose

Figure 5.3. A Manteño
incensario from the collec-
tions of the Museo Antro-
pologica del Banco Central
del Ecuador; photo by
Antonio Pareja from
Ecudor: La Tierra y el Oro by
Rosangela Adoum and Olf
Holm (Ayuntamiento de
Madrid, 1992).

with clenched fists resting on his knees, and the physical characteristics suggest that these are adolescent boys rather than mature males or elders. (For
a discussion of the clenched fist motif, see Guinea 2004:10–14.) They usually boast prominent ear spools and an elaborate necklace or collar, together
with other forms of body decoration either painted or tattooed on their upper torso and shoulders (Guinea 2004:25–28). The headpiece flares out to form
the broad, everted lip of the vessel. Some stools upon which the young man
sits have a stepped base analogous to the stepped form of the boundary separating the upper and lower design fields on the stelae described below.

The elaborate collared necklaces comprising multiple rows of beads and
plaques merit close scrutiny because of the design on the central pendant.
One bears a stepped design with spiral volutes similar to the design on a
Manteño clay seal used to apply body decoration (Parducci Zevallos 1968).
Another has an abstract motif consisting of a diamond within a notched
square that is also found on the clay seal nested within the contours of this
stylized seat form (Figure 5.4). Parducci Zevallos proposes that the contours

Figure 5.4. Clay seal with a diamond motif enclosed within a notched square.

of the seal are molded to fit the coccyx and buttocks and notes that "on the platform of the seal, that is the upper part that covers the impressed plane, there is a broad incised line that crosses the seal in its central part, making a vertical (axis), which served as orientation for the one applying the seal."[2]

We can infer that the spinal column of the subject provided the appropriate axis of alignment for applying the seal, which would likely have been used for repeated applications of the design on different individuals. As the ritual participant was seated, the abstract motif would be translated onto the horizontal plane and in this position would intersect with the vertical axis of the sitter's spine.[3] The iconography on this seal establishes an interesting insight into what presumably was a general practice of applying body paint in the course of seating rituals involving young males. A significant detail is found on either side of the central motif of a diamond within a notched square. Just above each of the out-turned arms of the seat symbol is a stylized face. The one on the right is an abbreviated rendering of a toadlike head (see below for discussion of this element as the "Composite Being"), while the other is the head of a snake. These hint at the seasonal oppositions and temporal axes around which some of the important seating rituals probably revolved. Other, perhaps related, aspects of these kinds of rituals are shown in a further group of ceramic figurines featuring naked male figures standing on either a feline or on a crouching human figure.

The corpus of figurines showing a range of seated individuals offers insights into the different kinds of ritual contexts in which they were used. One group involves high-ranking males standing in seats. The fact that the seats are of different sizes suggests they probably reflect the status of the owner and his place in a hierarchical seating arrangement. Another group might have formed part of initiation ceremonies in which young men have body paint and other ornaments applied and are ritually seated.

Manteño Stelae at Cerro Jaboncillo

The association between seats and stelae is corroborated by shared iconographic elements that firmly link the two classes of sculpture. The stelae consist of monolithic slabs made from the same range of limestone, submarine tuff, and sandstone as the stone seats and likely quarried from the same local sources. The majority have apparently been found in and around Cerro Jaboncillo. By all accounts, few have been discovered on other Manteño hilltop sites in the area, such as Cerro de Hojas, Cerro Jupa, and Cerro La Roma. So far as we know, the stelae are restricted to these hilltop locations and have not been reported from other Manteño settlements. Perhaps as few as 30 to 40 complete stelae survive today in museum and private collections.[4] I have restricted the scope of this study to the stelae that Saville found on Cerro Jaboncillo and that are therefore securely provenanced to this particular site.[5] Here they were found distributed among structures located along the upper reaches of the tributary spurs and on the summit plateau. The stelae range from approximately 1 to 1.5 m in height, are from 10 to 15 cm in thickness, and are usually slightly tapered from top to bottom. They bear incised designs only on the frontal surface. The back and edges are always undecorated. The lower third of each stela is also invariably left blank, suggesting that they stood upright with the undecorated basal portion embedded in the earth. Saville discovered a number of intact stelae as well as many fragments on or close to the ground surface. In some cases, he notes which stelae were found within which structures. I will comment on this in more detail below.[6]

Description of Stela Iconography

The stelae show intriguing regularities in the formal arrangement of their designs and in their subject matter. They are nearly all consistently divided into an upper and lower domain designated here as Field A and Field B, respectively. A distinctive stepped band (Boundary 1) separating the two fields extends across the breadth of the stelae. Beneath Field B, a horizontal serrated band (Boundary 2) separates the decorated upper portion of the stela from its undecorated base.[7] The stelae feature a principal figural subject that always appears in Field B. I have identified four different principal subjects and have divided the stelae into four groups accordingly (Figure 5.5).

I have juxtaposed a selection of images from each group in a provisional, integrated schema that helps visualize how the horizontal and vertical relationships that I have been discussing might be combined.

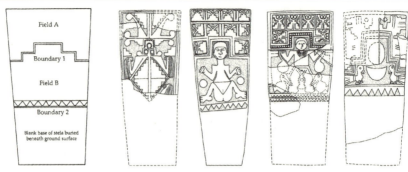

Figure 5.5. Manteño stelae with the four principal subjects: (from left to right follow-ing the key) the Composite Being, the Displayed Female, the Standing Figure, the Orb and Crescent.

Group 1: The Composite Being

In seeking an appropriate term to describe the Composite Being figure in the context of Manteño art, it is tempting to assign a term that has already been applied to similar figures found elsewhere in pre-Columbian iconography,[8] such as earth monster, earth toad, reptilian, or batrachian.[9] These terms, how-ever, confer a specificity of identification that can be misleading. The Man-teño figure defies easy categorization, and I have elected to call it the Com-posite Being. This neutral term recognizes the polymorphous attributes that the figure embodies without prejudging its identity and enables me to build a more objective argument about its iconographic relationships with the re-lated corpus of material.[10]

The Composite Being is depicted as if seen from the back squatting with its head directed upward. The spinal column forms a conspicuous vertical axis underlining the fact that the figure has been transposed from the horizontal to the vertical plane.[11] It is composed of the following elements:

Field A. Pairs of conventionalized volutes project upward as if emanating from the snout of the Composite Being beneath. The first pair curl inward and the upper one, two, or three pairs curl outward. In one case there is a con-trast between a round spiral at the end of one volute and a rectangular spiral at the end of the other. Other elements are placed on the central axis nested between the volutes. These include a bat, a disk, an extra pair of volutes, and a vertical bifurcated column. The latter can be compared to the small designs filling Field A on other stelae. Disks are also found flanking the arms of the volutes in one example.

Clear parallels can also be drawn between the form of the volutes extend-ing above the squared snout of the Composite Being and the form of the stone seats.[12] The volutes are centrally placed, sitting directly on the plane of articulation between the upper and lower fields. They can be equated with the small, conventionalized form of a stepped motif with volutes, which I will also refer to as a "seat symbol." These small seat symbols appear on other stelae as repetitive elements in Field A framing either the Displayed Female or the Standing Figure in Field B.

Field B. The head is shown facing upward as though seen from the back. It features a pronounced snout and hachured dentition along the upper edge. The eyes are represented by a distinctive element comprising two circles joined by a semicircular loop. The head is squared by being embedded within the stepped form of Boundary 1. On either side of the head are other stepped motifs and volutes or spirals.

The abdomen is outlined as a conventionalized diamond by a single bold line. On one stela, the body contains a stepped diamond comprising a stepped motif that unfolds around both the horizontal and vertical axes. On other stelae, the abdomen is portrayed with rounded haunches. The back is always bisected vertically by a spinal column. This usually has a filler element consisting of a herringbone design or nested triangles with adjacent parallel rows of circles that reveal the vertebrae as if in X-ray.[13]

The limbs are represented in splayed fashion like those of most reptiles including lizards, toads, and frogs. Elongated digits appear at the extremities of both the forelimbs and the rear limbs. Three or four elongated digits are shown, plus an attenuated, recurved "thumb" on the forelimb. This hooked thumb is not always shown on the rear limb, or it may be displaced to the outside.

An appendage sometimes extends from beneath the spinal column. In one case, this curves to one side and is curled like a monkey's tail. Another example is clearly bifurcated and might represent a penis or even exaggerated female genitalia. There is, therefore, an element of ambiguity in the Composite Being's sexual identity.[14]

Group 2: The Displayed Female

The central figure is a frontal, naked female sitting on the ground with arms and legs spread wide apart in a displayed pose.[15] The figure is subtly emphasized by deep areal excision of the background on either side, thus conveying the visual impression that it is recessed beneath Boundary 1 and Field A above.

Field A. Field A above Boundary 1 is filled by a series of small, repeated geometric motifs that run around the upper border of the stelae.[16] The double step motif (or a variant of it) is most frequently deployed and, as I noted above, can be described as an abbreviated seat symbol. This motif often in-

than change. The discovery of a unique origin for split representation would leave unanswered the question of why this means of expression was preserved by cultures that, in other respects, evolved along very different lines. External connections can explain transmission, but only internal questions can account for persistence (Lévi-Strauss 1958:258).

The question that all these studies hold in common is how to explain the regularity apparent in the basic organization of the constituent elements of a particular widespread motif and the systematic reproduction of this motif within differing social contexts. No matter how common a given motif may be, its specificity of meaning must, nevertheless, be derived from the internal logic of the way in which it is deployed in particular contexts.

Group 3: The Standing Figure

The third group is made up of a Standing Figure, which is usually male. Occasionally a standing female is shown, who may possibly represent a high-ranking woman fulfilling a "male" leadership role.

Field A. Field A is filled with a repeated stepped motif flanked by small disks similar to that found in Field A of the Displayed Female.

Field B. Two stelae depict a male frontal Standing Figure with arms raised. In either hand he holds or displays a pair of disks or bags. He wears a simple, unadorned coiffure or head-cap, a necklace but no ear spools, and a loincloth hanging from his waist. He is flanked by two birds shown in profile standing at ground level facing inward. Another stela depicts a male figure with his arms by his side wearing a tunic with a quadripartite design (for a discussion of dual division and quadripartition as an organizing principle in Manteño culture see Silva 1985).

One stela features a standing female who is naked, with her arms by her sides and with pierced earlobes. The anthropomorphic figures and lozenge motifs that run along the upper register and down either side differ from the geometric motifs that frame the male figures. The rectangular spiral motifs that terminate each end of the semicircular design that arches above the figure's head are analogous to those flanking the entrance to a building on one of the seals, suggesting that the female is standing in a doorway.

Group 4: The Orb and Crescent

A fourth group of stelae features an orb as the principal motif. The orb may appear by itself or nested into a crescent form beneath.

Field A. Field A is filled with a repeated stepped motif flanked by small disks similar to Groups 2 and 3.

Field B. Within the recessed space in one case, the orb has a crescent beneath and is flanked by two birds facing inward toward each other. In another example, a crescent below an orb is shown with "wings" similar to those on the stone seats. This representation is flanked by two small disks that are substituted for the pair of birds in the same manner that the disks replace the monkeys in the case of the female figures. The Orb and Crescent are also depicted poised above the arms of a seat.

In several kinds of stone sculpture, the disk is joined to the crescent beneath by a vertical element. This particular combination is found on the vertical portion of columns with stepped bases carved from the same stone as the seats and the stelae. I have encountered many of these columns in the course of surveying and mapping the architectural complexes at Agua Blanca. They are often found toward the front of structures and were perhaps used as architectural elements to support vertical posts, including those of the facade and the overhanging roof.

A similar motif is found on at least one seat. In several examples, a disk is shown positioned between the winged arms of a seat.

Discussion and Analysis

The contextual association, formal similarities, and shared motifs on the stelae enable me to consider them as a related body of material. Moreover, the formal regularities in the arrangement of the design fields and the standardization of the principal themes together imply systematic expression of a fundamental set of concepts. I will now address the relationships between the groups, following the order in which they have been presented. In a sense the starting point is arbitrary, since it will become apparent that the iconographic links between them could equally well be made by beginning with any one of the others. I will first consider how the principal figure in each group relates to that of the next group along a horizontal axis. I will then examine the hierarchical relationships between the groups and show how they can be arranged along a vertical axis to reflect this. Finally, I integrate the data into an overall interpretive model that will enable me to pose a further set of more specific questions concerning the significance of the thematic material, the contrasts and transformations that are effected, and the temporal contexts in which they might have been used.

Comparison between the Composite Being and the Displayed Female

Similarities and contrasts between the Composite Being and the Displayed Female invite comparison. The Composite Being has splayed limbs and is shown squatting on its haunches. This pose can be compared with the widespread arms and legs of the female who sits in contact with the earth. Both figures have a conventionalized diamond-shaped abdomen, which underscores their essential relatedness. The rounded haunches of some of the Composite Beings can be likened to the rounded buttocks of the Displayed Female. In one instance, a Displayed Female on a seat is shown with the elongated digits that typically characterize the Composite Being.

There are, however, important contrasts. The Composite Being is seen as though from the back, while the perspective is reversed for the Displayed Female, who is portrayed frontally. The skeletal spinal column of the Composite Being receives special emphasis, whereas the Displayed Female is always depicted as a fleshy, nubile figure. The spinal column of the Composite Being forms a pronounced vertical axis, while the abdomen of the Displayed Female is bisected by a horizontal line. In the case of the Composite Being, the vertical unfolding of the flanking stepped motifs across the horizontal plane of articulation between Fields A and B emphasizes the vertical, hierarchical relationship between these two domains. This contrasts with the horizontal unfolding of the Displayed Female and her attendant profile motifs, which emphasizes that she is sexually open and receptive. Earlier I noted that the form of the volutes emanating from the snout of the Composite Being can be compared with the small seat symbols that appear as the repetitive elements filling Field A above the Displayed Female in Field B. The curvilinear form of the single set of volutes contrasts with the ordered array of the smaller symbols. In both cases, a disk or disks are positioned between the arms of the volutes. This may be a single disk, a pair of equal size, or a larger disk flanked by two smaller ones.

The points of comparison between the Composite Being and the Displayed Female taken together with their reversed perspectives and contrasting attributes suggest that the one is the obverse of the other. They stand in complementary opposition to one another.

Comparison between the Displayed Female and the Standing Figure

There are fundamental similarities as well as contrasts between the groups of stelae that feature as the central figure the Displayed Female or the Standing Figure. Both are framed by carefully ordered rows of the small seat symbols in Field A. The systematic repetition of the seat symbols contrasts with the naturalistic central figure in Field B. The stepped boundary enclosing the recessed niche of Field B can be compared to the entrances of large buildings represented on pottery seals.[19] In turn, the way in which the seat symbols in Field A are arranged around the stepped boundary can be compared to the design elements depicted on the facades of these buildings. The seat symbols usually run in one or two rows horizontally across the top of Field A and are then rotated 90 degrees to run sideways on either side of Field B. I suggest that this is perhaps a graphic device deployed to render the three-dimensional depth of the interior space of the building on the two-dimensional surface of the stelae.[20] It may therefore also offer clues about the arrangement of the seats inside.

While both the Displayed Female and the Standing Figure are framed within the same kind of ordered space, a hierarchical distinction can be made between them on the basis of their flanking motifs. The female is flanked by a pair of monkeys shown in profile. Elsewhere in Manteño art, monkeys are associated with licentious sexual behavior and this underscores the Displayed Female's condition of sexual openness.[21] The way in which the flanking figures are depicted in profile is therefore used as a graphic device to reveal and to emphasize the chthonic connotations of the displayed pose. The Standing Figure is also portrayed frontally in a version of the displayed pose with raised, flexed arms that can be directly compared with that of the female. The Standing Figure is flanked by a pair of birds seen in profile. Just as the flanking profile monkeys reinforce the salient female attributes, so too do the flanking profile birds signal an association between the male figure and the sky. Thus the contrast between the two pairs of flanking figures (the birds flanking the male figure associated with the sky and the monkeys flanking the female denoting the terrestrial realm) establishes a hierarchical distinction between the Standing Figure and the Displayed Female.

There is a further interesting aspect that both the Displayed Female and the Standing Figure have in common. The flanking animals seen in profile on some stelae are substituted by a pair of flanking disks on others. In the female figure this is a straightforward replacement, so that the monkey is replaced by an interarthral disk positioned between the elbow and the knee of the female. On the basis of the comparative studies made by Carl Schuster, these can be equated with genealogical joint marks (Schuster and Carpenter 1986, 1996). The substitution of the disks for the birds flanking the male is not quite so straightforward, for it also entails a transformation of the man himself. I consider this in the comparison between the Standing Figure and the Orb and Crescent below.

Comparison between the Standing Figure and the Orb and Crescent

I have already noted that the birds in profile flanking the Standing Figure are substituted by flanking disks in the same way that the disks replace the monkeys on either side of the Displayed Female. The Standing Figure himself is substituted by a larger oval or circular symbol that I have designated the Orb to distinguish it from the smaller disk symbols. Thus on one stela, the Standing Figure in the center is replaced by an orb superimposed above a crescent, and the retention of the flanking birds clearly signals that the combined Orb and Crescent motif can be equated with the Standing Figure. On another stela, the pair of birds is substituted by a pair of disks, and at the same time the crescent assumes the unmistakable form of the U-shaped winged seat. The superimposition of an Orb above a crescent or the U form of the seat establishes a vertical opposition between the two elements. Since they occur together beneath Boundary 1, they can be directly compared to the figure of the Displayed Female. The U form of the seat is analogous to the rounded buttocks of the female and her splayed legs. However, while the female's displayed pose conveys a condition of openness and receptivity, by contrast, the uninterrupted, rounded form of the seat signals symbolic closure. The Orb can therefore be equated with a male celestial principle and the U-shaped form with a terrestrial feminine principle. The relationship between the two is made explicit in one case where the celestial Orb is poised between the arms of a classic Manteño seat with high arms. The vertical connection between the two symbols is emphasized on other sculpture such as columns and a seat where they are linked by a vertical axis. This in turn can be compared with the Standing Figure engraved on the front of other stone seats and the ceramic figurines showing priests standing on seats.

Comparison between the Orb and Crescent and the Composite Being

To complete this set of comparisons between the groups, the Composite Being can be compared directly to the Orb and Crescent. The pose of the Composite Being with its upturned head and batrachian attributes clearly associates it with the subterranean realm. By contrast, the Orb and Crescent, flanked as they are by the pair of birds, are linked to the celestial sphere. These two groups also embody a further set of opposed but complementary principles, the significance of which will become apparent as I turn to consider the hierarchical relationships between them.

The Hierarchical Relationships between the Groups

To begin to address the hierarchical relationships between the groups I will first return to the vertical orientation of the Composite Being. The vertical connection between the lower domain of Field B and the upper domain of Field A is reinforced by the way that the vertical axis of the spinal column of the Composite Being in Field B is emphasized and aligned with other design elements in Field A above. In one example, a bifurcated vertical column is directly aligned with the spinal column of the Composite Being below. The snout and jaws of the Composite Being are not only positioned at the interface between Fields A and B, but in fact intrude from the lower into the upper domain. This draws the two fields into a dynamic relationship by juxtaposing elements in the upper part of Field B with elements in Field A on the same horizontal plane. The manner in which the volutes are extruded upward from the snout of the Composite Being imparts an unmistakable directionality to the contact from below to above and establishes an explicit vertical connection between the lower domain occupied by the Composite Being and an upper domain congruent with the earth's surface. There is clearly an intent to underline the conjunction of these upper and lower domains and to manifest the active nature of the connection between them. These details combine to suggest that the Composite Being can be placed below the Displayed Female on a vertical axis.

I have already commented on the formal congruence between Field A as it frames the Displayed Female and the Standing Figure and the facades of large buildings bearing seat motifs. I infer that the naturalistic depictions of the human figures framed within this architectural setting allude to activities taking place within temples or cult buildings dedicated to this purpose. In this human realm, as I noted earlier, a hierarchical distinction is made between the Standing Figure and the Displayed Female.

Another kind of vertical connection is established by the relationship between the Orb and Crescent and the Standing Figure. The Orb and Crescent indicates that the upper domain can be equated with the sky and contrasted with a lower domain relating to the earth's surface signaled by the Standing Figure. The fact that a seat is positioned below the orb reinforces the notion of vertical movement in relation to a position of rest, analogous to the act of sitting itself. The fact that the celestial orb is transposed into the person of the Standing Figure, who is framed by the ordered sets of conventionalized seat symbols occupying Field A, implies that this conjunction of the upper celestial realm with earthly activity is likewise consummated within a temple setting.

Three realms are therefore represented: celestial, earthly, and underworld (Figure 5.5). Special emphasis is placed on the vertical connections between both the underworld and the earth and the celestial realm and the earth. There is a sexual division of earthly activities with a hierarchical distinction being made between male and female. I will now summarize the relationships between these realms and add some further comments.

Combining the Relationships into an Overall Model

So far I have presented the argument for the different set of relationships in terms of a visual logic and have refrained from making interpretive statements. However, enough information has now been discussed to justify an attempt at stating how this visual logic might be read.

The Composite Being combines various characteristics such as the splayed limbs and elongated digits that link it to the general class of batrachians including reptiles, toads, and frogs. It is marked by its sexual ambiguity, and its skeletal spine carries connotations of the ancestral world of the dead. Various ethnographies from northwest South America offer a rich source of comparative material that helps link this archaeological iconography to ethnographic accounts of orally transmitted mythologies and folklore. Throughout tropical lowland societies, frogs are closely connected with concepts of fertility and are widely recognized as harbingers of rain (Wassen 1934:333). Green stones are often fashioned into frog pendants and used as an important medium of exchange, not least for prospective wives (Boomert 1987). Frog-women feature prominently in South American creation mythologies. A Kogi myth tells how the Sun's first wife was a toad who was later banished for being unfaithful. Frogs and toads may have male as much as female characteristics identified and are thought of as embodying sexual desire. In the Bolivian highlands the earth (Pachamama) is said to assume the form of a toad and to walk about at night (Harris 2000:210). Frogs and toads also appear in mythology as devourers of the moon or of fire, and reptiles in general are associated with the primordial world of creation and ancestral time.[22]

I suggest that the Composite Being incorporates many of these characteristics and can be identified as an ancestral being linked with primordial time and chthonic powers. I have emphasized that the way in which the volutes are extruded upward from it establishes an explicit connection between the lower and upper realms. Just as the volutes that emerge from the snout of the Composite Being are transposed to become the ordered sets of conventionalized seat symbols occupying Field A, so the qualities and attributes of the Composite Being are similarly transposed to the Displayed Female. They are revealed in the human realm by the device of the displayed pose. The Composite Being can be seen to project vital qualities into the upper domain and infuse it with these powers. The curvilinear character of the volutes suggests that these powers impel the process of vegetative sprouting and may therefore represent the life forces driving new growth. While these forces are visibly manifest in plant growth, there is an essential invisible dimension entailed, and it is likely that the volutes allude to these powerful, invisible sources of life.

One of the Displayed Females has the same kind of elongated digits that characterizes the Composite Being and this also suggests a shared preoccupation with growth. Being fleshy, fully human, and sexually open, the Displayed Female can be seen as embodying concerns with human fertility, while the flanking monkeys allude to the origins of licentious sexual behavior before this was bound by cultural rules and constraints. The relationship between the Composite Being and the Displayed Female can be read as a transformation of the sub-earthly, chthonic sources of life into a concern with human fertility and procreation. The substitution of the disks in place of the

flanking monkeys implies that the emphasis has shifted to the vital repro-
ductive role of the female in the cultural realm.

By contrast, the Standing Figure is linked to a different set of relationships. Here the emphasis is placed on the vertical connection between the celestial realm and the earth's surface as the setting for human activity. The juxtaposition of the Orb above the seat implies that sitting is entailed. The Orb
can be associated with the sun as the dominant celestial object and identified as male. The "sitting of the sun" might on the one hand be taken to indicate the solstices in June and December, because this is when the sun is at
rest on the horizon, "sitting in its seat." Without continuous movement along
the horizon, this period of stasis underlines a concern with verticality. Alternatively, it is possible that zenith and antizenith passages of the sun also
provide a rationale for a similar focus on verticality. Two fundamental sets of
relationships are paramount: the vertical connection between the subterranean and the earthly realm, and its corollary between the celestial sphere and
the earth. I have shown that seat iconography plays a vital intermediary role
in both sets of relationships. Seating is instrumental in effecting the vertical connection and conjunction between these realms, and the timing of the
vertical relationships established by celestial phenomena may give the clue
to the timing of the seating rituals themselves.

I have argued that the naturalistic female and male figures may allude
to ritual practice in a special category of buildings, such as temples or cult
shrines set apart from everyday concerns. Based on a possible interest in vertical connections made around the time of the solstices, it is possible to hypothesize that one kind of building might be invested with the chthonic,
ancestral powers derived from the relationship with the Composite Being,
while another could have closer connections to the celestial realm, depending upon the time of year.

One clue that might offer a visual signifier identifying these kinds of buildings is found in the meanders that flank the snout of the Composite Being
and in the way that the volutes terminate in spirals. These can be compared
with the temple facades represented on seals, on which the meanders flank
the entrance to the building and the spiral motifs are transposed to the roof
crest. This idea is supported by the way that the distinguishing elements on
the Composite Being's snout, namely the eyes and the dentition, are likewise
transposed to become the masks over the building doorways. Thus the upturned head of the Composite Being is transposed on the earthly plane into
the frontal facade of the temple.[23] The facades are decorated with distinctive
motifs that signal their sacred character marking the threshold and entrance
to an ancestral domain.

In sum, I have suggested that there is a concern with two main aspects of verticality expressed in the stela iconography. One is focused on the sub-earthly figure of the Composite Being that embodies powers of growth that are transposed upward into the human realm. The second vertical relationship connects an upper celestial realm with the earthly plane. In both cases, it is evident that seats are positioned on the earthly plane at the interface between the sub-earthly realm on the one hand and the upper celestial realm on the other.

Two questions present themselves at this point. First, at what time or times of the year was there a heightened awareness of the conjunction and interpenetration of these realms? Second, what kind of formal ritual activity might have been linked to this? Some material clues as to where and when rituals were enacted might lie in the location of the stelae at Cerro Jaboncillo. Evaluating this involves looking at the distribution of the stelae among the buildings positioned on the summit plateau and adjacent ridges, combined with the arrangement of stelae within specific buildings. The information that can be extracted from Saville's notes about the provenience of individual stelae is limited. He gives a secure structure provenience for a total of eight stelae. This is scant evidence upon which to base an argument, but I will venture some initial observations and suggestions.

Two stelae are said to have come from Structure 17 on the Northern Arm, both of which feature the Displayed Female with flanking monkeys.[24] Farther upslope on the same ridge, two more stelae come from Structure 29. Again, both feature the Displayed Female but this time with flanking interarthral disks replacing the monkeys. In the Mound Group, two stelae come from Structure 46, one representing the Standing Figure flanked by two birds and the other the upper half of a Displayed Female. Also from Structure 40 in the Northern Group on the plateau comes the upper fragment of a stela with the Orb and Crescent positioned above the arms of a seat. Based on this information, it is possible to surmise that the stelae might have been arranged to follow a sequence progressing from the foot of Cerro Jaboncillo up to the summit plateau. If this were the case, it would give grounds for suggesting that a ritual progression could have been keyed to this sequence.[25]

It is notable that two stelae are reported from several structures, and in the cases of Structures 17 and 29 these are paired, though not identical. If this is taken at face value, and given that the stelae bear designs on just one side that were presumably intended to be seen, then some possible permutations for their arrangement within a given structure can be suggested. I have already noted that across the site as a whole, there seem to be many more seats than stelae at Cerro Jaboncillo and, insofar as can be determined, this also seems to be the case within individual structures. On the basis of the exca-vated evidence at Agua Blanca, one potential arrangement is that the seats were aligned along the side walls and faced inward toward the middle of the building. This might suggest that two (or perhaps more) stelae could have been placed in the central space, and perhaps even back to back in order to facilitate viewing from both sides of the building. Alternatively, they could have been placed side by side against the rear wall of a structure, conceiv-ably flanking a seated individual, or perhaps themselves flanked by seats. There is no firm evidence at the moment to suggest which may be correct or whether there were different permutations as opposed to a single prescribed arrangement.

In sum, the buildings with stelae seem to have housed one or two each. Since the bases of the stelae were buried, once placed they are not likely to have been moved. The buildings therefore offered a permanent setting for gatherings of small groups of individuals engaged in formal seating rituals at prescribed times of the year.

Summary Discussion of Ceramic Figurines Showing Seats

The different groups of ceramic figurines provide key insights into the differ-ent kinds of ritual contexts in which seating played a role. The main corpus of young, naked, seated male figures with body paint shown on the *incensarios* likely represents the culmination of what was probably a sequence of cere-monies in which naked males have body ornament applied and are then for-mally seated signaling their transition from adolescence to adulthood. These would be occasions for imparting esoteric lore about the origins of life and the creation of social order in human communities. The stepped form of the bases marks the boundary between the sub-earthly domain and the earth's surface upon which the seat rests.

In contrast, another significant group involves senior male figures and possibly priests standing in seats, and some of these too have stepped bases. The figures' elaborate attire signals their rank and status in the community. The fact that they are standing underlines the vertical connections to the celestial realm. The elaborate necklace of incised beads worn by one figure suggests that these individuals may be charged with responsibility for calen-drical calculation and notation and, by implication, with the timing of the festivals and ceremonies. Some of the standing figures have lime flasks sus-pended on their chests. This establishes a connection with other seated se-nior males shown with lime flasks and spatulas in hand ingesting lime to mix with the quid of coca leaves that is often visible in their cheeks.

These two groups suggest two contrasting kinds of seating rituals, one

connected with initiation rites for young men and the other linked to senior males gathered, it might be surmised, to engage in deliberations and
discussion.

On the other hand there is a limited corpus of material related to women.
While some occupy seats, others are seated on the ground. The latter find
their counterpart in other Andean traditions in depictions of presumably
women in displayed pose linked hand to hand in rows. These collective ceremonies may represent aspects of the female initiation ceremonies that are the
counterpart to the male rituals involving stools. A kind of feminine arche-
type for the displayed pose is found in the Taíno female ancestress engraved
as a petroglyph at the ceremonial center of Caguana, Puerto Rico. Together
with a male ancestor, she forms the focus of an array of other mythical beings, as well as images of significant species of fish, birds, and other creatures
(Oliver 1998).

On Being and Becoming: Seats and Seating Rituals

In a fundamental way, the natural *meseta* topography with plateaulike geological structures overlooking the flat coastal plain was surely influential in
the decision to designate Cerro Jaboncillo as a special-purpose site. Its location on a "hilltop in the clouds" amid the permanent verdure of the cloud
forest suggests a connection to a "primordial" time of fertile abundance. The
extraordinary assemblage of stone sculpture confirms that this was an important setting for significant ritual events. The topography naturally helped to
accentuate the contrast between the dry xerophytic vegetation typical of the
plain and the more luxuriant green vegetation of the tops sustained by the *garua* mists and fogs. Human intentionality likely found expression in the idea
of using this secluded location to address ritual concerns revolving around
the annual cycle of fertility and procreation and the mystery of the origins of
life. Linked to temporal solar and lunar rhythms, these must have focused in
turn on the creation of social order with seasonal events drawing congrega-
tions of participants from surrounding settlements and farther afield. Fieldwork currently under way on the lower flanks of Cerro Jaboncillo is revealing
extensive residential complexes that bear this out (Richard Lunniss, personal
communication 2011). The recurring nature of these activities would have affirmed and reinforced the transmission of oral and visual cultural traditions.

The iconography on the stelae offers key insights into these ritual concerns. Based on the principal figure on each stela, I have identified four main
groups: the Composite Being, the Displayed Female, the Standing Figure,
and the Orb and Crescent. I have demonstrated how they are linked to each
other by a set of transformational relationships and how they reveal an over-
riding concern with the vertical alignment between the underworld, the earth,

and the celestial realm. The landscape setting and the architectural and sculptural contexts, in which this suite of motifs was deployed, bear comparison with other ceremonial centers such as San Augustin and Caguana.[26]

The iconographic links between the stelae and the stone seats and the fact that they are found together with other sculpture in an architectural context on Cerro Jaboncillo confirm that they are integral elements of the same ritual complex. The fact that the seats and other sculpture are distributed up the length of the Northern Arm and across the summit plateau means that visitors to the site had to follow an ascending path up the ridge, passing individual buildings and groups of buildings housing seats and stelae. I have considered whether, in the course of this ascent, there might be evidence for a prescribed ritual order in which the sculptures were to have been visited and viewed. Alternatively, is it possible to posit that the distribution could reflect a representation of different geographical groups at the ceremonial center— each, for example, with its own house or shrine? A corollary to this is to ask whether any spatial order or ranking can be detected, and whether this culminates in a distinctive order or spatial arrangement at the summit complexes with their associated sculpture.

Evidently, the seats are much more numerous than the stelae. In at least one case, anthropomorphic and zoomorphic seats were housed in the same structure. Both anthropomorphic and feline seats are found at Cerro Jaboncillo, so clearly they were used in conjunction with each other, perhaps expressing an opposed and complementary relationship alluded to earlier. However, stone stools with lower wings are also found, hinting that there was probably a hierarchy of seats as well as different kinds of seating rituals. Nor can we discount the use of seats in wood, metal, or even ceramic, for which little or no evidence now exists. As many as a dozen seats are found in a single structure, while there appear to have been only one or two stelae per structure. This is suggestive of the kind of formal seating arrangements documented at Agua Blanca.

In attempting to propose a temporal framework for these events, I have drawn on the data obtained from Agua Blanca as well as the internal evidence derived from the iconographic analysis of seats and stelae at Cerro Jaboncillo. The dry-to-wet-season transition in December is of critical importance, and I suggest that this is the primary reason for the attention that has been paid to the December solstice. The cosmological turning point represented by the reversal of the sun's movement across the horizon would have been matched by a ritual concern with the approaching transition from the dry season to the critical winter rains upon which the earth's fertility and the life of the community ultimately depended. I suggest, therefore, that the concerns with earthly fertility were matched by a preoccupation with human sexuality and that the initiation rituals preparing the young boys for the transition from adolescence to adulthood could well have been carried out at precisely this time of the year.

In addition, there is a corpus of figurines from Cerro Jaboncillo depicting senior males chewing coca. These form part of a wider pattern in Andean archaeological traditions of seated figures chewing coca that can be linked to ethnographic accounts of coca use among both highland and lowland peoples today. The initiation rituals inferred at Cerro Jaboncillo are likely to have taken place in the presence of senior males and there may also have been an autonomous set of seating protocols involving senior males representing their respective communities. Together they affirm the significance of this hilltop as the setting for enacting the enduring traditions that underpinned the creation of social order.

Notes

1. Many are said to come from Cerro Jaboncillo but they are probably not restricted to this site alone. I have seen one example brought down from an unknown location in the hills east of Agua Blanca.

2. "En la plataforma del sello, o sea la parte superior que cubre el plano impreso, hay una linea incisa ancha cual cruza el sello en su parte central, haciendo una vertical, la cual servia como orientacion al que estampaba" (Parducci Zevallos 1968:77, Figure 1a).

3. This recalls the designs painted on Tukano stools that often emphasize a central axis (McEwan 2001). Some Manteño figurines also depict priests standing on seats, underlining the significance of the vertical axial relationship.

4. While the stelae in the Saville collection and some of those held by the Anthropological Museums of the Banco Central in Quito and Guayaquil have been published, an unknown number of others are scattered in both museum and private collections. No photos are available for these and, in parallel with future work on the seats, there is an obvious need to assemble a comprehensive archive of images and to combine this with the analysis of samples to determine their geological provenience.

5. As with the stone seats, I am sure that on stylistic and geological grounds it will eventually be possible to securely provenience the whole range of stone sculpture including all the stelae held in museums and private collections.

6. Since at least some of the stelae were found within structures, it is possible that they were placed against a wall. There is, however, no published account of a stela base being excavated in situ to substantiate this. Clearly, they were intended to be viewed frontally rather than in the round.

7. A boundary meander motif consisting of repeated rectangular spiral elements runs around the outer edge of one stela. A similar meander motif is found running around the leading edge of a number of stone seats.

8. Beginning with Saville, the Composite Being and the Displayed Female in Manteño art have been compared with other similar representations in pre-Columbian iconography. Saville, for example, compared the Displayed Woman as a frontally posed figure with the Aztec goddess Tlazolteotl. Fraser noted that the images of a monster with clawed hands and feet framed in a stepped pyramid and with open jaws pointing upward have a disk above, like those found flanking the Displayed Female figure. He observed that these "strongly suggest an earth monster or sun-swallower, a creature that in so many parts of the world daily devours the sun or moon and becomes by extension a symbol of death" (Fraser 1966:45). Fraser conflated the two images by suggesting that "the similarity of form and posture support the view that she represents the Great Earth Mother from which all life is reborn" (Fraser 1966:54). Such ancestral earth goddesses who reveal birth-giving as well as apotropaic aspects are well known in Mesoamerica (e.g., Cordy-Collins 1982).

9. The term *batrachian* has been used by anthropologists in the Caribbean and Northern Andes to refer to the order of reptiles that embraces frogs, toads, lizards, alligators, and caimans.

10. There are, of course, many examples in pre-Columbian iconographic traditions that combine a range of zoomorphic and anthropomorphic attributes.

11. Another well-known Andean monument depicting a reptilian similarly transposed from the horizontal to the vertical is the Tello Obelisk, showing a pair of caimans on an axial plinth.

12. In a general way these volutes can be compared to the spiral volutes grasped by the seated figures portrayed in certain Quimbaya cast-gold objects.

13. The vertebrae of frogs and toads are often very visible just under the surface of the skin. Some have dorsal markings that emphasize the spinal column. Certain reptiles including iguanas have a serrated back.

14. The Composite Being appears on other rare archaeological objects such as a hammered silver plaque and two conical headpieces that are among rare surviving Manteño metal objects in the collections of the Museo Antropologico del Banco Central (Guayaquil). These may have formed a set. The plaque has small perforations around its circumference, which suggest that it could have been sewn onto a textile and worn as a pectoral. Both objects feature the Composite Being portrayed in a pose identical to that on the stelae. Just as on the stelae, the Composite Being is represented in dorsal view, oriented vertically with its snout facing upward. The vertical spinal column and elongated digits are emphasized, as is the conventionalized diamond-shaped abdomen. The figure on the crown explicitly shows the volute motifs emanating directly from its snout. This provides an important link to the ritual events connected to the stelae and the seats. I am grateful to Olaf Holm for drawing my attention to these objects, although I regret that I have no additional information on their provenience.

15. Since their original publication by Saville, the displayed females on the Man-

teño stelae from Manabí have appeared in several treatments of cross-cultural themes in primitive art (Abramson 1990:154, Figure 3; Fraser 1966:74–77; Schuster 1951:4, Figure 1). They are also illustrated in standard texts such as Meggers 1966 and Willey 1971.

16. These designs have been variously interpreted as headdresses (Schuster 1951:42), as being "textile-like" (Kubler 1962:232), or as being derived from a stepped gable pattern that appears above Bahía seated figures (Fraser 1966:76–77; cf. Estrada and Meggers 1961:Figure 1a).

17. This had its origins in Germany with the Kulturkreis school. Diffusionist ideas were subsequently developed by a variety of European and North American anthropologists, among them Heine-Geldern, Eckholm, Fraser, and others.

18. Outstanding among these is Carl Schuster, who devoted a lifetime to assembling a comprehensive archive of materials organized thematically. This work culminated in the series of volumes published by Schuster and Carpenter (1986) and summarized in Schuster and Carpenter (1996). Schuster avoided forcing his material into a diffusionist framework but rather sought to develop a more objective methodology as a basis for comparative studies.

19. I suggest that the designs on pottery stamps represent the facades of large buildings, some with figures standing at the entrance. The stepped boundary motif also demarcates the threshold or juncture between an upper and lower domain elsewhere in Manteño art, especially in the ceramic figurines of individuals standing or sitting in seats. It is analogous to the stepped base of the seat pedestal, and the volutes can be compared to the arms of the seat. Implicitly, this design embodies the idea of a stepped or elevated surface: land or mountain, in terms of topography, or a platform mound or pyramid as a cultural construction.

20. One example from Mesoamerica that deploys this convention to depict a seating arrangement within an architectural setting is the Mapa Quinatzin.

21. One figurine illustrated by Saville shows a seated monkey masturbating, suggesting sexual incontinence. Part of the design is "airbrushed" out to preserve propriety.

22. The iguana commonly found on the coast of Ecuador lives in underground burrows. There the female lays and hatches her eggs only when the rains have come. The young have a skin that shines an iridescent, shimmering green in keeping with the sprouting green of new vegetation. Later this fades to a dark green/brown-red pelage as the reptile matures.

23. The large zoomorphic images sculpted in stone that Saville found on Cerro Jaboncillo and characterized as feline heads might in fact be identified with the Composite Being of the stelae.

24. Saville's information here is not consistent. He states in the text that five fragments that together composed one whole stela were recovered from within this structure. Elsewhere he illustrates two stelae attributed to Structure 17.

25. The fact that the Displayed Female appears on the summit and that an elaborately attired Standing Figure is found at Structure 18 on the ridge (between 17 below and 29 above) undermines the argument for this kind of straightforward progression. An alternate rationale for explaining the distribution of structures and their associated stone sculpture is outlined in the conclusion.

26. A similar context is offered by the suite of petroglyphs at the Taíno ceremonial center of Caguana in Puerto Rico that form the subject of a study by José Oliver (1998).

References Cited

Abramson, J.
  1990   Structural Aspects of Visual Art Design and Their Relation to Broader Sociocultural Contexts. *Empirical Studies of the Arts* 8(2):149–191.
Boomert, Arie
  1987   Gifts of the Amazons: Green Stone Pendants and Beads as Items of Ceremonial Exchange in Amazonia and the Caribbean. *Antropologica* 67:33–54.
Burger, Richard L.
  2008   Chavín de Huántar and Its Sphere of Influence. In *Handbook of South American Archaeology,* edited by Helaine Silverman and William H. Isbell, pp. 681–703. Springer, New York.
Chávez, Sergio J.
  2004   The Yaya-Mama Religious Tradition as an Antecedent of Tiwanaku. In *Tiwanaku: Ancestors of the Inca,* edited by Margaret Young-Sánchez, pp. 70–93. Denver Art Museum and University of Nebraska Press, Lincoln.
Cordy-Collins, Alana
  1982   Earth Mother/Earth Monster Symbolism in Ecuadorian Manteño Art. In *Pre-Columbian Art History: Selected Readings,* 2nd ed., edited by Alana Cordy-Collins, pp. 205–230. Peek Publications, Palo Alto, California.
Estrada, Emilio
  1957   *Prehistoria de Manabí.* Publicación 4. Museo Victor Emilio Estrada, Guayaquil, Ecuador.
  1962   *Arqueología de Manabí Central.* Publicación 7. Museo Victor Emilio Estrada, Guayaquil, Ecuador.
Estrada, Emilio, and Betty Meggers
  1961   A Complex of Traits of Probable Transpacific Origin on the Coast of Ecuador. *American Anthropologist* 63:913–939.
Fraser, Douglas
  1966   The Heraldic Woman: A Study in Diffusion. In *The Many Faces of Primitive Art,* edited by Douglas Fraser, pp. 36–99. Prentice Hall, Englewood Cliffs, New Jersey.

Guinea, Mercedes

2004   Los Símbolos del Poder o el Poder de los Símbolos. In *Símbolismo y Ritual en los Andes Septentrionales,* edited by Mercedes Guinea, pp. 9–49. Ediciones Abya-Yala, Quito.

Harris, Olivia

2000   The Mythological Figure of the Earth Mother. In *To Make the Earth Bear Fruit: Ethnographic Essays on Fertility, Work and Gender in Highland Bolivia,* edited by Olivia Harris, pp. 201–219. Institute of Latin American Studies, London.

Holm, Olaf

1992   *Cultura Manteño-Huancavilca.* Museo del Banco Central, Guayaquil, Ecuador.

Kubler, George

1962   *The Shape of Time: Remarks on the History of Things.* Yale University Press, New Haven, Connecticut.

Lévi-Strauss, Claude

1958   *Structural Anthropology.* Penguin, London.

McEwan, Colin

2001   *Seats of Power: Axis and Access to Invisible Worlds in Unknown Amazon: Culture in Nature in Ancient Brazil,* edited by Colin McEwan, Christiana Barreto, and Eduardo Neves, pp. 176–197. British Museum Press, London.

2004   And the Sun Sits in His Seat: Creating Social Order in Andean Culture. Unpublished Ph.D. dissertation, Department of Anthropology, University of Illinois, Urbana.

McEwan, Colin, and Florencio Delgado-Espinoza

2008   Late Pre-Hispanic Polities of Coastal Ecuador. In *Handbook of South American Archaeology,* edited by Helaine Silverman and William H. Isbell, pp. 505–525. Springer, New York.

Meggers, Betty J.

1966   *Ecuador.* Thames and Hudson, London.

Oliver, José R.

1998   *El Centro Ceremonial de Caguana, Puerto Rico: Simbolismo Iconografico, Cosmovision, y el Poderio Caciquil Taino de Boriquen.* BAR International Series, 727. Archaeopress, Oxford.

Parducci Zevallos, Resfa

1968   Un Sello Excepcional. *Cuadernos de Historia y Arqueología,* año XVIII, 34-5:75ff.

Saville, Marshall H.

1907   *The Antiquities of Manabí, Ecuador: Preliminary Report.* Contributions to South American Archaeology 1. Heye Foundation, New York.

1910   *The Antiquities of Manabí, Ecuador: Final Report.* Contributions to South American Archaeology 2. Heye Foundation, New York.

Schuster, Carl

 1951   Joint-Marks: A Possible Index of Cultural Contact between America, Oceania and the Far East. *Koninklijk voor Tropen, Medeleling* 44. *Afdeling Culturale en Physiche Anthropologie* 39:3–51.

Schuster, Carl, and Edmund Carpenter

 1986   *Materials for the Study of Social Symbolism in Ancient and Tribal Art.* 10 vols. Rock Foundation, New York.

 1996   *Patterns That Connect: Social Symbolism in Ancient and Tribal Art.* Harry N. Abrams, New York.

Silva, Maria-Isabel

 1985   Dual Division Quadripartition and Hierarchical Organization among the Manteño Polities of Late Pre-Columbian Coastal Ecuador. Paper presented at the International Congress of Americanists, Bogota, July 1985.

Wassen, Henry S.

 1934   The Frog-Motive among the South American Indians: Ornamental Studies. *Anthropos* 29:319–370.

Willey, Gordon R.

 1971   *South American Archaeology.* Prentice Hall, Englewood Cliffs, New Jersey.

Williams, Carlos

 1985   Monumental Architecture of the Central Coast of Peru. In *Early Ceremonial Architecture in the Andes,* edited by Christopher B. Donnan, pp. 227–240. Dumbarton Oaks Research Library and Collection, Washington, D.C.

Zuidema, R. Tom

 1998   Introduction. In *El Centro Ceremonial de Caguana, Puerto Rico: Simbolismo Iconografico, Cosmovision, y el Poderio Caciquil Taino de Boriquen,* by José R. Oliver, pp. ii–iii. BAR International Series, 727. Archaeopress, Oxford.

6
Hopi Clan Traditions and the Pedigree of Ceremonial Objects

Wesley Bernardini

Hopi clan migration traditions have appealed to archaeologists because they include lists of named, identifiable archaeological sites, details that inspired early researchers like Jesse Walter Fewkes to try to trace contemporary Hopi clans directly back into the archaeological record (e.g., Fewkes 1900). Yet a disjuncture between the time spans covered by clan oral traditions and the life spans of the clans who hold them calls into question the historical veracity of these stories. Hopi clan traditions often cover hundreds of years, but small kinship units rarely survive the whims of fertility and mortality for more than a few generations (e.g., Gaines and Gaines 1997).

Resolving this apparent paradox requires a reassessment of how clan traditions are transmitted across generations. Although traditional Hopi ethnography depicts clans as corporate units, historical evidence demonstrates that clan traditions are not transmitted genealogically as part of the inheritance package of a unilineal descent group. Instead, the control of ceremonies passes among clans over generations, suggesting that clan traditions do not recount the history of a single, unilineal group. Rather, clan traditions are argued to trace the history of ceremonies, control of which is legitimized by possession of ritual objects and the ritual knowledge attached to them. In essence, then, migration traditions thus recount not a genealogy of people but a *pedigree of objects.*

Hopi Clan Migration Traditions

According to Hopi *navoti* (traditional knowledge), upon emergence into this world from the *Sipápuni,* the place of emergence, Hopi ancestors entered into a spiritual contract with *Maasaw,* Guardian of the World, to migrate until they reached *Tuuwanasavi,* the earth center on the Hopi Mesas (Dongoske et al. 1997:603; Leigh Kuwanwisiwma, personal communication

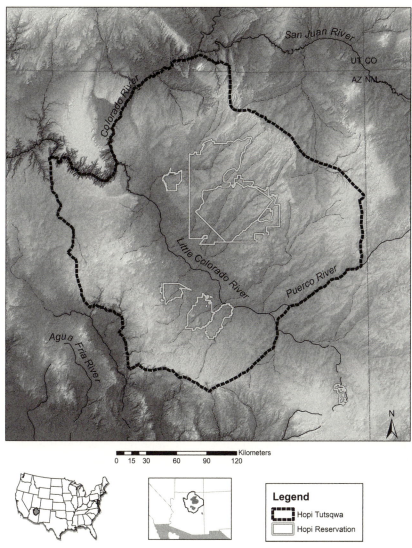

Figure 6.1. *Tuuwanasavi,* the earth center on the Hopi Mesas, in the middle of the Hopi Tutsqwa, the area of traditional Hopi land use bounded by shrines.

1998) (Figure 6.1). At various points along their migrations, groups of travelers acquired an affiliation with a *wuya,* or totem, which provided them with a name and a symbolic association. Some groups also acquired the knowledge to perform ceremonies, the potency of which determined whether or not they were accepted into villages they petitioned for entrance and their status once they entered (Eggan 1950:64; Fewkes 1900:585).

Movement was frequent in this migration period, often occurring on a subgenerational frequency (Bernardini 2005a:61–69; Parsons 1939:14), and it was such a defining aspect of life for ancestral Puebloans that they have been described as "urbanized nomads" (Fox 1967:24). A tradition of movement remains deeply ingrained in Pueblo thought (Naranjo 1995), with life conceptualized as a journey on a road (Fowles 2011; Parsons 1939:17). In fact, the Hopi conceptualize ancestral territories in ways similar to hunter-gatherer groups, as linear pathways of travel rather than as two-dimensional geographic blocks (Bernardini 2005a:168, 2005b; cf. Ingold 1980:155).

The migration pathways described in clan migration traditions were complex, overlapping, and irregular. Cosmos Mindeleff (1900:645) described them as "a little trickling stream of humanity, or rather many such streams, like little rivulets after a rain storm, moving here and there as the occurrence of areas of cultivable land dictated, sometimes combining, then separating, but finally collecting to form the pueblo groups as we now know them." The nature of these migration traditions is well illustrated by a portion of the Horn Clan story recorded by Fewkes:

> After the Horn clans parted from the Snake people in their migration southward from Tokonabi, they drifted into an eastern place called Lokotaaka. How far eastward they went is not known, but from Lokotaaka they moved to Kisiwi, and then to Monpa, where ruins are still to be seen. Continuing in their migration, which, after they left Lokotaaka, was toward the west, they came to a pueblo they called Lenyanobi, "Place of the Flute" (clans). There they evidently united with the Flute people, and from that time the group was composite. The combined clans did not remain at Lenyanobi, but moved by way of Wikyaobi to a point called Kwactapabi, where they were well within the present Hopi reservation. The route from Kwactapabi to Walpi, where they joined the Snake pueblo, was by Wipo, Kanelba, and Lenyacupu, or Kokyanba (Spider Spring) [Fewkes 1900:590].

The Nature of Hopi Clans

Although kinship (real or fictive) is extended to all members of a clan, clan ancestors are not tracked or venerated, and little interest is shown in tracing genealogy beyond the third or fourth generation (Kroeber 1917:129; Titiev 1944:46). Tooker (1971) traces a lack of emphasis on genealogical descent in certain societies to a lack of inheritable property. For ancestral Puebloan farmers, the spatial and temporal variability of rain-fed fields may have weakened the development of formal inheritance practices that are usually well established in agricultural societies. A social landscape defined by movement on a subgenerational frequency would also reduce concern with the inheritance of fixed resources, in addition to obscuring genealogical ties.

As Whiteley (1985, 1986) has shown, clans are not corporate groups united in their control of land and ceremony. Rather, a clan consists of a core household surrounded by a number of other groups in an "orbital" arrangement of dependence and support (Connelly 1979:542–543). The senior woman of the core household is signified by the modifier "*yü'amü*," which means "clan their mother," for example, *Suwi'inwüñwu yü'amü*, "Deer clan its mother" (Parsons 1969:70, 1048). The brother of the clan mother typically serves as the *wimmomngwit*, or chief priest of the ceremony "handed" (as the Hopi say) by the clan (Parsons 1922:284). Offices and privileges are thus held "not in the clan as a whole, but in a maternal family or lineage in the clan" (Parsons 1933:23). Lowie (1929:330) clarified that "whenever the statement is made that a certain office or ceremonial privilege belongs to a clan, concrete data always show that transmission is, above all, within the narrow circle of actual blood-kin and only secondarily extends to unrelated clansmen."

Core households are marked in several ways, most obviously through control of a ceremony. Ceremonial performance is the means by which clans are integrated into a community, giving "meaning to the clan and to the individual, for it is through the performance of one's clan-ascribed ceremonial duties as much as through anything else that one feels oneself a part of Hopi society and, more broadly, the cosmos under the guidance of spirit beings" (Schlegel 1992:382). Since the exercise of a ceremony is regarded as essential to the common welfare, all clans are bound together in an "organization of interdependence" (White 1959:157). Preservation of the ceremony, in fact, is more important than preservation of the clan. In some ways, clan is merely a "verbal convenience"; it was the ceremony that provided a benefit to the community and was therefore indispensable (Parsons 1936:231).

The special status of the core segment of a village clan is also marked with the term *pas* (meaning "real")—for example, Pashonanngyam ("Real Badger"), the core segment, vs. Masihonanngyam ("Gray Badger"), an orbiting segment (Titiev 1944:53; Whiteley 1986:74). At Zuni, the appellation for these core segments is *mossiye* or *ashi'I*, meaning "clan people name having" (Kroeber 1917:133). Informants rarely miscategorize the members of the "real" clan, but individuals outside this core may be classified in a variety of ways depending on their perceived proximity to the core. Thus, a village clan's identity is most clearly embodied by the core household.

Further, it is within the core segment that most of the traditional knowledge of the clan is held. Parsons (1921) distinguishes between esoteric and exoteric tradition—the first known only to special persons, the second being general knowledge. Exoteric clan migration traditions, known to all clan members, are general stories recounting the experience that gave a clan its name (e.g., an encounter with a badger) and a general sense of the origin and route of the clan's migrations. The esoteric migration traditions held by the clan chief, however, contain an "abundance . . . of *localization details*" (Parsons 1921:209–210 [emphasis added], 1933:35)—that is, lists of places the clan has lived. These place lists are occasionally sung by clan chiefs in the *wü'wü'yum lavai'ita*, "old men's speech" (Parsons 1969:713–714).

Finally, and most important for this study, the core household is marked by its custodianship of the fetish (or figurine or mask) and other ceremonial paraphernalia used in the ceremony controlled by the clan (Parsons 1969:70). All other markers of the status of the core household follow from its possession of the fetish, without which it lacks legitimacy.

The Clan Fetish

William Duncan Strong (1927) called attention to a pattern found across Pueblo society, as well as parts of southern California, that he termed the "group house, group-fetish, group-priest complex." This pattern revolves around control of a group fetish, called a *ma'swut* among southern California groups like the Serrano and Cahuilla, that is kept in the clan house by the clan mother. Among the Hopi these ritual objects are called *wiimi*, paramount among which are the *tiiponi*, the fetish or palladium of a clan chief that "bears in its womb all seeds, hence is mother of all" (Fewkes 1901:214; Parsons 1969:1305). These objects "are so sacred that they are regarded as the 'heart' of the clan" (Parsons 1922:289; Titiev 1944:55).

It is possession of the fetish that legitimizes control of a ritual by the core segment of a village clan. Thus, clan mothers are important "not because they perpetuate the clan but because in their houses they look after the fetishes of the ceremonies" (Parsons 1936:231). Alexander Stephen (Parsons 1969:1073) recorded that "the holder of the *tiiponi* is the chief of the society and head of the clan," deliberately phrasing this observation to show that it is possession of the object that makes the officer, rather than that an officer signifies his status through possession of an object. The term *nanakpétotá* is used to refer to "those who are trustees or owners of a ceremony," which translates as "they pass it [the *tiiponi*] along" (Parsons 1933:65). Although inheritance of the *wiimi* ideally remains within the genealogical line of the core household, it can and does pass out of it without losing any legitimacy in the eyes of the community, for it is the object that conveys authenticity upon the group, not the reverse. In fact, there are no actual totems of Hopi clans (e.g., a crane figurine for the Crane Clan), "because the fetish is primarily associated with the ceremony and only derivatively with the clan" (Parsons 1936:231). The intimate bond between the fetish and the ceremony is demonstrated by the fact that there are no *tiiponis* that symbolize village offices, such as *kikmongwi* (Village Chief) or Town Crier (Bradfield 1973:14–15; Parsons 1969:1074). Instead, possession of the *tiiponi* of a ceremony carried with it the responsibility of filling a village office, for example, the Soyal *tiiponi* for the office of *kikmongwi* at Oraibi. In fact, the term *wiimi* actually has two meanings: the first indicating a ceremony, the second the altar objects necessary to perform that ceremony (Parsons 1969:1318).

Possession of the clan fetish is so critical to the performance of ceremony and therefore the existence and identity of the clan that the migration of a village clan is in fact more accurately described as the movement of the fetish. Thus, "when a Hopi refers to migration of clan he is really referring to a migration by a fetish-holding maternal family . . . in native philosophy it is the clan fetish or the clan mask . . . which holds the group together" (Parsons 1922:289, 1933:37). For instance, when the Hopi village of Oraibi split in 1906, the Spider maternal family took the *tiiponi* of the Antelope ceremony to the village of Hotavilla; from then on, the ceremony was celebrated at Hotavilla but not Oraibi (Parsons 1922:289 n. 14). The ceremony authenticated by a fetish features prominently in clan migration traditions, with ceremony and clan name serving as almost interchangeable monikers for the group. For example, "the Patki clan came from where the sun rises; they had with them the Gray Flute ceremony" (Voth 1905:28–30), and "the Parrot and Crow clans, who had the Blue Flute cult . . . The Crane and Eagle clan brought the Drab Flute and Marau cult . . . The Sand Clan, with the Lagon, Soyal, and Snake cult" (Voth 1905:47–48).

Critically, "tradition of provenience accompanies the *wiimi* and is more reliable than tradition of clan provenience or origin" (Parsons 1939:970). That the pedigree of ceremonial objects is very much in the consciousness of Hopis is evident from information given by Pautiwa (Ned Zeena), a Tobacco Clan chief at Walpi, about fetishes from Awat'ovi, a Hopi village destroyed by other Hopi villages in 1700. Pautiwa told the anthropologist Harold Courlander that, prior to the destruction of Awat'ovi, "the Tobacco Clan leader [Taapalo] took all the sacred *tiponi* and brought them here." Courlander notes, "The narrator here refers not only to Tobacco Clan paraphernalia, but to the altars and other sacred objects of the Two Horn, the Wuwuchim, and the Tataukyam kiva societies." Pautiwa continued, "All the sacred things that we have now are from Awat'ovi . . . the other villages just copied those things. But the original ones, we still have them in Walpi" (Courlander 1982:20–21; this narration is discussed in greater detail in Whiteley 2002:153–154). Thus, more than 300 years after the destruction of Awat'ovi, the pedigree of ritual objects is still the basis for identifying "real" clans and ceremonies. It is important to note that although Pautiwa may be a genealogical descendant of Taapalo, he did not claim such descent to substantiate his statement. Pautiwa knew the history of these objects because he was in the line of custodian core households charged with maintaining them.

Kroeber (1917:167) recognized the importance of fetishes in Zuni society, arguing that "the truest understanding of Zuni life . . . can be had by setting the *ettowe* (fetishes) as a center. Around these, priesthoods, fraternities, clan organization, as well as most esoteric thinking and sacred tradition group themselves, while in turn kivas, dances, and acts of public worship can be construed as but the outward means of expression of the inner activities that radiate around the nucleus of the physical fetishes and the ideas attached to them. In other words, he who knows all that is knowable concerning the (fetishes) must necessarily understand substantially the whole of Zuni society." While fetishes have not received the same level of attention at Hopi, Titiev (1944:55 n. 57) came to realize their importance and lamented that he "deeply regret[ted] that circumstances have prevented me from studying this subject more fully while I was in the field." Access to fetishes is very restricted, making them very difficult to study; even ritual performers outside the core segment may not touch them, and they should never be seen by a *pahana,* or white person (Parsons 1933:37).

The Genealogy of People vs. the Pedigree of Objects

We now see that Hopi clan migrations record not a sequence of ancestors, nor even a history of a group per se, but rather the pedigree of ritual objects and the ceremonies they authenticate. Weiner's (1992) idea of "inalienable possessions," recently applied to the American Southwest by Mills (2004), is a useful concept in explaining the role played by these ritual objects. Inalienable objects require special knowledge to produce, knowledge that is passed down through specific chains of individuals, and in contrast to "prestige goods" (Friedman and Rowlands 1977) are rarely circulated. As a consequence of their restricted distribution, limited to those controlling esoteric tradition, inalienable objects become repositories of restricted knowledge, and thus are often featured in ceremonies of authentication and commemoration. Because of these qualities, inalienable possessions help to establish social differentiation "by validating or legitimizing the identity and claims of individuals who are unequal in terms of access to knowledge and resources" (Mills 2004:240).

Migrating groups may have settled on ownership of inalienable objects to signal identity and trace ancestry, rather than genealogy and kinship, because of the fluid, high-mobility social landscape in which they lived. As Parsons (1940:217) notes, "Peripatetic religionists have to work on what they can carry with them. The precious things they live by, their 'bundles,' their altars, they have to transport on their backs, at four days' notice." Orientation of a descent group around durable objects linked to the performance of public ritual provided a social identity that could be readily transferred as communities formed, dissolved, and reformed. Fetishes would also have provided an important check on the profusion of groups claiming ownership of ceremonies, preserving the authenticity and potency of rituals in a new community.

The prehistoric social landscape was thus populated by durable fetishes and ceremonies, owned by descent groups with fluctuating composition, size, rules of membership, symbolic affiliation, and relationships to other descent groups. But because it was essential to be able to demonstrate the pedigree of the fetish to authenticate the ceremony (to both insiders and outsiders), the historical trajectories recorded by clans would still have historical validity. Thus, for example, the fetish-holding core segment of what is now known as the Snake Clan may have been known as the Lizard Clan or the Cactus Clan in the past (segments that today are considered to be "orbiting" the core Snake segment), yet the fetish and the esoteric knowledge at the core of the fetish-ceremony complex could have persisted relatively unchanged. This situation allowed the traditional knowledge held by fetish-holding groups to persist for far longer than it would have if it was transmitted genealogically.

The durability of Hopi ritual objects and knowledge is not hypothetical, as demonstrated by the so-called Magician's Burial, excavated from Ridge Ruin, a small, twelfth-century site 20 miles east of Flagstaff, Arizona (McGregor 1943). The burial, a 35- to 40-year-old male, was accompanied by more than 600 objects, making it among the richest ever recorded in the Southwest. Several Hopi consultants who independently viewed the grave objects identified them as associated with the Momtsit, a Hopi ceremonial warrior society, and the deceased as a member of this society. One of the Hopi consultants was shown only a part of the assemblage and was able to correctly predict in detail other objects that should have been found in association with them, specifying, for example, "a clublike object with serrated edges, a double-horn-like object, and a cap with a point on the top" (Figure 6.2). This consultant also correctly identified the approximate geographical provenience of the burial site based on his clan's ancestral connection to the area (a connection that authorized his clan's continuing right to gather eagles from it). This consultant was apparently a member of the Spider Clan, which controlled the Momtsit ceremony at the Hopi village of Oraibi in the early twentieth century (Levy 1992:74), and thus would have been in a position to hold esoteric knowledge about the pedigree of Momtsit objects. Even Mason (2000:251), who opposes potentially unverifiable uses of oral tradition in archaeology, acknowledged the ability of Hopi consultants to interpret the 800-year-old Magician's Burial as a "powerful example of analogical reasoning backed up and verified by successful prediction from an incomplete test sample."

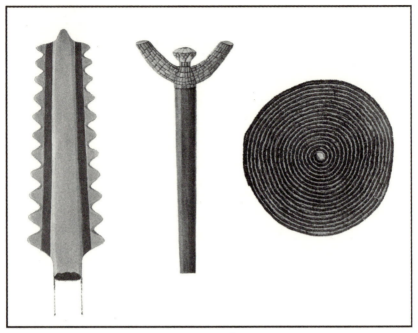

Figure 6.2. Objects interred with the Magician's Burial.

Conclusion

The use of inalienable ritual objects as a vehicle for the transmission of information across generations permits information to persist beyond the lifespan of any given curating group. Understanding this mechanism of transmission helps to explain how Hopi clan traditions can contain historical information that, as in the case of the Magician's Burial, is of greater antiquity than any lineage within the clan. To be sure, the relative insulation of Hopi villages from European and American interference has also helped to preserve cultural knowledge. But the organization of identity-laden group histories around durable ritual objects was the critical mnemonic strategy that accounts for the antiquity of Hopi traditional knowledge.

Accurate transmission of ritual knowledge was likely not a goal in its own right, but rather a strategy that emerged in the context of frequent movement and subgenerational community turnover. Frequent residential mobility would have disrupted genealogical links and weakened the role of lineages in establishing claims on fixed resources like land or water. Coupled with the temporal and spatial unpredictability of rainfall, frequent mobility makes it unsurprising that status differences in ancestral Puebloan societies typically did not revolve around control of productive resources. Hopi tradition recounts that high social status was achieved initially by primacy of place, with first-arriving clans generally acquiring the highest status (Eggan 1966:124–125). This explains, for example, the Bear Clan's role as village chief across all Hopi villages. Yet if the Bear Clan was to maintain its high status in a new setting it would either need to make perpetual preemptive moves or devise a portable means of legitimizing status. The attachment of esoteric historical knowledge to ceremonies and ritual objects provided just such a tool for authenticating difference in a new village and of excluding others from making claims to such status for themselves (Mills 2004).

Acknowledgments

The ideas presented in this chapter developed in part through helpful conversations with Leigh Kuwanwisiwma, Peter Whiteley, T. J. Ferguson, and Warren DeBoer. Their assistance does not imply responsibility for, or endorsement of, this chapter's content.

References Cited

Bernardini, Wesley

2005a   *Hopi Oral Tradition and the Archaeology of Identity.* University of Arizona Press, Tucson.

2005b   Reconsidering Spatial and Temporal Aspects of Prehistoric Cultural Identity: A Case Study from the American Southwest. *American Antiquity* 70: 31–54.

Bradfield, Robert M.

1973   *A Natural History of Associations: A Study in the Meaning of Community,* Vol. 2. International Universities Press, New York.

Connelly, John

1979   Hopi Social Organization. In *Southwest,* edited by A. Ortiz, pp. 539–543. *Handbook of North American Indians,* Vol. 9, William Sturtevant, general editor. Smithsonian Institution, Washington, D.C.

Courlander, Harold

1982   *Hopi Voices: Recollections, Traditions, and Narratives of the Hopi Indians.* University of New Mexico Press, Albuquerque.

Dongoske, Kurt, M. Yeatts, Roger Anyon, and T. J. Ferguson

1997   Archaeological Cultures and Cultural Affiliation: Hopi and Zuni Perspectives in the American Southwest. *American Antiquity* 62:600–608.

Eggan, Fred

1950   *Social Organization of the Western Pueblos.* University of Chicago Press, Chicago.

1966   *The American Indian: Perspectives for the Study of Social Change.* Aldine, Chicago.

Fewkes, Jesse W.

1900   *Tusayan Migration Traditions.* Bureau of American Ethnology Annual Report 19, Pt. 2, pp. 573–634. U.S. Government Printing Office, Washington, D.C.

1901   The Owakulti Altar at Sichomovi Pueblo. *American Anthropologist* 3:211–226.

Fowles, Severin

2011   Movement and the Unsettling of the Pueblos. In *Rethinking Anthropological Perspectives on Migration,* edited by Graciela Cabana and Jeffrey Clark, pp. 45–67. University of Florida Press, Gainesville.

Fox, Robin

1967   *The Keresan Bridge: A Problem in Pueblo Ethnology.* Monographs on Social Anthropology 35. London School of Economics, London.

Friedman, John, and Michael Rowlands

1977   Notes toward an Epigenetic Model of the Evolution of "Civilization." In *The Evolution of Social Systems,* edited by John Friedman and Michael Rowlands, pp. 201–276. Duckworth, London.

Gaines, Sylvia W., and Warren M. Gaines

1997   Simulating Success or Failure: Another Look at Small Population Dynamics. *American Antiquity* 39:683–697.

Ingold, Timothy

1980   *Hunters, Pastoralists, and Ranchers.* Cambridge University Press, Cambridge.

Kroeber, Alfred L.

1917   Zuni Kin and Clan. *Anthropological Papers of the American Museum of Natural History* 18(2):39–204.

Levy, Jerrold E.

1992   *Orayvi Revisited, Social Stratification in an "Egalitarian" Society.* School of American Research Press, Santa Fe, New Mexico.

Lowie, Robert H.

1929   Notes on Hopi Clans. *Anthropological Papers of the American Museum of Natural History* 30(6).

Mason, Ronald J.

2000   Archaeology and Native North American Oral Traditions. *American Antiquity* 65:239–266.

McGregor, John C.

1943   Burial of an Early American Magician. *Proceedings of the American Philosophical Society* 86(2):270–298.

Mills, Barbara

2004   The Establishment and Defeat of Hierarchy: Inalienable Possessions and the History of Collective Prestige Structures in the Pueblo Southwest. *American Anthropologist* 106:238–251.

Mindeleff, Cosmos

1900   *Localization of Tusayan Clans.* Bureau of American Ethnology Annual Report 19, Pt. 2, pp. 639–653. U.S. Government Printing Office, Washington, D.C.

Naranjo, Tessie

1995   Thoughts on Migration by Santa Clara Pueblo. *Journal of Anthropological Archaeology* 14:247–250.

Parsons, Elsie C.

1921   The Pueblo Indian Clan in Folk-Lore. *Journal of American Folklore* 34(132): 209–216.

1922   Contributions to Hopi History. *American Anthropologist* 24:253–298.

1933   *Hopi and Zuni Ceremonialism.* Memoirs 39. American Anthropological Association, Menasha, Wisconsin.

1936   The House-Clan Complex of the Pueblos. In *Essays in Anthropology Presented to A. L. Kroeber,* edited by Robert H. Lowie, pp. 229–231. University of California Press, Berkeley.

1939   *Pueblo Indian Religion.* University of Chicago Press, Chicago.

1940   Relations between Ethnology and Archaeology in the Southwest. *American Antiquity* 5:214–220.

Parsons, Elsie C. (editor)

1969   *The Hopi Journal of Alexander M. Stephen.* AMS Press, New York.

Schlegel, Alice

1992   African Political Models in the American Southwest: Hopi as an Internal Frontier Society. *American Anthropologist* 94:376–397.

Strong, William D.

1927   An Analysis of Southwestern Society. *American Anthropologist* 29:1–61.

Titiev, Mischa

1944   *Old Oraibi: A Study of the Hopi Indians of Third Mesa.* University of New Mexico Press, Albuquerque.

Tooker, Elizabeth

1971   Clans and Moieties in North America. *Current Anthropology* 12:357–376.

Voth, Henry R.

1905   *The Traditions of the Hopi.* Publication 96, Anthropological Series Vol. 8. Field Columbian Museum, Chicago.

Weiner, Annette

1992   *Inalienable Possessions: The Paradox of Keeping-while-Giving.* University of California Press, Berkeley.

White, Leslie

1959   *The Evolution of Culture: The Development of Civilization to the Fall of Rome.* McGraw-Hill, New York.

Whiteley, Peter M.

1985   Unpacking Hopi "Clans": Another Vintage Model out of Africa? *Journal of Anthropological Research* 41:359–374.

1986   Unpacking Hopi "Clans," II: Further Questions about Hopi Descent Groups. *Journal of Anthropological Research* 42:69–79.

2002   Re-imagining Awat'ovi. In *Archaeologies of the Pueblo Revolt: Identity, Meaning, and Renewal in the Pueblo World,* edited by Robert W. Preucel, pp. 147–165. University of New Mexico Press, Albuquerque.

7
Remembering Emergence and Migration in the Southwest Pueblos

Kelley Hays-Gilpin

> The figures in the eternal procession at Barrier Canyon [southeastern Utah]
> are related to us in story. We do not know the story, but we see its enact-
> ment on the face of the earth, that it reaches from the beginning of time
> to the present to a destiny beyond time. We do not know what the story
> means, but more importantly we know that it means, and that we are deeply
> involved in its meaning.
> —N. Scott Momaday (Kiowa) 1993

Half a century ago, the culture area view of North American ethnology defined the Southwest Pueblos as communities who speak diverse languages
but share worldview, a subsistence pattern based on maize agriculture, architectural styles, and certain material culture styles and technologies. The Uto-
Aztecan–speaking Hopi are relatively isolated in northern Arizona; Zuni is
a language isolate in western New Mexico; Keresan is spoken in several villages in western and northern New Mexico. Communities who speak several Tanoan languages are spread along the Rio Grande from northern New
Mexico to El Paso, Texas. Ancestral Pueblo communities extend from the
Las Vegas, Nevada, area on the west to the edge of the Great Plains on the
east, from southern Utah and Colorado on the north to Casas Grandes and
the cliff dwellings of the Sierra Madre in Chihuahua on the south. Ethnographic studies of diversity within this Puebloan culture area have focused
on linking ecological differences (dry farming vs. irrigation) with social organization (matrilineal clans vs. dual divisions); Fred Eggan's (1950) comprehensive synthesis provides the best example and is often cited by archaeologists today.

Only recently have ethnologists and archaeologists examined indigenous
views of the differences among Pueblos or diversity within communities (for

Hopi examples, see Bernardini 2005; Colwell-Chanthaphonh 2003; Colwell-Chanthaphonh and Ferguson 2006; Ferguson et al. 2004; Ferguson and Loma'omvaya 1999; Kuwanwisiwma and Ferguson 2004; Whiteley 2002a, 2002b). Lack of attention to indigenous views is partly due to Pueblo scholars' reluctance to engage in comparative analysis. This reluctance is partly a reaction against previous anthropological generalizations and partly a focus on contemporary needs to develop local histories for local purposes.

Is it appropriate for outsiders to engage in types of analysis that insiders find inappropriate, or at least not very useful? That depends, I think, on one's intentions and one's ability to engage in collaborative discussion about the many possible roles of archaeological methods in assisting indigenous communities. Archaeology may have a role in pressing matters such as land claims and water rights, formulating more accurate representations of historic and contemporary lives in museums and media, and developing cultural and historical curricula for community schools that must balance local desires with mandated state standards. In this chapter, I will offer an outsider's view of long-term Pueblo history that takes into account not only archaeological evidence but also some Puebloan views of historical relationships among communities and of the diverse histories of social groups within some of them. My intention is not only to point the way to more accurate information about long-term history, but also to demonstrate one way out of the static, inaccurate, and not very useful culture area approach to archaeology in the American Southwest and elsewhere. Arguably, this is a foundational step toward understanding the roots of Pueblo religious traditions: Pueblo histories, as conceptualized by Pueblo people, are inextricably parts of Pueblo religion. There is no timeless cosmological template for Pueblo religion. It is all movement, change, landscape, social groups, and encounters among different peoples and deities. Religion here is about remembering and enacting emergence into this world, migration, pilgrimage, earth stewardship, seasons, and life cycles.

I will discuss a few impressions of Puebloan views of the past, based on literature review and on some recent interviews with Hopi cultural specialists, including artists.[1] I do not intend for Hopi examples to represent other Pueblos. Over the past century, archaeologists have tended to use the Hopi and Zuni as somehow typical of all Pueblos, mainly because more published information was available about these western communities but also because Spanish colonization and forced religious conversion were less intense at Hopi than in the New Mexico Pueblos. In addition, the Hopi dry-farming economy is more generalized than the specialized irrigation economy of the Rio Grande Pueblos and thus more closely resembles the economies of most prehistoric Puebloan communities. Unfortunately for my argument about

Pueblo diversity, by virtue of my location at a university and a regional museum in northern Arizona and the collaborative nature of relationships among Northern Arizona University, the Museum of Northern Arizona, and the Hopi Cultural Preservation Office, I am most familiar with Hopi discourse on this subject. The Hopi are not a model for other Pueblos, but the internal diversity of Hopi communities and religion serves as illustration enough of the point I am trying to make about the diverse foundations of Pueblo religion and the roles of diversity in maintaining a rich and resilient religious tradition.

Each Pueblo community has dual divisions, religious sodalities, and kin groups with distinct migration histories, though as Eggan (1950) and others (see especially Ware 2001, 2002; Ware and Blinman 2000) have explained, emphases on different structures vary from east to west. All Pueblos tell stories of emergence, migration, and convergences at center places, though details differ. All Pueblos share flexible networks of symbols and meanings for clouds, water, caves, serpents, birds, certain animals, blue and green stones, shell, maize, directional colors, and more (Schaafsma 1999, 2001; Taube 2000, 2001). Archaeological traces, or "footprints of the ancestors," in the Hopi view (Ferguson and Loma'omvaya 1999; Kuwanwisiwma and Ferguson 2004), connect Pueblo ancestors across language groups and ecological niches. These traces connect some Pueblo ancestors with far-flung ethnic groups in Mexico and beyond. At the same time, different configurations of iconography and specific histories preserve deliberate differences among the Pueblos and heterodoxy within villages.

In the Pueblo view, where something happened is more important than when. When showing a pottery vessel to Hopi consultants, their first question is likely to be "where is it from?" rather than "how old is it?" For example, an image painted on the interior of a fifteenth-century Sikyatki Polychrome bowl (Figure 7.1) reminds some Hopi consultants of a performance called the Ladder Dance that is recounted in traditional histories although it has not been performed since at least the nineteenth century and probably earlier. After identifying the picture as an illustration of this dance, consultants sometimes recall which Hopi villages—no longer inhabited— performed this dance. They may describe the deep, round holes in bedrock at the mesa's edge that held tall poles. These pole sockets can still be seen today, although some archaeologists identify them as bedrock mortars. Some consultants point out that similar dances are still performed by indigenous groups in Mexico, such as the Totonac. This similarity is interpreted as evidence of ancient migration connections. The age of the bowl and the timing of such migrations are less important.

M. Jane Young's interviews about petroglyphs with Zuni consultants re-

Figure 7.1. Sikyatki Polychrome bowl with Shalako, a large katsina or deity with a clacking beak (center), and the Ladder Dance (to one side). To the other side is a line of dancers wearing textiles decorated with a tie-dye pattern reminiscent of earlier textiles from Chaco Canyon, Aztec, and Canyon de Chelly in New Mexico, as well as Mesoamerica. (Field Museum of Natural History, catalog number 156.21130. Drawing by the author.)

sulted in a wide variety of responses to different kinds of images in different landscape settings. She writes, "In some cases they [petroglyphs] are a 'message from the ancestors' rarely explicitly understood but signs of the ancestors' involvement with and concern for contemporary Zunis" (Young 1988: 232). Hopi consultants usually view potsherds, petroglyphs, and remains of habitation structures (so-called ruins) as deliberate messages from ancestors. Following explicit instructions from the first being to inhabit this earth, migrating clans deliberately left their footprints in this form. Some express the view that paintings in murals and pottery were done as a way of telling stories. Although we cannot tell the details of those stories, we can recognize and appreciate that the painters intended to make contact with us. The act of communication, then, is more important than the specific content of messages. The overall message is that "we were here and thinking of those who are coming after us." This message connects to family and clan histories, migration, and the social ordering of ritual and ecological responsibilities within each community. This message also reinforces the ethic of taking only what one needs to survive and leaving resources and knowledge for those who will come behind us.

Hopi consultants point out that each matrilineal clan in each village has its own history and that it is not appropriate to know another group's stories. Maternal uncles have the responsibility to transmit these stories to their nephews, and to certain others related by initiation, but to nobody else. Clan mothers have the responsibility of caring for certain items used in ritual and do not share these with outsiders. Hopi clans are ranked according to who arrived first to a particular locality and by the responsibilities assigned to each newcomer. In this way, Hopi communities deliberately maintain diverse histories with different versions of the same symbols and ritual practices and different layers of meaning. When one needs to tell a story to outsiders, a "folk tale" version can be generated, or the teller may refer to the dominant clan's version. For example, different Hopi clans locate the site of the original emergence into this world in different places, but the "public" version of emergence takes place in the Grand Canyon at the feature known as the *Sipapuni*. Other Pueblos have their own emergence locations with similar names, such as the Keresan *Shipap* and Tewa *Nan Sipu* or Earth Navel. Sometimes stories identify a specific location; sometimes the location is simply known to lie in a particular direction. Emergence places can be symbolized (or, more accurately, embodied or enacted) as features in kivas, plazas, or shrines outside the village. Pilgrimage to the Hopi *Sipapuni* or to sacred lakes of the Rio Grande Pueblos or ritual visits to particular shrines reenact migration. Placement of clan symbols at the Hopi petroglyph site of Tutuveni (Willow Springs) is a good example of this: like the ancestors who placed their footprints on the landscape, each Third Mesa man who makes the Salt Pilgrimage leaves his clan mark at this particular shrine (Bernardini 2005). Every man taking part encodes his own family's history into the collective process. In contrast, First Mesa men make a Salt Pilgrimage to the Zuni Salt Lake, probably referencing the large number of First Mesa clans who have their origins among communities who have settled in what is now New Mexico. Depression-era painter Fred Kabotie (of Second Mesa) chose this pilgrimage to illustrate Hopi connections to landscape in a mural inside the Painted Desert Inn, a historic structure located in Petrified Forest

National Park, because the historic trail passed nearby. Stories about places should be told in or near those places.

Sometimes iconography in rock art or pottery reminds consultants of the concept of center place and four directions (Figure 7.2), which in turn recalls emergence, migration to different directions, and return to center. The spiral can refer to migration and the movement of the sun, seasons, and water, as well as the movement of people. The enclosed cross can remind one of the start of a plaited basket, which might be used in rock art to refer to "the beginning of something," as can a spiral, the figure formed when starting a coiled basket or pottery vessel. The enclosed cross might represent the area of the earth for which Hopi people are responsible as stewards, and it might be interpreted as the symbol for a particular clan, placed in various localities as a "footprint" in its migrations. The enclosed cross can thus refer simultaneously to four directions, center place, and earth stewardship. Significantly, I think, Hopi consultants have never identified the enclosed cross as the planet Venus, its meaning in the Maya glyph system, though many rock art enthusiasts and new-agers are wont to make this connection. Rather, in the Hopi way, a simple image like this can have many meanings and references depending on the gender, clan, and village of the individual making the identification and on the particular context of the image or the context of the interview. This is not to say that the Hopi have somehow lost an original Maya meaning (Venus) or that they are hiding such a deep meaning from rock art researchers. But the day will surely come when Hopi individuals deploy a Maya-derived meaning in order to make a point about long-distance connections.

Interpretive diversity and ritual heterodoxy are almost certainly a long-standing pattern, not the result of cultural decay, as a degenerationist view espoused by some archaeologists would have it. Of course culture has changed, some traditions have been lost, and some have changed in their function and details. But in my experience and that of many of my colleagues, contemporary Pueblo people have not forgotten their own traditions. Nor does reluctance to discuss proprietary clan information with outsiders indicate that Hopi people are hiding the loss of traditions, or living in fear of Spanish and American oppression and exploitation, though certainly the continued exploitation of Hopi religious knowledge by new-agers and others remains a serious problem. Rather, secrecy is a strategy that preserves internal diversity and identities while (anthropologists would say) minimizing strife over competing versions. As in biology, in cultural diversity lie strength and tools for survival in changing natural and social environments. Not only do the Hopi retain many clan histories of migrations to and from the other Pueblos, but New Mexico Pueblos also relate stories of both small- and large-scale popu-

Figure 7.2. Enclosed crosses and spirals in basketry and rock art. Top row: left, enclosed cross petroglyph at V-Bar-V Ranch site in the Verde Valley, Arizona; right, spiral petroglyph with clan symbols, Wupatki National Monument, Arizona. Center and bottom (close-ups) rows: left, Hopi plaited yucca leaf sifter basket by Leota Poneoma, 1960 (Courtesy of the Museum of Northern Arizona, catalog number E8580); right, Second Mesa Hopi coiled basket, unknown weaver. (Courtesy of the Museum of Northern Arizona, catalog number E4363. Photos by the author).

lation movement, borrowing and "purchasing" ritual societies among different communities and harboring refugees following factional disputes, epidemics, famines, and political conflicts. (Anecdotally, collaborations between archaeologists and New Mexico Pueblo cultural specialists also reveal more internal diversity than has been widely reported.)

This sort of ongoing interaction has probably been the norm since at least the mid-1400s, and it can be illustrated with kiva murals of Antelope Mesa on the eastern edge of the Hopi Mesas and Pottery Mound near Albuquerque (Hays-Gilpin 2006; Hays-Gilpin and LeBlanc 2007; Hibben 1975; Schaafsma 2007; Smith 1952). Clothing and textiles depicted in kiva murals include local styles and techniques, as well as many introduced to the Hopi area from southern Arizona and perhaps northern Mexico (Webster 2007; Webster and Loma'omvaya 2004). Many Hopi consultants for the Museum of Northern Arizona's mural research project say that the murals illustrate rituals, clothing styles, and symbolism of the New Mexico Pueblos and that these communities were founded by immigrants from the east (see, for example, Polingyouma 2008). Some of their descendants returned to New Mexico, and some became incorporated into Hopi communities. Nonetheless, these murals serve as messages from the past that are relevant today. Particular images in the murals can be used to illustrate values that are still vital in all the Pueblos, such as the importance of prayer, reciprocity with the spirit world, reciprocity between men and women, and the metaphorical conflation of people and maize, which is shared throughout the Pueblos and Mesoamerica.

Hopi traditional histories also refer to interactions with Paiute, Ute, Navajo, Apache, Havasupai, Chemehuevi, and other non-Puebloan groups, and contemporary Hopi increasingly express interest in historical connections with indigenous groups in Mexico and even South America. New Mexico Pueblos have long traded with (and been raided by) Utes, Navajos, and Plains tribes. Now, members of different tribal communities meet at boarding schools, at universities, on job sites, and in other contexts. In many ways, the Pueblo world is expanding rather than contracting as might be expected in the face of the assimilating forces of American capitalism, language loss, drought, and other forces. I would suggest, based on archaeological evidence as well as traditional histories, that the Pueblo world was always multivalent, multiethnic, and innovative.

The story of Palatkwapi is a good example of the persistent importance of the past in the present and how Hopi traditional histories and those who tell them can adapt to changing circumstances. Palatkwapi, "Red-masonry House" (Hopi Dictionary Project 1998), also called Palatpavi, "Red Lake," in some versions (M. Kabotie, personal communication 2007), is an important place somewhere far to the south of the Hopi Mesas. As many as 30 clans have traditions placing them at Palatkwapi/Palatpavi. Some versions of the migration stories say the people who became Palatkwapi clans emerged from the *Sipapuni* in the Grand Canyon with everyone else, went south, and then returned north. Some identify an alternative "beginning place" for these clans as *Yayniwpu* (beginning place), far to the south, rather than the *Sipapuni*. Today, some clan elders identify *Yayniwpu* as the Valley of Mexico (Ferguson et al. 2004:12). Still other accounts say the people emerged somewhere far away and then took a long sea voyage.

All agree that after emergence, Hopi ancestors migrated in various directions and some met up at Palatkwapi, a large town with red masonry walls, or near a red sandstone butte, where large numbers of people lived, many rituals were performed, and social hierarchy was based on ritual power. As in almost all Hopi stories about the destruction of previous worlds and the depopulation of villages, the people of Palatkwapi became corrupt, stopped respecting their elders, and committed all kinds of bad behaviors (a condition called *koyanisqatsi*, life out of balance), so the community leaders conspired to destroy the evil people and move on with those who remained true to the right way of life.

What is unique to the Palatkwapi story, and always included, is the destruction of the town by a giant water serpent who caused the earth to shake, walls to fall, and the earth to turn upside down so that water spurted forth from the fireplaces and kivas. The plaza and ultimately most of the village flooded. Many were killed, many fled in various directions. The migrating clans sequentially founded a series of villages in their northward migration. The last four, including Chavez Pass Pueblo (Nuvakwewtaqa[2]) and two of the Homol'ovi village sites near Winslow, Arizona, are clearly identified and have been investigated archaeologically (archaeologists date them to the fourteenth century).

In a version of the Palatkwapi story recorded in about 1897, Jesse Walter Fewkes writes that Palatkwapi "is said to have been near San Carlos in the Gila Valley, southern Arizona" (Fewkes 1900:597). In a 1905 publication, Voth identifies Palatkwapi as "somewhere southeast of Flagstaff, in Southern Arizona" (Voth 1905:48). In the 1960s, archaeologist Charles Di Peso (1974) identified Casas Grandes/Paquimé as Palatkwapi. By 1971, Harold Courlander's narrators agreed that Palatkwapi was far enough south to be in Mexico (Courlander 1971). Recently, an elder from Second Mesa told ethnographers, "We know we came from Mexico, from the Sipapuni. I'm from Palatkwapi" (Colwell-Chanthaphonh 2003:18). Several other men from Palatkwapi clans recently have told me that Palatkwapi is in Mexico. Some say that some clans came on reed houseboats from South America to Mexico, then walked north to the Hopi Mesas. In summary, around 1900, Palatkwapi was said to be in southern Arizona, and its location has been moving farther south ever since as archaeological and cultural similarities among regions become apparent to Hopi and Euroamerican scholars alike.

In the way of archaeologists, we look for internal clues such as environmental descriptions that might fit particular regions or localities. Some say Palatkwapi was located in a land where giant cactus grew; others say the agave plants grew tall there. The Phoenix and Tucson basins and Sonora have giant saguaro cactuses, but the term could also describe the cardón, which grows even farther south. Large agave plants grow as far north as the Verde Valley, Arizona, only a couple hundred kilometers from the Hopi Mesas, but the largest agave plants are surely found in northern, western, and central Mexico. No published version of the story provides more useful locational detail than this, perhaps a clue that the story is a conflation of many different times and places, perhaps a result of the abbreviation of very long stories for the benefit of ethnographers and other outsiders who must publish and then move on. The story can function to unite some of the Hopi clans who came from the south, with a shared history, and yet set them apart from the clans who arrived first at the Hopi mesas, the *Motisinom,* or first peoples, and from the clans who arrived later, mostly from the New Mexico Pueblos.

In summary, Hopi traditional histories are diverse and flexible enough to accommodate other ways of knowing, including archaeology. This diversity and amenability to change is part of traditional functions and processes, not a result of degeneration or corruption. Deliberate diversity and heterodoxy may be more pronounced at Hopi than among other Pueblos. Details are not shared, and in many cases, major deities and ritual organizations are not shared. But the facts of diversity and resilience probably are shared. Finally, the many meanings and references of material remains such as architecture, pottery, petroglyphs, and landscape features (whether modified or not) remain extremely important to Pueblo people in recalling their emergence, migration, and coalition into communities. For Hopi, this process of coming together was a process of accommodation in which different clans took up responsibility for a part of the elaborate annual ritual calendar that structures Hopi life and religion (M. Kabotie, personal communication 2007). Before the coming together of the clans, then, there were only separate clan rituals. While the cosmologies underlying these practices might have been similar at a deep and ancient level, that deep structure appears to be more important to anthropologists than to Pueblo people, for whom the differences and the history of accommodation and differentiation are what should be emphasized.

Acknowledgments

I would like to dedicate this chapter to the late Michael Kabotie, artist and "mythic archaeologist," of the Snow Clan, Songòopavi Village, Second Mesa. Mike helped me understand much of the material presented here, but I alone am responsible for errors. Thanks also to Leigh J. Kuwanwisiwma and his staff at the Hopi Cultural Preservation Office, the Field Museum of Natural History, the collections staff at the Museum of Northern Arizona, and an anonymous reviewer. Some of the material presented here was previously published in the proceedings of the Second *Vías del Noroeste* conference, held in Real de Catorce, San Luis Potosí, Mexico, in 2004. Many thanks to Carlo Bonfiglioli and Marie-Areti Hers of the Universidad Nacional Autónoma de México for their kind invitation to take part.

Notes

1. The interviews are part of a collaborative project between the Museum of Northern Arizona and the Hopi Cultural Preservation Office. One goal of the Hopi Iconography Project is to plan an exhibit that will illustrate continuity in important Hopi values and worldview with pottery, mural painting, basketry, textiles, and works in other media, past and present. Because this chapter is outside the intended use of the interview transcripts, I will avoid quotes and instead speak generally and briefly when I refer to interview results.

2. This site lies about 200 km south of the present-day Hopi villages. Each village had its own traditional name for the fourteenth-century settlement there. Anecdotally, when the Coconino National Forest archaeologist needed a Hopi name for the site, consultants reached consensus on the name Nuvakwewtaqa, "one wearing a belt of snow," because it described what the mesa edge looks like in winter, not because it was a term any of them had heard in clan migration traditions.

References Cited

Bernardini, Wesley
  2005   *Hopi Oral Tradition and the Archaeology of Identity.* University of Arizona Press, Tucson.
Colwell-Chanthaphonh, Chip
  2003   Signs in Place: Native American Perspectives of the Past in the San Pedro Valley of Southeastern Arizona. *Kiva* 69:5–29.
Colwell-Chanthaphonh, Chip, and T. J. Ferguson
  2006   Memory Pieces and Footprints: Multivocality and the Meanings of Ancient Times and Ancestral Places among the Zuni and Hopi. *American Anthropologist* 108:148–162.
Courlander, Harold
  1971   *The Fourth World of the Hopis: The Epic Story of the Hopi Indians as Preserved in Their Legends and Traditions.* University of New Mexico Press, Albuquerque.
Di Peso, Charles C.
  1974   *Casas Grandes: A Fallen Trading Center of the Gran Chichimeca,* Vol. 3. Amerind Foundation, Dragoon, Arizona.
Eggan, Fred
  1950   *Social Organization of the Western Pueblos.* University of Chicago Press, Chicago.

Ferguson, T. J., Chip Colwell-Chanthaphonh, and Roger Anyon

2004   One Valley, Many Histories: Tohono O'odham, Hopi, Zuni, and Western Apache History in the San Pedro Valley. *Archaeology Southwest* 18(1):1–14.

Ferguson, T. J., and Micah Loma'omvaya

1999   *Hoopoq'uaqam niqw Wukoskyavi (Those Who Went to the Northeast and Tonto Basin): Hopi-Salado Cultural Affiliation Study.* Report on file at Hopi Cultural Preservation Office, Kykotsmovi, Arizona.

Fewkes, Jesse W.

1900   *Tusayan Migration Traditions.* Bureau of American Ethnology Annual Report 19, Pt. 2, pp. 573–634. U.S. Government Printing Office, Washington, D.C.

Hays-Gilpin, Kelley A.

2006   Icons and Ethnicity: Hopi Painted Pottery and Murals. In *Religion in the Prehispanic Southwest,* edited by C. S. VanPool, T. L. VanPool, and D. A. Phillips Jr., pp. 67–80. AltaMira, Walnut Creek, California.

Hays-Gilpin, Kelley A., and Steven LeBlanc

2007   Sikyatki Style in Regional Context. In *New Perspectives on Pottery Mound Pueblo,* edited by Polly Schaafsma, pp. 109–136. University of New Mexico Press, Albuquerque.

Hibben, Frank

1975   *Kiva Art of the Anasazi at Pottery Mound.* KC Publications, Las Vegas, Nevada.

Hopi Dictionary Project

1998   *Hopi Dictionary, Hopiikwa Lavaytutuveni, A Hopi-English Dictionary of the Third Mesa Dialect.* University of Arizona Press, Tucson.

Kuwanwisiwma, Leigh J., and T. J. Ferguson

2004   Ang Kuktota: Hopi Ancestral Sites and Cultural Landscapes. *Expedition* 46(2):24–29.

Momaday, N. Scott

1993   Address to the United Nations at the Cry of the Earth Gathering in November 1993. Electronic document, http://www.wisdomoftheelders.org/prog1 /transcript01_ew.htm, accessed September 1, 2008.

Polingyouma, Eric

2008   Awatovi: A Hopi History. In *Remembering Awatovi: The Story of an Archaeological Expedition in Northern Arizona, 1935–1939,* by Hester Davis, pp. xv–xviii. Peabody Museum of Archaeology and Ethnology, Harvard University, Cambridge, Massachusetts.

Schaafsma, Polly

1999   Tlalocs, Kachinas, Sacred Bundles, and Related Symbolism in the Southwest and Mesoamerica. In *The Casas Grandes World,* edited by Curtis F. Schaafsma and Carroll L. Riley, pp. 164–192. University of Utah Press, Salt Lake City.

2001   Quetzalcoatl and the Horned and Feathered Serpent of the Southwest. In *The Road to Aztlan: Art from a Mythic Homeland,* edited by Virginia M. Fields and Victor Zamudio-Taylor, pp. 138–149. Los Angeles County Museum of Art, Los Angeles.

Schaafsma, Polly (editor)

2007   *New Perspectives on Pottery Mound Pueblo.* University of New Mexico Press, Albuquerque.

Smith, Watson

1952   *Kiva Mural Decorations at Awatovi and Kawaika-a.* Papers of the Peabody Museum of Archaeology and Ethnology, Vol. 37. Harvard University, Cambridge, Massachusetts.

Taube, Karl A.

2000   Lightning Celts and Corn Fetishes: The Formative Olmec and the Development of Maize Symbolism in Mesoamerica and the American Southwest. In *Olmec Art and Archaeology in Mesoamerica,* edited by John E. Clark and Mary E. Pye, pp. 297–337. National Gallery of Art, Washington, D.C.

2001   The Breath of Life: The Symbolism of Wind in Mesoamerica and the American Southwest. In *The Road to Aztlan: Art from a Mythic Homeland,* edited by Virginia M. Fields and Victor Zamudio-Taylor, pp. 102–123. Los Angeles County Museum of Art, Los Angeles.

Voth, Henry R.

1905   *The Traditions of the Hopi.* Publication 96, Anthropological Series Vol. 8. Field Columbian Museum, Chicago.

Ware, John

2001   Chaco Social Organization: A Peripheral View. In *Chaco Society and Polity: Papers from the 1999 Conference,* edited by Linda S. Cordell, W. James Judge, and June-el Piper, pp. 79–93. Special Publication 4. New Mexico Archaeological Society, Albuquerque.

2002   Descent Group and Sodality: Alternative Pueblo Social Histories. In *Traditions, Transitions, and Technologies: Themes in Southwestern Archaeology,* edited by Sarah H. Schlanger, pp. 94–112. University Press of Colorado, Boulder.

Ware, John, and Eric Blinman

2000   Cultural Collapse and Reorganization: Origin and Spread of Pueblo Ritual Sodalities. In *The Archaeology of Regional Interaction: Religion, Warfare, and Exchange across the American Southwest and Beyond,* edited by Michelle Hegmon, pp. 381–409. University Press of Colorado, Boulder.

Webster, Laurie

2007   Ritual Costuming at Pottery Mound: The Pottery Mound Textiles in Regional Perspective. In *New Perspectives on Pottery Mound Pueblo,* edited by Polly Schaafsma, pp. 167–206. University of New Mexico Press, Albuquerque.

Webster, Laurie, and Micah Loma'omvaya

2004   Textiles, Baskets, and Hopi Cultural Identity. In *Identity, Feasting, and the*

Archaeology of the Greater Southwest, edited by Barbara J. Mills, pp. 74–92. University Press of Colorado, Boulder.

Whiteley, Peter M.

2002a   Re-Imagining Awat'ovi. In *Archaeologies of the Pueblo Revolt: Identity, Meaning, and Renewal in the Pueblo World,* edited by Robert W. Preucel, pp. 147–165. University of New Mexico Press, Albuquerque.

2002b   Archaeology and Oral Traditions: The Scientific Importance of Dialogue. *American Antiquity* 67:405–416.

Young, M. Jane

1988   *Signs from the Ancestors: Zuni Cultural Symbolism and Perceptions of Rock Art.* University of New Mexico Press, Albuquerque.

Part III
Balancing Stability and Change

8
Continuity and Discontinuity in Southwestern Religions

Stephen H. Lekson

The Southwest is a poster child for continuity. The New Mexico Tourism Department touts the depth of the state's history and prehistory, urging vacationers to stay a few days longer to take it all in. The Pueblo of Acoma claims to be the oldest continuously occupied village in the country (and so does Oraibi, over at Hopi). Pueblos, in particular, are marketed as timeless and eternal, never-changing. Of course, Pueblos that lost lands to colonial governments would challenge that claim, but the timelessness marketed in Santa Fe and Sedona refers not to land lines and legalities, but to cosmological verities. It pleases us to think that Southwestern Native American ideologies and worldviews are and were, in effect, permanent. And there is some truth to that: Southwestern religions and ideologies have deep roots.

For archaeology—and particularly for archaeology's contributions to our understanding of Southwestern religions—continuity has been the default assumption. From the very earliest days of Southwestern archaeology, we have assumed rather teleologically that the goal of the ancient peoples was to turn into Pueblos, as those were known in turn-of-the-last-century ethnologies. The back-story beginning of modern Pueblos began with the first great Southwesternist, Adolph Bandelier. The pioneering Swiss saw a steady, cumulative, boring progression from rough, rude beginnings to modern Pueblo life: "The picture which can be dimly traced into this past is a very modest and unpretending one. No great cataclysms of nature, no waves of destruction on a large scale, either natural or human, appear to have interrupted the slow and tedious development of the people before the Spaniards came" (Bandelier 1892:592).

We would not put it that way today of course. We know there were a few bumps on the road. The Great Drought of 1275 to 1300, for example, qualifies as a mild cataclysm. But a century after Bandelier and his "slow and tedious development," we still favor versions of the past that turn ancient people into modern Pueblos as quietly and efficiently as possible. Slow and tedious, perhaps, but along a fairly straight line leading from a hunter-gatherer Archaic to the modern Pueblos—serene, spiritual, communal, eternal. That's the version you see in museum exhibits, hear at Mesa Verde campfire talks, read in Santa Fe coffee-table books.

Slow and tedious development was codified in the master narrative of Pueblo archaeology, the Pecos Classification, with its sequence of Basketmaker II and III followed by Pueblo I, II, III, IV, and V. The Pecos Classification was first proposed in 1927 (Fowler 2000:315–318) and is still in use. It defined developmental stages or horizons and not spans of actual time, incrementally adding the elements necessary to modern Pueblo life: corn first, then pottery, then pueblos, then kivas, then kachinas, and so forth until all the pieces were in place for Hopi, or Acoma, or San Juan. That's not history; it's ontogeny.

A few archaeologists, even at the time, thought there was more to the story than a steady plodding march to Pueblodom. Frank Roberts proposed a modification of the Pecos stages, with a rise-and-fall plot (Roberts 1935):

Basketmaker (Basketmaker II)
Modified Basketmaker (Basketmaker III)
Developmental Pueblo (Pueblo I and Pueblo II)
Great Pueblo (Pueblo III)
Regressive Pueblo (Pueblo IV)
Historic Pueblo (Pueblo V)

The first acts of Roberts's story were set in the Four Corners—the San Juan Hypothesis, which suggested Mesa Verde was the original hearth of Pueblo history. The denouement took place in the Rio Grande pueblos, at Zuni and Hopi. Roberts thought Pueblo history peaked in the Four Corners—*Great Pueblo!*—and then skidded into the Rio Grande and the western pueblos: the *Regressive Pueblo* period. "Great" and "Regressive" clearly signaled the cultural peak at Mesa Verde, followed by a cultural decline in the later, proto-historic era. That offended archaeologists working in later time periods, especially in the Rio Grande. In part that was merely turf and amour propre: nobody wants to be told his or her research area was a dark age or a periphery. But even more, "regressive" was deliberately counter to the steady, slow, and tedious development master narrative. The master narrative prevailed: the term *regressive* was hissed off the stage, and today it simply *isn't said* in polite archaeological discourse. "Steady on" pretty much sums it up.

But there *was* a rise and fall—or rather, a series of rises and falls—in the history of the ancient Southwest (Lekson 2009). The region had history or, rather, several histories: rises and falls, heroes and villains, successes and failures, kings and commoners, war and peace: all the elements of history we know from every other agricultural region of the world. History is not about steady states, it's about events and change. In large part, history is the story of discontinuities. I think the discontinuities in Southwestern archaeology are far more interesting, and probably more important, than the undeniable continuities.

The Southwest is conventionally divided into three regions: Anasazi (ancestral Pueblo), on the Colorado Plateau around the Four Corners; Hohokam, in the Sonoran deserts around Phoenix and Tucson, Arizona; and Mogollon, in the narrow highlands separating the Plateau and the Sonoran desert, and spilling into the Chihuahuan desert of southern New Mexico and northern Mexico. The histories of each of these three regions were marked by dramatic discontinuities. I will briefly highlight a few.

Hohokam, in public perception, comes in a distant second to Anasazi. Everyone knows Mesa Verde; few people have heard of Snaketown. But the denizens of the desert were in almost every way more impressive, more developed, and more interesting than Chaco Canyon or Mesa Verde. They were precocious, living in large farming towns long before similar settlements appeared on the Plateau. The canal systems on the Salt and Gila rivers eclipsed Anasazi building programs, and in fact they were larger than anything comparable in Mexico (Doolittle 1990). We have to look to the Andean region for canals as large and complex as Hohokam's. The social and ideological system behind the remarkable Hohokam achievement manifests itself archaeologically as a complex of ball courts (earthen ovals, a local form of the Mesoamerican originals), cremation burial ritual, new art styles, and related institutions. These transformed the deserts around 650–700 C.E. The appearance of these elements, as a package, was so sudden and dramatic that the dean of Hohokam studies, Emil Haury, concluded that they represented an intrusion (migration? cult?) from Mesoamerica (Haury 1976). Haury's suggestion ran counter to the master Southwestern narrative of steady, cumulative, development. (The Pecos Classification was for Pueblos, which did not include Hohokam, but the belief in slow, tedious development was pan-Southwestern.) Reacting to Haury, archaeologists rushed to demonstrate continuities from pre-650 to post-650 Hohokam, but those arguments failed. Today, the complex of ball courts, burial ritual, and so forth is generally described as an explosive cult, which indeed transformed Hohokam society (e.g., Wallace et al. 1995). And a few archaeologists are even coming full circle, entertaining Haury's original idea of Mesoamerican origins. In any event, the discontinuities between pre-650 and post-650 Hohokam were indeed revolutionary. For several centuries, Hohokam became one of the most remarkable social developments in North America.

And then it fell apart. Around 1050 and certainly by 1075, ball courts fell out of use. By 1150, all were abandoned (Wilcox 1991). Burial rituals lost their rigid formality, and a variety of practices coexisted. Indeed, the old Hohokam region balkanized, breaking into a half-dozen local districts. New ideologies arose or arrived, directed by new elite families living in great houses elevated on huge platform mounds. Those were all novel things for Hohokam. Indeed, "Hohokam" in some senses no longer existed. People whose grandparents saw ball games marched to a new order, more authoritarian and (in the end) less successful. Around 1450, the once-thriving Hohokam heartland was all but depopulated (Hill et al. 2004).

So there were at least three major discontinuities: first, the transformation of pre-650 desert peoples into Hohokam with the sudden appearance of ball courts and other complex developments; second, the ragged end of Hohokam from 1050 to 1150 and the replacement of its ideologies with more authoritarian models; and third, of course, the discontinuity of regional collapse around 1450.

The Mogollon region saw its share of discontinuities, too. I focus here on the Mimbres Mogollon subregion of southwestern New Mexico and northern Chihuahua (Lekson 2006). Mimbres is famous for its black-on-white pottery, with arresting images of people, bugs, birds, and fish and astonishing depictions of myths and alternate realities. That pottery, made between 1000 and 1150 C.E., might not have been highly valued by neighbors to the Mimbres: it was not widely traded, compared to other Southwestern types. But it was extremely important to Mimbres people, many of whom were buried with a black-on-white bowl inverted over their heads. Mimbres ideologies were expressed in other media (rock art and amazing wooden objects found in Mogollon mountain caves), but the pottery was probably the most public expression of Mimbres beliefs. For over a century, extraordinary artistic energies were invested on the interior of black-on-white bowls (bowl exteriors were only roughly finished, and decorated jars were remarkably rare). Then, around 1125–1130, it was as if someone threw a switch: bowl interiors almost overnight switched from the principal canvas for complex ideological imagery to anti-designs: unpainted, smudged black, burnished interiors that acted like dull concave mirrors, faintly reflecting the viewer's eyes—and nothing more. After 1150 jar exteriors became the primary field for pottery design. Complex geometric designs (continuing a strong Mimbres interest in geometrics) became common on water jars—in contrast to earlier Mimbres pottery.

More than pottery changed: people left their stone pueblo villages and moved out into the deserts, building adobe towns. Something big happened between 1125 and 1150, which completely transformed Mimbres society—so great a discontinuity that archaeologists argue whether the area was abandoned by Mimbres and quickly reoccupied by black burnished, adobe people; or whether the history was one of Mimbres "changing clothes" and turning their backs on a vibrant ideological and artistic tradition. Whatever Mimbres ideologies and religions might have been at 1100, they were no longer at 1200.

But perhaps the biggest Mogollon discontinuity was what came next: Casas Grandes, with its remarkable capital, Paquimé, in northern Chihuahua (Di Peso 1974). The Rio Casas Grandes was the southern edge of the old Mimbres region. Mimbres ended around 1150; a century later, around 1250–1300, the great city of Paquimé rose in a valley that was previously only moderately populated. By 1400, Casas Grandes was probably the most heavily populated region in the Southwest (Lekson et al. 2004). It more certainly was the busiest, most cosmopolitan, and most politically complex development in the history of the Southwest. Monumental effigy mounds (for example, a football-field-long plumed serpent) shared ceremonial space with Mesoamerican ball courts (not the Hohokam earthen ovals, but real I-shaped courts, like those of Tula). Paquimé was a commercial hub with ties to west Mexico: Paquimé boasted amazing quantities of west Mexican metal artifacts and tropical macaws. Paquimé was the capital of an impressively large region (the Casas Grandes region), and could easily qualify as a small, secondary state—a spin-off or knock-off of Mesoamerican states to the south.

Where'd *that* come from? There was little in Mimbres to suggest anything like Paquimé, and a century of desert wanderings separated the two. (But some elements of Mimbres continued in Casas Grandes [Lekson 1999].) The site's excavator, Charles Di Peso, was so struck by the discontinuities that he argued strongly that Paquimé was a direct and deliberate Mesoamerican intervention (Di Peso 1974), a suggestion supported by later researchers (Riley 2005) and played in various variations (Lekson 1999). Recent work at the site emphasizes smaller-scale, local developments in the story of Casas Grandes (Whalen and Minnis 2001, 2003), and surely local environments, economies, and populations played key roles, but Paquimé simply will not fit any master narrative of slow, tedious development. Paquimé was an event! And the most interesting kind of discontinuity.

And in the Pueblo and Anasazi area? It was Pueblo prehistory that gave rise to the slow, tedious Pecos Classification. Neither Hohokam nor Mogollon was under the same teleological constraints as Anasazi, because neither Hohokam nor Mogollon led so obviously to descendant communities. In the early days of Southwestern archaeology, it was not at all clear that Hohokam became Pima, or Mogollon became Zuni, or any other candidate group. But everyone knew that Anasazi became Pueblo.

One of the first great steps on that road happened at Chaco Canyon, but perhaps not the way you think. Tree rings told us that the massed, terraced "pueblo" form appeared first at Chaco, so it was natural to see it as the source of the communal Pueblo societies. Indeed, Lewis Henry Morgan ("the Father of American Anthropology") pegged Chaco as the font and origin of New World communalism, based on its architecture (Lekson 2005). But it turns out that the big, impressive buildings at Chaco were not communal pueblos. They were, instead, monumental palaces. Chaco was a city of palaces, of wannabe kings who appear clearly in archaeology and in Native American traditions (Lekson 2009; Lekson et al. 2006). Chaco's would-be kings and princes, inspired by the Mesoamerican Postclassic or even Mississippian lords, were not particularly successful. They picked the wrong time and place to start up a state, but how could they know that? They tried a bait-and-switch, moving the capital 60 km north to a site now known as Aztec Ruins National Monument, and from that second city they tried to rule the Anasazi region. That, too, failed. The rain did not fall, violence escalated, and villages surrounded themselves with defensive walls or moved to the safety of alcoves high in canyon walls, the cliff dwellings of Mesa Verde. Things got ugly: Chacoan princes at Aztec Ruins tried to enforce their failing rule by acts of brutal repression (Turner and Turner 1999). That was the last straw: families, clans, and whole villages began to leave the Four Corners, decades before the Great Drought, which set the final punctuation on the Chacoan collapse.

Between 1200 and 1300, tens of thousands of people voted with their feet and left the Four Corners. They were fleeing bad times and bad rulers. Most settled at existing villages on the southern fringe of the Chacoan world, from Hopi on the west, through Zuni and Acoma, to the Rio Grande on the east. The influx of newcomers strained those farming communities almost to breaking, but elders and leaders instituted new ideologies and ceremonies to hold things together.

One thing they did *not* try was kings. The people had endured four centuries of kings, princes, and hierarchies at Chaco Canyon and Aztec Ruins. They very deliberately and consciously rejected those forms of government and developed new ways of living—communal, egalitarian, and ritually based—which allowed medium-sized farming towns to exist and prosper *without kings*. They became, in a word, pueblos.

We know this because Chaco's palaces (the most obvious evidence of hierarchy) were never recreated; those forms stayed behind in the Four Corners. Even things that characterized commoner life in the Four Corners, such as family "kivas" and the distinctive Mesa Verde mug ceramic form, were left behind and never used again. Like Mimbres, the Anasazi-Pueblo people *changed,* distancing themselves geographically and ideologically from the immediate past. A period of intense, post-Chaco ritual experimentation is archaeologically visible in the explosion of ideologically charged art after 1300. Pottery, rock art, murals, and other media all show an unmistakable break from the past, with new colors, new compositions, new symmetries, and new content (e.g., Schaafsma 2007).

I opened this essay with the suggestion that the U.S. Southwest is a poster child for continuity. In stark contrast, the Anasazi-Pueblo world, before and after 1300, is a case study in discontinuity. Of course they were the same *people:* Anasazi was indeed "ancestral Pueblo." But the structure and fabric of societies before and after 1300 were apples and oranges, cheese and chalk. They couldn't be more different: ostentatious kings at Chaco, trying to create a Postclassic secondary state; poor self-effacing priests at Zuni, smoothing the progress of communal life in an egalitarian village.

Pueblo people recall these events. Pueblo "migration stories" are stories of change and discontinuity: how they did something wrong here, learned an important lesson there, and finally—after a long series of events and revelations—they came to rest at a center place. One story, in particular, is illustrative: that of White House, a great city where people lived in rich prosperity until certain individuals acquired power over other people. That is, kings and lords. The moral of the story is that those roles were wrong for Pueblo peoples, and (along with other transgressions) the rise of kings resulted in the fall of White House. (The term *king* is not used, although some Native Americans suggest it would accurately describe what happened at Chaco [Lekson 1999, 2009].)

Native Southwestern societies show admirable, even inspirational, continuity in the face of five centuries of colonial oppression. Pueblos today continue practices and philosophies that rose in the fourteenth-century reaction against Chacoan hierarchies. Given the impacts of Spanish, Mexican, and American occupations, that's truly remarkable. Some of those practices may have pre-Chaco roots. But as archaeologists and historians we should not let their remarkable persistence blind us to the discontinuities that shaped Pueblo and Southwestern prehistory. The history of the ancient Southwest was anything but a slow and tedious progression.

References Cited

Bandelier, Adolph F.
   1892   *Final Report of Investigations among the Indians of the Southwestern United States, Carried on Mainly in the Years from 1880 to 1885.* American Series, Vol. 3-4, Archaeological Institute of America, Cambridge, Massachusetts.

Di Peso, Charles C.

1974   *Casas Grandes: A Fallen Trading Center of the Gran Chichimeca,* Vols. 1–3. Amerind Foundation, Dragoon, Arizona.

Doolittle, William E.

1990   *Canal Irrigation in Prehistoric Mexico: The Sequence of Technological Change.* University of Texas Press, Austin.

Fowler, Don D.

2000   *A Laboratory for Anthropology: Science and Romanticism in the American Southwest, 1846–1930.* University of New Mexico Press, Albuquerque.

Haury, Emil W.

1976   *The Hohokam: Desert Farmers and Craftsmen.* University of Arizona Press, Tucson.

Hill, J. Brett, Jeffery J. Clark, William H. Doelle, and Patrick D. Lyons

2004   Prehistoric Demography in the Southwest: Migration, Coalescence, and Hohokam Population Decline. *American Antiquity* 69:689–716.

Lekson, Stephen H.

1999   *The Chaco Meridian: Centers of Political Power in the Ancient Southwest.* AltaMira, Walnut Creek, California.

2005   Complexity. In *Southwest Archaeology in the Twentieth Century,* edited by Linda S. Cordell and Don D. Fowler, pp. 157–173. University of Utah Press, Salt Lake City.

2006   *The Archaeology of the Mimbres Region, Southwestern New Mexico.* BAR International Series, 1466. Archaeopress, Oxford.

2009   *A History of the Ancient Southwest.* School for Advanced Research Press, Santa Fe, New Mexico.

Lekson, Stephen H., Michael Bletzer, and A. C. MacWilliams

2004   Pueblo IV in the Chihuahuan Desert. In *The Protohistoric Pueblo World, A.D. 1275–1600,* edited by E. Charles Adams and Andrew I. Duff, pp. 53–61. University of Arizona Press, Tucson.

Lekson, Stephen H., Thomas C. Windes, and Peter J. McKenna

2006   Architecture. In *The Archaeology of Chaco Canyon, New Mexico,* edited by Stephen H. Lekson, pp. 67–116. School of American Research Press, Santa Fe, New Mexico.

Riley, Carroll L.

2005   *Becoming Aztlan: Mesoamerican Influences in the Greater Southwest, AD 1200–1500.* University of Utah Press, Salt Lake City.

Roberts, Frank H. H., Jr.

1935   A Survey of Southwestern Archaeology. *American Anthropologist* 37:1–35.

Schaafsma, Polly (editor)

2007   *New Perspectives on Pottery Mound Pueblo.* University of New Mexico Press, Albuquerque.

Turner, Christy G., II, and Jacqueline A. Turner

1999   *Man Corn: Cannibalism and Violence in the Prehistoric American Southwest.* University of Utah Press, Salt Lake City.

Wallace, Henry D., James E. Heidke, and William H. Doelle

1995   Hohokam Origins. *Kiva* 60(4):575–618.

Whalen, Michael E., and Paul E. Minnis

2001   *Casas Grandes and Its Hinterland: Prehistoric Regional Organization in Northwest Mexico.* University of Arizona Press, Tucson.

2003   The Local and the Distant in the Origin of Casas Grandes, Chihuahua, Mexico. *American Antiquity* 68:314–332.

Wilcox, David R.

1991   The Mesoamerican Ballgame in the American Southwest. In *The Mesoamerican Ballgame,* edited by Vernon L. Scarborough and David R. Wilcox, pp. 101–125. University of Arizona Press, Tucson.

9
The Importance of Being Specific
Theme and Trajectory in Mississippian Iconography

James Brown and John Kelly

Arguably, one archaeological finding has enlivened the debate about Southeastern contacts with Mesoamerica and the Caribbean more than any other: the demonstration that earthwork construction was of great age, some 7,000 years old, in the Lower Mississippi Valley (Saunders et al. 1997). The realization that planned earthworks of substantial monumentality predated known mound-building in Mesoamerica has undercut entrenched preconceptions about the priority of that area as the privileged source for certain cultural elements held in common with the Eastern Woodlands (Clark and Knoll 2005). The lesson to be drawn from this realization is that the history of interregional contact and cultural exchange was undoubtedly much more complex than hitherto thought. More than a simple center–periphery relationship has to be involved (White 2005). The time is ripe for a reevaluation based on the little concrete information we have in hand, rather than pouring resemblances into an old familiar scheme based on the age-area hypothesis refined in the 1920s as a substitute for a genuine history (Ford 1969; Steward 1947). Clark and Knoll (2005) and Widmer (2005) have offered important discussions on this topic.

The past 50 years of research has altered the terms of debate over intercontinental connections. The scope of relevant material has expanded far beyond the cultural traits used in the debate originally. Furthermore, absolute dating has meant that material elements need not be used to anchor a chronology while simultaneously providing content for comparison. Out of these factors emerged the realization that changes of major scale are autochthonous to each area. One of the consequences is that Southeastern cultural connections with Mesoamerica and with northern South America via the Caribbean have become fast-developing subjects of interests (White 2005; White and Weinstein 2008). The debate has been enriched by improved cultural chronologies in all three areas and by in-depth restudy of relatively neglected information from the Eastern Woodlands having to do with distant trade items, earthwork engineering, iconography, art history, comparative folklore, comparative linguistics, and related subjects (Barker et al. 2002; Brain and Phillips 1996; Brown 1997; Hall 1997; Kozuch 2002; Phillips and Brown 1978, 1984; Reilly and Garber 2006; Townsend 2004; White and Weinstein 2008). Indicative of the impact that new sources of information have provided, the past decade has seen much new thinking on the scope and history of hemisphere-wide connections (Brown 2004b; Clark 2004; Clark and Knoll 2005; Cobb et al. 1999; Hall 1997; Kehoe and Reilly 2003; Peregrine and Lekson 2006; White 2005; White, ed. 2005).

The issue of what constitutes evidence for intercontinental contact has to be examined seriously. Not all apparent resemblances are sustainable as cultural connections. Many reviews have made this point in the case of platform mound construction (Griffin 1980). Not only are resemblances subject to cherry-picking, but the architectural contexts in which platform mounds are typically embedded early in the Southeast bear little resemblance to the mound and plaza arrangements in Mesoamerica (Cobb et al. 1999). Previous reviews have tried to make similar-looking platform mounds into testimony of past contact (Webb 1989; Wicke 1965). If so, their presence in Hopewellian times puts these rather weak similarities into a time line well before the Mississippian period when the appearance of so many large and well-defined examples provided the instances that have raised some of the ideas dealt with in this chapter.

The reverse is also true. The documents for contact may be veiled by intervening changes over time and by our inability to recognize historically valid connections. Clearly, our dependence upon the shortcomings of a material record has to hamper this enterprise.

Continuity of platform mound construction can be documented in the American Bottom of the Mississippi River valley where the town of Cahokia arose (Kelly 1990a, 1996). Small rectilinear platform mounds appear at several sites in the American Bottom at the beginning of the eleventh century (Kelly 1990b, 2006b). At about this time, these mounds appear with fine ceramic wares whose stylistic and vessel morphologies connect with those present to the south and to the west of the Mississippi River (Trans-Mississippi South) (Kelly 1991). Prior to the incorporation of the platform mound into the Late Emergent Mississippian villages the larger villages were configured around a central plaza flanked by small courtyards (Kelly 1990a; Kelly et al. 2007). At the west end of the George Reeves phase (ca. 950–1000 C.E.) a large (41.5 m^2) structure was erected with numerous rebuildings. However, it is clear that the creation of the platform mound is the final act that completes the ritual processes that started by erecting buildings that were then destroyed. By the onset of the Mississippian in the region a mound of monumental size resulted from the repeated performance of these rituals (see Pauketat 1993; Smith 1977).

The debate over intercontinental connections has had a long history that we do not need to go into. According to the once prevailing age-area paradigm, the Eastern Woodlands were culturally peripheral to the Mesoamerican source of major innovations. A considerable lag took place for these innovations to reach the Eastern Woodlands, a lag that was in proportion to the distance from the Mesoamerican center. Revised dating of earthworks and other innovations has nullified this paradigm. But before we move on to other reasons, we should point out that the age-area paradigm still exercises an unfortunate influence on archaeological perspectives to this day. Berle Clay (2005) has shown how the Adena culture arose as a conceptual bridge to the cultural complexity of Ohio Hopewell deeply centered in the eastern Midwest. The Adena of the upland South became the necessary intermediary to an earlier mound-building culture situated hypothetically along the Gulf Coast. As a consequence of the legacy of the age-area paradigm, Adena culture retains a place in continental-scale narratives only because of its importance to Eastern Woodlands history. The revised history of mound-building north of the Gulf Coast renders this position on the necessary importance of Adena completely obsolete (Clay 2005).

While the terms of debate have been altered, advances in social theory have necessitated a deconstruction of the diffusion paradigm. Intergroup power relations, including World Systems Theory, have provided a model for all intergroup relationships that has remained largely unquestioned.

In the brief space allotted for what we regard as a complex subject, we want to make two points. The first is to challenge the prevailing assumption that the more complex of the two cultures must dominate the relationship between them. We will call the domination-from-the-center or cultural core as the "radio-transmitter model," with its barrage of signals falling onto foreign ears in distant lands—with or without direct contact. In the absence of evidence for direct contact, this model has enjoyed acceptance as the model of choice—nowadays regarded as down-the-line trade or trade by other means. Eric Wolf characterized it this way: "The European and American diffusionists traced the movement of culture traits over wide geographical areas, implying by their studies that groups, or tribes, or social entities merely served as relay stations in the transmissions of traits and were connected in far-reaching networks of communication" (Wolf 2001:322).

The second point is that complex networks of interconnectedness became important particularly in the wake of capitalistic systems (Wolf 2001). These connections create power gradients that easily can be conflated with far more modest connections that require constant rejuvenation. In that regard what age-area proposals enact is an ancient replica of a modern capitalistic net-work. The dominating influence of the projection-of-power paradigm has more to do with the gaze of capitalists than most would acknowledge (Clay 2005). Intercultural connections become recast in terms of their exploitative potential. It is as if age-area enthusiasts think that it is natural for arts and technology to be accepted because of their potential for monetary return. Only capitalistic practices adopt this exploitative posture. It hardly applies to situations in which the basis of power is tenuous and is constantly under-going challenge.

Contemporary concepts of agency provide some help on the issues. In-tention, choice, and the exercise of power relations on the part of individu-als become the appropriate level for explanation for cultural transmission, not the abstract transfer of so-called "beneficial" ideas and practices. Be-cause the various aspects to intentionality become the focus, it is evident that there is logic to transfers of one kind or another (Sewell 1992). Sherry Ortner (2006) has distinguished between the relations of power and those of simple intentionality—or what she terms a disposition to the enactment of specific projects for limited purposes. A familiar example of this kind of agentic re-lationship is the one developed by Mary Helms (1988). The form of inter-continental relationship of the power type has had little traction for eastern North America. This leaves the field clear to seriously consider its alternative.

The scale within which power relations have operated in aboriginal North America has been described by Kent Flannery (1968). They were manifest in material culture by direct contact or a chain of contacts. He drew force-fully upon the dominating relationships that Northwest Coast groups had upon the cultures of more simply organized inland groups. But the geographic scale was relatively confined and is one that defies export to the Mesoameri-can relationship with the Southeast. Approximately 900–1,000 km separate Mesoamerica from the westernmost outposts of Mississippian culture (Grif-fin 1980) (Figure 9.1).

Recent theoretical considerations in the archaeology of colonial encoun-ters allow us to consider the Helms principle in other ways (Stein 2004). Briefly, the power to dominate or even to influence peoples on the outside has been enunciated by Gil Stein as one conditioned by distance. The far-ther the distance from the homeland center of power, the less weight a visitor can have. Stein has illustrated this principle by the measly power that Uruk tradespeople had in the Anatolian Highlands. Cheek by jowl with locals, the Uruk material culture was not only confined to a residential compound, it had a very restricted impact upon the material culture of the indigenous hosts. Contact for trade yes, but the impact of state-level cultural domination is not in evidence, unless one grants it some impact on future generations.

The barrier that distance throws up is clearly shown by the meager number

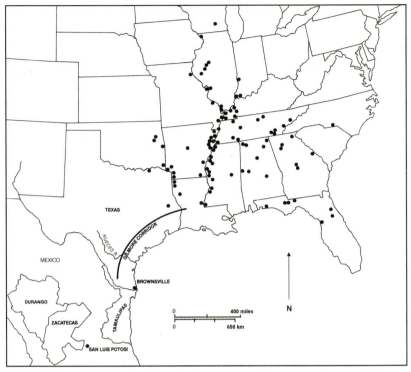

Figure 9.1. Locations of major Mississippian centers with respect to the potential inter-
action corridor that separates them from the nearest contemporary centers in northeast
Mesoamerica. Courtesy of the Center for American Archeology, Kampsville, Illinois.
(From Griffin 1980, *Early Man* 3(2):14.)

of items of Mesoamerican origin that show up in Southeastern sites compared with the more substantial amount from the Southwest (Barker et al.
2002; Cobb et al. 1999). The same is true of cotton cloth, obsidian, and Gulf
of California *Olivella dama* shells ending up at Spiro, located at the western edge of the Southeast (Barker et al. 2002; King and Gardner 1981; Kozuch 2002). In summarizing formerly common models of long-distance interaction, Cobb and colleagues (1999:179) pinpoint an unmet need to identify "the
mechanism by which this continental scale interaction may have occurred."

   Contact usually is dismissed as having any serious impact on the developmental histories. The World Systems model offered by Peregrine (1991,
1995; Peregrine and Lekson 2006) advocates the opposite, at least in principle. In the Eastern Woodlands case the chain of contacts is internal to
the Eastern Woodlands with relatively few instances of external connections
(Brown 2004b; Muller 1995). We have already pointed out the failure to hold
water of the old-line explanations for the list of innovations. Even the cir-

cumstances of development in the American Bottom leading to Mississippian culture document a history in which key innovations do not appear simultaneously, but are separated in time (Beck et al. 2007). In the American Bottom some of the key cultural features associated with Mississippian culture came together hundreds of years prior to its standard beginning at 1050 C.E. For example, stylistic elements such as the beginnings of the Braden style whose impact was felt throughout the Southeast had their early expression in the recesses of caves and rockshelters in east-central Missouri (Diaz-Granados 2004) and southwest Wisconsin (Salzer 2005; Salzer and Rajnovich 2001) during the early eleventh century. A primary image is one identified with Birdman or the Red Horn of late nineteenth-century Siouan myths. Birdman is the precontact form of Morning Star that is visible in the predawn sky. This example allows us to examine the intercontinental connections without invoking the "profound impact" of a power gradient in this massive network cited by Peregrine (1995:248).

As a challenge to the foregoing radio-transmitter model, Helms (1988:58–59) has provided a sterling example of the agency of intentionality. Backed by extensive Central American ethnography, her model is a version of the "projects" level of agency. Helms's research illustrated how spiritual leaders and secular chiefs undertook far-distant trips to acquire the astounding objects and powerful knowledge that validated their claims to divine connections. The beliefs, practices, and objects that they acquired validated their standing as having truly powerful medicine. The logic is obvious. In a world in which sources of power are eagerly sought after, finding or accessing an ontologically prior power is the ultimate attainment. In this climate, the race toward accessing the ultimate source of power is won by the individual who can claim such priority more than any other competitor. A successful trip well beyond what ordinary travelers have accomplished provides that certification of power. Kate Spielmann applies Helms to the Ohio Hopewell in the following words:

> The conquest of distance, to make a trip beyond the known world and return successfully, is a testament to the exceptional qualities the traveler possesses. Successful traveling can be used to enhance one's political prestige, the pieces of place being evidence that the journey actually occurred. . . . This unique material became proof that one had entirely left the world of the Eastern Woodlands. Helms calls this form of journeying power questing [Spielmann 2009:181].

Although the prize of enhanced power at home has been attained by the journey, the quest remains a project initiated locally and achieved by means of resources under the command of individuals.

A potential case in point may be the way in which Aztec tobacco (*Nicotiana rustica*) entered eastern North America. It has not been identified in the east prior to 1100 C.E. (Wagner 2000; but see Jones and Dunavan 2006). Archaeological specimens of tobacco prior to that time have been identified as *N. quadrivalvis*. Some have expressed the opinion that *N. rustica* was transferred to the East through early European contact after the plant was acquired from communities along the coast of Brazil. It only came to the Southwest after Spanish contact (Winter 2000). Consequently, it may be one plant that arrived in the East from northeast Mesoamerica rather than via the Southwest.

Helms (1988:116–118) argues that a similar logic likewise applies to the crafting of particularly fine objects. Instead of invoking the stimulation provided by contact, one need only draw upon observations that direct attention to what it takes to achieve distinction in any endeavor. Gladwell (2008:35–68) popularized the thesis that something on the order of 10,000 iterations of an operation, artistic or otherwise, was essential to have mastered the most difficult steps in a project. When repeated practice yields a superior level of craftwork and artistry, these skills need not have emanated from foreign lands. The capacity lies entirely within the homelands after work effort attains a certain intensity of practice. Refinement in artistry then is not conditioned on contact with superior talents, but upon the honing of local talent to new heights.

We think that a distance of over 1,000 km would constitute a barrier to the impact of domination or even reciprocal trade between the various Mesoamerican centers and the Southeastern chiefdoms. Griffin (1980) concluded from his review that direct contact was highly improbable, had little substantive basis, and in any case contact was more likely to be by down-the-line trade. But the impressive geographical scale of any such contact would provide an appropriate distance with which to validate contact with the ultimate of supernaturals and to return with some token(s) of their power.

Mississippian and Mesoamerican Imagery

Southeastern iconography of the Mississippian period has had a difficult time shedding the lingering perception that the so-called similarities with Mesoamerican depictions are indicative of an ultimate derivation from that continental center.

We will not delve into the commonplace practice of perceiving Mesoamerican resemblances in Southeastern artistic representations, particularly those of the human imagery expressed in the Classic Braden style of the Mississippian period. On this matter Phil Phillips (Phillips and Brown 1978, 1984) rendered an invaluable service by showing that the resemblances were merely just that, a combination of minor potential connections within a multitude of coincidences.

Speaking from the standpoint of the Mississippian connections to earlier Adena-Hopewellian times, Phillips stated:

> In the context of iconography, both traditions are parts of a vast system whose dimensions border on the hemispheric. For explanatory purposes common membership in such a system is of little power. It is for exactly the same reasons that connections between the arts of the Southeast and Mesoamerica have proved so difficult to establish [Phillips and Brown 1978:157].

The archaeologically based historiographies of these images can now be sketched. They reveal a sequence of imagery quite at variance with the thesis that Mesoamerica is the direct source for specific resemblances. The archaeological record reveals cultural roots for Mesoamerican traits going back to the Hopewellian period, 2,000 years ago, as Bob Hall (1989) argued on the basis of a much smaller pool of data. Hall summarized his argument for connections with the statement,

> I have drawn comparisons from the literature of Mesoamerican archaeology and oral tradition that show that the worldviews and belief systems of Mesoamerica and the eastern United States were quite close over a period of many centuries, perhaps millennia. More specific evidence of contacts between Mesoamerica and the eastern United States is found in the Osages' apparent awareness of the Mesoamerican date Thirteen Reed and its association with the birth of the sun, in the strong parallel between the Iowa/Winnebago myth of Red Horn and the experiences of the character One Hunter in the Quiche Mayan *Popol Vuh*, in the similarity of origin myths of the Choctaws and Aztecs, and in the use of the Greater Cahokia area of blood autosacrifice in a form and with a function like that found in Mexico [Hall 1989:278].

Each of these are elements of ritual or are plausibly connected with ritual. In such a role they could readily belong to projects entered into on the part of the practitioners themselves.

Stylistic Histories

Superficial similarities between images of each region notwithstanding, an examination of the stylistic histories of relevant Mesoamerican and Mississippian regions reveals a strong level of independent development in each.

Since the completion of Phillips's monumental study of Spiro engraved marine shell, evidence has accumulated from a variety of quarters to show that the "realism" of the Classic Braden style (or the Braden A School of Phil Phillips) has a long history in the eastern prairies of the Midwest in Illinois, Missouri, and Wisconsin (Brown and Kelly 2000; Muller and Brown 2012). This so-called realism has been the source for Mesoamerican speculations since William Holmes's (1883) declarations on the subject (Brown 2004a). Characterized this way, Classic Braden becomes the poster child for civilized sophistication among otherwise unbenighted local cultures. Such a dismissive approach to indigenous artistic achievements is undermined in two respects. The style complex is now recognized as encompassing a broad stretch of the Mississippi River valley, from Vicksburg to the Wisconsin area. One of the two regions we know most about covers the eastern prairies of the Midwest (Brown 1989, 2004a). The center of creativity for this region is Cahokia, where the most refined expressions of work in shell and copper are known for the thirteenth century (Brown and Kelly 2000). Evidence exists from several sites in the region that the style has preceding history reaching back to the tenth century at least (Muller and Brown 2012). Ironically, the early manifestations are known from the Midwest, even more remote from the supposed Mesoamerican source than the Southeast proper (Brown 2004a).

Hawk and falcon imagery has long been the focus for speculation about Aztec eagle inspiration. The alleged correspondence is superficial. First, the falcon is a symbol for rebirth through cosmic combat with the life-taking forces, which does not correspond with the place of the eagle in an iconology south of the international border (Brown 2004a, 2007; Brown and Dye 2007). Second, falcon symbolism has persistent cultural associations from pre-Mississippian times to the present in the eastern prairies (Brown 2011). Third, its cosmic role is readily explained by its natural history. Because the peregrine falcon undertakes annual migrations from Canada to South America along the Mississippi River valley, the cliffs that flank the valley in southern Illinois and Missouri constitute a unique hunting habitat not replicated elsewhere (Grossman and Hamlet 1964). Other hawks and falconids reside in the area year-round, but the abrupt appearance and subsequent disappearance of the falcon in myth and legend contributes to the bird's appropriately mysterious powers (Radin 1948). Through the Morning Star symbolism the bird's cycle of appearance and disappearance accords with the semiannual dominance of planet Venus in the predawn sky. Hence, it is logical for observers of nature to conceive of a connection between the behavior of the bird and the "star."

Radiocarbon dating has been particularly revealing about the antiquity of the falcon in the humanoid spirit form of Birdman. Well-realized imagery of this and other spirits probably makes its appearance during Emergent Mississippian times. The Picture Cave example is not alone (Muller and Brown 2012). The earliest recognized form of this and other spirits in the engraved marine shell art are the engraved cups bearing human figures of the Classic Braden style (Brown 2004a). The surfaces of selected pottery are likewise treated in this style (Brown and Kelly 2000). A distinctive attribute of the pre-1050 work in shell is the champlevé effect that was achieved by carving out the background around the engraved imagery (Phillips and Brown 1978:Cup 1). This effect was achieved by removing the shell matrix around the imagery midway into the body of the shell.

Birdman can be traced by one of his three identifiers—namely, the Long Nosed God, the bi-lobed arrow, and the single long braid (Brown 2005). The first of these is readily identified in the archaeological record by the maskette ear ornaments in copper and shell. The other two are represented in depictions in rock art, shell, and copper work. A particularly splendid example on one of the walls of Picture Cave in Missouri provided pigment that was dated at least to 1000 c.e., if not earlier (Diaz-Granados et al. 2001).

The history of the major art styles in the Mississippian period helps frame the discussion of diffusion into the Southeast. From the beginning around 1050 c.e. this period exhibits strong regionalism beneath the common veneer of platform mound ceremonialism and a shell-tempered technology for making pottery. First of all, the eastern prairies, of which the lower portion was once part of the greater Southeast, provides the basic inspiration for what was to unfold in the Mississippian period. As cited above, the Birdman myth cycle was well established in the preceding Emergent Mississippian period. Its rootedness in the eastern prairies is likely to have been predicated by past expression of the Hopewell phenomenon in a particularly vigorous form.

The Classic Braden style seems to belong to a cluster of styles established early in several regional forms (Figure 9.2). One of these, the Bellaire style, which was centered on the Lower Mississippi River valley in the vicinity of the Plaquemine culture, has been segregated from core contemporary Classic Braden examples (Knight et al. 2008). The knotted double-headed snake is probably a specialty of this regional expression. To this image can be added a distinctive focus on the owl and the panther (Knight et al. 2008). By the mid-thirteenth century this Lower Valley expression and the now redefined Classic Braden changed into something that can be called the Late Braden style group. Coexisting within this expanded Braden style group were less distinctive and more idiosyncratic styles of expression.

In the twelfth century an impressive corpus of human and human/animal sculptures was fabricated in the American Bottom area from a redstone,

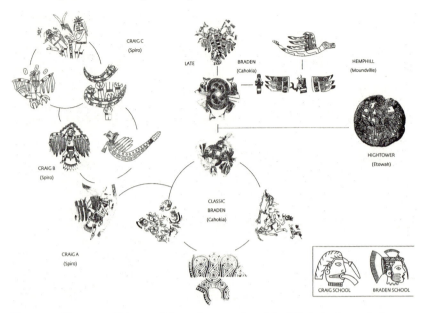

Figure 9.2. Conceptual history of the major art styles of the Mississippian period as a tree. (Layout from the Art Institute of Chicago. Additional images were adapted from Philip Phillips and James A. Brown, *Pre-Columbian Shell Engravings from the Craig Mound at Spiro, Oklahoma,* Vols. 1 through 6, Peabody Museum Press, Harvard University, Figures 179, 189, 262. Copyright 1975, 1979, 1980, and 1982 by the President and Fellows of Harvard College.)

known commercially as fireclay or flintclay, available from exposures in nearby Missouri (Emerson et al. 2003). Reilly (2004) and others (Brown 2011; Emerson 1989; Prentice 1986) have argued that these images represent hero-spirits or gods and goddesses. By 1200 C.E. redstone figure production declines, or even halts altogether, to be replaced by image-making conventions executed in light-colored stones (Brown 2004a; Kelly 2006a).

Sufficient information is available to present a model of stylistic development of imagery from 900 to 1500 C.E. Although some of these images are commonly emphasized to compose a Southeastern Ceremonial Complex, the selection is arbitrary. It ignores their separate histories as discrete motifs and independent stylistic elements (Brown 2004a; Brown and Kelly 2000; Knight 2006). If one were to suppose that the Classic Braden style at Cahokia represented the trunk of a style tree, its direct descendant, Late Braden, would lie on the central branch (Figure 9.2). A major side branch to the left delineates the Craig stylistic sequence of A, then B, and finally C, centered on the Arkansas and Red River watersheds. The Craig style was preeminently

Figure 9.3. Close iconic similarities in engraved marine shell between eastern Tennessee/ northern Georgia and northeastern Mesoamerica. Left, Hightower style gorget, Big Toco type, Birdman; right, Huastecan style sectoral, "Mixcoatl." (Image adapted from Philip Phillips and James A. Brown, *Pre-Columbian Shell Engravings from the Craig Mound at Spiro, Oklahoma*, Vol. 1, Peabody Museum Press, copyright 1975 by the President and Fellows of Harvard College, Figures 177, 180.)

associated with the Spiro site although little evidence exists of its production there. The Hightower and the Hemphill styles from the Etowah–Upper Tennessee and Moundville areas, respectively, appear to be branches as well (Brown 2004a:109).

Two examples of external agentic connections of the project type stand out for comment. First of these is the provocative resemblance of a particular Huastecan marine shell gorget from the northeastern edge of Mesoamerica with a Hightower style gorget from the southern Appalachian Southeast (Figure 9.3; Phillips and Brown 1978:128). Although the latter is commonly called the Big Toco "style" (Brain and Phillips 1996:44–49), it is more appropriate to regard it as just one type of image within a more embracing Hightower style (King 2011; Muller 1989, 1997; Reilly and Garber 2011). The posture and design layout of this and allied types focus around a frontally seated winged figure. The raptorial claws communicate a Birdman connection in the Big Toco type variation. When two figures compose the image, they are shown in a combative pose. In other variations, the right hand holds either an elongated swordlike object or an object that Knight and Franke (2007) identify as the sphinx moth. They supply convincing evidence that the sphinx moth is the primary natural prototype. These connections hold our attention because this moth is a pollinator of the tobacco plant. Knight and Franke (2007) point to the mothlike patterning of the fanlike wings. They also reveal that the peculiar serpentine element in the hand has a forked end that mimics the chrysalis of an emerging moth. Each of these lepidopteron elements joins with human ones to create a series of interconnected images combining Birdman with a supernatural moth. The quintessential message of human rebirth is affirmed by the presence of two bi-lobed arrows positioned in the composition above the outstretched arms of Birdman (Brown 2005, 2007). The age of Hightower style gorgets at Etowah is around 1300 C.E..

The imagery of the Huastecan gorget stands apart, as far as we are aware, from the many other gorgets from the area (Beyer 1933). Neurath (1992:4) identifies the central figure as a god cognate with Mixcoatl or Huitzilopochtli, deities associated with the hunt and with the stars (Figure 9.3, right). Note that the insect in the right hand is impressively analogous to another species of insect in the same position on the Hightower style warrior gorgets (Knight and Franke 2007). In both cases we are dealing with what has been identified independently as the Morning Star hero (Brown 2007; Neurath 1992). Although the stylistic rendering and details of costume made it absolutely Huastecan, the elements and their deployment in the composition clearly replicate the Big Toco type of the Hightower gorget. So far as we are aware, the Huastecan gorget is without local parallels (Beyer 1933). The implications are strong that the Huastecan artist took a template from Tennessee or Georgia to create a composition that employed locally understood format and detail.

The second example includes more specimens and does not involve the great distances exemplified in the first. The resemblance between the famous winged human figure on a Craig B shell cup and certain kiva designs of the "Knife-Wing Being" type in the Rio Grande region has been remarked upon for years (Cobb et al. 1999:180; Holmes 1883:Plate 76) (Figure 9.4). Since Phillips's study we can acknowledge that the Birdman so displayed belongs to a historical sequence of such figures that go back to 1000 C.E. at least in the radiocarbon-dated example from Picture Cave in Missouri (Diaz-Granados et al. 2001). The similarity with the Kiva 9 painting at Pottery Mound pueblo in New Mexico is strong enough to merit comparison (Figure 9.4, left; Schaafsma 2000). Although the frequently illustrated Museum of the American Indian image example of Craig B style has borne the burden of comparison, details in the bird's claws point more convincingly to the less well-known corpus of later Craig C examples (Phillips and Brown 1984:Plates 200 and 302) (Figure 9.4, right). Bear in mind that the aforementioned stereotypic Craig B example has human legs and feet (Phillips and Brown 1984:Plate 203). In both the Kiva 9 example and in the many examples in the Spiro corpus, the claw is drawn within the confines of a circle. This is quite unlike the more naturalistic claws of Craig A and Craig B in which the claws are depicted more linearly and with the rear talon in oppo-

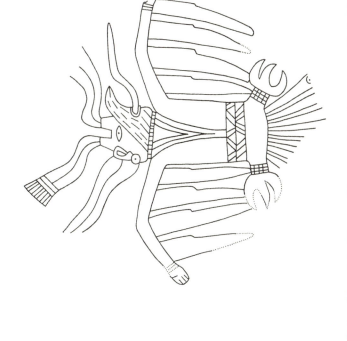

Figure 9.4. Close iconic similarities between the 1350–1450 C.E. Pottery Mound site Kiva 9 wall image and the circa 1400 C.E. Craig Mound (Spiro) Great Mortuary marine shell cup engraving in Craig C style. Left, Knife-Wing Being; right, Birdman (Morning Star) Craig C style. Note the parallels in the blocky bodies and the circular outline claws. (Left-hand image courtesy of K. C. VanDooven, KC Publications, Wickenburg, Arizona. Reproduced from Schaafsma 2000:Figure 3.34. Right-hand image adapted from Philip Phillips and James A. Brown, *Pre-Columbian Shell Engravings from the Craig Mound at Spiro, Oklahoma*, Vol. 6, 1982:Plate 302, Peabody Museum Press, copyright 1982 by the President and Fellows of Harvard College.)

sition to the front ones. The age of the Pottery Mound example is bracketed between 1375 and 1450 C.E. (Schaafsma, ed. 2007); the Spiro Great Mortuary contexts of the shells date around 1400 C.E. or a little later (Brown 1996).

The Birdman image on the Museum of the American Indian cup is relevant to this discussion because of the presence of the stepped cloud motif surmounting our Birdman hero (Figure 9.5). Lankford (2006) has combed the literature for examples of what is regionally called the terrace motif, which occurs on both Classic and Late Braden shell art and on Craig A examples as well. The dating is tricky because the contexts have special problems if they are known at all. But based on the work undertaken at Moundville, an age between 1200 and 1300 C.E. seems to bracket most examples. Lankford (2006) concluded that the motif was a result of cross-Plains contact with the direction from the Southwest to the Southeast.

Around 1250 C.E. is the time that Schaafsma (2000, 2007) estimates the Knife-Wing Being made its appearance in the Southwest. The picture that emerges from this two-way transfer of theme and motif is a complex cross-Plains interaction over at least one hundred years. It does not seem to be a one-off happening because the Knife-Wing Being at Pottery Mound is coordinated stylistically with a 1400s Craig style detail. Thus an ongoing transfer seems to have been repeated many times. Of course many questions go begging with this and other examples. In the case of the Knife-Wing Being, is this an example of cult transmission from east to west, or the reverse? And what role did the seeming eastward transfer of the cloud device have in this process? Again in both cases the hero image is that of a spiritual being associated with fertility and warfare: Morning Star.

Explaining Resemblances

An enlarged circle of resemblances discloses geographic continuities between the regions that call for explanation. The genealogy of the Birdman theme has a strong connection with the western edge of the Southeast, as conventionally considered, that persisted from Woodland times through the Mississippian period. If one were to include ethnological correlates its presence would have to be acknowledged well into the early twentieth century. The associations with a cult in which Morning Star triumphs over enemies in war, reanimates the dead, and fosters the continued procreation of the human line are very strong. The imagery is that of raptorial boldness of the falcon and a continued line of descendants likened to the flight of a sacred arrow. Bob Hall (1997) has demonstrated the presence of Birdman imagery (e.g., bi-lobed arrow) and practices connected with honoring the falcon (e.g., calumet ceremonialism, particularly in its early form) as permeating the precontact archaeological record. Although they appear to be quite disparate in their presence, they make more sense as part of one or more cults. The exis-

Figure 9.5. Craig B style Birdman from the Great Mortuary at Spiro. Note the terraced cloud motif. (Image adapted from Philip Phillips and James A. Brown, *Pre-Columbian Shell Engravings from the Craig Mound at Spiro, Oklahoma,* Vol. 5, 1980:Plate 203, Peabody Museum Press, copyright 1980 by the President and Fellows of Harvard College.)

tence of a core of belief and practice, however, is essential to unify disparate images, symbols, objects, and even practices.

An emphasis on one-to-one correspondence at the artifact or symbol level, however, is bound to yield fruitless results. At the conceptual level, a great deal can be said in favor of the transmission of cultic practices by way of inspired quests. But let us be concrete. Cults have a derived power. When acquired through personal contact from far-distant places, cults assume an ontological superiority that cements whatever social and political relations are ongoing at the time. Their real power in this light is that they have the capability of enduring well past the time they were initially acquired and as such form the basis of other, different religious movements later. They can become the basis for political power to come. What cultic transmissions are not is any projection of power from some distant place. As a consequence models that derive from that kind of projection are clearly not suitable in the eastern United States case.

Acknowledgments

We would like to express our indebtedness to Prof. F. Kent Reilly III, who has been a constant font for productive ideas. On more than one occasion discussions held during his annual workshop on Mississippian Iconography at Texas State University have helped to sharpen these and other positions. However, we take responsibility for the views expressed herein.

References Cited

Barker, Alexander W., Craig E. Skinner, M. Steven Shackley, Michael D. Glascock, and J. Daniel Rogers

    2002   Mesoamerican Origin for an Obsidian Scraper from the Precolumbian Southeastern United States. *American Antiquity* 67:103–108.

Beck, Robin A., Jr., Douglas J. Bolander, James A. Brown, and Timothy K. Earle

    2007   Eventful Archaeology: The Place of Space in Structural Transformation. *Current Anthropology* 48:833–860.

Beyer, Hermann

    1933   Shell Ornament Sets from the Huasteca, Mexico. Department of Middle American Research, Tulane University. *Middle American Research Series* 5, pp. 153–215. New Orleans.

Brain, Jeffrey P., and Philip Phillips

    1996   *Shell Gorgets: Styles of the Late Prehistoric and Protohistoric Southeast.* Peabody Museum Press, Harvard University, Cambridge, Massachusetts.

Brown, James A.

    1989   On Style Divisions of the Southeastern Ceremonial Complex: A Revisionist Perspective. In *Southeastern Ceremonial Complex: Artifacts and Analysis: The Cottonlandia Conference,* edited by Patricia K. Galloway, pp. 183–204. University of Nebraska Press, Lincoln.

    1996   *The Spiro Ceremonial Center: The Archaeology of Arkansas Valley Caddoan Culture in Eastern Oklahoma.* 2 vols. Memoirs of the Museum of Anthropology No. 29. University of Michigan, Ann Arbor.

    1997   The Archaeology of Ancient Religion in the Eastern Woodlands. *Annual Review of Anthropology* 26:465–485.

    2004a   The Cahokia Expression: Creating Court and Cult. In *Hero, Hawk, and Open Hand: American Indian Art of the Ancient Midwest and South,* edited by Richard F. Townsend and Robert V. Sharp, pp. 104–123. Art Institute of Chicago, Chicago.

    2004b   Exchange and Interaction to A.D. 1500. In *Southeast,* edited by Raymond D. Fogelson, pp. 677–685. *Handbook of North American Indians,* Vol. 14, William C. Sturtevant, general editor. Smithsonian Institution, Washington, D.C.

2005   Beyond Red Horn: Where Ethnology Meets History. Paper presented at the 70th Annual Meeting of the Society for American Archaeology, Salt Lake City.

2007   On the Identity of the Birdman within Mississippian Period Art and Iconography. In *Ancient Objects and Sacred Realms: Interpretations of Mississippian Iconography,* edited by F. Kent Reilly III and James F. Garber, pp. 56–106. University of Texas Press, Austin.

2011   The Regional Culture Signature of the Braden Art Style. In *Visualizing the Sacred: Cosmic Visions, Regionalism, and the Art of the Mississippian World,* edited by George E. Lankford, F. Kent Reilly III, and James Garber, pp. 37–63. University of Texas Press, Austin.

Brown, James, and David Dye

2007   Severed Heads and Sacred Scalplocks: Mississippian Iconographic Trophies. In *The Taking and Displaying of Human Body Parts as Trophies by Amerindians,* edited by Richard J. Chacon and David H. Dye, pp. 274–294. Kluwer Academic/Plenum, New York.

Brown, James, and John Kelly

2000   Cahokia and the Southeastern Ceremonial Complex. In *Mounds, Modoc, and Mesoamerica: Papers in Honor of Melvin L. Fowler,* edited by Steven R. Ahler, pp. 469–510. Scientific Paper 55. Illinois State Museum, Springfield.

Clark, John E.

2004   Surrounding the Sacred: Geometry and Design of Early Mound Groups as Meaning and Function. In *Signs of Power: The Rise of Cultural Complexity in the Southeast,* edited by Jon L. Gibson and Philip J. Carr, pp. 162–213. The University of Alabama Press, Tuscaloosa.

Clark, John E., and Michelle Knoll

2005   The American Formative Revisited. In *Gulf Coast Archaeology: The Southeastern United States and Mexico,* edited by Nancy Marie White, pp. 281–303. University Press of Florida, Gainesville.

Clay, R. Berle

2005   Adena, Rest in Peace? In *Woodland Period Systematics in the Middle Ohio Valley,* edited by Darlene Applegate and Robert C. Mainfort, pp. 94–110. The University of Alabama Press, Tuscaloosa.

Cobb, Charles, Jeffrey Maymon, and Randall H. McGuire

1999   Feathered, Horned, and Antlered Serpents: Mesoamerican Connection with the Southwest and the Southeast. In *Great Towns and Regional Polities in the Prehistoric American Southwest and Southeast,* edited by Jill E. Neitzel, pp. 165–181. University of New Mexico Press, Albuquerque.

Diaz-Granados, Carol

2004   Marking Stone, Land, Body, and Spirit: Rock Art and Mississippian Iconography. In *Hero, Hawk, and Open Hand: American Indian Art of the An-*

cient Midwest and South, edited by Richard F. Townsend and Robert V. Sharp, pp. 138–149. Art Institute of Chicago, Chicago.

Diaz-Granados, Carol, Marvin W. Rowe, Marian Hyman, James R. Duncan, and John R. Southon
2001   AMS Radiocarbon Dates for Charcoal from Three Missouri Pictographs and Their Associated Iconography. *American Antiquity* 66:481–492.

Emerson, Thomas E.
1989   Water, Serpents, and the Underworld: An Exploration into Cahokian Symbolism. In *Southeastern Ceremonial Complex: Artifacts and Analysis: The Cottonlandia Conference,* edited by Patricia K. Galloway, pp. 45–92. University of Nebraska Press, Lincoln.

Emerson, Thomas E., Randall E. Hughes, Mary R. Hynes, and Sarah U. Wisseman
2003   The Sourcing and Interpretation of Cahokia-Style Figurines in the Trans-Mississippi South and Southeast. *American Antiquity* 68:287–313.

Flannery, Kent V.
1968   The Olmec and the Valley of Oaxaca: A Model for Inter-regional Interaction in Formative Times. In *Dumbarton Oaks Conference on the Olmec,* edited by Elizabeth P. Benson, pp. 79–110. Dumbarton Oaks, Washington, D.C.

Ford, James A.
1969   *A Comparison of Formative Cultures in the Americas.* Smithsonian Contributions to Anthropology 11. Smithsonian Institution Press, Washington, D.C.

Gladwell, Malcolm
2008   *Outliers: The Story of Success.* Little-Brown, New York.

Griffin, James B.
1980   The Mesoamerican-Southeastern US Connection. *Early Man* 3(2):12–18.

Grossman, Marie Louise, and John Hamlet
1964   *Birds of Prey of the World.* Clarkson H. Potter, New York.

Hall, Robert L.
1989   The Cultural Background of Mississippian Symbolism. In *Southeastern Ceremonial Complex: Artifacts and Analysis: The Cottonlandia Conference,* edited by Patricia K. Galloway, pp. 238–278. University of Nebraska Press, Lincoln.
1997   *An Archaeology of the Soul: North American Indian Belief and Ritual.* University of Illinois Press, Urbana.

Helms, Mary W.
1988   *Ulysses' Sail: An Ethnographic Odyssey of Power, Knowledge, and Geographic Distance.* Princeton University Press, Princeton, New Jersey.

Holmes, William H.
1883   *Art in Shell of the Ancient Americans.* Bureau of American Ethnology Annual Report 2, pp. 185–305. U.S. Government Printing Office, Washington, D.C.

Jones, Volney H., and Sandra L. Dunavan

2006   Tobacco. In *Environment, Origins, and Population,* edited by Douglas H. Ubelaker, pp. 447–451. *Handbook of North American Indians,* Vol. 3, William C. Sturtevant, general editor. Smithsonian Institution, Washington, D.C.

Kehoe, Alice B., and F. Kent Reilly III

2003   A Mohican Meets Mesoamericans. In *A Deep-Time Perspective: Studies in Symbols, Meaning, and the Archaeological Record,* edited by John D. Richards and Melvin L. Fowler, pp. 267–297. *The Wisconsin Archeologist* 84(1-2).

Kelly, John E.

1990a   Range Site Community Patterns and the Mississippian Emergence. In *The Mississippian Emergence,* edited by Bruce D. Smith, pp. 67–112. Smithsonian Institution Press, Washington, D.C.

1990b   The Emergence of Mississippian Culture in the American Bottom Region. In *The Mississippian Emergence,* edited by Bruce Smith, pp. 113–152. Smithsonian Institution Press, Washington, D.C.

1991   The Evidence for Prehistoric Exchange and Its Implications for the Development of Cahokia. In *New Perspectives on Cahokia: Views from the Periphery,* edited by James B. Stoltman, pp. 65–92. *Monographs in World Prehistory,* Vol. 2. Prehistory Press, Madison, Wisconsin.

1996   Redefining Cahokia: Principles and Elements of Community Organization. In *The Ancient Skies and Sky Watchers of Cahokia: Woodhenges, Eclipses, and Cahokian Cosmology,* edited by Melvin L. Fowler. *The Wisconsin Archeologist* 77(3-4):97–119.

2006a   The Ritualization of Cahokia: The Structure and Organization of Early Cahokia Crafts. In *Leadership and Polity in Mississippian Society,* edited by Brian M. Butler and Paul D. Welch, pp. 236–263. Occasional Paper 33. Center for Archaeological Investigations, Southern Illinois University, Carbondale.

2006b   Washausen and the "Big Bang": Understanding the Context of the Ripple Effect. Paper presented at the 60th Annual Meeting of the Southeastern Archaeological Conference, Little Rock, Arkansas.

Kelly, John E., Steven J. Ozuk, and Joyce A. Williams

2007   *The Range Site: The Emergent Mississippian, George Reeves and Lindeman Phase Components.* ITARP, Transportation Archaeological Research Reports 18. University of Illinois, Urbana-Champaign.

King, Adam

2011   Iconography of the Hightower Region of Eastern Tennessee and Northern Georgia. In *Visualizing the Sacred: Cosmic Visions, Regionalism, and the Art of the Mississippian World,* edited by George E. Lankford, F. Kent Reilly III, and James Garber, pp. 279–293. University of Texas Press, Austin.

King, Mary Elizabeth, and Joan S. Gardner

1981   The Analysis of Textiles from Spiro Mound, Oklahoma. In *The Research Potential of Anthropological Museum Collections,* edited by Anne-Marie E. Cantwell, James B. Griffin, and Nan A. Rothschild, pp. 123–139. *Annals of the New York Academy of Science* 376.

Knight, Vernon James, Jr.

2006   Farewell to the Southeastern Ceremonial Complex. *Southeastern Archaeology* 25:1–5.

Knight, Vernon James, Jr., and Judith A. Franke

2007   Identification of a Moth/Butterfly Supernatural in Mississippian Art. In *Ancient Objects and Sacred Realms: Interpretations of Mississippian Iconography,* edited by F. Kent Reilly III and James F. Garber, pp. 136–151. University of Texas Press, Austin.

Knight, Vernon James, Jr., Robert Sharp, and George Lankford

2008   Report on Lower Mississippi Valley Iconography. Prepared for the 2008 Mississippian Iconographic Workshop, San Marcos, Texas.

Kozuch, Laura

2002   Olivella Beads from Spiro and the Plains. *American Antiquity* 67:697–709.

Lankford, George E.

2006   Some Southwestern Influences in the Southeastern Ceremonial Complex. *The Arkansas Archeologist* 45:1–25.

Muller, Jon D.

1989   The Southern Cult. In *Southeastern Ceremonial Complex: Artifacts and Analysis: The Cottonlandia Conference,* edited by Patricia K. Galloway, pp. 11–26. University of Nebraska Press, Lincoln.

1995   Regional Interaction in the Later Southeast. In *Native American Interactions: Multiscalar Analyses and Interpretations in the Eastern Woodlands,* edited by Michael S. Nassaney and Kenneth E. Sassaman, pp. 317–340. University of Tennessee Press, Knoxville.

1997   Review of Brain and Phillips, *Shell Gorgets: Styles of the Late Prehistoric and Protohistoric Southeast. Southeastern Archaeology* 16:176–178.

Muller, Jon D., and James Brown

2012   Tradition and Horizons in Southeastern Representation: Lessons from the Picture Cave. In *Picture Cave Interdisciplinary Project,* edited by Carol Diaz-Granados and F. Kent Reilly. University of Texas Press, Austin.

Neurath, Johannes

1992   Mesoamerica and the Southern Ceremonial Complex. *European Review of Native American Studies* 6:1–8.

Ortner, Sherry

2006   *Anthropology and Social Theory: Culture, Power, and the Acting Subject.* Duke University Press, Durham, North Carolina.

Pauketat, Timothy R.

1993   Temples for Cahokia's Lords: Preston Holder's 1955–1956 Excavations of Kunnemann Mound. Memoirs of the Museum of Anthropology No. 26. University of Michigan, Ann Arbor.

Peregrine, Peter N.

1991   *Mississippian Evolution: A World-Systems Perspective.* Prehistory Press, Madison, Wisconsin.

1995   Networks of Power: The Mississippian World-System. In *Native American Interactions: Multiscalar Analyses and Interpretations in the Eastern Woodlands,* edited by Michael S. Nassaney and Kenneth E. Sassaman, pp. 247–265. University of Tennessee Press, Knoxville.

Peregrine, Peter N., and Stephen H. Lekson

2006   Southeast, Southwest, Mexico: Continental Perspectives on Mississippian Polities. In *Leadership and Polity in Mississippian Society,* edited by Brian M. Butler and Paul D. Welch, pp. 351–364. Occasional Paper 33. Center for Archaeological Investigations, Southern Illinois University Carbondale.

Phillips, Philip, and James A. Brown

1975   *Pre-Columbian Shell Engravings from the Craig Mound at Spiro, Oklahoma,* Vol. 1. Peabody Museum Press, Harvard University, Cambridge, Massachusetts.

1978   *Pre-Columbian Shell Engravings from the Craig Mound at Spiro, Oklahoma, Part 1.* Peabody Museum of Archaeology and Ethnology, Harvard University, Cambridge, Massachusetts.

1979   *Pre-Columbian Shell Engravings from the Craig Mound at Spiro, Oklahoma,* Vol. 4. Peabody Museum Press, Harvard University, Cambridge, Massachusetts.

1980   *Pre-Columbian Shell Engravings from the Craig Mound at Spiro, Oklahoma,* Vol. 5. Peabody Museum Press, Harvard University, Cambridge, Massachusetts.

1982   *Pre-Columbian Shell Engravings from the Craig Mound at Spiro, Oklahoma,* Vol. 6. Peabody Museum Press, Harvard University, Cambridge, Massachusetts.

1984   *Pre-Columbian Shell Engravings from the Craig Mound at Spiro, Oklahoma, Part 2.* Peabody Museum of Archaeology and Ethnology, Harvard University, Cambridge, Massachusetts.

Prentice, Guy

1986   An Analysis of the Symbolism Expressed by the Birger Figurine. *American Antiquity* 51:239–266.

Radin, Paul

1948   *Winnebago Hero Cycles: A Study in Aboriginal Literature.* Indiana University Publications in Anthropology and Linguistics, Bloomington.

Reilly, F. Kent, III

2004   People of Earth, People of Sky: Visualizing the Sacred in Native American Art of the Mississippian Period. In *Hero, Hawk, and Open Hand: American Indian Art of the Ancient Midwest and South,* edited by Richard F. Townsend and Robert V. Sharp, pp. 124–137. Art Institute of Chicago, Chicago.

Reilly, F. Kent, III, and James F. Garber

2011   Dancing in the Otherworld: The Human Figural Art of the Hightower Style Revisited. In *Visualizing the Sacred: Cosmic Visions, Regionalism, and the Art of the Mississippian World,* edited by George E. Lankford, F. Kent Reilly III, and James Garber, pp. 294–312. University of Texas Press, Austin.

Reilly, F. Kent, III, and James F. Garber (editors)

2006   *Studies in Mississippian Iconography I.* University of Texas Press, Austin.

Salzer, Robert J.

2005   The Gottschall Site: 3,500 Years of Ideological Continuity and Change. In *Native Symbolic Expression around the Great Lakes and Beyond,* edited by W. A. Fox and R. J. Pearce. *Ontario Archaeology* 79/80:109–114.

Salzer, Robert J., and Grace Rajnovich

2001   *The Gottschall Rockshelter: An Archaeological Mystery.* Prairie Smoke Press, St. Paul, Minnesota.

Saunders, Joe W., Rolfe D. Mandel, Roger T. Saucier, E. Thurman Allen, C. T. Hallmark, Jay K. Johnson, Edwin H. Jackson, Charles M. Allen, Gary L. Stringer, Douglas S. Frink, James K. Feathers, Stephen Williams, Kristen J. Gremillion, Malcolm F. Vidrine, and Reca Jones

1997   A Mound Complex in Louisiana at 5400–5000 Years before Present. *Science* 277:1796–1799.

Schaafsma, Polly

2000   *Warrior, Shield, and Star: Imagery and Ideology of Pueblo Warfare.* Western Edge Press, Santa Fe, New Mexico.

2007   Head Trophies and Scalping: Images in Southwest Rock Art. In *The Taking and Displaying of Human Body Parts as Trophies by Amerindians,* edited by Richard J. Chacon and David H. Dye, pp. 90–123. Kluwer Academic/Plenum, New York.

Schaafsma, Polly (editor)

2007   *New Perspectives on Pottery Mound Pueblo.* University of New Mexico Press, Albuquerque.

Sewell, William H., Jr.

1992   A Theory of Structure: Duality, Agency, and Transformation. *American Journal of Sociology* 98:1–29.

Smith, Harriet M.

1977   The Murdock Mound: Cahokia Site. In *Explorations in Cahokia Archae-*

ology, 2nd rev. ed., edited by Melvin L. Fowler, pp. 49–88. Bulletin 7, Illinois Archaeological Survey. University of Illinois, Urbana.

Spielmann, Katherine A.

2009   Ohio Hopewell Ritual Craft Production. In *Footprints: In the Footprints of Squier and Davis: Archeological Fieldwork in Ross County, Ohio,* edited by Mark J. Lynott, pp. 179–188. Midwest Archeological Center Special Report No. 5. U.S. Department of the Interior, National Park Service, Midwest Archeological Center, Lincoln, Nebraska.

Stein, Gil J. (editor)

2004   *The Archaeology of Colonial Encounters.* School of American Research, Santa Fe, New Mexico.

Steward, Julian H.

1947   American Culture History in the Light of South America. *Southwestern Journal of Anthropology* 3:85–107.

Townsend, Richard F., and Robert V. Sharp (editors)

2004   *Hero, Hawk, and Open Hand: American Indian Art of the Ancient Midwest and South.* Art Institute of Chicago, Chicago.

Wagner, Gail E.

2000   Tobacco in Prehistoric Eastern North America. In *Tobacco Use by Native North Americans: Sacred Smoke and Silent Killer,* edited by Joseph C. Winter, pp. 185–201. University of Oklahoma Press, Norman.

Webb, Malcolm C.

1989   Functional and Historical Parallelisms between Mesoamerican and Mississippian Cultures. In *Southeastern Ceremonial Complex: Artifacts and Analysis: The Cottonlandia Conference,* edited by Patricia K. Galloway, pp. 279–293. University of Nebraska Press, Lincoln.

White, Nancy Marie

2005   Prehistoric Connections around the Gulf Coast. In *Gulf Coast Archaeology: The Southeastern United States and Mexico,* edited by Nancy Marie White, pp. 1–55. University Press of Florida, Gainesville.

White, Nancy Marie (editor)

2005   *Gulf Coast Archaeology: The Southeastern United States and Mexico.* University Press of Florida, Gainesville.

White, Nancy Marie, and Richard A. Weinstein

2008   The Mexican Connection and the Far West of the U.S. Southeast. *American Antiquity* 73:227–277.

Wicke, Charles R.

1965   Pyramids and Temple Mounds: Mesoamerican Ceremonial Architecture in Eastern North America. *American Antiquity* 30:409–420.

Widmer, Randolph J.

2005   A New Look at the Gulf Coast Formative. In *Gulf Coast Archaeology:*

The Southeastern United States and Mexico, edited by Nancy Marie White, pp. 68–86. University Press of Florida, Gainesville.

Winter, Joseph C. (editor)

2000   *Tobacco Use by Native North Americans: Sacred Smoke and Silent Killer.* University of Oklahoma Press, Norman.

Wolf, Eric R.

2001   *Pathways of Power: Building an Anthropology of the Modern World.* University of California Press, Berkeley.

10
Landscapes of Memory and Presence in the Canadian Shield

John Norder

In the study of rock art sites in archaeology, a substantial portion of research has emphasized symbolic and iconographic understandings. In other words, research has typically revolved around the following question: What did the images placed at a rock art site mean to the people who created them (e.g., Figure 10.1)? In pursuing these issues, one aspect of these sites that researchers have come to focus on is that part of their symbolic capital, in addition to the composition(s) present, is the location. Within this more inclusive perspective, the notion of "place" becomes part of how these sites are conceived. Subsequently, rock art sites have increasingly been studied as part of sacred landscapes, where rock art serves to mark locations of religious and cosmological significance of a given community (Arsenault 2004a, 2004b; Lewis-Williams 1977; Whitley 1998, 2000, 2001).

In contextualizing rock art sites within a sacred landscape, these places become part of a geography structured by spiritual and cosmological perceptions of the world that are grounded in a culture's religious belief and practice. Rock art sites in their image composition represent the unseen universe that is hidden from, but coexistent with, daily experience, and their placement on the landscape represents bridges between these worlds. However, the concept of a sacred landscape is also one that is only part of the equation of what rock art sites have the potential to represent. They are also part of a landscape of memory that embodies a community's identity and serves to guide human experience and action in manners that bridge these visible and invisible worlds. They also mark the presence of a community on the landscape. In this framework, the memory of a community may fail, and the stories of particular places may be forgotten, but the physical presence of rock art sites may endure for hundreds, if not thousands, of years. Thus these

Figure 10.1. Annie Island pictograph.

places serve as discursive points on the landscape where subsequent generations may encounter, rediscover, and redefine them as a means of maintaining or creating presence.

   This chapter examines these issues of memory in presence not just as part
of the sacred landscape but also as part of the broader social landscape, which
embodies not just the sacred but also the everyday. Within this frame of reference, rock art is a visible manifestation that is encountered both as a religious object and as a social one, engaged with in ways that serve to guide
human social interactions with each other as well as with the spirits that are
seen to inhabit these places. Landscape becomes multidimensional, also, existing not as a space defined and redefined by human actions and imagination, but as one that serves as a source of direction for human actions (Harkin
2000). By focusing on both archaeological and contemporary ethnographic
research done in the Lake of the Woods region of northwestern Ontario,

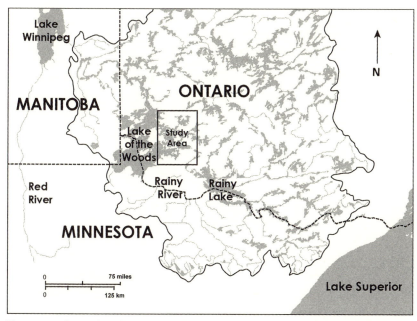

Figure 10.2. General study area along the western region of Lake of the Woods.

I will outline how these two concepts of landscape, memory and presence, serve to promote a more holistic understanding of the position of rock art not only at the time of its production and primary use but also in its role among contemporary Ojibwa communities within the region.

Rock Art Forms in the Lake of the Woods Region

The study area outlined here (Figure 10.2), located at the intersection between Minnesota and the Canadian provinces of Ontario and Manitoba, is, in terms of rock art style, considered to be part of the larger Canadian Shield Rock Art Tradition (Dewdney and Kidd 1967), which stretches from Saskatchewan in the west through Quebec, dipping down through Minnesota, Wisconsin, and Michigan. In regard to geographic coverage, it forms one of the largest contiguous rock art styles in the world and conforms more or less to the geographic distribution of northern Algonquian Indian cultures, to which this tradition has been attributed (Dewdney and Kidd 1967; Rajnovich 1994).

Rock art within the region comes in four types: pictographs, petroglyphs, petroforms, and lichenographs. Pictographs, which are the focus of this study, are the most numerous type found in the region. They are produced by an application of red ochre pigments to rock faces. Stylistically they are also the most complex forms, with images ranging from the naturalistic to complex geometrics. They are typically found on vertical or sheltered rock faces, overlooking or immediately on bodies of water. As a result, the only ways that they can be viewed are by watercraft or during the winter when the lakes are frozen over. Other examples that are located away from the water are rumored, but have not been confirmed in the region. The antiquity of pictographic rock art in the region is unknown, but circumstantial evidence based on the distributions of archaeologically defined cultures (Rajnovich 1994) and one dated context from the Canadian province of Quebec to the east (Alan Watchman, personal communication 2000) suggest that this form may date as early as 2,000 years ago. This would place it within a Middle Woodland period context, which in the region is called Laurel.

Petroglyphs, or images that are pecked or incised onto a stone surface, are found in the study region, but there are only a few examples of this form. Many of these sites have images that are only shallowly pecked into the stone surfaces on which they are found. As a result, it is often only at sunrise or sunset that the images are easily visible. Stylistically there is little difference between the images found at these sites and those on pictographic sites; however, geometric images tend to be the dominant type in all of the documented panels in the region, with only occasional naturalistic images. Within the study region, the known examples all occur on horizontal rock surfaces in areas next to bodies of water. One site is low enough that it is frequently inundated during the spring when water levels in the Lake of the Woods are at their highest. In terms of antiquity, one site was dated in the study region to approximately 3500 B.C.E. (Steinbring and Simpson 1983), suggesting that rock art may have begun among Archaic peoples rather than Woodland; however, this date is contested (C. S. "Paddy" Reid, personal communication 2005).

Petroforms, or boulder mosaics, are a well-documented phenomenon on the Great Plains (Mirau 1995) but are rare on the Canadian Shield. There are a few examples of this form in the study region. They are formed by arranging stones into particular shapes. Unfortunately, only three sites have been fully documented, two of which were identified during this project's 2005 field survey. Other sites have been noted in the region but were destroyed before they could be documented (archaeological site forms on file at the Ministry of Citizenship, Culture and Recreation, Thunder Bay Region). Stylistically, little can be said with only three examples known. One site consists of two small circular structures approximately 2 m in diameter constructed by stacking rocks up to a height of 40 to 50 cm. Another consists of a single ring of large stones, approximately 4 m in diameter, with gaps of 20 to 30 cm between each stone. An elder I discussed this site with referred to it as a "council ring," or meeting place where decisions were made. The third example fell stylistically within that of the larger Canadian Shield Rock Art Tradition. It was composed of at least three petroforms set in geometric configurations. The antiquity of these petroforms in the region is unknown, but speculation and relative dating of other examples to the immediate west suggest ages ranging from 1,500 to 3,000 years ago (Steinbring 1970).

The last of the rock art forms in the study region, lichenographs, are documented in the study region and around Lake Superior to the east but in few other places. These images are the easiest to produce but also the shortest lived. Created by scraping clean a surface covered with lichen growth to create the images, the exposed surface is reclaimed by that same growth over time. The geologist Louis Agassiz who stopped at a site on Lake Superior observed this when he commented, "these pictures were of various dates, as was shown by the various degrees of distinctness, as the rock was either laid quite bare, or the black lichens had more or less completely recovered possession of it" (quoted in Dewdney and Kidd 1967:148). Alternatively, as Selwyn Dewdney observed when he visited the same site a century later, lichen can also die, removing the image just as easily (Dewdney and Kidd 1967:148). From what little is known of these rock art sites, they seem to be consistent in style to the larger tradition in which they occur (Dewdney and Kidd 1967; archaeological site forms on file at the Ministry of Citizenship, Culture and Recreation, Thunder Bay Region). There is no information to indicate the age of these sites.

Previous Research in the Canadian Shield

Rock art studies in the Canadian Shield hold a unique and sometimes poorly known honor. Within the larger arena of North American rock art studies, Canada is where the first rock art research organization on the continent was established. Selwyn Dewdney, an author and artist, was a key figure in early research on the Canadian Shield Rock Art Tradition. In 1957, under the direction of anthropologist Kenneth Kidd, he began a program of systematically locating and documenting rock art sites around the Great Lakes region. While Dewdney's work examined issues of typology and dating, his most significant contribution was in ethnographic research that attempted to link rock art production to contemporary regional First Nations peoples. While he was not successful in linking the specific Algonquian-speaking peoples he interviewed with the production of rock art, his work did link the places that rock art sites were found with portals that allowed "specially gifted Ojibwa shamans . . . to enter the rock and exchange tobacco for an extremely potent 'rock medicine'" (Dewdney and Kidd 1967:14). This brings into focus the notion of landscape as an important contextual component of rock art sites.

Kenneth Kidd, who provided guidance on Dewdney's project, also observed the following:

> It is conceivable that there is some pattern or plan to the general loca-
> tion of rock paintings, but, if this is true, it has still to be worked out.
> Were they placed only at the abodes of spirits? Were they located hap-
> hazardly in remote as well as accessible places? Were they located only
> along important routes, or along routes used only at certain seasons for
> certain purposes? [Dewdney and Kidd 1967:168].

Later researchers followed up on Dewdney and Kidd's initial work and observations, focusing on the social and landscape contexts of the production of these sites. In terms of the social context, two main themes were followed. The first was to link the production of rock art sites solidly to Algonquian-speaking peoples such as the Cree and Ojibwa, among others living across the Canadian Shield. Joan and Roman Vastokas were critical figures in iden-tifying this linkage. Their work at the Peterborough Petroglyph site in north-eastern Ontario was among the earliest to examine ethnohistoric and ethno-graphic sources as a means of identifying the ancestral Algonquian creators of the site and its enduring role as a place of teaching for the descendant communities in the region (Vastokas and Vastokas 1973). Similarly, Thor and Julie Conway were able to do this with the Agawa Pictograph site on Lake Superior, only in this case, they were able to identify the specific person re-sponsible for some if not all of the images found there (Conway and Con-way 1990).

The second theme was derived from the first and looked to inform our knowledge of rock art compositions within the contexts of Algonquian re-ligious and cosmological beliefs. Both the Vastokases and Conways did this within their own works (also see Conway 1989, 1993), but it was Grace Rajno-vich who is, perhaps, more popularly known for her research on developing a framework for understanding rock art compositions. Using the work of the literary critic Northrop Frye, Rajnovich proposed that images used in his-torically documented Algonquian contexts could be used to inform those of precontact period rock art through analogy and assumptions of the conti-nuity of specific elements of traditional culture. In this case, she examined Ojibwa birch-bark scrolls, often used in the context of the Midéwiwin medi-cine lodge, which contained many images found in Canadian Shield rock art. The hypothesis she used to support the comparison was that "a culture does not change its basic myth structure over time but adds detail to it" (Rajno-vich 1989:181). Within this framework it was possible to use historic and con-temporary understandings of images used on birch-bark scrolls to interpret rock art. Ultimately, though, the approach proved difficult to apply. Rajnovich commented that pictographic symbols did not have simple meanings. Rather, they possessed multiple meanings that were encoded within cultural metaphors expressed in myth. For example, in discussing the use of a bear image on a particular scroll, she noted that "[t]he metaphor provides multiple imagery: the Bear equals fire equals powerful medicine equals the singer, a multiple meaning" (Rajnovich 1989:182).

In terms of landscape research, the earliest person to seriously consider the topic in the Canadian Shield was Brian Molyneaux. In considering the elements of cosmology and religious belief encoded within rock art images, he noted that one also had to consider the location of rock art sites as a significant element (Molyneaux 1980). Molyneaux, like others after him including Thor Conway (1993), Daniel Arsenault (2004b), and Jack Steinbring (1992), observed that the selection of rock art sites followed principles related to the four-world concept of Algonquian cosmology, which included sky, earth, underwater, and underground. In this framework, sites were places that were intersections between these worlds and were where spiritual power was concentrated and drawn from by those in Algonquian society who sought for it. In support of this assertion, Anastasia Shkilnyk, in her work among the Grassy Narrows Ojibwa, documented the following:

> Our people used to believe there is a spirit that dwells in those cliffs over there. Whenever the Indians thought something like that, they put a marker. And you can still see these markers on the old reserve. Sometimes you see paintings on rocks. These mean something; they were put there for a purpose. . . . The rock paintings mean that there is a good spirit there that will help us on the waters of the English River. You see a cut in the rocks over there; that's where people leave tobacco for the good spirit that inhabits that place [Shkilnyk 1985:71].

Within this statement are embedded both the spiritual conception regarding selected places on the landscape and the everyday practices associated with them. Such places were recognized as the abodes of spirits and were marked accordingly. At the same time, once marked, they became an active part of the cultural landscape requiring certain behaviors: in this case, leaving offerings that would aid in success in the pursuit of various activities related to life on the river.

The most recent and finessed treatment of Canadian Shield rock art as a component of a cultural landscape has been that of Daniel Arsenault (2004a, 2004b). Arsenault's research in Quebec and northeastern Ontario has focused considerably on the social context of the production of these sites

within the context of sacred landscapes (Arsenault 2004a:74). The significance of his approach is its promotion of a holistic method for interpreting
rock art in the Canadian Shield. In his view, such a methodology not only
is informed by archaeological methods and theories but also seeks to incor-
porate and recognize the inherent value of perceptual experience and oral
histories as tools that help reveal the "phenomenological" (Tilley 1994) dimensions of a sacred landscape, a factor that is typically elusive to standard
archaeological research. In application, Arsenault's research documents multiple dimensions of a site, examining imagery, geology, geomorphology, phenomenology, toponymy, ethnography, and oral traditions to develop a complete picture of how Cree and ancestral Algonquians created and perceived
the sacred landscapes that they inhabited (Arsenault 2004b).

Lake of the Woods Landscape Project

The research I have conducted was initially inspired in part by Dewdney,
Molyneaux, and Conway, with Arsenault's work serving as a contemporary
and complementary companion in the past few years. Early in my own research, Thor Conway, in particular, provided food for thought with the observation in his 1993 book *Painted Dreams* that he "was always greatly puz-
zled by the absence of images at seemingly perfect, sheer cliffs on lakes just
a few portages removed from existing pictograph sites" (Conway 1993:101).
Conway's observation harkened back to Kidd's comment quoted above that
suggested that there was a pattern to the placement of rock art sites in the
Canadian Shield. Drawing from the broader literature on landscape and
hunter-gatherer research of people like Richard Bradley (1991, 1997) working in Europe and Tim Ingold (1987) working among circumpolar hunter-
gatherers, I designed my research to examine the validity of this observation.

   Field survey was designed to document not only places where rock art was
found but also locations where it could have been placed but was not (Figure 10.3). In this case it would have been any cliff face on or overlooking the
water that was generally free of lichen cover and was within relatively easy
reach of a person sitting or standing. Using these criteria, and out of a sample
of over 40 bodies of water within the delineated area, there were over 400
possible choices. Of these, fewer than 20 were selected (Figure 10.4). Other
sites are included here that are outside the region but have been documented
elsewhere. In other words, it was clear that people were making choices in
terms of where they would or would not place rock art sites. This distribution was then cast against known and potential travel routes through the region (Figure 10.5). In analysis completed elsewhere, these water routes were
then compared with least-cost paths that were generated using geographic

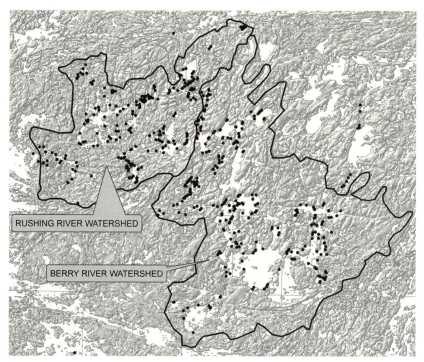

Figure 10.3. Locations available for the placement of rock art within the 2005 survey area.

information systems (GIS) and were found to match the least-cost paths in the lower half of the study area (Norder and Carroll 2011).

I did not ignore the meaning of rock art compositions. However, instead of performing a standard typological and stylistic study, I examined imagery through the work of Ralph Hartley and Anne Vawser (Hartley 1992; Hartley and Vawser 1998), who approached the production of rock art from the perspective of information theory. Using the Shannon-Weaver Information Measure, they calculated the information values of rock art compositions of sites in the Colorado Plateau region. The assumption of this particular measure is that the greater the redundancy of information in a rock art composition, the less ambiguous the message is to the observer. The results of their research suggested "that rock-art in prominent topographical situations functioned as one medium of information available for coping with the mobility demands of [the] environment" (Hartley and Vawser 1998:206). In other words, redundant image use, or lack thereof, in the composition of a given rock art site in combination with the placement of the site suggested that there were secular, functional roles of these sites outside of the typical religious interpretations

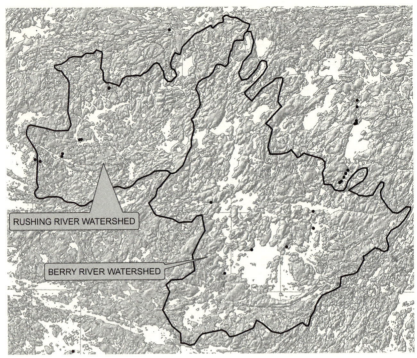

Figure 10.4. Locations of documented pictographic rock art sites within and outside of the surveyed watersheds as of 2005.

assumed of them. Applying this approach to my own research, I was able to identify three specific types of sites based on their information score (Figure 10.6) and geographic distribution.

While the work of Hartley and Vawser was critical in identifying the presence of site types in the Lake of the Woods region, it was important to also provide a culturally specific context in which these sites operated. To add this dimension to my interpretation, I drew from ethnohistoric data derived primarily from the observations of the use of culturally defined pictographs among Ojibwa communities by Henry Rowe Schoolcraft (1853), an Indian agent working in the Great Lakes region during the nineteenth century. He identified two broad categories of images, the *kekeewin* and *kekeenowin,* that were used only in particular contexts and composed of specific types of images. In general, though, the *kekeewin* images were typically simple or easily recognized objects, while those of the *kekeenowin* were more abstract and difficult to understand without explicit instruction as to their meaning. Adding this dimension to the site types identified with the Shannon-Weaver Information Measure results, I interpreted these site types in the following way:

Figure 10.5. Historical and contemporary canoe routes through the overall survey regions and locations of documented rock art sites as of 2005.

Type I: The first type included sites with single images, or with a high redundancy of the same image. These sites, I have argued elsewhere (Norder 2003), served as a means of facilitating travel by communicating the basic message that people are here, you should look for them, and you are headed in the right way to do so.

Type II: The second type included sites that had large numbers of images that were composed of familiar and naturalistic forms and had a high degree of redundancy. For example, one site located on Whitefish Bay on Lake of the Woods contained three representations of large mammals, possibly elk or moose, and nearly a dozen handprints as part of the overall composition. Type II sites are found mainly in the southern part of the study region in an area that is also known for its higher density of wild rice fields. This region would have been a seasonal aggregation area and the Type II sites would have communicated that you are in a place where people gathered.

Type III: The final site type had images that were often difficult to identify because of their abstract nature or that were composed of complex

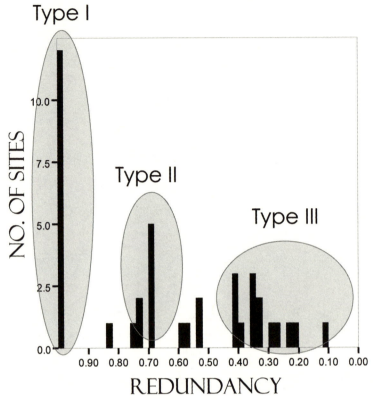

Figure 10.6. Shannon-Weaver Information Measure histogram indicating the three clusterings of potential site types.

human–animal forms typically associated with aspects of cosmology, as in the case here. Their locations are often in places that border on large expanses of water that can be difficult to travel on in inclement or windy weather. These sites were those most steeped in religious and cosmological belief, and their placement and content indicated that you are in a place of transition where powerful forces are in effect and that there are people in the area with knowledge to contend or communicate with those forces.

Overall, I would argue, the themes that unite these site types are their embodiment of memory and their communication of presence. In a landscape of sparse population where face-to-face contact is limited to certain times and certain places, these sites serve as mnemonic cues whose encoded symbolic capital has both specific and general meaning depending on the observer. There is no requirement that all individuals encountering any of the three site types have a detailed understanding of the composition, something that would be virtually impossible to begin with given the private nature of their creation. Rather, the existence of these places serves to populate the landscape with visual cues that evoke this cosmologically understood link between the four worlds and human beings and also the variability in which these linkages occur. The patterned placement of these sites provides an additional dimension to this relationship by creating and marking paths through the landscape that link spaces of communal engagement. As people move along these paths, whether they are local or not, they are guided, in a very practical way, through the visible world, but they are also confronted with the invisible world and must respond to this presence as well.

Ethnohistoric and Contemporary Ethnographic Fieldwork

As part of studying this relationship of memory and presence, I conducted ethnographic interviews with elders living on First Nations reserves in the region in order to assess the level of current traditional landscape knowledge and what role rock art sites played in their contemporary world. In many of the ethnographic and ethnohistoric resources, I found abundant references to the interaction between people and rock art sites in the Great Lakes region through the leaving of offerings. Through my interviews I found that this practice continued.

Elders frequently told me that they continued to leave, or remembered leaving, offerings at sites. The reasons varied, depending on what activities people were undertaking. Often offerings were left as a means of obtaining blessings for safe travel. Sometimes they were for success in hunting or fishing. Other times, and less commonly, they were offerings left in prayer for guidance during times of crisis. Oral tradition continues to name places throughout the region and provide us with the means through which memory and identity are encoded for these communities. As with Keith Basso's landscape study of Western Apache naming practices (Basso 1996), the region is given meaning not only through a physical inscription upon the landscape through the practice of rock art, but also through a discourse of naming, storytelling, and active engagement with the land. The active presence of the Ojibwa in the region is marked through offerings, which in turn honor and reinforce communal memory and identity.

While these practices continue they are also endangered. They have diminished over the years as youth, representing a community's future, have engaged less and less with the traditional landscape around their reserve communities. With reduced economic opportunity around communities, and with greater access to the global world through a variety of media formats, youth have either left these communities looking for opportunity elsewhere or chosen to engage the world through information technology rather than traditional teaching.

Conclusion

While the past has continued to impact the present in the sense that rock art sites remain an active, albeit reduced, element of traditional society, their role as mnemonics and linkages between the imagined and experienced worlds remains. Rock art sites in the region continue to structure human engagement with the landscape, and their presence has led to their incorporation into broader realms of human experience. Cultural tourism in the region has developed around these places, and people, typically non–Native Americans, experiencing these sites are encouraged to engage with them in manners that are respectful of the presence and memory of the people who produced and continue to use them today.

At the same time, marking of the landscape with rock art has not vanished completely. New traditions of marking presence and creating identity have developed and elaborations of the traditional form have periodically appeared. At this transformative point in history, the ways in which these new practices are embraced or rejected will determine the future of their role within both First Nations and non-Native societies in the region.

References Cited

Arsenault, Daniel

2004a   Rock Art, Landscape, Sacred Places: Attitudes in Contemporary Archaeological Theory. In *The Figured Landscapes of Rock-Art: Looking at Pictures in Place,* edited by C. Chippendale and G. Nash, pp. 69–84. Cambridge University Press, Cambridge.

2004b   From Natural Settings to Spiritual Places in the Algonkian Sacred Landscape: An Archaeological, Ethnohistorical and Ethnographic Analysis of Canadian Shield Rock-Art Sites. In *The Figured Landscapes of Rock-Art: Looking at Pictures in Place,* edited by C. Chippendale and G. Nash, pp. 289–317. Cambridge University Press, Cambridge.

Basso, Keith

1996   *Wisdom Sits in Places: Landscape and Language among the Western Apache.* University of New Mexico Press, Albuquerque.

Bradley, Richard

1991   Rock Art and the Perception of Landscape. *Cambridge Archaeological Journal* 1(1):77–101.

1997   *Rock Art and the Prehistory of Atlantic Europe: Signing the Land.* Routledge, New York.

Conway, Thor

1989   Scotia Lake Pictograph Site: Shamanic Rock Art in Northeastern Ontario. *Man in the Northeast* 37:1–23.

1993   *Painted Dreams: Native American Rock Art.* Northword Press, Minocqua, Wisconsin.

Conway, Thor, and Julie Conway

1990   *Spirits on Stone: The Agawa Pictographs.* Heritage Discovery Books, Echo Bay, Ontario, Canada.

Dewdney, Selwyn, and Kenneth Kidd

1967   *Rock Paintings of the Great Lakes.* 2nd ed. University of Toronto Press, Toronto, Canada.

Harkin, Michael

2000   Sacred Places, Scarred Spaces. *Wicazo Sa Review* 15(1):49–70.

Hartley, Ralph

1992   *Rock Art on the Northern Colorado Plateau: Variability in Content and Context.* Avebury, Brookfield, Vermont.

Hartley, Ralph, and Anne Vawser

1998   Spatial Behavior and Learning in the Prehistoric Environment of the Colorado River Drainage (Southeastern Utah), Western North America. In *The Archaeology of Rock-Art,* edited by C. Chippendale and P. S. C. Taçon, pp. 185–211. Cambridge University Press, Cambridge.

Ingold, Timothy

1987   *The Appropriation of Nature: Essays on Human Ecology and Social Relations.* University of Iowa Press, Iowa City.

Lewis-Williams, J. David

1977   Led by the Nose: Observations on the Supposed Use of Southern San Rock Art in Rain-Making Rituals. *African Studies* 36:155–159.

Mirau, Neil

1995   Medicine Wheels on the Northern Plains: Contexts, Codes, and Symbols. In *Beyond Subsistence: Plains Archaeology and the Postprocessual Critique,* edited by P. Duke and M. Wilson, pp. 193–210. The University of Alabama Press, Tuscaloosa.

Molyneaux, Brian

1980   Landscape Images: Rock Paintings in the Canadian Shield. *Rotunda* 13(Fall): 6–11. Royal Ontario Museum, Toronto, Canada.

Norder, John

2003   Marking Space and Creating Place in Northern Algonquian Landscapes: The Rock-Art of the Lake of the Woods Region, Ontario. Unpublished Ph.D. dissertation, Department of Anthropology, University of Michigan, Ann Arbor.

Norder, John, and Jon Carroll

2011   Applied Geospatial Perspectives on the Rock Art of the Lake of the Woods Region of Ontario, Canada. *International Journal of Applied Geospatial Research* 2(4):77–92.

Rajnovich, Grace

1989   Visions in the Quest for Medicine: An Interpretation of the Indian Pictographs of the Canadian Shield. *Midcontinental Journal of Archaeology* 14: 179–225.

1994   *Reading Rock Art: The Indian Rock Paintings of the Canadian Shield.* Natural Heritage/Natural History, Toronto, Canada.

Schoolcraft, Henry Rowe

1853   *Information Respecting the History, Condition, and Prospects of the Indian Tribes of the United States, Part III.* Lippincott, Grambo, Philadelphia.

Shkilnyk, Anastasia

1985   *A Poison Stronger than Love: The Destruction of an Ojibwa Community.* Yale University Press, New Haven, Connecticut.

Steinbring, Jack

1970   The Tie Creek Boulder Site in Southeastern Manitoba. In *Ten Thousand Years: Archaeology in Manitoba,* edited by W. Hlady, pp. 223–268. Manitoba Archaeological Society, Winnipeg, Canada.

1992   Phenomenal Attributes: Site Selection Factors in Rock Art. *American Indian Rock Art* 17:102–108.

Steinbring, Jack, and David Simpson

1983   The Mud Portage Site (DkKr-4): A Preceramic Context for Petroglyphs in Northwest Ontario. *American Indian Rock Art* 10:145–156.

Tilley, Christopher

1994   *A Phenomenology of Landscape: Places, Paths and Monuments.* Berg, Oxford.

Vastokas, Joan, and Roman Vastokas

1973   *Sacred Art of the Algonkians: A Study of the Peterborough Petroglyphs.* Mansard Press, Peterborough, Ontario, Canada.

Whitley, David S.

1998   Finding Rain in the Desert: Landscape, Gender and Far Western North American Rock-Art. In *The Archaeology of Rock-Art,* edited by C. Chippendale and P. S. C. Taçon, pp. 11–29. Cambridge University Press, Cambridge.

2000   *The Art of the Shaman: Rock Art of California.* University of Utah Press, Salt Lake City.

2001   Science and the Sacred: Interpretive Theory in U.S. Rock Art Research. In *Theoretical Perspectives in Rock Art Research,* edited by K. Helskog, pp. 124–151. Institute for Comparative Research in Human Culture, Oslo.

Part IV
Recognizing Deep-Time Traditions

11
Cave Rituals and Ritual Caves in the Eastern United States

Cheryl Claassen

Cave use by Late Prehistoric peoples in the eastern United States for ritual or mortuary function is now well documented (e.g., Simek, Cressler et al. 2001; Simek, Frankenberg et al. 2001). The relatively recent discoveries of Archaic art in caves (Simek et al. 1998) and the Archaic mortuary caves of Ohio (Pedde and Prufer 2001) open a window into much earlier ritual use of caves and rockshelters. In a previous paper (Claassen 2005), I have made the case for interpreting the records from Archaic levels of Dust Cave (northwest Alabama) and Russell Cave (northeast Alabama) and the Early Woodland Salts/Mammoth Cave (central Kentucky) as evidence of ritual use and their status as *ritual* caves, not habitation loci. For this chapter I will review two more caves with Archaic records, Graham Cave and Rodgers Shelter, both in Missouri, while hinting at the type of evidence to be suspected and the possible meaning of the rituals that might have been carried out at and in these caves. Further thoughts on Archaic rituals and a ritualized landscape can be found in two other recent studies (Claassen 2007, 2010).

Ritual Evidence

To look for ritual behavior in caves and to identify a cave as a permanent ritual site, I have turned to the fast-growing body of evidence of cave rituals and ritual caves produced by archaeologists working in Mexico and Mesoamerica. I have derived a list of expectations for offerings found in Mayan caves (relying on Benson 1997 and Pohl 1983) when the purpose of the offering is to solicit the aid or favor of one or more earth and/or underworld deities. These deities control rain and thus thunder, lightning, fertility, and the actual animals and plants that humans depend on.

1. Caves with flowing water inside are the most sacred.
2. Items of personal adornment are left as cave offerings.
3. Offerings are frequently burned and/or broken.
4. Artifacts not of personal adornment used in rituals are weaving equipment (spindle whorls and awls), bone needles, old textiles, tools, wooden objects, miniature dishes and jars, tiny or full-sized manos and metates, and water vessels.
5. Breaking of stalactites and stalagmites is ubiquitous in Maya caves. Caches of them were made.
6. Children, juveniles, and adults were sacrificed in some cave rituals.
7. Fauna used in rituals are all types of birds, especially water birds and songbirds, freshwater and marine shell, reptiles (snakes, turtles), fish (particularly catfish), frogs, deer, turkey, dog, and opossum.
8. Characteristics of the fauna are burning, smallness (rats, bats, shrews, and songbirds), immature animals, incomplete carcasses, a disproportionate number of left-side elements or hind elements or skulls and wings.

I have used this list of characteristics subsequently to peruse the site reports of several U.S. caves and believe that there is ample evidence of rituals at them, with some variations on the list of characteristics as expected. At this time I will review briefly several observations on nonhuman bone, mollusks, hematite, and stone in these archaeologically important caves utilized during the Archaic (10,000 to 3,500 years ago).

Bone

Probably at least two important aspects of bone govern the ritual use and deposition of bones we find in caves; these are bone as a repository of the soul and a great time depth to the deities. The belief that the deities emanate from an earlier creation (as do the ancestors) is visualized in smallness (Pohl 1983). Songbirds, baby mammals, reptiles, amphibians, and human babies are appropriate for their small size. Human babies are appropriate for their purity and as reciprocal gifts as fruits of the human body (Arnold 1991:229). Thus, many offerings to earth and underworld deities include small animals, which many zooarchaeologists assume are noncultural introductions. The offering often does not include the entire animal (or plant) but just an important part, such as the head or left side. The ritual itself, however, may require one or more living animals to be sacrificed for a blood offering with the entire carcass left at the ritual location.

Another belief is that of bone soul, the concept that one of several manifestations of the soul of living beings is captured in hard substances, such as bone and stone (Furst 1995). From the bones or shells or other body parts, the animal can be regenerated. In order to ensure the continuation of the desired species, it is necessary to offer the bones, feathers, and shells (as well as seeds, fruits, or flowers for plants) to the responsible spirits who dwell inside the earth and are approachable through a cave or rockshelter (Brown 2005). Based on the ritual characteristics enumerated above, there are probable offerings, evidence of rites, and bone soul deposits in several of the caves.

At Russell Cave, over 30,000 pieces of bone were recovered, representing at least 66 species. Small terrestrial mammals were represented in greater or equal proportions to deer in both Early Archaic (10,000–8000 B.P.) and Middle Archaic (8000–6000 B.P.) levels (Goldman-Finn 1994:219). Mammals and birds dominate the species list. Deer were uncommon at Russell. Black bear was present in all layers except the later Middle Archaic. Porcupine occurs here quite south of its modern range. Thirteen species of birds were recovered. Passenger pigeons, loons, teal, wood duck, red-tailed and red-shouldered hawks, barred owl, and red-bellied woodpecker were recovered from the excavations in Room Two. Feathers from several of these species were left as historic offerings in Ludlow Cave, South Dakota (Sundstrom 1996). At least 20 turkeys and 155 gray squirrels were retrieved from one layer. Amphibians and reptiles were numerous as well, and at least 12 fish species were present, drum and catfish being the most common species. Partial skeletons (for example, heads of birds and hindquarters of deer) were common (Griffin 1974).

The bone debris from these early levels at Russell Cave suggests that this place was used repeatedly during the Archaic for rites related to earth renewal. I know of no cases of feasting occurring inside of a cave, only the conduct of rites. The deposit of a human infant as the deepest human burial in this cave also suggests a ritual use related to fertility, continuation, earth renewal, and an acknowledgment of a reciprocal arrangement with the entities responsible for earth renewal.

The hundreds of burned bones in the vestibule of Salts Cave (Mammoth Cave system) also suggest numerous rituals, some of which may have occurred in the Late Archaic given Late Archaic (6000–4000 B.P.) evidence of exploration of deep portions of this cave system (Kennedy 1996). In particular, the burning of bones and the inclusion of human bone in the mix, much of it involving body parts typically taken as trophies, suggest offerings, as do other characteristics of the fauna. Raccoons were represented predominantly by skull fragments and deer by their mandibles and legs (Duffield 1974:128). Several turkeys were brought into the cave whole, but "most of the identified turkey bones are from the anterior portion of the bird" (Duffield 1974:128). The other taxa present have but a few individuals—striped skunk, red fox, gray fox, snakes, and others—and probably were not accidentals, says

Duffield (1974:130), because their skeletons are incomplete. Fish, particularly catfish and bass, were recovered from the deepest horizon. A sample of faunal material recovered from the vestibule of Mammoth Cave by Nelson (1917) adds black bear, opossum, porcupine, elk, and a crane to the list.

Not just the vestibules were staging places for renewal rituals. Just past the vestibule of Salts Cave, in the Iron Gate vicinity, were found a turkey and a groundhog skeleton, and beyond that a catfish bone, turkey bones, and deer bone fragments, all on the surface.

Yet another aspect of cave rituals is evident in several apparent offerings recognizable as bone clusters in Salts and in Rodgers Shelter. At Salts Cave, one pocket of concentrated turkey bones and another of concentrated human bones were encountered in the vestibule excavation (Watson 1974:94). Feature 7A contained one piece of raccoon, an immature deer, large mammal bones, one small bird, and a turkey rib. Feature 7D contained a right distal humerus of a turkey, 57 large mammalian bones, and two bird bones. Feature 7F had six large mammal bone fragments. Similar features were recorded inside Rodgers Shelter (Feature 8233) in the Middle Archaic Horizon 8 (Kay 1982). One pit included one finely flaked point, a human humerus and tibia, a bison tooth, a large bird bone, a terrapin shell fragment, cottontail parts, squirrel parts (humerus, calcaneus, and radius fragments), and a pharyngeal fragment of a drum. Six inches away sat a hematite processing slab (Feature 8242). A second pit feature contained the pelvis and sacrum of a deer, one bison phalanx, rabbit parts (teeth, ulna, and radius), terrapin shell, a turkey ulna and corocoid, a canis premolar, and a squirrel radius. In these signs of ritual acts we see a high diversity of species yet low number of individuals.

Different rituals are probably apparent in the *burial* of an animal inside of a cave, rather than the placement of an animal on the surface such as was mentioned above. Here I call attention to the burial of large birds (geese, swans) and dogs. A Dalton aged feature in Rodgers Shelter (ca. 10,000 B.P.) contained most of the skeleton of a trumpeter swan (Kay 1982). A cache of goose humeri was uncovered in Dust Cave (Walker and Parmalee 2004) also in a Late Paleoindian context. (These two examples suggest Paleoindian ritual use of caves and that the use of these particular caves began that early, underscoring the concept of *ritual caves in opposition to habitation sites*.) Dog burials are also found in Dust Cave (Walker et al. 2005) and in Rodgers Shelter in Archaic contexts. I have discussed elsewhere the ritualized use of dogs in the Americas to lead and judge the dead (Claassen 2008).

Mollusks

Shells are commonly associated with primordial time and with the renewal of time and life (Claassen 2005, 2008). The spiraling form of the gastropods, particularly the large marine whelks and conchs, was emblematic of the winds, eternity, and the turning movement of the world at the dawn of creation (e.g., Bassie-Sweet 1996). Winds emanate from caves. Gastropods, of course, also have their own caves (as do paired bivalves), as do women with their uteruses, so that caves, women, and gastropods are often equivalent metaphors for fertility and useful in fertility and renewal rites. From these associations, we should consider the possibility that shells in a cave are part of a renewal rite and are themselves offerings. There are historic examples of offered shells in the northern Great Plains caves and rockshelters (Sundstrom 1996) and today in Mesoamerica (Halperin et al. 2003).

Shells are also returned to caves as acts of thanksgiving. An informant asked about the significance of small gastropods in caves in southern Mexico told an archaeologist that since jute live in springs and springs have water that comes out of caves, jute live in sacred water. People eat jute broth or meat to ingest sacred food, and then men return the jute to the caves to give thanks to Mother Earth (Halperin et al. 2003).

The souls of dead babies are also seen as the stars that shine at night. These white stars are but the white shells of the watery underworld that rotates into the upper position each night (Bassie-Sweet 1996). Therefore shells placed in caves, the entrance and exit points for the day and night skies, can petition for more births. As mentioned above, shells, like bone, feather, seeds, and other items, should also be returned to the earth deity to ensure their continuation.

At Russell Cave, 4,710 freshwater snails and bivalves were brought from the Tennessee River, over six miles distant. Large quantities of mollusks were recovered from the Early and Middle Archaic levels in Dust Cave. The Salts Cave vestibule had a number of shells, many burned and mixed with fragmented human and animal bone. A feature filled with bivalves and aquatic gastropods was found inside Rodgers Shelter in the Late Archaic horizon. Mollusk shells were found in Graham Cave as well. The often large quantities of shells found in caves and shelters contributes to the conclusion that caves were habitation loci; however, because shells are imbued with much symbolism (Claassen 2008), their ritual role should be considered first.

Hematite

The quantity of hematite evident in the deposits inside Graham Cave was commented on by several archaeologists (e.g., Klippel 1971). At Rodgers Shelter, the hematite was even more remarkable. In Middle Archaic Horizon 7 there were two hematite grinding areas with large quantities of powdered hematite, hematite-stained grinding slabs, pieces of ground hematite, and adjacent hearths. Kay points out that the complex supports the "idea that chunks of hematite were purposely fired both to enhance the color and make the hematite softer" (Kay 1982:571). Like the quarrying of salts and chert inside a cave, and the reduction of chert inside a cave, the choice of a cave for the processing of hematite suggests that the cave context imbued the target substance with more power than would otherwise accrue.

Rock Features

Three possible structures were identified by Kay in the Horizon 7 Middle Archaic levels inside Rodgers Shelter. Structures 1 and 2 were rings of rock 1.52 m (5 feet) in diameter. Structure 2 incorporated three pieces of hematite, one hammerstone, five cores, two biface preforms, three projectile points, one scraper, four utilized flakes, a tooth, and one piece of galena. Structure 3, which was 2.04 m (6.7 feet) in diameter, had two ground stone fragments, five cores, one biface preform, and one projectile point. Both Ahler and McMillan (1976) and Kay (1982) allowed that these might be ceremonial structures inside Rodgers Shelter. A circle of large stones was also uncovered inside Graham Cave. I propose that they are either altars or shrines. There may be sweatlodges inside caves and rockshelters as well.

Lithics

Finished stone tools and their manufacturing debris are ubiquitous at these caves. Rather than being evidence of mundane occupation, however, there are beliefs attached to stone that would give tools and flakes a ritual role.

As tools, arrow points, knives, drills, and scrapers are appropriate offerings. However, Hall discusses the symbolic and ritual significance that arrows have as windpipes, pipestems, and the conceiving spirit-breath (Hall 1997:56). There are a number of historical associations between arrows and caves among Great Plains groups. Sundstrom (1996) clearly documented the use of arrows as cave offerings in Ludlow Cave, where 339 points were recovered.

There is also an association of lightning with the sparks that can be produced when two stones strike one another. Individuals who have been struck by lightning are destined for ritualized roles in several cultures. In central Mexico these people specifically undergo training rites in caves (Heyden 2005: 25). Some groups identified axes they found as the manifestation of lightning strikes (Bassie-Sweet 1996). Since caves were viewed as the exit for lightning, wind, and rain, making lightning in a cave could be a ritual way to call forth the relevant spirit or deity. Flint-knapping at caves may well be the activity of the ritual specialists and apprentices who thus show their ability to handle lightning. Lightning and water are, of course, fertility symbols, so it is fitting that among central Mexicans, babies were referred to as "the chips, the flakes" of the ancestors (Furst 1995:125). In this regard, I find the tremendous amount of debitage around the entrance to Austin Cave (Barker and Breitburg 1992) on the Cumberland River in Kentucky to be highly suggestive of fertility rituals, as are the tens of thousands of flakes and the chert mining in caves like Third Unnamed Cave in Tennessee (Franklin 2001).

Unmodified round and heart-shaped stone are also the home of *yolia*, that part of the soul that animates, and worked stone is the home and manifestation of *tonalli*, that part of the soul that imbues personality and fate in the thought of many Mexican groups (Furst 1995). The hundreds of points, preforms, and scrapers found in these caves could be offerings to the spirit dead, even a returning of the souls of the dead to the cave.

I am proposing a long history for many of these ritual elements and a long tradition of cave rituals in the eastern United States. It has not been possible in the space allotted to highlight the human burial programs at these caves that have strong indications of sacrifice or consecration, such as the initial deposits of infants at Russell and Dust Caves and the mixtures of human remains found in the vestibule of Salts Cave and several Ohio Late Archaic rockshelters and sinks. Nor has it been possible to talk about the idea that desiccated bodies in caves were actually intentional and tended as oracles. It has also not been possible here to develop the idea of the importance of pilgrimages and that these caves were destination places for pilgrimages or were points visited on pilgrimages to other destinations such as the shell mounds or Poverty Point. I hope to develop these ideas in future papers.

If these were indeed ritual caves during the Archaic, they were so for 8,000 or more years. It is possible to see the growth of such dedicated places throughout the following 4,000 years with a significant increase in ritual caves during the Woodland period—for burial in particular—and during the Mississippian period—for deep cave rituals involving image production. It is possible to see the morphing of many of these rituals. For instance, shells are one of the more common items in caves and rockshelters of the Woodland period (3500–1200 B.P.). Incomplete fauna are found in the later burial caves and rockshelters of Ohio, eastern Tennessee, and southwestern Virginia. Even the particular fauna retain symbolic significance, such as seen in the swan burial in the Dalton levels of Rodgers and the swan remains in the feasting pit under Mound 51 at Cahokia (Kelly and Kelly 2007), and the minerals too continue to play a role, such as the galena found both in the Middle Archaic level at Rodgers (Missouri) and in the Copena mortuary caves in Alabama.

Much research remains to be done on these rites and their loci of enactment. Caves are so important in historic accounts of origins and homes of deities and culture heroes that rather than defaulting to camping to explain the material culture found in caves, the default explanation should become ritual. This ritual use of caves is masking a great deal of craft production and energy consumption; our failure to assume ritualized uses is masking a great deal of ancient life. Furthermore, the ritual use of caves needs to be viewed as one element in a highly ritualized landscape that also included mountaintops, waterfalls, bluffs, springs, sinkholes, rockshelters, riversides, shell mounds, shell rings, dirt mounds, and embankments (Milne 1994).

References Cited

Ahler, Steven, and Bruce McMillan
  1976   Material Culture at Rodgers Shelter: A Reflection of Past Human Activities. In *Prehistoric Man and His Environments: A Case Study in the Ozark Highlands,* edited by W. Wood and R. McMillan, pp. 163–199. Academic Press, New York.
Arnold, Philip
  1991   Eating Landscape: Human Sacrifice and Sustenance in Aztec Mexico. In *To Change Place: Aztec Ceremonial Landscape,* edited by David Carrasco, pp. 219–233. University Press of Colorado, Boulder.
Barker, Gary, and Emanuel Breitburg
  1992   Archaic Occupations at the Austin Site (40Rb82). Paper presented at the 49th Annual Meeting of the Southeastern Archaeological Conference, Little Rock, Arkansas.
Bassie-Sweet, Karen
  1996   *At the Edge of the World: Caves and Late Classic Maya World View.* University of Oklahoma Press, Norman.
Benson, Elizabeth P.
  1997   *Birds and Beasts of Ancient Latin America.* University Press of Florida, Gainesville.
Brown, Linda
  2005   Planting the Bones: Hunting Ceremonialism at Contemporary and Nineteenth-Century Shrines in the Guatemalan Highlands. *Latin American Antiquity* 16:131–146.
Claassen, Cheryl
  2005   Putting Ritual Back into Eastern US Caves. Paper presented at the 22nd Annual Meeting of the Kentucky Heritage Council, Lexington.
  2007   Newt Kash Rock Shelter, A Menstrual Retreat. Paper presented at the 72nd Annual Meeting of the Society for American Archaeology, Austin, Texas.
  2008   Archaic Rituals: Rebalancing with Dogs. Paper presented at the 65th Annual Meeting of the Southeastern Archaeological Conference, Charlotte, North Carolina.

2008   Shell Symbolism in North America. In *Early Human Impact on Megamolluscs*, edited by Andrzej Antczak and Roberto Cipriani, pp. 37–43. BAR International Series, S1865. British Archaeological Reports, Oxford.

2010   *Feasting with Shellfish: Archaic Sacred Landscape and Ritual.* University of Tennessee Press, Knoxville.

Duffield, Lathel

1974   Nonhuman Vertebrate Remains from Salts Cave Vestibule. In *Archeology of the Mammoth Cave Area*, edited by Patty Jo Watson, pp. 123–133. Academic Press, New York.

Franklin, Jay

2001   Excavating and Analyzing Prehistoric Lithic Quarries: An Example from Third Unnamed Cave, Tennessee. *Midcontinental Journal of Archaeology* 26: 199–217.

Furst, Jill

1995   *The Natural History of the Soul in Ancient Mexico.* Yale University Press, New Haven.

Goldman-Finn, Nurit

1994   Dust Cave in Regional Context. *Journal of Alabama Archaeology* 40:212–231.

Griffin, John (editor)

1974   *Investigations in Russell Cave.* U.S. Department of the Interior, National Park Service, Washington, D.C.

Hall, Robert L.

1997   *An Archaeology of the Soul: North American Indian Belief and Ritual.* University of Illinois Press, Urbana.

Halperin, Christina, Sergio Garza, Keith Prufer, and James Brady

2003   Caves and Ancient Maya Ritual Use of Jute. *Latin American Antiquity* 14: 207–209.

Heyden, Doris

2005   Rites of Passage and Other Ceremonies in Caves. In *In the Maw of the Earth Monster: Mesoamerican Ritual Cave Use*, edited by James Brady and Keith Prufer, pp. 22–28. University of Texas Press, Austin.

Kay, Marvin (editor)

1982   *Holocene Adaptation within the Lower Pomme de Terre River Valley, Missouri.* Report submitted to the U.S. Army Corps of Engineers, Kansas City District.

Kelly, Lucretia S., and John E. Kelly

2007   Swans in the American Bottom during the Emergent Mississippian and Mississippian. *Illinois Archaeology* 15-16:112–141.

Kennedy, Mary

1996   Radiocarbon Dates from Salts and Mammoth Cave. In *Of Caves and Shell*

Mounds, edited by Kenneth C. Carstens and Patty Jo Watson, pp. 48–81. The University of Alabama Press, Tuscaloosa.

Klippel, Walter

1971   *Graham Cave Revisited: A Reevaluation of Its Cultural Position during the Archaic Period.* Memoir 9. Missouri Archaeological Society, Columbia.

Milne, Courtney

1994   *Sacred Places in North America: A Journey into the Medicine Wheel.* Stewart, Tabori and Chang, New York.

Nelson, N. C.

1917   Contributions to the Archaeology of Mammoth Cave and Vicinity, Kentucky. *Anthropological Papers of the American Museum of Natural History* 22(1).

Pedde, Sara, and Olaf Prufer

2001   Hendricks Cave, Rockshelters and Late Archaic Mortuary Practices in Ohio. In *Archaic Transitions in Ohio and Kentucky Prehistory,* edited by O. Prufer, S. Pedde, and R. Meindl, pp. 328–354. Kent State University Press, Kent, Ohio.

Pohl, Mary

1983   Maya Ritual Faunas: Vertebrate Remains from Burials, Caches, Caves, and Cenotes in the Maya Lowlands. In *Civilization in the Ancient Americas: Essays in Honor of Gordon R. Willey,* edited by Richard Leventhal and Alan Kolata, pp. 55–104. University of New Mexico Press, Albuquerque.

Simek, Jan, Alan Cressler, Charles Faulkner, T. Ahlman, B. Creswell, and Jay Franklin

2001   The Context of Late Prehistoric Cave Art: The Art and Archaeology of 11th Unnamed Cave, Tennessee. *Southeastern Archaeology* 20:142–153.

Simek, Jan, Sarah Frankenberg, and Charles Faulkner

2001   Toward an Understanding of Prehistoric Cave Art in Southern Appalachia. In *Archaeology of the Appalachian Highlands,* edited by Lynne Sullivan and Susan Prezzano, pp. 49–64. University of Tennessee Press, Knoxville.

Simek, Jan, Jay Franklin, and Sarah Sherwood

1998   The Context of Early Southeastern Prehistoric Cave Art: A Report on the Archaeology of Third Unnamed Cave. *American Antiquity* 63:663–677.

Sundstrom, Linea

1996   *The Material Culture of Ludlow Cave (39HN1), Custer National Forest, Harding County, South Dakota: A NAGPRA Evaluation.* Report submitted to USDA Forest Service, Custer National Forest, Billings, Montana.

Walker, Renee, Darcy Morey, and John Relethford

2005   Early and Mid-Holocene Dogs in Southeastern North America: Examples from Dust Cave. *Southeastern Archaeology* 24:83–92.

Walker, Renee, and Paul Parmalee

2004   A Noteworthy Cache of Goose Humeri from Late Paleoindian Levels at Dust Cave, Northwestern Alabama. *Journal of Alabama Archaeology* 50: 18–35.

Watson, Patty Jo

1974   Prehistoric Cultural Debris from the Vestibule Trenches. In *Archeology of the Mammoth Cave Area,* edited by Patty Jo Watson, pp. 83–105. Academic Press, New York.

12
Reopening the Midéwiwin

Warren DeBoer

> There is a hallowed binary that separates America's original inhabitants into two types: prehistoric and historic. The former settled and created its landscapes, yet are knowable only through mute material evidence of the kind archaeologists piece together. The latter exist only insofar as they come into contact with the invader, being in this sense a pure extension of Western historiography.
> —Gordon Brotherston (1992:174)

In Native North or South America (but excluding literate Mesoamerica), Brotherston's charge in the epigraph above could be reduced to a mere definition. Obviously, there can be no *prehistoric* history if history is restricted to written documents rather than to the more generally conceived *historein*, "inquiry" of the Greeks, an enterprise carried out by a *hist_r*, or "sage." In this etymological sense, an Ojibwa priest who relies upon birch-bark scrolls, notched counters, and songs as mnemonic aids while reciting the origins of the Midéwiwin, or medicine lodge, is certainly doing history. That the priest is not speaking in an archaeological idiom nor following the methods of a would-be scientific archaeology is hardly disqualifying, but rather should prompt anthropological curiosity concerning the varying ways that historical knowledge is created and mobilized. It is uncharitable to begin by claiming that *our* (pre)history seeks reliable knowledge of the past while the priest's narration claims something else. Nor is it helpful to undermine the historical project altogether by viewing the past merely as an arena for ethnic cheerleading or as an arsenal for contemporary power plays. There should be a middle ground of the kind discussed by Whiteley (2002).

Upon first consideration, the Midéwiwin, a religious society of the Upper Great Lakes region, would seem poorly equipped for crossing the protohistoric Rubicon separating prehistory and its text-driven sequel. According to Harold Hickerson (1963), this society arose during the early historic period, crystallizing first among the Ojibwa and later spreading to neighboring Algonquian and Siouan groups, where it took diversifying forms. In Hickerson's view, the Midéwiwin was a nativist development geared to the integration of multiclan and multiethnic settlements formed during the fur-trade era. From the perspective of its members, however, it served to con-fer the good life through the observance of proper behavior and through the acquisition of knowledge needed to stave off illness and otherwise ma-neuver through a difficult world. The society, headed by a priesthood, was or-ganized into four or, rarely, eight degrees symbolically identified with world levels. Each degree demanded progressively costly payments on the part of initiates. Following functionalist logic, Hickerson argued that these graded payments served to channel new wealth obtained through the fur trade. Jay Miller (1999), however, has emphasized that, while food was widely shared in Native North America, spiritual information typically had to be acquired through the giving of appropriately valued gifts. The notion of spiritual ar-cana as the currency that counts is a widespread and deep-seated feature in North America, one unlikely to have originated in the fur-trade era.

Hickerson's case for a short Midéwiwin history has been accepted by a majority of scholars. Even Karl Schlesier (1990), the champion of extending Native American ethnography into deep time, has embraced Hickerson's short chronology. A few scholars, however, notably Robert Hall (1997:74) and Michael Angel (2002), have suggested earlier roots. I wish to be added to their number.

Historical Evidence

Figure 12.1 plots historical accounts pertaining to Midéwiwin or Midéwiwin-like practices as recorded ethnographically. The hedging simile "Midéwiwin-like" seems appropriate, for, whenever its inception as a named cultural in-stitution, the Midéwiwin was presumably composed of elements having prior cultural roots. In this regard, it is of interest to note the cognate appellation *mete:wini*, glossed as "mystic rite," appears in Aubin's (1975) Proto-Algonquian dictionary. Although not ensuring an ancient pedigree, such an entry is none-theless intriguing.

During his 1623–1624 sojourn in Huronia, the Recollet Gabriel Sagard (Wrong 1939:209) reported a Neutral ceremony in which the name and so-cial identity of a deceased individual were bestowed upon a successor. Al-though Sagard's account is brief, it recalls the Menomini Obliteration Cere-mony as observed three centuries later by Alanson Skinner (1920:183). In both cases, ceremonial resurrection took place a year after death. In contrast to the Neutral case, however, the Menomini rite was explicitly associated with the *mitäwin* (the Menomini term for Midéwiwin). In a later example from 1636, the Jesuit Jean de Brébeuf described a secret "Brotherhood of Lunatics" as-sembled to assist a Huron sorcerer-in-training (Thwaites 1896–1901:10:209). Following a frenzied dance, the candidate was shot with bear claws, eagle's

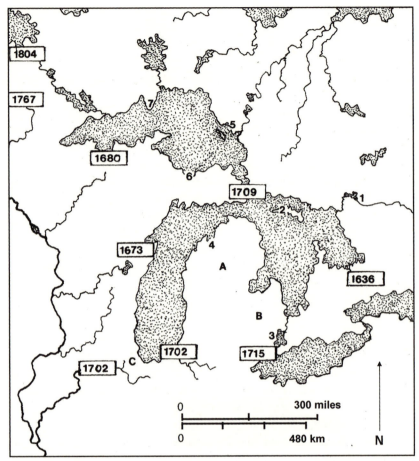

Figure 12.1. The Upper Great Lakes with selected sites pertinent to Midéwiwin history. Boxed dates refer to earliest regional occurrences of Midéwiwin or Midé-like practices: 1636, Huron "Brotherhood of Lunatics" (Thwaites 1896–1901:10:209); 1673, the cross incident at Green Bay (Kinietz 1965:215); 1680, Chequamegon (Hickerson 1963); 1702, St. Joseph (Blair 1996:2:86–88) and Illinois Rivers (Kinietz 1965:401–402); 1709, Sault Sainte Marie (Kinietz 1965:372–374); 1715, Detroit (Keesing 1971:49); 1767, Red Lake (Carver 1813); 1804, Lake of the Woods (Harrison 1982:Table 2). Letters indicate archaeological sites: (A) Missaukee Earthworks; (B) Younge; (C) Anker. Numbers indicate Midé-related landmarks: (1) Allumettes Island (Thwaites 1896–1901:9:277); (2) Manitoulin Island (Smith 1995:30); (3) Lake St. Clair (Vennum 1978:782); (4) Traverse Bay (Blackbird 1887:74); (5) Nanibojou Island (Henry 1966 [1809]:212–213); (6) Grand Island (Vennum 1978:763); (7) Thunder Bay (Reid 1963:94).

talons, and other missiles, only to be later revived, a practice recalling the Midé drama of killing and then reviving initiates. Magically animated effigies also appeared in this Huron performance and, as Hall (1997:62) notes, are matched by the puppet show or "sacred amusement" accompanying later Menomini rites.

The opening years of the eighteenth century produced a spate of possible Midéwiwin sightings among the Miami (Blair 1996:2:87–88; Kinietz 1965:216–219), the Saulteur Ojibwa (Kinietz 1965:329, 373), and the Potawatomi, the latter calling the ceremony "medelinne" (Hickerson 1963:76). These reports vary in detail but all mention the shooting of participants with claw or feather missiles, in one case from an otter-skin medicine bag, followed by revivification. It is clear that early versions of the Midéwiwin were in full swing by the early eighteenth century. One notable difference, however, is the choice of ammunition. In the recent Midéwiwin, cowry shells native to the Indian Ocean are the standard missiles. According to Dewdney (1975:71), Hudson Bay traders introduced cowries during the early to mid-nineteenth century. They came to supersede bird talons, animal claws, and the small "bean-like" shells mentioned in the 1760s by Jonathan Carver (1813:154). This replacement, however, was not total. Both Radin (1991:188–189) and Harrison (1982:107) mention grizzly bear claws and even polar bear canines for Midé shootings. As both the bear and the color white are Midé power symbols, a white bear was doubly potent (Blessing 1977:82, 113). Ursine parts and exotic shells, of course, have a long history as valued trade items in North America. The cowry is but a recent example.

Other early historic references are contested. En route to his famous discoveries of 1673, Marquette toured the Green Bay area and, during a stopover at a combined Miami-Kickapoo-Mascouten village, noted with enthusiasm what he took to be a Christian cross "adorned with white skins, red belts, and bows and arrows" (Thwaites 1896–1901:59:103). In a later appraisal of this remark, Hoffman was quick to equate Marquette's cross with the fourth-degree pole of the Midéwiwin (Figure 12.2) and identified the affixed trappings as Midéwiwin gifts and not, as Marquette marveled, offerings to the Christian God (Hoffman 1891:155). In further support, it can be added that Marquette's visit took place during the early days of June, a favored time for Midéwiwin initiations (Bray 2004:200).

Hickerson countered Hoffman's interpretation by pointing out that it was missionary practice to erect crosses at Indian villages and that these crosses had been incorporated into Native ritual life well before Marquette's visit (Hickerson 1962). Thus Marquette was indeed observing the Christian icon. This inference, however, is beside the point. As symbol of the world quarters, the cross is one of the more widespread and ancient motifs of Native America.

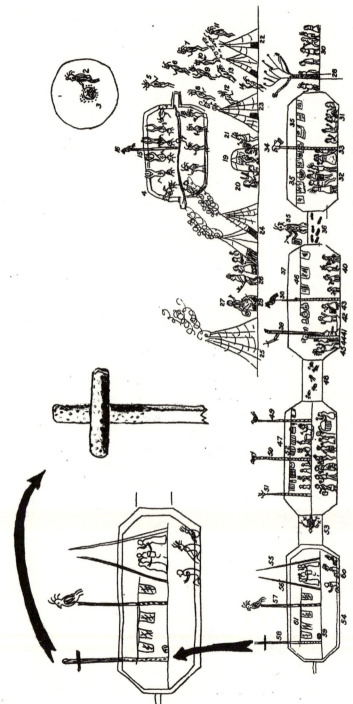

Figure 12.2. Painted cross of the fourth degree of Midéwiwin on a Midé scroll copied from an original said to have a La Pointe provenance, early nineteenth century (Hoffman 1891:Plate VIII).

It would seem unnecessary to require a late introduction from Christian Europe. More likely, it served briefly as a point of wishful, if radically misunderstood, commonality between Jesuit and Native American priests. Certainly the white deerskin tied to the cross is a Native American sacrament.

The cross aside, Hickerson raised a more telling objection. If the Midéwiwin were truly aboriginal, then evidence for its seventeenth-century occurrence is oddly skimpy when compared to the numerous and rich descriptions pertaining to other ceremonies such as the Feast of the Dead. What might explain this difference? Both Ritzenthaler (1978:755) and more recently Angel (2002) address this issue. Whereas the Feast of the Dead was a public, salient, and thereby hard-to-miss spectacle, the Midéwiwin, although staging some events for public view (such as the Obliteration Ceremony mentioned previously), was primarily a private society based upon the acquisition of restricted knowledge. Its pictographic scrolls, intelligible to the select, concealed meaning from the uninitiated (Landes 1968:86, cf. Kohl 1985 [1860]:289). Midéwiwin songs, medicinal recipes, and myths, especially those belonging to the higher degrees, were guarded by threats of sorcery (Coleman 1937:43). Ritual knowledge was further protected by the use of archaic or foreign speech only partly understood by the laity and unintelligible to the public at large (Coleman 1937:45). Thus Winnebago and Iowa Midé songs, for example, were sung in Ojibwa (Skinner 1915:693). The hidden is not designed to attract unknowing foreigners, especially of the hit-and-run variety. In 1846, Paul Kane found Midéwiwin practitioners "displeased" by inquiries (Kane 1968 [1859]:48). Later ethnographers also encountered such wariness. Skinner (1920:11–12) admitted that his own research was possible because informants feared the imminent demise of their society. Among the Winnebago, Paul Radin relied on converts to the growing peyote religion to reveal the inner workings of the Medicine Society (Hall 1997:68). Reo Fortune fared no better in his investigation of the related Water Monster society of the Omaha. There the unsanctioned disclosure of society secrets was believed to cause grave misfortune, while theft of such information was equated with homicide (Fortune 1932:67).

On the basis of the historical record alone, Midéwiwin antiquity remains contestable.

Oral Traditions

No consensus exists concerning the historicity of oral traditions; however, even the sternest of text-privileging critics, a group including such luminaries as Robert Lowie (1917) and George Peter Murdock (1959:3), usually stop short of dismissing all oral traditions as fabrications cobbled together for immediate ends. Even in what is otherwise a comprehensive dismissal of oral traditions as a source of reliable history, Ronald Mason (2006) concedes that this or that story, myth, legend, or whatever might serendipitously carry usable historical information (also see Brown and Roulette 2005). Traditions chartering the Midéwiwin are noteworthy for their attention to time and place. If a summary, or meta-myth, is permitted: Far to the east, perhaps on the Atlantic seaboard or even in Palestine (!) in a Christianized version cited by Dewdney (1975:31), the Manitous atoned for human mortality by granting the Midéwiwin to a reluctant Nanabozho, the protean Algonquian culture hero. In turn, Nanabozho entrusted this knowledge to a messenger or messengers—bear, otter, crane, or cowry shell, depending on the account—that carried the ceremony up the St. Lawrence and then through the Great Lakes, ultimately to reach western Lake Superior. The journey is recorded in bark migration scrolls, some of which have been handed down or recopied over generations (Dewdney 1975:72–73), and, as mapped in Figure 12.1, is commemorated in numerous landmarks including the "swirling eddies" of Lake St. Clair (Vennum 1978); Pewanagoing or "flinty point" on Grand Traverse Bay (Blackbird 1887:73–74); Mackinac, where the culture hero stopped to net fish; Nanabozho (Nanibojou) Island in Michipicoten Bay (Henry 1966 [1809]:212–213); Grand Island off the south shore of Lake Superior (Vennum 1978:763); and the "Sleeping Giant" overlooking Thunder Bay (Reid 1963:94). This toponym-studded route charts the east-to-west flow of Midéwiwin power. Johann Kohl expressed the Ojibwa view in 1860: "The farther east a prophet lives, the more powerful he is" (Kohl 1985 [1860]:458).

Based on a genealogy inscribed on a plate of copper, William Warren, the Ojibwa historian, proposed that the Ojibwa people accompanied by the Midéwiwin arrived at Chequamegon in the late fifteenth century (Warren 1984 [1885]:89). Hickerson, as seen, shortened Warren's chronology by shunting it forward into the historic period. Based on an examination of the scrolls, Dewdney (1975) seconded this move. All three scholars—Warren, Hickerson, and Dewdney—advanced their interpretations on the basis of textual materials, whether an inscribed plate, Midé scrolls, or Jesuit *Relations* (Schenck 1996).

Although there are no definite procedures for wringing time out of oral traditions, Brown and Brightman (1988) have assembled evidence for Cree and Northern Ojibwa Earth-diver myths that harbor chronological implications. The Earth-diver myth is one of the world's great creation narratives, with variants stretching from Hungary to Huronia (Count 1952; Kongas 1960; Reichard 1921). In North America, the myth displays a coherent distribution centering on a massive block of northern Athapaskan and Algonquian speakers but also including outliers assignable to variable language families (Figure 12.3). About 30 percent of motifs tabulated in Brown and Brightman's study span the entire 160-year period covered by available rec-

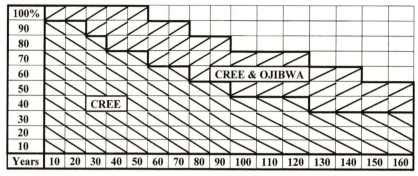

Figure 12.3. Duration of motifs in Cree Earth-diver myths recorded by Brown and Brightman (1988) supplemented by Ojibwa variants given in Barnouw (1977), Blackbird (1887), Bourgeois (1994), Carson (1917), Chamberlain (1891), Coleman et al. (1962), Dorson (1980), Jenness (1935), Jones (1917), Josselin de Jong (1913), Radin and Reagan (1928), Simms (1906), Skinner (1911), and Speck (1915).

ords, while the average motif "half-life" is about a century. If the sample is expanded to encompass cognate myths from the Ojibwa, the collective half-life is raised to 150 years. These estimates are compatible with those offered by the Ojibwa scholar Irving Hallowell (1937:666–668) and correspond to Vansina's more general appraisal of limits to error-free maintenance of oral tradition (Vansina 1985). None of these estimates, of course, should be likened to radiometric dates based on largely invariant rates of decay, and other scholars have been more charitable in their assessments of high fidelity, if not error-free, transmission over time. For example, Wesley Bernardini (2005 and this volume) and T. J. Ferguson (2007) have argued that Hopi and Zuni migration narratives, when taken in their intended idiom, can shed light on prehistory.

Nonetheless, the time depth for which oral traditions may have historical value remains disputed, and the merging of oral traditions with archaeological evidence has its own problematic past (Fewkes 1900). In contrast to a large experimental literature on memory, we know comparatively little about the long-term fidelity of cultural transmission in nonexperimental and nonliterate settings, although ongoing research projects promise to remedy a topic largely neglected for several decades (e.g., Lancy et al. 2010; O'Brien and Shennan 2010; Stark et al. 2008). In a sense, all of culture can act as a cross-indexed mnemonic device that channels behavior into expected patterns. For example, among the Ojibwa and many other Native Americans, winter nights were prime time for myth-telling, and specialists noted for their large repertoire and oratorical talents were avidly sought and rewarded for their services. Among the Ojibwa, such skilled orators joined Midé priests and tribal historians as "preservers" (Vennum 1978:754). In 1858 the Missisauga

George Copway remarked that he knew storytellers "who would commence to narrate legends in the month of October and not end until quite late in the spring" (Vecsey 1983:84). One imagines a discerning audience delighted by novel variations yet rejecting major mutations in the telling. Without such deviation-limiting processes at work and without recourse to a credible theory of prepotency, it is difficult to account for the numerous and specific similarities characterizing such far-flung creation myths as Earth-diver. Although Midéwiwin chartering narratives most commonly stand alone, they may also accompany Earth-diver myths, seemingly as insertions. Vecsey (1983:99) takes this inserted occurrence to indicate a graft during historic times, but a more reasonable conclusion would be the limited and uncontroversial one that Earth-diver myths are earlier than their Midéwiwin inclusions, whenever the latter were added. Adsorption and retrieval of discrete motives are common processes in oral traditions. For example, the Cheyenne separate the genesis story for their Massaum ceremony from world creation via earth-diving. The Massaum charter and its associated ritual, however, focus upon the exploits of two brothers, the younger drowned by underwater beings and later revived (Schlesier 1993:76–78). The parallel to Nanabozho and his Wolf brother, protagonists in Midéwiwin origin accounts (see below), is evident and suggests derivation from a common source. This datum qualifies Hallowell's otherwise well-taken observation that "the absence of the Midéwiwin among the Plains Algonkians would make it appear that the ceremony must have had its rise and spread after these people had become detached from the main stock" (Hallowell 1936:34).

The appearance of Midé elements in Earth-diver contexts is charted in Figure 12.4. This is not the occasion to itemize all elements and mythemes upon which this figure is based, but a brief summary is in order. Taken together, elements 34–38 and 53–54 address Nanabozho's consuming grief upon the death of his wolf companion at the hands of underwater beings. Alarmed by his cosmos-threatening despair, Manitous of Sky and Earth convene to confer upon Nanabozho the life-restoring powers of the Midéwiwin. Balancing the forces of Sky and Earth and finding a place for both Life and Death are more than whimsical addenda to what otherwise is merely a whopping good story of battles with horned panthers, cataclysmic floods, and diving muskrats who surface clutching the stuff for a new world. They are bedrock theological matters that Midé members came to master as they advanced through the society. Such mastery was costly and lengthy. Ritual roles had to be rehearsed and the candidate was expected to be able "to recount the legends exactly" (Vennum 1978:754). Presumably, these demands for faithful transmission, buttressed by scroll mnemonics and memorable songs, were keys to perpetuating a tradition carried by a restrictive, if not totally secret,

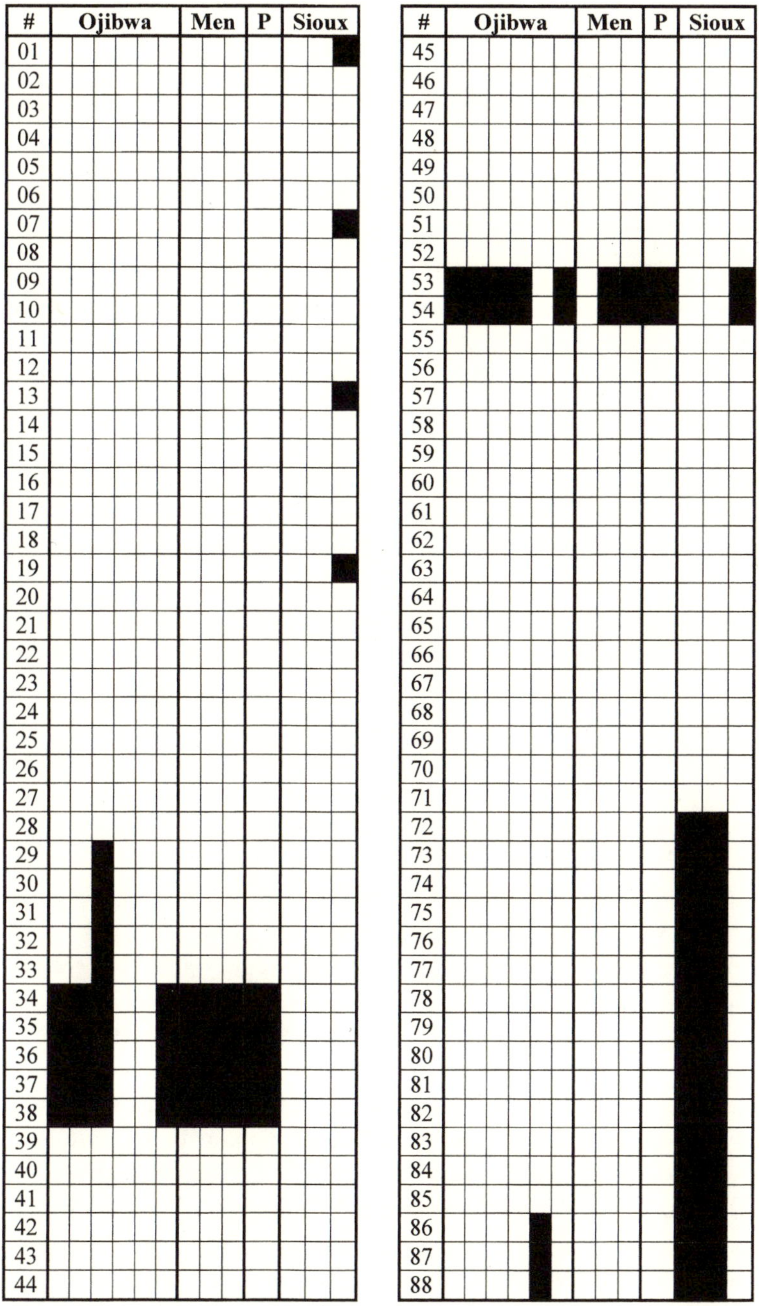

#	Ojibwa	Men	P	Sioux
01				■
02				
03				
04				
05				
06				
07				■
08				
09				
10				
11				
12				
13				■
14				
15				
16				
17				
18				
19				■
20				
21				
22				
23				
24				
25				
26				
27				
28				
29	■			
30	■			
31	■			
32	■			
33	■			
34	■	■		
35	■	■		
36	■	■		
37	■	■		
38	■	■		
39				
40				
41				
42				
43				
44				

#	Ojibwa	Men	P	Sioux
45				
46				
47				
48				
49				
50				
51				
52				
53	■	■	■	■
54	■	■	■	■
55				
56				
57				
58				
59				
60				
61				
62				
63				
64				
65				
66				
67				
68				
69				
70				
71				
72				■
73				■
74				■
75				■
76				■
77				■
78				■
79				■
80				■
81				■
82				■
83				■
84				■
85				■
86		■		■
87		■		■
88		■		■

Figure 12.4. Distribution of Midé-related elements (black squares) in Earth-diver narratives of the Ojibwa, Menomini (Men), Potawatomi (P), and Siouan groups. Ojibwa cases drawn from those listed in Figure 12.3. Menomini are taken from Densmore (1932), Hoffman (1896), Michelson (1911), and Skinner (1920); Potawatomi from Alexander (1916); Siouans from Dorsey (1892), Fortune (1932), and Skinner (1925).

society (cf. Barth 1989). On the basis of oral tradition, nonbelievers might concede that Midé origins remain up for grabs.

Archaeology

A recent article claims to "decisively defeat the ethnohistorical argument that [Midé] ritual was a consequence of European contact" (Howey and O'Shea 2006:275). This strong claim rests on a remarkable interpretation of Michigan's Missaukee Earthworks. The site consists of two circular enclosures with diameters of about 50 m that are situated about 600 m apart on an east–west line with a spring-fed swampy area to the south. Each enclosure has a pair of openings. The eastern circle is associated with a concentration of fire-cracked rock that may mark the presence of a sweatlodge. This occurrence would be significant as sweatlodges, typically located eastward of the medicine lodge proper, were obligatory components of Midé rites (see Figure 12.2, upper right). The western circle, having a large boulder at its center, is associated with two large pots and a grinding stone. Whether the latter remains are sufficient to indicate a special area devoted to food preparation is arguable. Finally, exotic flints indicate that the Missaukee Earthworks were part of a far-reaching trade network or, perhaps, a destination for pilgrims from distant lands.

According to Howey and O'Shea, the layout of Missaukee and its surrounding topography can be read as a monumental projection of a Midé origin narrative, specifically one that Will Rogers or Hole-in-the-Sky, a Midé priest at the Red Lake reserve, illustrated for Ruth Landes in 1933 (Landes 1968:18). Based on Hole-in-the-Sky's drawing and accompanying origin narrative, the western enclosure with its central boulder ("what we are sitting on"), can be viewed as the site of Bear's emergence from the underworld. From this emergence site, Bear then followed the floor of the sea (Lake Superior) until surfacing to meet daylight in the east (the eastern enclosure). On his submarine return to the west, Bear recrossed the sea (represented by Missaukee's swampy ground), periodically surfacing to dispense medicines from his Midé pack. These stopping points continue to be well-known landmarks.

The mapping of Missaukee onto Hole-in-the-Sky's Midé drawing is ingenious but as critics have pointed out is also underspecified if not totally fanciful (Mason 2009). For example, if two enclosures connectable by putative paths are sufficient to identify the Midéwiwin, then the Newark Works of Ohio Hopewell would qualify, extending Midé-like activities back 1,700 years. At Newark, there is a well-defined east–west causeway that connects the Newark square to the famed Newark octagon (Squier and Davis 1998 [1848]:Plate XXV). The Newark causeway also matches the Missaukee plan by skirting a large pond, whether natural or artificial, to the south. One might even equate four- and eight-sided polygons with the four and eight Midé degrees. These comparisons are not mere fancy, but more on the order of useful imaginative exercises. In fact, Midéwiwin architecture, artifacts, myths, and other accoutrements can provide insightful trains of thought for animating Ohio Hopewell (DeBoer 2006), whether or not the Midéwiwin as such existed at such great time depths. This is so because both Midéwiwin and Hopewell participate in a grand, deeply seated tradition of Northeastern religious beliefs and ceremonies. If the Hopewell example seems strained in comparison to the Missaukee–Midéwiwin connection, it is because the latter gains credence through proximity in time and space and not, as claimed by some, because matters of prehistoric meaning and ancient belief are unknowable (Whitley 2009, contra Howey and O'Shea 2009).

Without the Missaukee Earthworks, the archaeological record for the Midéwiwin is sparse. No prehistoric bark scrolls can be expected nor can definitive rock art be cited. An alleged Midé drumstick has been claimed for an Archaic site in southern Ontario (Two Shoes 1995). Unfortunately, the specimen appears to be a quite ordinary raccoon baculum. Drumming accompanied all Midé services, and the *midé gwakik,* or traditional water drum, was laden with both Midé and Earth-diver imagery. The drumstick was often a loon beak, symbolizing quick descent from the sky; the membrane was an otter skin held taut by a snakeskin tie; the water inside, the mythic flood (another Earth-diver connection); and the turtle stopper at the base, the island where Nanabozho delivered the first Midé rites to Otter (Harrison 1982: 165–166). Excavations in the Chequamegon region, the "traditional Ojibwa capital," and on Grand Island, another hotspot in Ojibwa history, yield no recognized traces of Midé activity (Birmingham 1992; Skibo et al. 2004).

A suitable archaeological signature, one oddly missing from the Missaukee analysis, might be the distinctive *midéwigan,* or medicine lodge itself. These ceremonial lodges were built in clearings near settlements and were typically of light construction, often hastily erected for the ceremony at hand. They could be refurbished or rebuilt for subsequent usage, and the Midéwiwin site, if not the lodge, was a permanent installation, typically located a short walk away from the hosting village. Figure 12.5 plots length against width of historic medicine lodges and compares them to the dimensions of late prehistoric or protohistoric Oneota and Iroquois Huron longhouses. Such a comparison is justified given that the medicine lodge can be seen as a special-use longhouse (Bushnell 1919:615). Although length is not discriminating, medicine lodges tend to be narrower than residential longhouses. This tendency is real: medicine lodges comprise 16 of 37 structures having widths below the median value of 6.4 m (21 feet), while they comprise only 4 of 36 cases above the median. Two of these structures, however, have unusual properties that warrant inspection.

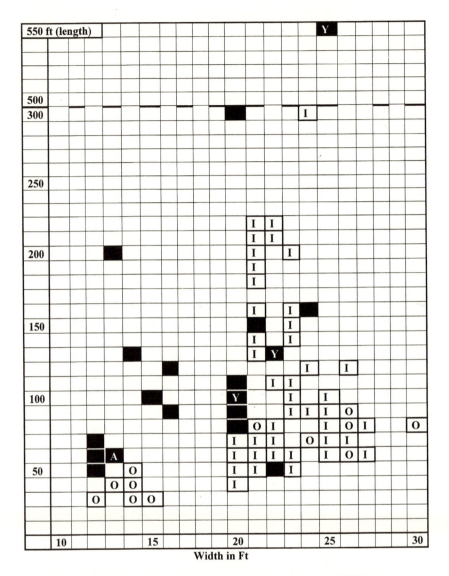

Black squares: Midewigan; O: Oneota; I: Iroquois; A: Anker site; Y: Younge site.

Figure 12.5. Dimensions of *midéwigan* and Huron-Iroquois and Oneota longhouses. *Midéwigan* figures drawn from Angel (2002:55), Coleman (1937:45), Densmore (1910:36, 1979:92), Hilger (1992:66), Hoffman (1891:187, 1896:103), Kohl (1985 [1860]:41), Landes (1968:155), Lyford (1953:22), Pond (1986:94), Reagan (1933:503), Schoolcraft (1868:3:286), and Warren (1984 [1885]:187). Huron-Iroquois and Oneota dimensions from Bluhm and Fenner (1961), Bluhm and Liss (1961), Funk and Kuhn (2003), Hart (2000), Hollinger (1995), McKusick (1973), and Ramsden (1989).

The 16.8-m-long (55 feet) lodge from the Anker site near Chicago was constructed of rather flimsy poles and yielded a peculiar material assemblage (Bluhm and Liss 1961). This assemblage included an otter skull with copper-lined eye sockets—presumably the remnants of a medicine bag—as well as imported marine shells and an assortment of small fancy pots and disk pipes. With respect to the latter two, Densmore (1910:13) noted that "each leader has a pipe which he smokes only at meetings of the Midewiwin," while the use of special vessels in feasts and mortuary rites was commonplace (Angel 2002:222). This exotic array of objects came largely from burials in a nearby but associated cemetery. The affairs of death, however, were also concerns of the Midéwiwin, rites of which dealt specifically with the ordered transition of the soul from the earthly lodge administered by Nanabozho to the Ghost Lodge headed by his Wolf brother. Anker dates to the fifteenth century (Brown and Asch 1990:153), more than a full century before the pan-Northeastern elaboration of curing artifacts and rites that Fitzgerald (2001:43) relates to introduced European diseases.

Over 70 years ago, Emerson Greenman excavated a set of very unusual structures at the Younge site, now the eponym for a late prehistoric complex. Unencumbered by Hickerson's later arguments, Greenman noted that the Younge structures could be likened to medicine lodges. His Enclosure One extended over 152.5 m (500 feet) and pointed toward a small oval structure 61.0 m (200 feet) to the east. This layout recalls the positioning of lodge and accompanying sudatory in the Midéwiwin (Greenman 1937:90). Enclosure Two, located 91.5 m (300 feet) to the south, apparently represents two aligned lodges, each sized in keeping with historic medicine lodges. Although Younge lacked the flamboyant materials found at Anker, Greenman was impressed by the abundance of smoking pipes and the puzzling paucity of domestic rubbish. As at Anker, burials were present, and Greenman was torn between a Midéwiwin or Feast of the Dead interpretation of the remains. At 1200 C.E. or so, however, the distinction between Feast of the Dead and Midéwiwin-like institutions may not have been sharply drawn. As late as the early eighteenth century, Cadillac observed an Ottawa "feast for the dead" that took place in a 36.6-m-long (120 feet) midéwigan-like structure (Kinietz 1965:283). As recently as 1910, the "ghost society" component of the Nett Lake Midéwiwin still incorporated a "feast of the dead." This feast could be a farewell meal for the recently deceased, one designed to speed their journey to the Land of Mysteries, or, alternatively, a welcoming feast, held at the grave site one year after death, at which the deceased revisited the living to bestow his or her social identity onto an adopted successor (Reagan 1933).

Reagan's report on the Nett Lake ceremony inadvertently opens up one of those connections that so infuriate critics of ethnographic analogy. A photograph sandwiched between pages 502 and 503 of this report shows an initiate wearing a sign badge bearing an embroidered design in the form of a headless human figure. The figure does not resemble any of the *nindoodem*, or clan markings, recently discussed by Bohaker (2010). In the context of the Midéwiwin, Johnston (1982:147) notes that dismembered figures of this kind portray the dead, including the initiates who must die to be reborn during the ceremony. In the Shawnee Society of Doctors, how these bodies lost their heads and limbs is described:

> When they were about to receive a young member, they assembled in some retired spot with the applicant and their house dogs. The boy was knocked down with a club, and his head and limbs were severed from his body. The head was preserved and the dogs were called to devour the mangled limbs. After they had done so, they were driven away, and then a bed of leaves was prepared in the middle of the lodge, the head was deposited upon the leaves, and the dogs called back. These animals being overcharged with the food which they had eaten were kept near the head, where they vomited and discharged all they had eaten. The society danced around the lodge to the right four times in quick succession, the oldest men sung very violently, and at the end of the dance, the boy, having exactly the appearance which he had had before being killed, arose and took his place among the members [Kinietz and Voegelin 1939:36].

The Shawnee did not have the Midéwiwin but homologous practices are evident in the above description. Intriguing archaeological parallels are also apparent. Limbless cutouts from Ohio Hopewell sites recall in detail the badge worn by the Nett Lake woman (see Mills 1922:Figures 67, 76, and Shetrone 1926:Figure 46), while a Copena style stone pipe in the form of a human-devouring canid found at the Seip mound offers an explicit parallel (Shetrone and Greenman 1931:Figure 40). In addition, the well-known Wray figurine from Newark that Lepper (1996) identifies as a "Bear Shaman" could easily be matched by fourth-degree Midé priests garbed in bear robes. Mounting in number and specificity, these comparisons leave the realm of baseless analogy and come to resemble concordances culled from the same deep tradition.

Conclusion

The ethnohistoric record with respect to Midéwiwin origins is inconclusive and occasionally suffers from definitional and tautologous reasoning in which history perforce begins with written testimony. It is as if the peoples of prehistory wandered through a temporal fog of short-term memory and fable. Oral traditions, once a central concern of Americanist anthropology, should be revisited and new methods for wringing time depth from these alternative sources need to be devised. Knowing the past is too difficult to dismiss bodies of evidence, however intractable they may appear, and too important to be left to an archaeology that claims uncontested sovereignty over the past. Although less than definitive, current archaeological evidence offers tantalizing, if fleeting, glimpses of Midéwiwin predecessors in late prehistory, while Midé-like activities can be traced back into deep time, a verdict that will not surprise many Native Americans. This is not to suggest that the Midéwiwin was, in any sense, a static institution. Even a preliminary analysis of the kind presented here undermines such an essentialist and ahistorical point of view. Diagnostic features found in the historic institution were often assembled from separate sources. An example is the widespread practice of magically reviving candidates from death. Contrary to much popular discourse in archaeology, however, it can be argued that human creativity, although vital, is rare, that terms such as reinvention, transformation, and agency are often misused in a wishful way, and that the lot of most human behavior is retrieval, recycling, and recombining baggage bestowed by the past. Without such continuity, there would be no movement at all and the story of Midéwiwin beginnings, whether as historical chronicle or mythic genesis, could neither be told nor understood.

References Cited

Alexander, Hartley Burr
   1916   *North American Mythology.* Marshall Jones, Boston.
Angel, Michael
   2002   *Preserving the Sacred: Historical Perspectives on the Ojibwa Midewiwin.* University of Manitoba Press, Winnipeg, Canada.
Aubin, George F.
   1975   *A Proto-Algonquian Dictionary.* Mercury Series, Canadian Ethnology Service, Paper 29. National Museum of Man, Ottawa, Canada.
Barnouw, Victor
   1977   *Wisconsin Chippewa Myths and Tales.* University of Wisconsin Press, Madison.
Barth, Fredrik
   1989   *Cosmologies in the Making.* University of Cambridge Press, Cambridge.
Bernardini, Wesley
   2005   *Hopi Oral Tradition and the Archaeology of Identity.* University of Arizona Press, Tucson.
Birmingham, Robert A.
   1992   Historic Period Indian Archeology at La Pointe in Lake Superior: An Overview. *Wisconsin Archeologist* 73(3-4):177–198.

Blackbird, Andrew J.
  1887   *History of the Ottawa and Chippewa Indians of Michigan.* Ypsilanti Job Print-
          ing House, Ypsilanti, Michigan.

Blair, Emma Helen
  1996   *The Indian Tribes of the Upper Mississippi Valley and Region of the Great Lakes.*
          2 vols. University of Nebraska Press, Lincoln.

Blessing, Fred K.
  1977   *The Ojibway Indians Observed: Papers of Fred K. Blessing, Jr., on the Ojibway
          Indians.* Minnesota Archaeological Society, Fort Snelling.

Bluhm, Elaine A., and Gloria J. Fenner
  1961   The Oak Forest Site. In *Chicago Area Archaeology,* edited by Elaine A. Bluhm,
          pp. 139–162. Bulletin 3, Illinois Archaeological Survey. University of Illinois,
          Urbana.

Bluhm, Elaine A., and Alan Liss
  1961   The Anker Site. In *Chicago Area Archaeology,* edited by Elaine A. Bluhm,
          pp. 89–137. Bulletin 3, Illinois Archaeological Survey. University of Illinois,
          Urbana.

Bohaker, Heidi
  2010   Rethinking Anishinaabe Identities: Meaning and Metaphor in Nindoo-
          dem Pictographs. *Ethnohistory* 57:11–33.

Bourgeois, Arthur P. (editor)
  1994   *Ojibwa Narratives of Charlotte Kawbawgam and Jacques LePique, 1893–1895.*
          Wayne State University Press, Detroit.

Bray, Martha C. (editor)
  2004   *The Journals of Joseph N. Nicollet.* Minnesota Historical Society Press,
          St. Paul.

Brotherston, Gordon
  1992   *Book of the Fourth World: Reading the Native Americas through Their Litera-
          ture.* Cambridge University Press, Cambridge.

Brown, James A., and David L. Asch
  1990   Cultural Setting: The Oneota Tradition. In *At the Edge of Prehistory: Hu-
          ber Phase Archaeology in the Chicago Area,* edited by James A. Brown and
          Patricia J. O'Brien, pp. 145–154. Center for American Archeology, Kamps-
          ville, Illinois.

Brown, Jennifer S. H., and Robert Brightman
  1988   *"The Orders of the Dreamed": George Nelson on Cree and Northern Ojibwa Re-
          ligion and Myth, 1823.* Minnesota Historical Society Press, St. Paul.

Brown, Jennifer S. H., and Roger Roulette
  2005   Waabitigweyaa: The One Who Found the Anishinaabeg First. In *Algon-
          quian Spirit: Contemporary Translations of the Algonquian Literatures of North
          America,* edited by Brian Swann, pp. 159–169. University of Nebraska Press,
          Lincoln.

Bushnell, David I., Jr.

1919   Ojibway Habitations and Other Structures. *Annual Report of the Smithsonian Institution for 1917,* pp. 609–617. U.S. Government Printing Office, Washington, D.C.

Carson, William

1917   Ojibwa Tales. *Journal of American Folklore* 30:491–493.

Carver, Jonathan

1813   *Three Years' Travels throughout the Interior Parts of North America.* Isaiah Tecmas, London.

Chamberlain, A. F.

1891   Nanibozhu amongst the Otchipwe, Mississagas, and Other Algonkian Tribes. *Journal of American Folklore* 4:193–213.

Coleman, M. Bernard

1937   The Religion of the Ojibwa of Northern Minnesota. *Primitive Man* 10(3-4):33–57.

Coleman, M. Bernard, Ellen Frogner, and Estelle Eich

1962   *Ojibwa Myths and Legends.* Ross and Haines, Minneapolis.

Count, Earl W.

1952   The Earth-Diver and the Rival Twins: A Clue to Time Correlation in North-Eurasiatic and North American Mythology. In *Selected Papers of the 29th International Congress of Americanists,* edited by Sol Tax, pp. 55–62. University of Chicago Press, Chicago.

DeBoer, Warren R.

2006   Salient Representations of the American Past. In *A Pre-Columbian World,* edited by Jeffrey Quilter and Mary Miller, pp. 137–186. Dumbarton Oaks, Washington, D.C.

Densmore, Frances

1910   *Chippewa Music.* Bulletin 45, Pt. 1, Bureau of American Ethnology. U.S. Government Printing Office, Washington, D.C.

1932   *Menominee Music.* Bulletin 102, Bureau of American Ethnology. U.S. Government Printing Office, Washington, D.C.

1979   *Chippewa Customs.* Minnesota Historical Society Press, St. Paul.

Dewdney, Selwyn

1975   *The Sacred Scrolls of the Southern Ojibway.* University of Toronto Press, Toronto, Canada.

Dorsey, James Owen

1892   Nanibozhu in Siouan Mythology. *Journal of American Folklore* 5:293–304.

Dorson, Richard M.

1980   *Bloodstoppers and Bearwalkers. Folk Traditions of the Upper Peninsula.* Harvard University Press, Cambridge, Massachusetts.

Ferguson, T. J.

2007   Zuni Traditional History and Cultural Geography. In *Zuni Prehistory:*

Toward a New Synthesis of Southwestern Archaeology, edited by David A. Gregory and David R. Wilcox, pp. 377–406. University of Arizona Press, Tucson.

Fewkes, Jesse W.

1900   *Tusayan Migration Traditions.* Bureau of American Ethnology Annual Report 19, Pt. 2, pp. 573–634. U.S. Government Printing Office, Washington, D.C.

Fitzgerald, William R.

2001   Contact, Neutral Iroquoian Transformation, and the Little Ice Age. In *Societies in Eclipse: Archaeology of the Eastern Woodlands Indians, A.D. 1400–1700,* edited by David S. Brose, C. Wesley Cowan, and Robert C. Mainfort Jr., pp. 37–47. Smithsonian Institution Press, Washington, D.C.

Fortune, Reo

1932   *Omaha Secret Societies.* Columbia University Press, New York.

Funk, Robert E., and Robert D. Kuhn

2003   *Three Sixteenth-Century Mohawk Iroquois Village Sites.* Bulletin 503. New York State Museum, Albany.

Greenman, Emerson F.

1937   *The Younge Site.* Occasional Contributions 6. Museum of Anthropology of the University of Michigan, Ann Arbor.

Hall, Robert L.

1997   *An Archaeology of the Soul: North American Indian Belief and Ritual.* University of Illinois Press, Urbana.

Hallowell, A. Irving

1936   The Passing of the Midewiwin in the Lake Winnipeg Region. *American Anthropologist* 38:32–51.

1937   Temporal Orientation in Western Civilization and in a Pre-literate Society. *American Anthropologist* 39:647–670.

Harrison, Julia D.

1982   The Midewiwin: The Retention of an Ideology. Master's thesis, Department of Anthropology, University of Calgary, Calgary, Canada.

Hart, John P.

2000   New Dates from Classic New York Sites. *Northeast Anthropology* 60:1–22.

Henry, Alexander

1966   *Travels and Adventures in Canada.* University Microfilms, Ann Arbor,
[1809]   Michigan.

Hickerson, Harold

1962   Notes on the Post-contact Origin of the Midewiwin. *Ethnohistory* 9:404–423.

1963   The Sociohistorical Significance of Two Chippewa Ceremonials. *American Anthropologist* 65:67–85.

Hilger, M. Inez

1992   *Chippewa Child Life and Its Cultural Background.* Minnesota Historical Society, St. Paul. Originally published 1951, Bulletin 146, Bureau of American Ethnology.

Hoffman, Walter J.

1891   *The Mide'wiwin or "Grand Medicine Society" of the Ojibwa.* Bureau of American Ethnology Annual Report 7, pp. 143–300. U.S. Government Printing Office, Washington, D.C.

1896   *The Menomini Indians.* Bureau of American Ethnology Annual Report 14, pp. 3–328. U.S. Government Printing Office, Washington, D.C.

Hollinger, R. Eric

1995   Residence Patterns and Oneota Cultural Dynamics. In *Oneota Archaeology: Past, Present, and Future,* edited by William Green, pp. 141–174. Office of the State Archaeologist Report 20. University of Iowa, Iowa City.

Howey, Meghan C. L., and John M. O'Shea

2006   Bear's Journey and the Study of Ritual in Archaeology. *American Antiquity* 71:261–282.

2009   On Archaeology and the Study of Ritual: Considering Inadequacies in the Culture-History Approach and Quests for Internal "Meaning." *American Antiquity* 74:193–201.

Jenness, Diamond

1935   *The Ojibwa Indians of Parry Island, Their Social and Religious Life.* National Museum of Canada Publication 78. Canada Department of Mines, Government Printing Bureau, Ottawa.

Johnston, Basil

1982   *Ojibway Ceremonies.* University of Nebraska Press, Lincoln.

Jones, William

1917   *Ojibwa Texts.* Publications of the American Ethnological Society 7(1). E. J. Brill, Leyden.

Josselin de Jong, J. P. B., de

1913   *Od_ibwe Texts with English Translation.* Baessler-Archiv, Beiträge zur Völkerkunde 5. B. G. Teubner, Leipzig, Germany.

Kane, Paul

1968   *Wanderings of an Artist among the Indians of North America.* Charles E. Tuttle, Rutland, Vermont.
[1859]

Keesing, Felix M.

1971   *The Menomini Indians of Wisconsin.* Johnson Reprint, New York. Originally published 1939, American Philosophical Society, Philadelphia.

Kinietz, W. Vernon

1965   *The Indians of the Western Great Lakes, 1615–1760.* University of Michigan Press, Ann Arbor.

Kinietz, W. Vernon, and Erminie W. Voegelin (editors)

1939   *Shawnese Traditions by C. C. Trowbridge.* Occasional Papers 9. Museum of Anthropology, University of Michigan, Ann Arbor.

Kohl, Johann G.

1985   *Kitchi-Gami: Life among the Lake Superior Ojibway.* Minnesota Historical
[1860]   Society Press, St. Paul.

Kongas, Elli Kaija

1960   The Earth-Diver. *Ethnohistory* 7:151–180.

Lancy, David F., John Bock, and Suzanne Gaskins (editors)

2010   *The Anthropology of Learning in Childhood.* AltaMira, Lanham, Maryland.

Landes, Ruth

1968   *Ojibwa Religion and the Midéwiwin.* University of Wisconsin Press, Mil-
waukee.

Lepper, Bradley T.

1996   The Newark Earthworks and the Geometric Enclosures of the Scioto Valley: Connections and Conjectures. In *A View from the Core: A Synthesis of
Ohio Hopewell Archaeology,* edited by Paul J. Pacheco, pp. 224–241. Ohio Archaeological Council, Columbus.

Lowie, Robert H.

1917   Oral Tradition and History. *Journal of American Folklore* 30:161–167.

Lyford, Carrie A.

1953   *Ojibwa Crafts.* U.S. Department of the Interior, Bureau of Indian Affairs,
Washington, D.C.

Mason, Ronald J.

2006   *Inconstant Companions: Archaeology and North American Indian Oral Traditions.* The University of Alabama Press, Tuscaloosa.

2009   Bear's Journey and the Study of Ritual in Archaeology: Some Comments
on Howey and O'Shea's Midewiwin Paper. *American Antiquity* 74:184–192.

McKusick, Marshall

1973   *The Grant Oneota Village.* Office of the State Archaeologist, Report 4. University of Iowa, Iowa City.

Michelson, Truman

1911   Menomini Tales. *American Anthropologist* 13:68–88.

Miller, Jay

1999   *Lushootseed Culture and the Shamanic Odyssey.* University of Nebraska Press,
Lincoln.

Mills, William C.

1922   Exploration of the Mound City Group. *Ohio Archaeological and Historical
Quarterly* 13:245–408.

Murdock, George Peter

1959   *Africa: Its Peoples and Their Culture History.* McGraw Hill, New York.

O'Brien, Michael J., and Stephen J. Shennan (editors)

2010   *Innovation in Cultural Systems.* MIT Press, Cambridge, Massachusetts.

Pond, Samuel W.

1986   *Dakota Life in the Upper Midwest.* Minnesota Historical Society, St. Paul.

Radin, Paul

1991   *The Road of Life and Death: A Ritual Drama of the American Indians.* Princeton University Press, Princeton, New Jersey. Originally published 1945, Pantheon, New York.

Radin, Paul, and Albert B. Reagan

1928   Ojibwa Myths and Tales: The Manabozho Cycle. *Journal of American Folklore* 41:61–146.

Ramsden, Carol N.

1989   *The Kirche Site: A Sixteenth Century Huron Village in the Upper Trent Valley.* Copetown Press, Dundas, Ontario, Canada.

Reagan, Albert B.

1933   Some Notes on the Grand Medicine Society of the Bois Fort Ojibwa. *Americana* 27:502–529.

Reichard, Gladys A.

1921   Literary Types and Dissemination of Myths. *Journal of American Folklore* 34:269–307.

Reid, Dorothy M.

1963   *Tales of Nanabozho.* Oxford University Press, Toronto, Canada.

Ritzenthaler, Robert E.

1978   Southwestern Chippewa. In *Northeast,* edited by Bruce G. Trigger, pp. 743–759. *Handbook of North American Indians,* Vol. 15, William C. Sturtevant, general editor. Smithsonian Institution Press, Washington, D.C.

Schenck, Theresa

1996   William W. Warren's History of the Ojibway People: Tradition, History, and Context. In *Reading beyond Words: Contexts for Native History,* edited by Jennifer Brown and Elizabeth Vibert, pp. 242–260. Broadview Press, Peterborough, Ontario, Canada.

Schlesier, Karl H.

1990   Rethinking the Midewiwin and the Plains Ceremonial Called the Sun Dance. *Plains Anthropologist* 35:1–27.

1993   *The Wolves of Heaven: Cheyenne Shamanism, Ceremonies, and Prehistoric Origins.* University of Oklahoma Press, Norman. Originally published in English 1987.

Schoolcraft, Henry Rowe

1868   *Archives of Aboriginal Knowledge.* 6 vols. J. B. Lippincott, Philadelphia.

Shetrone, Henry C.

1926   Explorations of the Hopewell Group of Prehistoric Earthworks. *Ohio Archaeological and Historical Quarterly* 35:1–227.

Shetrone, Henry C., and Emerson F. Greenman

1931   Exploration of the Seip Group of Prehistoric Earthworks. *Ohio Archaeo-logical and Historical Quarterly* 40:343–509.

Simms, Stephen Chapman

1906   Myths of the Bungees or Swampy Indians of Lake Winnipeg. *Journal of American Folklore* 19:334–340.

Skibo, James M., Terrance J. Martin, Eric C. Drake, and John C. Franzen

2004   Gete Odena: Grand Island's Post-Contact Occupation at Williams Land-ing. *Midcontinental Journal of Archaeology* 29:167–190.

Skinner, Alanson

1911   Notes on the Eastern Cree and Northern Saulteaux. *Anthropological Papers of the American Museum of Natural History* 11(1):7–177.

1915   Societies of the Iowa, Kansa, and Ponca Indians. *Anthropological Papers of the American Museum of Natural History* 11(9):678–801.

1920   *Medicine Ceremony of the Menomini, Iowa, and Wahpeton Dakota, with Notes on the Ceremony among the Ponca, Bungi, Ojibwa, and Potawatomi.* Indian Notes and Monographs 4. Museum of the American Indian, Heye Foundation, New York.

1925   Traditions of the Iowa Indians. *Journal of American Folklore* 38:425–506.

Smith, Theresa S.

1995   *The Island of the Anishnaabeg.* University of Idaho Press, Moscow.

Speck, Frank G.

1915   *Myths and Folk-lore of the Timiskaming Algonquin and Timagami Ojibwa.* Canada Department of Mines and Geological Survey, Memoir 71. Government Printing Bureau, Ottawa, Canada.

Squier, Ephraim G., and Edwin H. Davis

1998   *Ancient Monuments of the Mississippi Valley.* Smithsonian Institution Press,
[1848]   Washington, D.C.

Stark, Miriam T., Brenda J. Bowser, and Lee Horne (editors)

2008   *Cultural Transmission and Material Culture.* University of Arizona Press, Tucson.

Thwaites, Reuben Gold (editor)

1896–   *The Jesuit Relations and Allied Documents. Travels and Explorations of the Je-*
1901   *suit Missionaries in New France, 1610–1791.* 73 vols. Burrows Brothers, Cleveland.

Two Shoes, Minnie

1995   Oral History Confirmed by "Modern Science." *New from Indian Country* 9(24):1, 5.

Vansina, Jan

1985   *Oral Tradition as History.* University of Wisconsin Press, Madison.

Vecsey, Christopher

1983   *Traditional Indian Religion and Its Historical Changes.* American Philosophical Society, Philadelphia.

Vennum, Thomas, Jr.

1978   Ojibwa Origin-Migration Songs of the Mitewiwin. *Journal of American Folklore* 9:753–791.

Warren, William W.

1984   *History of the Ojibway People.* Minnesota Historical Society Press, St. Paul.
[1885]

Whiteley, Peter M.

2002   Archaeology and Oral Tradition: The Scientific Importance of Dialogue. *American Antiquity* 67:405–416.

Whitley, David S.

2009   Comments on Howey and O'Shea's "Bear's Journey and the Study of Ritual in Archaeology." *American Antiquity* 74:183–188.

Wrong, George M. (editor)

1939   *The Long Journey to the Country of the Hurons.* The Champlain Society, Toronto, Canada.

13
Resolving Contradictions as a Methodology for Investigating Maya Calendar History and Its Cosmological Associations

Robert L. Hall

In a recent book Prudence Rice (2004:9) speaks of the "tyranny of the epigraphic record," one of whose dangers is placing too much reliance upon surviving stone inscriptions to gain insights into some historical aspects of ancient Maya society. She is not speaking so much of the danger of accepting the rhetoric of the inscribed texts as historical truth as the danger of not considering what might be fact just because it was not cut in stone.

There is an implicit early background for the Classic Maya calendar that does not appear on any inscribed monument or surviving written text in the form of actual dates. The background is implicit because it exists mainly in the form of certain contradictions that presume the sometime existence of a calendar other than that known for the Classic Period. Archaeologists are understandably reluctant to speculate on "what might have been" in the absence of clues of a material sort. It can be headline news today (interior section, of course) when an archaeologist finds an object that suggests the Middle Preclassic existence of an element of the Maya calendar such as a day sign because, among other things, it suggests the existence of writing. Yet, for a century and more there have been clues, some overlooked, others just not fully appreciated, that the Maya calendar had a long and complex history before the first date ever appeared on stone. The evidence is in the form of contradictions.

Contradictions Preserved in Our Calendar

Contradictions can provide valuable clues to past events. In the area of calendar studies, the very names of our own "Christian" calendar months and days are good examples. To begin with, the names of the months contain the names of some very un-Christian pagan deities. Mars and Juno were the eponymous Roman gods of the months March and June, for example. Our Wednesday lightly conceals the name of Woden, a god in the Germanic background of the English language, while in countries with stronger Roman imperial histories the same day derives from the name of the Roman god Mercury.

December is the twelfth month of our calendar, but the name is based on the Latin word *decem*, which translates as "ten." September is currently the ninth month but has a name based on the Latin word *septem*, or "seven," and so on for the names October and November as well. This is because the Christian calendar once began with March (Aveni 1989:176). This clue is preserved in the contradictions.

Russia's October Revolution was an October revolution only in the reckoning of the Julian (Julius Caesar's) calendar still in use in Russia in 1917. In countries that had earlier adopted the Gregorian calendar, starting in 1582, it was a revolution in November. Such discrepancies provide clues to calendar reform of another sort. In this case, it is a readjustment in the length of the year after the shift from the Julian calendar to the Gregorian calendar. Russia's official religion was Russian Orthodoxy, whose patriarchs did not wish to follow the lead of Rome in calendar reform. Other kinds of religious history are also vaguely concealed in our calendar and present other contradictions.

The selection of December 25 as the official day of Christ's birth at the Council of Nicea (325 C.E.) was influenced by the birth on the December solstice of the Persian god Mithras, the Unconquered Sun, whose worship was an official Roman religion competing with Christianity at the time. The December solstice falls on the twenty-first of the month and not the twenty-fifth, of course. Because of the difference in the length of the Julian calendar year and that of the actual tropical year, the date of the solstice had moved forward four days by the time of the Council of Nicea.

Contradictions Preserved in the Maya Calendar and Ritual Practice

The Yucatec Mayas that Diego de Landa knew and wrote of had a year whose month names seemed to contain contradictions. Yaxkin was the sixth month of the Yucatec year but had a name based on the words *yax*, or "new, green," and *kin*, "sun, day." The preceding month was Xul, which translates as "end." There is an implication here that there had once been a year that ended with the month Xul and began with the month Yaxkin.[1] In Gates's (1937:74) commentary on Landa, he remarked on the possibility that there had once indeed been a Maya calendar beginning with the month Yaxkin. Yet, there is no year on record for the Mayas, nor for any other Mesoamerican people for that matter, that began and ended with the months Yaxkin and Xul. Can a calendar reform be inferred from this contradiction? In Tozzer's (1941:158 n. 808) own commentary on Landa, he pointed out that the Yucatecs performed rites on the last five days of Xul that "recall the same details in the ritual held on the Uayeb days." Uayeb was the five-day intercalary month that concluded the year in the Maya calendar and in that calendar came between the months Cumku and Pop, the last month of one year and the first month of the following year.

The ancient Maya year typically had 18 months of 20 days each, followed by the five-day month to bring the total to 365, producing a solar year that the Mayas knew as the *haab*. The combination of 360 + 5 days was the case also for all sun-based calendars in ancient Mesoamerica. This was a distinctive year that was not only found throughout Mesoamerica but was also one of the defining characteristics of the Mesoamerican culture area itself, as set forth by Paul Kirchhoff (1943). In a year that, for argument, began with Yaxkin, the second half of the year would have begun with Pax. The Yucatec word *pax* translates as "broken" and its Quiché cognate *paxih* as "split, divide" (Kelley 1976:135); the glyph for Pax incorporates the glyph for *tun*, a Maya unit of 360 days. Pax was a name that would be appropriate for a month that begins on day 180 of a year that starts with the month Yaxkin—it splits the year—but why else? The patron deity of the month Pax was the jaguar god representing the midnight sun. Such a deity would have been appropriate for a year when Yaxkin began with the June solstice, because the December solstice would then have fallen in the month Pax. In a sense the December solstice is to the year as midnight is to the day. Through time a Maya month can coincide with all of the principal markers of the solar year—equinoxes, solstices, and zenith and nadir passages. Because the Maya 365-day year is a quarter of a day shorter than the years in our own calendar, it moves away from the tropical (365.2422-day) year by one day every four years until after 1,507 tropical years or 1,508 Maya years the two calendars once more are in sync. This is called a "solar era" (Edmonson 1988) or "tropical year drift" (Powell 1997) and will be referred to in the present work as "solar drift cycle."

The Yucatec year in Landa's time began with the month Pop, or "mat," as did all Maya years for which there is any kind of written record. A year beginning with Yaxkin would thus have had to belong to a very ancient era indeed. The preparations for a new year amounted to a vigil that lasted through the five-day intercalary month Uayeb. In a year that began and ended with the months Yaxkin and Xul, the five-day intercalary month could be expected to have preceded Yaxkin rather than Pop, under whatever names these months would have had at the time. The names used here are merely the Yucatec names as reported by Landa. There were many languages in the Mayan family, not to mention languages of the Mixe-Zoque family that logically must be considered. Mixe-Zoque is the language family believed to be that of the archaeological Olmecs.

Another contradiction involves the names of days that can be the first day or New Year day of any given year. In the Classic Maya calendar the Yucatec names of these days are Ik, Manik, Eb, and Caban. In other variants of the Maya calendar the possible names are Akbal, Lamat, Ben, and Etznab for a year used late in the Classic Period. During the Postclassic Period Kan, Muluc, Ix, and Cauac were used by the Yucatecs of Landa's day in the so-called Mayapán calendar. Yet, in the Maya book known as *The Book of Chilam Balam of Chumayel* there is a clear reference to a day 1 Chuen as the first day of the first *uinal* or 20-day month (Roys 1967 [1933]:116–117). This implies a year in which the days Chuen, Cib, Imix, and Cimi can be the New Year days. Yet, there is no known Maya calendar with New Year days of this group. Another enigma. Another contradiction.

Some Characteristics of Mesoamerican Calendars

Mesoamerican years were distinguished by the days from which they took their names, the so-called year-bearer days. In both the Classic and Postclassic Maya year this day was the first day, the New Year day. This was the case also for the Zapotec year in Oaxaca, but the succeeding Mixtec year took its name from the 360th day, the one just preceding the five-day intercalary month. In Central Mexico the Aztecs and others were following the latter practice when the Spanish arrived. This poses the question, was the Postclassic Aztec and Mixtec practice of terminal naming an innovation or was it a marginal survival from an earlier calendar?

One essential element of the Mesoamerican calendar is the existence of a 260-day sacred or almanac year, also called the *tzolkin*, that is produced by the permutation of a set of 13 numerals and a set of 20 day names. Any one combination of day name and numeral repeats after 260 days (13 × 20 = 260), generating names that follow the sequence, for instance, of 11 Manik, 12 Lamat, 13 Muluc, 1 Oc, 2 Chuen, and so on.

Given the above details of the Classic Maya year in relation to other Mesoamerican years generally, is there any additional reason for believing that there is an undiscovered past for the Classic Maya calendar? One answer lies in the relation of the Classic Maya year to the tun or 360-day year of the Long Count (LC). One feature that distinguishes the calendars of the Maya Classic period from most other calendars in Mesoamerica is the supplemental use of a measure of elapsed linear time—the LC. Like all calendars that measure elapsed time, the LC had a base date, but unlike most such calendars, the Maya base date lies not in the historical past but in the mythical past. Base dates that lie in the historical past include any that measure time from an actual historical event—the birth of Christ (A.D. or Anno Domini) or the founding of Rome (A.U.C. or Ab urbe condita), and so on. The Maya era base was projected back to a mythical period of Creation in 3114 B.C.E. Because a year zero must be allowed for in astronomical calculations, 3114 B.C.E. equals astronomical -3113. The units of the LC are the *baktun, katun, tun, uinal,* and *kin* with the following relationship:

1 *baktun* = 20 katuns = 144,000 days
1 *katun* = 20 tuns = 7,200 days
1 *tun* = 18 uinals = 360 days
1 *uinal* = 20 kins = 20 days
1 *kin* = 1 day

There is a major contradiction in the relationship of the tun in the LC to the Classic Maya year that can be illustrated as follows: name-day position, three hundred sixtieth day vs. first day; New Year day group, Imix, Cimi, Chuen, Cib vs. Ik, Manik, Eb, Caban; year-bearer day group, Chicchan, Oc, Men, Ahau vs. Ik, Manik, Eb, Caban. In other words, there is no compatibility between the tun of the LC and the Classic Maya year except for the basic idea of eighteen 20-day months. This is a major contradiction. There is no time in Maya history when the 360-day tun of the LC would have coincided exactly with the first 360 days of a Classic Maya year. It is difficult to imagine either year as a prototype of the other. It is unlikely that the authors of the LC were using the Classic Maya year when the LC was invented or instituted. Whoever created the tun of the LC must have had a 365-day year unlike the Classic Maya year in the direction of, well, the year presumed by the Creation story in *The Book of Chilam Balam of Chumayel* (Roys 1967 [1933]:116). In that story the first *uinal* began with a day 1 Chuen. In such a calendar the year-bearer day could be a day Ahau, and each *uinal* could end with a day Ahau, in one year out of four. In the LC each and every *uinal* ends with one of 13 possible days Ahau.

The Classic Maya and Other Maya Creations

The story of the Maya Creation presented by Freidel et al. (1993:65–69) from inscriptions found at Quirigua, Guatemala, and Palenque in Chiapas, Mexico, calls for an initial day of Creation during which the Three Stones of Creation were laid down to define a cosmic hearth. This happened on 4 Ahau 8 Cumku (Classic year), August 11, 3114 B.C.E. Five hundred forty-two days later there was a Sky Event on 13 Ik 20 Mol (= 13 Ik 0 Chen), February 3, 3112 B.C.E.[2]

According to *Chumayel* the Maya Creation occurred during a *katun* whose terminal or name day was 11 Ahau, which has consequently come to be referred to as the Katun of Creation (Roys 1967 [1933]:65 n. 1, 99). This itself is a contradiction because the Maya Creation story read from the inscriptions indicates that the first day of Creation was a day 4 Ahau 8 Cumku, which was the terminal or name day of a Katun 4 Ahau, and the second day of Creation was 452 days later during the subsequent Katun 2 Ahau (Freidel et al. 1993). Because the latter Creation story is chiseled in stone and is older, it has carried more weight than that in *Chumayel*, which was written in manuscript form during the postconquest period. The association of the Katun of Creation with a Katun 11 Ahau is typically written off as a reference merely to the fact that all katuns 11 Ahau begin with a day 1 Imix, which is the first day of the 260-day sacred year (e.g., Roys 1967 [1933]:185). But, does the day 1 Imix have no firmer association with the Creation?

The Chortí of Guatemala perform an annual ritual that corresponds closely in many respects to that read from the inscriptions. It is a world renewal rite and reenactment of the Creation, and it begins each year on a day 1 Imix in the sacred 260-day year and on February 8 in the solar year (Freidel et al. 1993; Girard 1948, 1949, 1966; Mathews and Garber 2004). The Chortí sacred year is unusual in that it does not repeat in the usual way. Typically the Maya sacred year runs from 1 Imix to the two hundred sixtieth day, 13 Ahau, and then resumes immediately with 1 Imix as the first day of the next sacred year. The Chortí sacred year always begins on February 8, runs its 260 days, ending on October 25 with a day 13 Ahau, and then has a 105-day time-out until the next February 8. The days February 8 to October 25 (October 24 in leap years) encompass the Chortí agricultural year from the cutting and burning of the *monte* before planting to the final harvest.

Like the Maya Creation of the inscriptions, the Chortí have a first day of Creation during which certain Stones of Creation are laid, followed later by a day during which there is a Raising of the Sky. The Stones of Creation in the Classic Maya story are three in number and define a hearth. The stones are five in number in the Chortí story and have no explicit connection with a hearth. The Chortí Creation is obviously a mixture of two Creation stories, one following the Classic Maya story in the acts performed and another reflecting a calendar that is implied in *Chumayel* with Creation events that can coincide with a day 1 Imix.

The choice of February 8 is less clear but arguably relates to the fact that at the latitude of the Chortí February 8 was an antizenith day, a day of nadir passage of the sun. On that day the sun was directly underfoot at midnight much as on days of zenith passage the sun is directly overhead at noon. February 8 is also the occasion for all-night vigils among the Mayas of San

Antonio in the Maya Mountains of Belize. This observance marks the start of the local agricultural year (Thompson 1930:41–42). Days of nadir passage of the sun may have had more significance for the Mayas than is generally believed, especially if associated with the Creation itself.

Munro Edmonson's "Olmec Year"

There is only one year in the Mesoamerican literature that meets the conditions for a year that could have been in use at the time of the innovation of the LC. That is a hypothetical year proposed by Edmonson (1988) to which he has given the name "Olmec year." No stela or monument recognizably bearing a date in such a system has ever been found. The Olmec year has been a victim, one might say, of the "tyranny of the epigraphic record." It should be noted, however, that Edmonson only named the year with its implication of an Olmec origin. The idea of a year beginning with the *uinal* Yaxkin had already been in the literature since Gates wrote of it in 1937. Edmonson defined his Olmec year to be terminal naming with days of the series Chicchan, Oc, Men, and Ahau; to begin with the month Yaxkin; to end with the month Xul; and to have the five-day month Uayeb following Xul rather than Cumku. Unlike the Classic Maya year, the 360-body of Edmonson's Olmec year was quite compatible with the 360-day tun of the LC. On April 12, 550 B.C.E., for example, the name day of Olmec year 13 Ahau coincided with the name day of tun 13 Ahau of the LC (Hall 1994).

Bricker and Spinden on the Invention of the *Uinal*

Victoria Bricker (1982) has suggested that the Yucatec names applied to certain months of the Maya year contain clues to the season of the year when they were first used and that this naming presumably occurred at a time when o Pop, the first day of the Classic Maya year, coincided with a winter solstice. She has suggested that this event took place around 550 B.C.E. She began by relating the first day of Pop to the winter solstice in the year 956 C.E., making this connection on the day December 16 in the Julian calendar, which is December 21 (winter solstice) in the Gregorian calendar of that year. By moving back one solar drift cycle of 1,507 years she arrived at the year 552 B.C.E., which was a year that she said had the same correspondence of days in our solar year and the Maya 365-day *haab*. It turns out, however, that Bricker (personal communication 1992) had made an error of calculation. December 21, 956, was actually a day 7 Pop and not o Pop. Zero Pop fell on December 21, 930, a half Calendar Round (26 years) earlier than 956. The date one solar drift cycle earlier consequently was 11 Manik o Pop, December 21, 578 B.C.E.

The Calendar Round (CR) day 11 Manik o Pop is just one day earlier than a CR day 12 Lamat 1 Pop that Kelley (1980) has inferred from an almanac of the Madrid Codex to be something like a day of conception of the astronomical gods with their births following in intervals appropriate to the synodical periods of the heavenly bodies involved. The birth of the sun on 13 Ben falls 365 days after 12 Lamat, for example. In fact, 12 Tochtli, the Aztec equivalent of 12 Lamat, was the day on which divine offspring were born to the Divine Pair in Aztec cosmology (Caso 1967:194). Kelley believed that the base New Year date 12 Lamat 1 Pop could be expected to fall on a winter solstice, which it does in fact in 578 B.C.E. This means that the CR day of the Creation inferred from the Madrid Codex by Kelley (1980) corresponds almost to the day to the time Bricker calculated for the origin of the *uinal*, as corrected. Bricker noted that the names of the uinals would also correlate with the wet and dry seasons and planting cycle still another solar drift cycle earlier, which would be 2085 B.C.E., but rejected this as too early. This rejection was based on her assumption that the seasonal associations of the *uinal* names were meant to be those current at the time the *haab* was created and that there could have been no Mesoamerican high culture capable of formulating a complex calendar in the year 2085 B.C.E. Such a date—2085 B.C.E.—would be a more logical year for the installation of the astronomical gods than 578 B.C.E. By then Olmec culture would have been rolling along very nicely without these gods for almost a thousand years, so why would 2085 B.C.E. not be a date more logical for the *mythical* installation of the uinals, as it was for the gods?

Using much the same logic as Bricker, Herbert Spinden concluded that the Mayas must have originally had two calendars, one an "agricultural year" beginning with the month Yaxkin and the other an "astronomical year" that began with the month Pop: "Carrying back o Pop from a position in Landa's era to a Preclassic time when it coincided with the winter solstice before the inscriptions gave 580 B.C.E. as a tentative beginning for the Mayan calendar" (Spinden 1924:129–130). This winter solstice was only two years earlier than that which figures in Kelley's inferences for the CR position of a day of Creation and in Bricker's estimated date for the origin of the *uinal*. Spinden's work with the months did not require the correlation of the Christian and Maya calendars. He came to his conclusions without the benefit of—actually despite—his now rejected thinking on the base date of the LC and the date of its invention. Spinden was working with CR days and the manner in which they intermeshed with days of the tropical year through time. The CR was a period of 18,980 days during which each day of the *haab* had the chance to be paired once with each day of the *tzolkin* (52 × 365 = 73 × 260 = 18,980). He was aware of the drift of the Mayan *haab* away from the tropical year and that completion of this solar drift cycle took 1,508 *haab*. Spinden (1924:174) expresses it as "the concordance between 29 calendar rounds and the complete lap gained by a 365-day year over one of 365.2421996 days," in other words, 29 × 52 × 365 = 1,508 × 365 = 1,507 × 365.2421996 days.

Spinden (1924:129) saw the agricultural year as originally beginning with the month of Yaxkin that extended through the 20 days of April 21 to May 10. During this time the rains could be expected to begin. Spinden's astronomical year began with the 20 days of Pop running from December 22 to January 10. The December solstice fell on the twenty-first in 580 B.C.E.

The meanings of the names of the months may have correlated with seasonal rainfall and dryness and with the several routines of maize agriculture in the second quarter of the sixth century B.C.E. as they occur in the Classic year. This did not mean that the Classic year was in use in the sixth century B.C.E. It means only that when the Classic year was eventually created it merely continued, by translating, earlier, presumably Olmec, names that were in use during the sixth century B.C.E. or earlier. When Classic years are discussed for this period it should be understood that these are years presumptively in the proleptic Classic calendar. A proleptic calendar is one that is extended back from a period when it was first adopted. All solar dates in this report, for instance, are given in the proleptic Gregorian calendar, because the Gregorian calendar was not created until 1582.

Spinden's agricultural calendar began April 21, 579 B.C.E., a day 12 Caban o Yaxkin (Classic Maya year). We know, although Spinden could not have known, that this day was followed after four days by the New Year day of Edmonson's Olmec year that began 3 Imix 4 Yaxkin, April 25; 4 Yaxkin (Classic year) is the same as o Yaxkin (Olmec year).[3] April 25 happens also to be the second of the two days each year that the Guatemalan Chortís celebrate as the anniversaries of the Creation and as the beginning of their agricultural year. The observance continued from April 25 until the rains came. At this latitude the first zenith passage of the sun is on May 1. This means that the tropical year date of one event in the Chortí Creation drama (a) coincided in 579 B.C.E. with the New Year day of Edmonson's Olmec year, (b) was within four days of Spinden's year and day of origin of a "Maya" agricultural year, (c) was within a year of the year of initiation of the *uinal* according to Bricker (as corrected), and (d) conforms closely as well with some of Kelley's expectations for the CR position of the day of the Creation as he interprets it from the Madrid Codex. Almost as a bonus, April 25, 581 B.C.E., was a day 1 Chuen o Yaxkin in the "Olmec" calendar (4 Yaxkin in the Classic calendar). This means that the particular day in the 260-day sacred year that was called the first day of the first *uinal* ever in Maya time reckoning, according to the *Chilam Balam of Chumayel,* coincided in 581 B.C.E. also with the New Year day of Edmonson's "Olmec" year and with the Gregorian year day of one of the two days of the Creation as years later it was celebrated by the Chortís of Guatemala. More importantly, all of the Creation associations discussed above for the Chortís and Yucatecs, all those from the writings of Bricker, Spinden, and Kelley for the early sixth century B.C.E., hold for the early twenty-first century B.C.E., as well. All of the seasonal associations of the uinals that held for the early sixth century B.C.E. hold also for the early twenty-first century B.C.E.

Rice (2007:57) indicates her belief that Bricker's (1982) assignment of the origin of the *uinal* and Maya 365-day calendar to the era of 550 B.C.E. may be too late and that a year 1,507 years earlier "is not an entirely unreasonable estimate." She suggests 2060 B.C.E., but 1,507 years before the corrected date of 578 B.C.E. for Bricker's suggested date of invention of the *uinal* would bring that earlier date to 2085 B.C.E. I myself believe that this is too early for the date of invention of the calendar, even by the Olmecs, but it is not too early for a mythical day of inauguration of the calendar projected backward from the actual day of invention. The year 2085 B.C.E. is teasingly close to a year 2091 B.C.E. for a mythical first year of the Olmec Creation proposed a decade ago (Hall 1998). The zero day for the calendar based on that year was 13 Ahau 8 Zip, February 10, 2091 B.C.E., with the first day of the Olmec era following a day later on 1 Imix 9 Zip. This date was calculated quite independently of my later discovery that two almanacs in the Madrid Codex do, in fact, suggest pre-Columbian knowledge of a sacred year beginning 1 Imix 9 Zip, February 11, 2091 B.C.E.

Two Madrid Codex Almanacs

The Madrid Codex contains an almanac beginning on August 9, 924 C.E., which is 13 Ik 10 Ceh in the Classic calendar, and a second beginning October 26, 924 C.E., which is 13 Ahau 8 Pax in the Classic calendar (Bricker and Bricker 1988; Vail and Bricker 2004:206–207). Each of these dates falls in a year in which February 10 coincides with the Classic Maya CR day of 1 Imix 9 Zip. This date follows 1 Imix 9 Zip, February 11, 2091 B.C.E. (above) by precisely two 1,507-year solar drift cycles. One can easily argue that these two Madrid Codex almanacs were perceived as falling within the two-solar-drift-cycle anniversary year of the Olmec Creation.

The Madrid day 13 Ahau 8 Pax, October 26, 924 C.E., calls to mind the days 13 Ahau, October 25, that are each year the final day of the Chortí agricultural year but also the last day of a sacred 260-day year that begins with an anniversary celebration of the Chortí Creation on 1 Imix, February 8. This should be a clue that the Chortí Creation story could owe less to the Creation story of the Classic Maya inscriptions than to a Creation story linked to the first year of an earlier Olmec era.

The *haab* day 9 Zip turns out to have an important ritual association of its own. On another such day 9 Zip in the sixteenth century Fray Diego Landa reported that the Yucatec fishermen "blessed a tall and thick pole, and set it upright" (Tozzer 1941:155–156). The hunters began with a dance on 7 Zip (Mayapán calendar), which was 8 Zip (Classic), that was followed on the next day by the raising of the pole on 9 Zip (Classic). Raising this pole suggests the Raising of the Sky in the Chortí ritual year and reminds us of 9 Zip as the first day of the discussed Olmec era (Hall 1998).

Discussion and Conclusion

Anthony Aveni (2009:67) has written that "the idea of encapsulating historical events in a closed chronological network of time loops likely came from the Olmec culture." This would be the use of natural (astronomical) and/or devised (*tzolkin?*) cycles of time within a formal calendar system. The Mayas were likely inheritors of this groundwork with its implications of a cyclicity of time and history. One well-known example is the belief of Postclassic Itza Mayas that knowledge of events associated with past katuns can be a guide to anticipating future events of the same nature (Edmonson 1982:xii). Katuns of the same name recurred through a cycle of 256 years.

Another Maya use of cycles was to give desired meanings to events of the present by relating them to events of the past. This was accomplished by bridging the dates with manipulations of time known as a "contrived numbers." "By showing that . . . two dates had the same shape in time, the Maya declared that the actions and the actors associated with those dates—gods for the mythical dates, kings for the historical ones—were also the same" (Schele and Miller 1986:321).

In the present essay the solar drift cycle was observed to relate two almanacs of the Madrid Codex to the initial year two solar drift cycles earlier of an Olmec era whose existence was reasoned in a previous publication (Hall 1998). The element of ancient intentionality here would have been to draw toward the present of 924 C.E. some of the creative energy of an Olmec year of Creation by shrinking time—2091 B.C.E. and 924 C.E. became as one because the Calendar Round days of each fell within the same positions in the tropical year. The Chortí Mayas reenact the Creation annually through ritual drama whose timing makes use of *tzolkin* and tropical year associations seemingly frozen to the year 924 C.E. and hence also to 2091 B.C.E. In effect this is a rite of world renewal that reconnects the agricultural year of the present with the first year of Creation.

It is the intended function of the present essay to provide reasons for more seriously considering clues to calendar history long existing in preserved manuscript records of the Postclassic period such as the Madrid Codex and

The Book of Chilam Balam of Chumayel. These clues exist as references that appear contradictory to received wisdom in calendar matters.

Notes

1. For the purpose of this chapter special terms in Mayan are italicized except when used in the plural, as with "katuns," to avoid mixing italic and Roman characters in the same word, since Mayan does not produce plurals by adding an *s.* Similarly, Mayan words are printed in Roman characters when there is a need for capitalization, as in the case of a proper noun.

2. These days August 11 and February 3 are reported as August 13 and February 5 in the original because of the use by Freidel and colleagues of the 584285 variant of the Goodman-Martínez-Thompson (GMT) family of correlation constants. The "correlation constant" is the Julian day number of the base date of the Long Count. In this case, August 11, 3114 B.C.E. (Gregorian) is Julian day 584283. Julian day numbers are not to be confused with days in the Julian or pre-Gregorian Christian calendar.

3. The New Year days of years in the Maya Classic Period do not coincide with those in the "Olmec" year because of the moving of the five-day Uayeb month from before Yaxkin to before Pop and because of the shift of the accompanying *tzolkin* day one day from, for example, Chuen to Eb or Imix to Ik.

References Cited

Aveni, Anthony F.

1989   *Empires of Time: Calendars, Clocks, and Cultures.* Basic Books, New York.

2009   *The End of Time: The Maya Mystery of 2012.* University Press of Colorado, Boulder.

Bricker, Victoria R.

1982   The Origin of the Maya Solar Calendar. *Current Anthropology* 23:101–103.

Bricker, Victoria R., and Harvey M. Bricker

1988   The Seasonal Table in the Dresden Codex and Related Almanacs. *Archaeoastronomy* (Supplement to the *Journal for the History of Astronomy*) 12(JHS19): S1–S62.

Caso, Alfonso

1967   *Los calendarios prehispánicos.* Universidad Nacional Autónoma de México, Instituto de Investigaciones Históricas, Mexico City.

Edmonson, Munro S.

1982   *The Ancient Future of the Itza: The Book of Chilam Balam of Tizimin.* University of Texas Press, Austin.

1988   *The Book of the Year: Middle American Calendrical Systems.* University of Utah Press, Salt Lake City.

Freidel, David, Linda Schele, and Joy Parker

1993   *Maya Cosmos: Three Thousand Years on the Shaman's Path.* William Morrow, New York.

Gates, William (translator and editor)

1937   *Yucatan before and after the Conquest by Friar Diego de Landa with Other Related Documents, Maps and Illustrations.* 2nd ed. Publication 20. Maya Society, Baltimore.

Girard, Rafael

1948   *El calendario maya-mexica: orígen, función, desarrollo y lugar de precedencia.* Editorial Stylo, Mexico City.

1949   *Los chortís ante el problema maya: historia de las culturas indígenas de America, desde su orígen hasta hoy.* Antigua Librería Robredo, Mexico City.

1966   *Los mayas: su civilización, sus vinculaciones continentales.* Libro Mex, Mexico City.

Hall, Robert L.

1994   Review of *The Book of the Year: Middle American Calendrical Systems* by Munro S. Edmonson (University of Utah Press, Salt Lake City, 1988). *Archaeoastronomy* 11:118–121.

1998   A Comparison of Some North American and Mesoamerican Cosmologies and Their Ritual Expressions. In *Explorations in American Archaeology: Essays in Honor of Wesley R. Hurt,* edited by Mark G. Plew, pp. 55–88. University Press of America, Lanham, Maryland.

Kelley, David H.

1976   *Deciphering the Maya Script.* University of Texas Press, Austin.

1980   Astronomical Identities of Mesoamerican Gods. *Archaeoastronomy* (Supplement to the *Journal for the History of Astronomy*) 2(JHS11):S1–S54.

Kirchhoff, Paul

1943   Mesoamérica: sus límites geográficos, composición étnica y caracteres culturales. *Acta Americana* 1:92–107.

Mathews, Jennifer, and James F. Garber

2004   Models of Cosmic Order: Physical Expression of Sacred Space among the Ancient Maya. *Ancient Mesoamerica* 15:49–59.

Powell, Christopher

1997   A New View on Maya Astronomy. Unpublished M.A. thesis, University of Texas at Austin.

Rice, Prudence M.

2004   *Maya Political Science: Time, Astronomy, and the Cosmos.* University of Texas Press, Austin.

2007   *Maya Calendar Origins: Monuments, Mythistory, and the Materialization of Time.* University of Texas Press, Austin.

Roys, Ralph L.

1967   *The Book of Chilam Balam of Chumayel.* University of Oklahoma Press, Nor-
[1933]   man. Originally published 1933, Carnegie Institution of Washington, D.C.

Schele, Linda, and Mary Ellen Miller

1986   *The Blood of Kings: Dynasty and Ritual in Maya Art.* George Braziller, New
         York.

Spinden, Herbert J.

1924   *The Reduction of Mayan Dates.* Papers of the Peabody Museum of Ameri-
         can Archaeology and Ethnology, Vol. 4, No. 4. Harvard University, Cam-
         bridge, Massachusetts.

Thompson, J. Eric S.

1930   *Ethnology of the Mayas of Southern and Central British Honduras.* Anthro-
         pology Series 17(2). Field Museum of Natural History, Chicago.

Tozzer, Alfred M. (translator and editor)

1941   *Landa's Relación de las Cosas de Yucatan.* Papers of the Peabody Museum of
         American Archaeology and Ethnology, Vol. 18. Peabody Museum, Harvard
         University, Cambridge, Massachusetts.

Vail, Gabrielle, and Victoria R. Bricker

2004   Haab Dates in the Madrid Codex. In *The Madrid Codex: New Approaches
         to Understanding an Ancient Maya Manuscript,* edited by Gabrielle Vail and
         Anthony Aveni, pp. 171–214. University Press of Colorado, Boulder.

Conclusion

Alice Beck Kehoe

Religion—in the sense of belief, and in the sense of rituals—has been claimed to be the means of maintaining community and permitting individuals to carry on lives that seem coherent. Both Durkheim (1947 [1912]), founding the French tradition of cultural analyses, and Malinowski (1954), teaching the British tradition, focused thus on religion, or shall I better say "religion": a Western cultural category. Thus it behooves archaeologists socialized in the Western cultural tradition to search for evidence of religion in the archaeological record. Thus this book.

An underlying theme in the book, set forth by editors Sundstrom and De-Boer, is the likelihood that religious concepts and symbols persist through many human generations, paralleling (but not in step with) ceramic and lithic technology and style traditions. To put it bluntly, because archaeologists recognize transmission over generations of ceramic and lithic artifact types and of house forms, an archaeologist may premise similar transmission of religious beliefs and seek evidence for such tradition. The essays in this volume illustrate how inchoate are such efforts. Data sets that seem not to serve biological necessities such as subsistence or shelter are postulated to have been created for inhabitants' "religion"—it used to be a joke that if one couldn't figure out a practical purpose for an artifact or feature, one should label it "ceremonial." Not many American archaeologists would say they are Marxists, yet most focus on material evidence of economics and seem to assume a superstructure of religion and ideology secondary to the pragmatics of everyday living. Methodologies to recognize, retrieve, and interpret economic data are well developed (technologies of subsistence practices, occupation features, zooarchaeology and paleobotany, demography, trade), in contrast to the varied avenues explored by the contributors to this book on religious traditions.

The chapters here could be clustered as follows, to explore the varied approaches taken by participants in the project.

Asserting the validity of oral histories of group movements and settlements
    (Bernardini, Hays-Gilpin, Lekson)
Premising millennia depth for concepts known ethnographically (Claassen,
    DeBoer, Clark and Colman, McEwan, Roe and Roe, Sundstrom)
Seeking principles and patterns in the data, to infer continuity with variation
    (Quilter) or significance of place (Norder)
Using textual and ethnographic data to infer history (Hall)
Arguing for independent-invention gradualism—a nineteenth-century axiom
    (Lyell 1830; Trigger 2006:564) (Brown and Kelly)

Oral history as "tradition" has been a staple of anthropology from its nineteenth-century beginnings and indeed from the late eighteenth-century early Romanticism efforts to preserve folk cultures, for example, by Walter Scott and his friends in Scotland. Scots had been literate for several generations by then, thanks to the Scottish Kirk's requiring primary schools in each parish, but so long as aged women and men in their humble thatched dark houses spoke in dialect, their ballads and tales were taken to be age-old tradition. By the late nineteenth century, professional anthropologists were taking down national ("tribal") histories from elder men. Whatever seemed unlikely could be labeled "myth." Among the Pueblos, the detailed histories of migrations by residence groups labeled "clans" by anthropologists were often dismissed as myth, because the Pueblos were stereotyped to be small communal egalitarian primitive societies, rooted in their soil as if wildflowers. Textbooks well into the mid-twentieth century contrasted such "primitive" societies with "dynamic" Western civilizations, the primitives' myths contrasted with Western "true histories." Come the Roosevelt New Deal's Indian Claims Commission, beginning in 1946, U.S. tribes struggled to document their claims to treaty-recognized territories. Florence Hawley Ellis was one of the archaeologists working with Pueblos to prove claims by excavation of occupation traces: she married oral traditions to archaeologists' ceramic style traditions, as well as excavating structure features in the places described in the oral histories. Both Bernardini and Hays-Gilpin carry on this project of reconciling Hopi "traditional" histories with archaeological data, seen also in the book by T. J. Ferguson and Chip Colwell-Chanthaphonh (2006) that ranges farther afield to document Pueblo occupations in southern Arizona.

Bernardini and Hays-Gilpin advance the study to a higher level by revealing that there is not one Hopi traditional history, but many, clan by clan, and Bernardini links oral-historical events to exercise of power in Hopi towns. We might call these studies historical thick description.

Stephen H. Lekson stands back from the particulars of Hopi histories to describe dramatic discontinuities in all three of the major regions recognized by archaeologists in the Southwest. These real human histories were at odds with the colonialist dogma of unchanging stable small villages. What makes Lekson's chapter interesting is his conclusion, asserting that *after the 1680 Pueblo Revolt,* the Pueblos were indeed unchanging: in the face of severe oppression by Spanish and then American invaders, they doggedly hung on to their religious beliefs and rituals. From Lekson's perspective, "traditional" Pueblo religions are those frozen by the social cataclysm of ruthless conquests. Unexamined in this essay are the changes and innovations that did occur through the generations after 1680, some because, for example, pilgrimages were curtailed by white settlement and some because demographic or resource changes forced abandoning, merging, or altering rituals, and overall, the intrusion of Christianities that did gain footholds. The Southwest's archaeological record does exhibit architecture and artifacts attesting to five centuries of Christian traditions superimposed on Pueblos and to differing degrees, integrated as had been the katsinas (Wilcox 2009).

Half the chapters in this volume deal with archaeological data that seem to reflect ethnographically known beliefs. It is standard procedure to consider whether post-European ethnographic descriptions fit earlier archaeological material. If the shoe fits, wear it. But might the shoe fit because it was rebuilt? Altered? We know that sixteenth-century Franciscan and Augustinian missionaries reinterpreted the Aztec sacrificed heart to be Christ's heart, whence François de Sales created the device of the sacred heart of Jesus to be the emblem of his Catholic Reformation Order of the Visitation (Kehoe 1979). We could separate the chapters in this group into those proposing that continuity is tied to critically important ecological factors—McEwan, Roe and Roe—and those citing sets of data that may reflect "metaphors we live by" (Lakoff and Johnson 1980), almost universal in human experience: trees as axes mundi, crosses representing the four directions, caves as earth wombs, mountains as power, relatively rare shiny minerals as power-invoking objects, large fierce birds symbolizing leadership and military might (Claassen cites finding remains of a trumpeter swan, which in the Northern Plains and Plateau is the greatest creature, flying higher, seeing and calling farther than any other being). That art depicting such widespread emotive habitus experiences continued to be used for millennia, and continues to be, does not seem an exorbitant claim. Clark and Colman ambitiously project Mesoamerican tradition onto the oldest kingdoms, the Olmec, as Miguel Covarrubias did decades ago (Covarrubias 1954, 1957). Crocodiles, rattlesnakes, caves from which emerge powerful figures, and mountains (in a land of volcanoes) are experienced today in Mesoamerica as they must have been three millennia ago. Similarly, the South American art in locations linkable to vital environmental phenomena, described by McEwan and Roe and Roe, is not unreasonably interpreted as evidence of longstanding symbolism. DeBoer's parallels between historic Midé and precontact northeastern Midwest sites are not as dramatic, but reasonable, given the caveat that Midé may have recast some older elements, as Christian sects recast theologies and rituals over two millennia. Sundstrom's projection of cosmograms on a broad landscape seems to me the boldest of these essays, not unjustified, but to be more persuasive, requiring a greater number of sites manifesting the characteristics she looks for. Increasingly digitalized archaeological data may very well permit rank-ordering large numbers of sites according to apparently more ritual or more domestic artifacts, and then Sundstrom's cosmograms may appear.

Quilter and Norder seek to sort out details to distinguish clusters and contrasts. Jeff Quilter challenges the easy interpretation that South Americans had for millennia worshipped a male deity bearing a staff of office; instead, he postulates the figures' stance communicates a fighter's power, a "dare" to confront him. Such an iconic stance, one might say a martial arts posture,[1] fits under the "metaphors we live by" heading, generalizing experiences of threatening animals as well as humans to communicate threatening power. Geographically and temporally spread societies laid upon this experienced stance a variety of particular referents. John Norder similarly analyzes Canadian Shield rock art by comparing and sorting, in this case drawing not upon primal postures but upon ethnography and sorting by location in the landscape. His interpretation that rock art sites signal presence of (native) people, rendezvous, or spirit being haunts is supported by his interviews with contemporary Ojibwa residents in the Lake of the Woods region. Both Quilter and Norder may be said to focus on "traditional" art as language, forcefully communicating information.

Maya are famous for the strength of their traditions, surviving like the Pueblos the five centuries of Spanish domination plus—unlike Pueblos in Lekson's estimation—two millennia before those invasions. Robert Hall's characteristically dense amassing of data—ethnohistorical, ethnographic, astronomical—leads him to first distinguish two Mayan creation accounts, somewhat uncomfortably merged in Chortí tradition, and then to link calendric rituals with seasons (like McEwan and Roe and Roe) to deduce that the Classic Maya basic calendar was constructed probably in the sixth century B.C.E. Typical of Maya, their calendar was projected backward a full 1,508-year solar cycle to claim a much earlier origin. Thus Hall recognizes not only a calendric tradition operating over more than two millennia but also a Maya *sense* of tradition inducing them to extend that tradition back, far earlier than (in Hall's opinion) its actual construction. We should note that Maya studies enjoy an extraordinary richness of data, from written texts and a wealth of representational art to half a millennium of European observation documents and numerous ethnographies of still-vital Maya communities.

Lastly, I will discuss the chapter by James Brown and John Kelly. Their perspective is on in situ development from eleventh-century "emergent" American Bottom settlement to what Brown termed the Classic Braden style, attributed to Cahokia a century and a half later. No one would expect that Cahokians at the hub of the Midwest would practice a Mesoamerican art style, yet, as a visit to any art museum will demonstrate, different strokes do not preclude common ideas. Brown and Kelly acknowledge this in their discussion of Morning Star (they state, "we are dealing with what has been identified independently as the Morning Star hero"). Morning Star as warrior captain has been widely recognized by Mesoamericanists (Carlson 1991). Schaafsma accepted Mexican sources for Morning Star and katsina ritual in 1994, as well as in the work cited by Brown and Kelly. Morning Star is one manifestation of Quetzalcoatl, who is frequently shown in Mississippian art wearing his iconic *ehécatlcoxcatl,* "wind jewel" pendant, a cut conch cross section or columella (Kehoe 2005:272). Conch columellae were found in Cahokia's Ramey Mound, along with Ramey knives that look like Quetzalcoatl's mother Flint Knife (Kehoe 2005:273). Southwestern archaeologists for many years dogmatically rejected Mesoamerican connections with their area (Lekson 2009:31). Although Brown and Kelly were familiar with the 2005 volume *Gulf Coast Archaeology,* they do not refer to the strong cases for Mississippian–Mesoamerican connections in the chapters by Wilkerson, Dávila Cabrera, Zaragoza Ocaña, and myself. Brown and Kelly state, "We think that a distance of over 1,000 km would constitute a barrier to the impact of domination or even reciprocal trade between the various Mesoamerican centers and the Southeastern chiefdoms," yet Chaco in northern New Mexico, exactly coeval with Cahokia, imported scarlet macaw feathers, and Paquimé (Casas Grandes), due south in northwestern Mexico, imported breeding pairs of live macaws thousands of kilometers from southeast Mexico. Compared with that overland portering, the big trading canoes seen by Columbus in the Gulf of Mexico made trans-Gulf trading easy (as argued by Wilkerson, Dávila Cabrera, and Zaragoza Ocaña in their 2005 papers). I can only say that I am disappointed that Brown and Kelly have not seriously weighed these data.[2]

It is a bit curious that no one raised the question whether to speak of "religion" in "Native America" is to impose a Western category liable to distort non-Western societal configurations (Edwards 2005). In the same vein, we might question whether "Native America" can be a reasonable category to encompass the thousands of indigenous societies in the two continents. Only a post-Columbian colonial perspective would lump all into "Native America," a perspective generally decried in the twenty-first century. On the other hand, the concept of Nuclear America has a solid foundation, maize. The vast area from the St. Lawrence Valley to Chile did share in a vital cultural tradition, growing a plant that cannot propagate itself. Knowledge and seed corn had to pass from person to person; it is not unreasonable to postulate transmission of beliefs and symbols—metaphors we live by—along with corn. We have abundant evidence of long-distance procurement of nonperishables such as chert as early as Paleoindian times and historical observations of First Nations people traveling half across the continent and back with new rituals and paraphernalia. Whether "religion" is the proper term for what sometimes may have been supposedly efficacious magic (another Western category) can be debated. Let us simply say that the contributors to this volume have sought evidence in the archaeological record for beliefs and symbols persisting through time and in some cases extending geographically. These would be cultural traditions. Our authors here present rich data evidencing enduring traditions in the Americas.

Notes

1. Wayne Van Horne and some other anthropologists familiar with martial arts traditions suggest that formal martial arts postures may be depicted in Mississippian, Olmec, and other First Nations art (Van Horne 2002).

2. Brown and Kelly imply the popular model of gradual cultural evolution. Of the principle of gradualism no longer premised by evolutionary biologists, Stephen Jay Gould said, "Lyell managed to elevate a testable claim about gradualism to . . . a received a priori doctrine . . . [that has] exerted a profound, and largely negative, influence" (Gould 2002:482).

References Cited

Carlson, John B.

1991   *Venus-Regulated Warfare and Ritual Sacrifice in Mesoamerica: Teotihuacan and the Cacaxtla "Star Wars" Connection.* Technical Publication 7. Center for Archaeoastronomy, College Park, Maryland.

Covarrubias, Miguel

1954   *The Eagle, the Jaguar, and the Serpent: Indian Art of the Americas.* Alfred A. Knopf, New York.

1957   *Indian Art of Mexico and Central America.* Alfred A. Knopf, New York.

Dávila Cabrera, Patricio

2005   Mound Builders along the Coast of the Gulf of Mexico and the Eastern United States. In *Gulf Coast Archaeology: The Southeastern United States and Mexico,* edited by Nancy Marie White, pp. 87–107. University Press of Florida, Gainesville.

Durkheim, Emile

1947   *The Elementary Forms of the Religious Life: A Study in Religious Sociology.*
[1912] Translated by J. W. Swain. Free Press, New York.

Edwards, David N.

2005   The Archaeology of Religion. In *The Archaeology of Identity: Approaches to Gender, Age, Ethnicity and Religion,* edited by Margarita Díaz-Andreu, Sam Lucy, Stasa Babíc, and David N. Edwards, pp. 110–128. Routledge, Abingdon, U.K.

Ferguson, T. J., and Chip Colwell-Chanthaphonh

2006   *History Is in the Land: Multivocal Tribal Traditions in Arizona's San Pedro Valley.* University of Arizona Press, Tucson.

Gould, Stephen Jay

2002   *The Structure of Evolutionary Thought.* Belknap, Cambridge, Massachusetts.

Kehoe, Alice B.

1979   The Sacred Heart: A Case for Stimulus Diffusion. *American Ethnologist* 6(4):763–771.

2005   Wind Jewels and Paddling Gods: The Mississippian Southeast in the Postclassic Mesoamerican World. In *Gulf Coast Archaeology: The Southeastern United States and Mexico,* edited by Nancy Marie White, pp. 260–280. University Press of Florida, Gainesville.

Lakoff, George, and Mark Johnson

1980   *Metaphors We Live By.* University of Chicago Press, Chicago.

Lekson, Stephen H.

2009   *A History of the Ancient Southwest.* School for Advanced Research Press, Santa Fe, New Mexico.

Lyell, Charles

1830   *Principles of Geology.* John Murray, London.

Malinowski, Bronislaw

1954   *Magic, Science and Religion.* Doubleday, Garden City, New York.

Schaafsma, Polly

1994   The Prehistoric Kachina Cult and Its Origins as Suggested by Southwestern Rock Art. In *Kachinas in the Pueblo World,* edited by Polly Schaafsma, pp. 63–79. University of New Mexico Press, Albuquerque.

Trigger, Bruce G.

2006   *A History of Archaeological Thought.* 2nd ed. Cambridge University Press, Cambridge.

Van Horne, Wayne

2002   War Clubs and Falcon Warriors: War Club Use in Southeastern Native American Chiefdoms. In *Combat, Ritual, and Performance: Anthropology of the Martial Arts,* edited by David E. Jones, pp. 209–222. Praeger, Westport, Connecticut.

Wilcox, Michael V.

2009   *The Pueblo Revolt and the Mythology of Conquest: An Indigenous Archaeology of Contact.* University of California Press, Berkeley.

Wilkerson, S. Jeffrey K.

2005   Rivers in the Sea: The Gulf of Mexico as a Cultural Corridor. In *Gulf Coast Archaeology: The Southeastern United States and Mexico,* edited by Nancy Marie White, pp. 56–67. University Press of Florida, Gainesville.

Zaragoza Ocaña, Diana

2005   Characteristic Elements Shared by Northeastern Mexico and the Southeastern United States. In *Gulf Coast Archaeology: The Southeastern United States and Mexico,* edited by Nancy Marie White, pp. 245–259. University Press of Florida, Gainesville.

Contributors

Wesley Bernardini is associate professor of sociology and anthropology at the University of Redlands, California. His work on migration and identity in the American Southwest has been published in two books as well as in articles in *American Antiquity, Journal of Anthropological Archaeology, Journal of Anthropological Research*, and *Kiva*.

James Brown is professor emeritus of anthropology at Northwestern University. He has published widely on topics of iconography of the Mississippian period (1000–1550 C.E.) in the eastern United States, as well as on the archaeology of burials.

Cheryl Claassen is professor of anthropology at Appalachian State University. Her research interests are sacred landscape, rituals, pilgrimage, caves, and gender in the pre-Columbian eastern United States and central Mexico.

John E. Clark has been doing research in southern Mexico for 32 years, with an emphasis on the Formative Period. His particular interest is the transition from hunting and gathering societies to the first villages, towns, and cities. He is a professor at Brigham Young University.

Arlene Colman works as an editor, researcher, and artist for the New World Archaeology Foundation.

Warren DeBoer is professor of anthropology at Queens College of the City University of New York. His research and publications deal with the prehistory and ethnoarchaeology of the Peruvian and Ecuadorian tropical forests with forays into North American Hopewell, games, and color systems. He is currently preparing a monograph on Shipibo children's art.

Robert L. Hall (1927-2012) was professor emeritus of anthropology at the University of Illinois at Chicago, where he taught from 1968 to 1998 after positions with the Wisconsin and Illinois State Museums, the University of South Dakota, and Marquette University. His many publications include the book *An Archaeology of the Soul: North American Indian Belief and Ritual* (1997).

Kelley Hays-Gilpin is professor of anthropology at Northern Arizona University and curator of anthropology at the Museum of Northern Arizona. She has nearly 30 years of experience studying rock art and pottery in the Southwest. She has authored numerous articles and books, including *Ambiguous Images: Gender and Rock Art* (2003), which won the 2005 Society for American Archaeology book award.

Alice Beck Kehoe is professor of anthropology, emeritus from Marquette University. She has published *North American Indians: A Comprehensive Account* (3rd edition 2006), *Controversies in Archaeology* (2008), *Shamans and Religion* (2000), and *The Ghost Dance* (2nd edition 2006).

John Kelly is a senior lecturer in archaeology in the Department of Anthropology at Washington University at St. Louis, where he has taught for the past 18 years. He has been for the past 40 years and is currently involved in research at Cahokia Mounds and the surrounding region, with numerous publications.

Stephen H. Lekson is curator and professor of anthropology at the Museum of Natural History, University of Colorado, Boulder. He has directed archaeological projects throughout the Southwest. His most recent publications include *A History of the Ancient Southwest* (2009); *The Architecture of Chaco Canyon* (2007); *The Archaeology of Chaco Canyon* (2006); and *Archaeology of the Mimbres Region* (2006).

Colin McEwan is head of the Americas Section at the British Museum and specializes in the art and archaeology of the Americas. From 1979 to 1991 he directed the Agua Blanca Archaeological Project focused on a major Manteño settlement in coastal Ecuador. His latest book is *Ancient American Art in Detail* (2009).

John Norder is a member of the Spirit Lake Tribe of North Dakota and associate professor in the department of anthropology at Michigan State University. His research and publications have focused on the intersections between contemporary First Nations and Native communities and their ancestral landscapes and biological heritage.

Jeffrey Quilter is deputy director for Curatorial Affairs at the Peabody Museum, Harvard University. He has conducted archaeological investigations in Peru and Costa Rica. His most recent book is *Treasures of the Andes* (2005).

Amy Roe is a doctoral candidate and research associate at the Center for Energy and Environmental Policy at the University of Delaware.

Peter G. Roe, Ph.D., professor in the department of anthropology, University of Delaware, Newark, combines archaeology and ethnography in his research on Caribbean and South Amerindians.

Linea Sundstrom is a private contractor specializing in North American archaeology, ethnogeography, and rock art. She is the author of *Storied Stone: Rock Art of the Black Hills Country* (2004).

Index